Exploring Current Issues in Educational Technology

Drew Tiene and Albert Ingram

Boston   Burr Ridge, IL   Dubuque, IA   Madison, WI
New York   San Francisco   St. Louis
Bangkok   Bogotá   Caracas   Lisbon   London   Madrid   Mexico City
Milan   New Delhi   Seoul   Singapore   Sydney   Taipei   Toronto

McGraw-Hill Higher Education

*A Division of The **McGraw·Hill** Companies*

EXPLORING CURRENT ISSUES IN EDUCATIONAL TECHNOLOGY

Published by McGraw-Hill, an imprint of The McGraw-Hill Companies, Inc., 1221 Avenue of the Americas, New York, NY 10020. Copyright © 2001, 1997 by The McGraw-Hill Companies, Inc. All rights reserved. No part of this publication may be reproduced or distributed in any form or by any means, or stored in a database or retrieval system, without the prior written consent of The McGraw-Hill Companies, Inc., including, but not limited to, in any network or other electronic storage or transmission, or broadcast for distance learning.

Some ancillaries, including electronic and print components, may not be available to customers outside the United States.

This book is printed on acid-free paper.

1 2 3 4 5 6 7 8 9 0 DOC/DOC 0 9 8 7 6 5 4 3 2 1 0

ISBN 0–07–230480–4

Vice president and editor-in-chief: *Thalia Dorwick*
Publisher: *Jane E. Vaicunas*
Sponsoring editor: *Beth Kaufman*
Developmental editor: *Teresa Wise*
Marketing manager: *Daniel M. Loch*
Project manager: *Mary Lee Harms*
Senior media developer: *James Fehr*
Production supervisor: *Laura Fuller*
Coordinator of freelance design: *David W. Hash*
Cover designer: *Lisa Gravunder*
Cover illustration: *Bradly Gravunder*
Senior photo research coordinator: *Lori Hancock*
Senior supplement coordinator: *Candy M. Kuster*
Compositor: *Black Dot Group*
Typeface: *10/12 Palatino*
Printer: *R.R. Donnelley & Sons Company/Crawsfordsville, IN*

Interior cartoons by *Tim Wallace*
A cubicle escapee of the Hi-Brow department at American Greetings, Tim Wallace has been producing cartoons and caricatures in Northeast Ohio since the mid-sixties. He is also employed as a humorous singer/songwriter and is currently cultivating a love/hate relationship with his computer.

Library of Congress Cataloging-in-Publication Data

Tiene, Drew
Exploring current issues in educational technology/Drew Tiene, Albert Ingram.— 1st. ed.
p.   cm.
Includes index.
ISBN 0–07–230480–4
1. Educational technology.   2. Constructivism (Education)   I. Ingram, Albert.   II. Title.

LB1028.3 .T58   2001   00–036129
371.33—dc21   CIP
www.mhhe.com

About the Authors

Drew Tiene is an Associate Professor in Instructional Technology at Kent State University in Ohio. Originally from New York, he received his Master's Degree from the University of Michigan and his Doctorate in Instructional Technology from the University of Texas. Dr. Tiene has written extensively about educational television, including the "Instructional Television" entry in the International Encyclopedia of Education. He has published articles in numerous journals, including *Educational Leadership, Journal of Educational Research,* and *Educational Technology.* His award-winning television productions have been distributed nationwide and have been shown overseas in translation. Dr. Tiene has also served as a juror at the Japan Prize, the world's most prestigious educational television contest, and worked internationally as a consultant for the World Bank and the U.S. Agency for International Development.

Albert L. Ingram is Assistant Professor of Instructional Technology at Kent State University. He received his Ph.D. in Educational Technology from Arizona State University in 1984. Since then, he has designed and developed instructional systems for a variety of organizations including the Digital Equipment Corporation, the Army Research Institute, The American College, and the Software Engineering Institute. He has taught at Governors State University and directed statewide instructional technology efforts at the University of Medicine and Dentistry of New Jersey. He is the author of papers in such journals as *Educational Technology Research and Development*, *Educational Technology*, and the *Journal of Educational Technology Systems*. Dr. Ingram's current research interests include computer-mediated communications, instructional design, and Web-based instruction.

To our parents,
who encouraged and guided our learning experiences
from the very beginning:

Charles and Dorothy Tiene
and Albert L. and Margaret S. Ingram

Contents

Preface: Why This Book Is Different   xv

Introduction   1

Selecting Your Scenarios: Chapter Overviews   3

From Video to Virtual Reality: Technology and Its Instructional Potential   15

From Conditioning to Constructivism: Learning Theories and Their Impact on How We Teach   25

SECTION 1

Curricular Concerns: Strategies and Skills   37

1. The Role of Research: Asking the Right Questions About Educational Technology   39

    Introduction   39
    Examining a Critical Issue: The Role of Technology in Instruction   40
    Challenges Involved in Researching   41
    Guidelines for Good Experimental Design   44
    Descriptive Research   45
    The Role of the Researcher   48
    Which Type of Research Is Best?   49

Recommended Reading   50
Other References   50
Scenario   50
Issues Inquiry   51

2. Surviving the Information Explosion: Researching on the World Wide Web   53

Introduction   54
Search Engines   54
How to Take Advantage of the Vast Resources on the Web   56
Levels of Cognitive Awareness   58
Recommended Reading   60
Other References   61
Scenario   61
Issues Inquiry   62

3. Deconstructing Constructivism: The Paradox of Planning Unstructured Units   63

Introduction   64
Constructivist Approaches to Teaching   64
Getting Situated   66
Successful Constructivist Projects   67
Planning Your Constructivist Lessons   69
Recommended Reading   72
Other References   72
Scenario   73
Issues Inquiry   74

4. How Can Technology Facilitate Constructivist Units?   75

Introduction   76
Information Access Through Communications Technologies   76
Creative Projects with Technology   78
A Sample Unit: Ancient Egypt   80
Deconstructing Pop Culture Images   82
Recommended Reading   84
Other References   84
Scenario   85
Issues Inquiry   86

SECTION 2

Difficult Decisions: Crucial Yet Complicated   87

5. TV or Not TV? That Is the Question: Commercialization of the Classroom   89

Introduction   89
    Opposition to the Channel One Project   89
    The Potential Advantages of Subscribing to Channel One   91
    The Nationwide Proliferation of Channel One Schools   92
    Research into the Effects of the Channel One Project   93
    Commercialism in the Schools   94
Recommended Reading   95
    Other References   95
Scenario   96
Issues Inquiry   97

6. Is a Computer's Place in the Lab or in the Classroom?   99

Introduction   100
    Advantages of a Computer Laboratory   100
    Teaching in a Lab   101
    Potential of Computers in Classrooms   102
    Curriculum Integration of Computers   103
    Computer Placement in Different Types of Schools   104
    Other Factors Influencing Computer Location   106
Recommended Reading   108
    Other References   108
Scenario   108
Issues Inquiry   110

7. Replacing Books with "Notebooks": Hard Copy Versus Software   111

Introduction   112
    Can Schools Afford It?   112
    The Book As an Instructional Medium   114
    Advantages of Electronic Text   115
    Compact Discs or Networking?   117
    Access to Other Electronic Resources   118
    Mere Replacement or Significant Shift?   119

Recommended Reading   120
Other References   120
Scenario   120
Issues Inquiry   121

8. Is Educational Technology Sometimes Just
    Too Expensive?   122

Introduction   123
Cost Categories   123
Estimating Cost   125
So, Is It All Worth It?   127
Recommended Reading   131
Other References   131
Scenario   131
Issues Inquiry   132

SECTION 3

Social Issues: Rights and Responsibilities   135

9. Internet Indiscretions: The Limits of Free Expression in
    Cyberspace   137

Introduction   137
What About Standards for the Internet?   138
Educational Examples   139
Major Controversy at Northwestern University   140
What Can People Place on the Web?   141
Acceptable Use Policies   142
Spamming   143
Filtering the Internet   144
Recommended Reading   146
Other References   146
Scenario   146
Issues Inquiry   148

10. It Takes a Global Village: Multicultural Studies Through
     Telecommunications   149

Introduction   150
Why Is Intercultural Awareness Important?   151
Incorporating Intercultural Experiences into the Curriculum   152

Culture Through the Lens   153
Culture on Compact Disc   155
Culture on the World Wide Web   156
Electronic Exchanges with Other Cultures   157
Beyond Text: Graphic Interfaces and Video-Based Exchanges   159
Making Connections   160
Recommended Reading   160
Other References   161
Scenario   161
Issues Inquiry   162

11.   Coming to Conclusions About Inclusion: What Role for
Assistive Technologies?   164

Introduction   165
Some Background About Educating Students with Disabilities   165
Physical Disabilities Encountered in the Classroom   166
Sensory Impairment: Blindness and Deafness   167
Cognitive Disabilities Faced by Young Learners   168
Assistive Devices for the Physically Impaired   170
Overcoming Sensory Impairments with Technology   171
Software and the Learning Disabled   173
Developing the Individualized Education Program   174
Approaches to Selecting Devices and Applications   175
Recommended Reading   176
Other References   177
Scenario   177
Issues Inquiry   179

12.   Fair Use: Copyright or Copywrong?   180

Introduction   181
What Constitutes Fair Use?   182
Questions of Interpretation   183
Permission or Paying Can Be Problematic   185
The Question of Enforcement   186
New Technologies Raise New Questions About Copyright   187
Online Issues: Are Hyperlinks a Copyright Violation?   188
Distance Education and Copyright: Issues of Scale   189
Future Issues   191
Recommended Reading   192
Other References   192
Scenario   193
Issues Inquiry   195

SECTION 4

New Opportunities: Engaging or Enraging?   197

13. Is Hypermedia Worth the Hype?   199

Introduction   200
    A Hyperattenuated History of Hypermedia   200
    How Hypermedia Helps   201
    Linking and Associative Learning   202
    Hypermedia and Constructivism   203
    Getting Lost in Hyperspace   204
    Issues in Hypermedia Design   206
Recommended Reading   207
    Other References   207
Scenario   208
Issues Inquiry   209

14. Digital Developments: Television's Technological
     Transformation   210

Introduction   211
    Improvements in Television Quality   211
    Sending Signals   213
    Television Becomes Video   214
    Shooting in a Gallery (or Museum, Craft Fair, Garage Sale, Etc.)   215
    Editing Goes Digital   217
    Television As a Presentation Device   218
    Video As an Archival Medium   219
    Telecommunicating Educational Experiences   220
    No Big Production   222
Recommended Reading   223
    Other References   223
Scenario   224
Issues Inquiry   225

15. Distance Education: So Far, So Good?   226

Introduction   227
    A Brief History of Distance Education   227
    Teleconferencing Technologies   228
    Online Instruction   230
    Distance Education Issues   232
Recommended Reading   233

Other References   233
Scenario   234
Issues Inquiry   236

16. Conceptual Connections: Establishing Online Learning Communities   238

Introduction   239
Electronic Mail   239
Mailing Lists   241
Newsgroups   242
Bulletin Boards   243
"Chat" Services   243
Applications of Computer-Mediated Communications in Education   245
Limitations of Computer-Mediated Communications   247
Recommended Reading   247
Other References   248
Scenario   248
Issues Inquiry   249

SECTION 5

Future Possibilities: Virtually No Limitations?   251

17. Teacher Training in Technology: The Trials and Tribulations of the Technophobes   253

Introduction   254
Keeping Up with the Latest and Greatest   254
Beyond the Basics with Technology   255
Integrating Technology into Classroom Instruction   257
Technology and Active Learning   258
Hands-on, Not Hands-off   259
Knowing It, Hands Down   261
Recommended Reading   261
Other References   261
Scenario   262
Issues Inquiry   263

18. Is Artificial Intelligence Better Than Authentic Stupidity?   264

Introduction   265
Expert Systems: Smart but Specialized   265

Pattern Recognition: Making Machines More Perceptive   267
Speech Recognition: My Machine Just Doesn't Understand Me   269
Intelligent Computer-Assisted Instruction: How Smart?   270
Deep Blue and Beyond   273
Recommended Reading   274
Other References   274
Scenario   275
Issues Inquiry   277

19. That's Virtually Impossible! (or Is It?): Virtual Reality in the
Classroom   278

Introduction   279
How VR Became a Reality   279
Real World Applications of VR   281
Multiuser VR on the Web   282
Experience Is the Best Teacher: VR in the Schools   283
From Pacman to Holodeck   285
Recommended Reading   286
Other References   286
Scenario   287
Issues Inquiry   288

20. The Third Millennium School: From Industrial to Information
Society   289

Introduction   290
Schools in a Changing Society   290
The New Curriculum   291
Information-Processing Skills   293
Instructional Technology in the Schools of the Future   294
From the Student's Perspective   297
New Roles for Teachers   298
New Approaches to Evaluation of Student Progress   299
Changes in School Structure   300
Recommended Reading   301
Other References   301
Scenario   302
Issues Inquiry   303

Glossary   305

Preface: Why This Book Is Different

Exploring Current Issues in Educational Technology deals with the appropriate application of new communications technologies, like computer-mediated communications, laptop computers, school television newcasts, hypermedia environments, distance education, virtual reality, artificial intelligence, and so on. It addresses how these new technologies can be used to inform and educate students. In doing so, the book explores a number of different issues that arise when educators consider teaching with technology.

So why is this book different, as the preface title claims? This is not a text that simply provides you with information that you are expected to memorize. Instead, it tries to get you to think. It presents problematic issues and asks for your perspectives on how best to deal with them. These problems are presented in a set of [scenarios], each of which describes a situation that we feel is relatively realistic. We suspect that either something like this has already happened, could conceivably have taken place, or might very well occur sometime in the near future.

Who is this book for? It is primarily designed for future teachers. Young people in education programs throughout this country and around the world will be expected to use communications technologies in their teaching. While some individuals may be uncomfortable with this prospect, most would agree that technology offers educational opportunities that teachers should take advantage of, if their students are going to learn as much as possible. Besides, new teachers with little awareness about technology risk being viewed as "dinosaurs" by their more technologically-savvy students. Speaking of dinosaurs, this book might also be extremely helpful for experienced teachers who need to expand their awareness of what educational technologies are currently available and who also need to acquaint themselves with the critical issues associated with the effective utilization of these new technologies. Finally,

Exploring Current Issues in Educational Technology is for instructional technology specialists who either already have an advanced degree or are working on one.

So how can you, the reader, most effectively use this book? As you peruse the table of contents, you will see twenty chapters, each of which tackles a different issue in the field of instructional technology. We have attempted to provide sufficient variety in the types of issues addressed so as to provide adequate coverage of the book's principal concern: how educational technologies can be implemented effectively in the classroom. But this variety is also designed to provide *choice* for the reader. In fact, it might be difficult for a college class to address all twenty topics in the typical fifteen-week semester. So the instructor, or better still the class, might select the topics that they are most interested in or that they feel are most important. Of course, if you happen to be reading this book on your own, feel free to focus on those issues that are most relevant to your own situation. We hope that a sufficient number of compelling topics are included for anyone involved in the instructional application of technologies.

Each chapter has three basic parts. The centerpiece is the aforementioned "Scenario," which poses a problem to the reader. However, each scenario is preceded by an "Introduction" section, which provides background material, so that the scenario can be more fully appreciated and so that readers can respond to the issues involved in more sophisticated ways. Each scenario is followed by a section entitled "Issues Inquiry," which contains some questions designed to help the reader think carefully about the key issues associated with each scenario.

CHAPTER INTRODUCTIONS

The Introduction section in each chapter should be helpful, especially for novices who know little about technologies or how they have been used in educational settings. We have provided some information about the topic area, so that readers can better understand the issues associated with the scenario. Most of the scenarios raise issues that are relatively complex, so a variety of different responses are possible. Often there are at least two sides to the issue. This Introduction section tries to present an objective overview of topics associated with the scenario situation. We may describe several facets of the problem to be addressed. It is up to the you, the reader, to make up your own mind about the best course of action to be followed in resolving the complicated situation described in the chapter's scenario.

We have tried to provide a clear explanation of why the issues raised in each scenario are important. But it is difficult to summarize such complex issues in the limited space allowed for each chapter in this book. Consequently, each introductory passage concludes with a list of recommended readings. If this book is to be used most effectively, its readers will need to pursue some readings in each chapter to more fully inform themselves about the topic and the issues involved. The most critical readings for each chapter have been listed immediately after the introductory section. This "Recommended Reading" usually includes a few journal articles (or other sources like book chapters, reports, conference presentations, etc.). Then, after this section, a longer bibliography of "Other References" is listed, so that those who are especially interested in a particular issue can pursue it in greater depth. But it is *highly recommended* that all readers find the "Recommended Reading" materials and read them carefully, before attempting to respond to the scenario. College instructors using this book are encouraged to place these materials on reserve for the class, to compile them in a class packet for student purchase, or to distribute them as handouts.

THE SCENARIOS

Each scenario asks you to place yourself in the position of someone who has to cope with a real-life problem. Usually this person is a teacher, and the problems are those commonly faced in classrooms. Sometimes the problem might more likely be addressed at a schoolwide level or perhaps even at the district level. But each scenario is designed for prospective teachers, so the issue will be relevant to the teaching experience in one way or another.

These twenty scenarios deal with a wide variety of different technologies. Some ask you to decide what technologies might be most appropriate for a given situation or a given set of objectives. But others address the potential use of a specific technology, like the World Wide Web, school television, distance learning, virtual reality, hypermedia, computer agents, and so on. One of the critical capabilities that teachers of the twenty-first century will need is an understanding of how certain technologies can be used effectively within the context of their own classrooms. These scenarios help readers learn more about a technology and to carefully consider its appropriate instructional application.

What kinds of issues are addressed in these scenarios? Many are, of course, instructional issues. What types of learning are facilitated by which applications of a given technology? How can a technology be creatively utilized to improve a curriculum unit? What kinds of learning activities can your students engage in with the computers in your room? How can students most effectively use the World Wide Web as an educational resource? How might students be guided to learn more about current events from a schoolwide telecast? How would you use technology to foster constructivist approaches to learning? How can other teachers most effectively be trained to work with technology?

Other issues address learner characteristics. What type of student can successfully negotiate a "hypertext" learning environment? How can you help a student with disabilities by using assistive technology? Is distance education a good way to provide advanced subject matter for gifted students? Is constructivism an appropriate approach for all kinds of students?

Some of the issues raised in the scenarios are more administrative. Do you want some computers in your room, or would you prefer to take your class to a computer laboratory? How would you design a "Classroom of the Future," and what role would technology play? Should computers replace textbooks whenever possible? How can the expense of many new technologies be justified in terms of learning outcomes?

Finally, there are more philosophical issues to be dealt with. Should the World Wide Web remain a medium where people can express any point of view, however controversial? Should television commercials be shown in the classroom? To what degree can a computer replace a teacher in the classroom? To what extent can virtual reality mimic real situations? How can research studies be designed so as to most effectively inform classroom teachers about critical instructional issues?

Generally, at the conclusion of the scenario, you will be asked to write a paper of several pages, in which you express your viewpoint regarding the issues raised. Often a kind of "position paper" is expected. But the written document may take different forms, depending on the situation described. Prepared speeches, debates, funding proposals, lesson plans, and curriculum units are asked for in some of the different chapters. As with the scenarios themselves, we have tried to make the written assignments as realistic as possible. The expected response, in most cases, would be similar to a response that might be expected of you as an educator who was dealing with a professional problem or a choice to be made that would affect the learning environment in your school.

"ISSUES INQUIRY" QUESTIONS

To assist you in thinking about the issues raised in this book, each scenario is followed by an "Issues Inquiry" section. Its questions will help guide your exploration of the topic. In the course of writing your response to the scenario, if you can answer most of the questions in this section, you will have sufficiently explored the key issues. Instructors using this text may find that the "Issues Inquiry" section will help clarify what the major points of class discussion might be. It can be used as a starting point for small-group discussion in class, as well as for whole-group discussions, about a chapter.

In each "Issues Inquiry," the most critical issue is usually raised first. Subsequent questions address more specific aspects of the topic or explore alternative ways of seeing it. You may not feel it necessary to address all of the questions, although you will probably need to address the first few items if you hope to adequately respond to the scenario. But you can decide which questions are most important or of most interest to you.

A major assumption of this book is that college students should be treated like the professionals they are striving to become. As a teacher, you need to make some important decisions about how to best provide instruction for all your students. It is up to you to address a series of challenges associated with the teaching profession. It is up to you to continue to educate yourself, so you keep up with the latest developments in the field. It is up to you to research subject matter as you prepare to teach it. It is up to you to develop appropriate methods by which to evaluate student performance. It will be up to you to communicate student progress to the students themselves, their parents, school administrators, and to the next set of teachers who will work with these children. So this book leaves the learning, to a large extent, *up to you*.

For each chapter, you will be expected to engage in research about the topics raised, using the reference material provided. Once you have sufficiently informed yourself about the topic, you will then need to think the issues through. You will need to examine your own value system and think about your own experiences. You will need to weigh the advantages and disadvantages of each proposed approach, so as to come to a decision regarding the best course of action. We hope your instructor will provide an opportunity for you to discuss each chapter topic with a small group of your classmates, before you write your reaction to the scenario, so that your paper reflects some shared deliberation. You will then need to develop a written document of several pages that summarizes your thinking about the scenario. You will also probably be asked by your instructor to express your thoughts in class discussions, first within a small group and then with the entire class. After hearing the perspectives of your classmates, you may wish to modify your own position on the topic and perhaps revise your paper.

A "CONSTRUCTIVIST" APPROACH

Some might describe the approach taken in this book as "constructivist." If you have not heard this term, you can read about this approach in an upcoming chapter entitled "From Conditioning to Constructivism." Described in simple terms, constructivist philosophy encourages learners to expand their awareness and develop their own perspectives, by researching topics on their own and discussing their findings with their peers. It leaves a great deal of the effort in the hands of the student. Often the teacher serves more as a facilitator than a dispenser of information. Rather than making pronouncements on a given issue, the instructor's role is to help students explore and express their own ideas.

This constructivist approach can benefit learners in significant ways, for it allows students to develop their own sense of what is important. It allows for self-development, one of the most important aspects of anyone's educational experience. This book supports this approach in the schools, even though it can be very challenging to implement with a large group of learners, and it is a departure from the more authoritarian teaching style that has been commonly used in our public schools for decades.

This book intends to introduce this constructivist learning approach to each reader (or to further expose some who are already familiar with the approach). If the most effective way to learn is to do something yourself, we hope that you, the reader, will learn about constructivism by actually engaging in it on your own in the course of working with this book. You can see for yourself whether you are comfortable with it. You can test how valid it is for you. You are far more likely to try it out with your own students if you have some experience with it, and if you believe it can be an effective way to learn.

Instructors using this book for a course are encouraged to require two additional assignments that should enhance the learning experience. One assignment is for students to evaluate the scenarios they read. This can be done in a number of ways. They could rank order them from best to worst. They could list their three favorites and their three least favorite. However this is accomplished, there ought to be written rationales for the evaluations made. These opinions should also be discussed in class, so each of you can see how others felt about the scenarios.

The second assignment is for students to develop their own scenarios, with accompanying references, and an "Issues Inquiry" section with questions for discussion. Providing an "Introduction" for the scenario, as we have done in each chapter, would be optional. These scenarios might also then be discussed in class. Classmates could critique one another's scenarios. If time permits, some of these student-developed scenarios could be assigned just as those in this book have been, culminating in a reaction paper and class discussion of the issues involved.

THINKING CAREFULLY ABOUT IMPLEMENTING TECHNOLOGIES IN THE CLASSROOM

Exploring Current Issues in Educational Technology also hopes to expand each reader's awareness about the potential of instructional technologies. Why is it appropriate to take a problem-based approach to learning about the use of communications technologies for teaching? Well, for one reason, a lack of awareness in the field of education about how to use new technologies has already resulted in many disappointing experiences with instructional media. An inability to make good choices about technology has plagued the field of education for decades.

In the 1950s, the Ford Foundation spent millions on instructional television in the United States, hoping that it would revolutionize education. Its directors believed that a "master teacher" could be broadcast to hundreds of classrooms, and thereby improve instruction. This plan failed miserably, mainly because few teachers wanted to play "second fiddle" to a master teacher on television. Later, educational television became more sophisticated, taking advantage of production techniques to hold the attention of its audience. *Sesame Street* was a hit with its preschool audience watching at home, often with encouraging parents close by. But within schools, educational television has never gained a significant audience. Television equipment has not become widely available in classrooms, and available programming has never been especially compelling for teachers, who rarely bother with it. Educational television has been a marginalized instructional endeavor for several decades. The Channel One Project has revived some classroom interest in the medium (see Chapter 5, "TV or Not TV? That Is the Question"), and it may yet make more substantial contributions to public schooling in the next few decades. But school television was an instructional technology fad that came and went. Today, this is mainly how it is viewed (or not viewed!).

In the 1980s, the microcomputer was heralded as the latest technological wonder, and many were sure it would transform education. It did not. There were never enough machines or enough pieces of software available to enable a machine designed for individual use to succeed in the group environment of the classroom. Much of the software was educationally weak, focusing on low-level cognitive activities like drill-and-practice. Teachers were never given the training necessary to help them use the new technology in the classroom. Twenty years later, the number of computers and software titles in many schools are finally beginning to approach levels at which the instructional impact might become significant. However, if educators fail to effectively orchestrate their efforts, the latest technology fad, the networking of schools, may well experience the same disappointments registered by previous so-called "educational revolutions."

Educators need to enhance their awareness of how technology has been used most effectively in the past and why it has often failed to live up to expectations. Educators also need to think more carefully about the complications associated with trying to implement technology effectively in the schools. Without understanding these complexities, educators will continue to bungle as they work with technology. The same mistakes have been repeated again and again by educators over the decades. They tend to think each situation is novel because the technology itself is new. But the basic circumstances of the classroom have remained constant for years, and certain fundamental principles can serve to guide efforts at integrating technology into the curriculum.

In working with this book, you should come to understand these principles as you address the questions raised by each scenario. We hope that the experiences described in the scenarios will help you approach the use of instructional technologies with greater sophistication. By thinking through situations in advance, you should be ready to address problematic circumstances that arise in your own classroom and to take full advantage of worthwhile opportunities that present themselves.

Introduction

Selecting Your Scenarios

CHAPTER OVERVIEWS

This book provides twenty scenarios on a variety of issues associated with using technology in the classroom. However, some readers may not be inclined to address all twenty scenarios. Instructors planning a semester's work with this book will not have that many weeks in a semester, so they will probably choose their favorites from among these twenty. Readers may wish to focus on certain topics and exclude others. Also, many readers may not wish to move linearly through the book, preferring instead to work with chapters in a different order in which they are listed. So this chapter is designed as a readers' guide providing an overview of each of the twenty scenario-based chapters. It will clarify what each chapter covers and what issues are addressed by each scenario, so that readers can decide how they wish to proceed through the book and instructors can develop strategies for using it.

TABLE OF CONTENTS: HOW THE BOOK IS ORGANIZED

In examining the table of contents, readers will note that the book begins with four special chapters that precede the twenty scenario-based chapters. These four chapters (the preface chapter and the three chapters in the introduction) describe the book's pedagogical approach and its many topics. Presumably readers have already read the preface, entitled "Why This Book Is Different," which explains the book's problem-based approach and its use of scenarios to prompt critical thinking and group discussion. As just mentioned, this chapter provides an overview of the chapters within each of five main sections. The two chapters which follow explain two critical content areas that will be addressed throughout the text: technology and instructional theory. The chapter "From Video to Virtual Reality: Technology and Its Instructional Potential" discusses new communications technologies, with a primary focus on the advances witnessed in the television industry and the rise of digital technologies associated with the computer. The introductory chapter, entitled "From

Conditioning to Constructivism: Learning Theories and Their Impact on How We Teach," addresses three important schools of psychology that have influenced instructional theory and classroom practice throughout the twentieth century: behaviorism, cognitive science, and constructivism.

The scenarios themselves can be found in each of the subsequent twenty chapters, which have been organized into five sections, each of which reflects a given theme. The table of contents identifies each of these five sections and its abiding concern. The first section, entitled "Curricular Concerns: Strategies and Skills," introduces chapters that deal primarily with educational approaches but also ask readers to describe how these techniques can be used in conjunction with technology. Section 2, "Difficult Decisions: Crucial Yet Complicated," includes chapters that raise controversial issues associated with the implementation of instructional technology. The scenarios found in this section are most likely to stimulate lively debate in classrooms. The third section, "Social Issues: Rights and Responsibilities," addresses social issues that arise from the use of technology. These scenarios can also be controversial, for they ask readers to address areas wherein the rights of one individual (or group) conflict with the rights of another. Chapters in this section also address the need to be sensitive to individual differences associated with cultural background or special circumstances. Section 4, "New Opportunities: Engaging or Enraging?," provides examples of new applications of technology, asking how teachers can best exploit these new opportunities and avoid the frustration that often accompanies experimentation with "cutting edge" technologies (sometimes sarcastically called *bleeding* edge!). Readers will be asked to think of creative activities using instructional technologies like hypermedia, new video formats, distance learning, and computer-mediated communications. The final section, "Future Possibilities: Virtually No Limitations?," raises future possibilities for instructional technology. Will such dynamic applications like virtual reality and artificial intelligence, currently in their infancy, mature into highly significant technologies in the classrooms of the twenty-first century? Finally, how will technology transform our schools by the end of this new millennium?

SECTION 1: CURRICULAR CONCERNS: STRATEGIES AND SKILLS

This first section of the book includes scenario-based chapters that focus on educational process. The first chapter encourages readers to show an interest in research findings regarding the use of instructional technologies. It also expresses the hope that as teachers, they may even be interested in designing some of their own research studies. Chapter 2 discusses how teachers should stimulate their students to think at levels beyond mere memorization. Presenting problems for students to solve encourages them to think more thoroughly. The World Wide Web can be a place for pupils to find the information necessary for solving teacher-developed problems. The third chapter describes constructivism, an educational approach that was introduced in the introductory chapter on learning theories. It asks readers to consider how this approach might be used in the classroom and how a teacher might develop lesson plans for such an open-ended, student-centered approach to learning. Chapter 4 follows up with the issue of how technology might most effectively be used to support constructivist units.

Chapter 1. The Role of Research: Asking the Right Questions About Educational Technology

How can educators determine whether technology can facilitate learning? Some have questioned whether a medium has any real impact on learning, stressing the importance of the content and how instruction is designed. They point to the fact that the vast majority of studies into the effectiveness of mediated lessons show no superiority to nonmediated lessons. On what basis should teachers be evaluating the merits of studies they read and how may they themselves effectively examine these kinds of issues? The basic tenets of both experimental and descriptive research are discussed. The scenario asks readers to design a study to determine the effectiveness of a computer laboratory for teaching language arts.

Chapter 2. Surviving the Information Explosion: Researching on the World Wide Web

The World Wide Web is potentially a tremendous resource. How can it best be used for instructional purposes? Finding specific information is difficult, because there is so much of it. Identifying worthwhile material is another challenge, since so much of the Web's information is of questionable value. Also, learners can find it difficult to maintain focus on a given line of inquiry, since it is so easy to link to other materials with hypertext. Unfortunately, the tendency has been for teachers to use the Web as just another source of facts. The typical approach to orienting students to the Web has been to send them on a scavenger hunt for trivial facts. While this can be fun, the Web can be used for the development of higher-level thinking skills. The chapter scenario asks readers to design a Web-based lesson plan that requires problem-solving skills.

Chapter 3. Deconstructing Constructivism: The Paradox of Planning Unstructured Units

Constructivism is an educational philosophy gaining favor with educators across the country. It encourages teachers to allow students to discover facts, ideas, and principles on their own. It stresses the importance of allowing each individual to come to his or her own conclusions about issues. If this approach is valid, then how should teachers adjust their planning? How can you effectively plan lessons that encourage students to work independently? How can objectives be set for open-ended activities? How can learning outcomes be tested, if they differ for each student? The scenario asks readers to plan a constructivist-based fourth-grade science curriculum.

Chapter 4. How Can Technology Facilitate Constructivist Units?

One of the reasons the open classroom movement of the early seventies did not last long is that it encouraged the development of learning centers to which children might gravitate and work independently. The idea was a good one, but implementing it demanded resources that few schools had. Nowadays, one of the challenges associated with constructivist teaching approaches is finding sufficient material for students to explore on their own. Fortunately, today's classroom technology is more developed than it was thirty years ago, and technology can be used to access a great variety of different types of information: videotaped programming, encyclopedias on compact disc, websites on the Internet, and so on. How can new information technologies contribute to the development of units that allow students to learn independently? This chapter's scenario asks readers to design such a unit and to describe specifically how it might be enhanced by the use of technology.

SECTION 2: DIFFICULT DECISIONS: CRUCIAL YET COMPLICATED

The second section of this book deals with a set of controversial issues involving school policy. Chapter 5 addresses the issue of corporate sponsorship in the schools and whether schools should allow television advertisements into the classroom in exchange for free television equipment and educational programming. Chapter 6 discusses whether school computers should be placed in a laboratory or in individual classrooms. It also explores the advantages and disadvantages associated with each approach. Chapter 7 examines whether school districts might benefit from diverting funds from textbook budgets to purchase portable laptop computer "notebooks" for students, which could be used to provide electronic versions of those texts. Finally, Chapter 8 asks whether technology is a cost-effective approach for schools and whether other needs should be addressed before schools embark upon wholesale investment in technology.

Chapter 5. TV or Not TV? That Is the Question: Commercialization of the Classroom

Corporate commercialism seems to be invading every aspect of our lives. One very visible example is the way in which sports facilities, and even the events played within them, are taking the names of their corporate sponsors. The next world chess championship may be the Microsoft Chess Challenge, held in Seattle's Key Arena, named for a giant bank. Schools also are beginning to experience the impact of corporate sponsorship. Many printed materials prominently display the names of the companies who produce and distribute them, often for free. The most recent corporate intrusion is the Channel One school telecast, which contains two minutes of television advertising. It comes with lots of freebies for the school: television equipment, the newscast, educational programming, and so on. This chapter's scenario asks readers to evaluate the pros and cons of accepting a Channel One-like plan and then to state their opinion as to whether schools should subscribe.

Chapter 6. Is a Computer's Place in the Lab or in the Classroom?

When schools purchase computers, they must deal with the crucial question of where to place them. For many years, schools that had the available space tended to place all the computers together in a "computer laboratory." But now many schools are placing the machines right in the classroom. There are, of course, advantages and disadvantages associated with each approach, and schools with enough equipment may opt for both strategies. This chapter's scenario asks readers to analyze the advisability of each of these strategies for computer placement and then to indicate which of the two approaches they think is potentially more effective.

Chapter 7. Replacing Books with "Notebooks": Hard Copy Versus Software

When encyclopedias first came out on CD-ROM, many educators began to wonder whether digitized information on optical discs might soon replace printed materials. After all, CD-ROMs had features that the printed encyclopedias did not provide: multimedia materials, like sounds and videos; efficient computerized searches by terms, with all results instantly provided; and hyperlinks to related material. The compact disc version was even considerably cheaper! When networking became more prevalent, it was also clear that digitized materials might be accessed online. Recently, the chairman of the Texas State Board of Education proposed that the state purchase laptops in lieu of texts with the funds in its textbook budget. This chapter's scenario asks the reader to consider this proposal. Might it make sense to spend school textbook money on inexpensive laptop computers, which can provide electronic versions of school materials and also access the wealth of information on the World Wide Web?

Chapter 8. Is Educational Technology Sometimes Just Too Expensive?

Although few dispute that technology can provide exciting, dynamic ways to learn, many educators worry about its price tag. The equipment is expensive, and the educational programming and software can be costly as well. It may only serve small numbers of students. It may not be used effectively (or at all!). It may not be as educationally worthwhile as other school purchases that could have been made with the same money spent on technology. Sometimes other needs may be more essential, like proper facilities or basic supplies. This chapter's scenario asks readers to compare the cost-effectiveness of some computers with that of a minilibrary of books that could have been bought for the same price. It then asks them to choose which of the two alternatives they might have purchased and why they chose that particular option.

SECTION 3: SOCIAL ISSUES: RIGHTS AND RESPONSIBILITIES

This section explores a series of important social issues associated with the use of technology. Chapter 9 examines the topic of when the rights of free speech on the World Wide Web clash with standards of acceptability. Chapter 10 addresses the concern that young people appreciate cultural differences and explores how technology can contribute to understanding between people of different countries. Chapter 11 raises the issues of how technology can help children with special needs and how much time, effort, and expenditure should be devoted to individuals with significant needs. Chapter 12 explores the complex issue of copyright. Under what circumstances does the teacher's responsibility to provide interesting materials for the classroom conflict with the rights of those who produced those materials to receive compensation for them?

Chapter 9. Internet Indiscretions: The Limits of Free Expression in Cyberspace

On the Internet, you can find material on almost any topic imaginable. You can also find opinions of every kind. To what extent do the constitutional rights of a free press protect written expression of ideas on the World Wide Web? To what extent is the graphic depiction of potentially offensive materials protected? If rights of expression have depended in the past upon "local" standards of decorum, whose standards would apply on the global Internet? This chapter's scenario asks readers how they feel about a Web page that declares the Holocaust never happened and asks them to develop an acceptable use policy for Web materials.

Chapter 10. It Takes a Global Village: Multicultural Studies Through Telecommunications

The United States is a highly pluralistic society, where people from many different cultures come to start a new life. Every day, more immigrants enter this country from around the world. Multiculturalism is an important aspect of American education, yet many teachers find it difficult to effectively implement. One way to acquaint children with other cultures is to use technology. Television can show them what goes on in foreign lands. The Web has a wealth of material about other countries. E-mail can provide direct exchanges with other children in remote locales. This chapter's scenario asks readers to develop a lesson plan that takes advantage of technology to teach students about other cultures.

Chapter 11. Coming to Conclusions About Inclusion: What Role for Assistive Technologies?

Many children in our schools suffer from disabilities that affect them either physically or cognitively and that may make learning more difficult. Technology can be used to help overcome some disabilities and to enhance individual learning needs. Students with physical or sensory disabilities can employ special devices that allow them to work effectively with computers, video equipment, and so on. Students with cognitive or learning disabilities can benefit from software that may be motivational and that allows students to learn at their own pace. But special devices can be expensive and difficult to properly install. Software appropriate for a child with special needs may not be appropriate for the rest of the class. And how much time and effort devoted to helping a disabled child can be expected from a classroom teacher, who has many other children to attend to? This chapter's scenario asks readers to discuss how they would deal with a child who has physical and learning disabilities, within the context of a fifth-grade classroom.

Chapter 12. Fair Use: Copyright or Copywrong?

Copyright has always been an important issue for educators. Teachers seeking to copy materials for class use are seldom sure whether they have violated copyright laws. Even the courts do not seem to have fully clarified what constitutes "fair use" of materials for educational purposes and what kinds of excerpting is allowable. With video programming and computer software, duplication can be even easier and cheaper than wholesale Xeroxing of printed materials. So the temptation to obtain these kinds of materials without paying for them is greater than ever, especially when the school budget will not allow for these kinds of expenditures. How can the rights of educators to provide worthwhile materials for their classes be balanced against the rights of authors and entrepreneurs to financially benefit from their efforts? This chapter's scenario asks readers to deal with a situation in which a media specialist claims a teacher has violated copyright restrictions, even though the violations seem marginal, at best. Readers must decide for themselves how to apply copyright standards and why they came to the conclusions they reached.

SECTION 4: NEW OPPORTUNITIES: ENGAGING OR ENRAGING?

This section describes a series of technologies that really came into mainstream use in the 1990s. They are increasingly important today. Chapter 13 addresses the educational potential of the hypermedia learning environment, which characterizes the World Wide Web, electronic encyclopedias, and a great deal of educational software. Chapter 14 looks at how television has evolved into a multifaceted, user-friendly medium that educators, and their students, can creatively use in the classroom to enhance learning. Chapter 15 explores the variety of forms of distance education now available for providing instruction to special students or under special circumstances. Finally, Chapter 16 explores the potential of online networking to provide exciting new educational opportunities for instructors and students to share their thoughts, their stories, and their efforts, around the state, across the country, and all over the world.

Chapter 13. Is Hypermedia Worth the Hype?

In the late 1980s, the field of instructional technology was very excited about the rise of new authoring languages like HyperCard, which allowed the designer to create links to other pages that connected at a click of the mouse. This so-called hypertext allowed readers to instantaneously link to related material in a different part of a document or in another document altogether. Hypermedia allowed for the same instantaneous connections to a media source, like pictures, sounds, or a video clip. Now many educational materials include these links and the Web itself is a hypertext environment. Many educators feel that such convenient linking may aid learning, allowing students to quickly move to related material of interest. But is there a potentially negative side to all of this "hyperactivity"? Can students get lost in hyperspace? This chapter's scenario asks readers to explore the potential of hypermedia-based materials and to analyse the conditions under which they are likely to be most instructionally effective.

Chapter 14. Digital Developments: Television's Technological Transformation

Television is a medium that has undergone a somewhat "quiet revolution." While much of the attention in the past two decades has been focused on the computer's remarkable advances, television has evolved to the point where it is now a technology for the masses to produce, as well as enjoy viewing. With light, portable camcorders and user-friendly videocassette recorders, even young children can shoot and play their own programming. Soon digital forms of television will be prevalent, allowing users to edit video footage within their own personal computers. The scenario in this chapter asks readers to suggest some creative video projects dealing with the sixties decade.

Chapter 15. Distance Education: So Far, So Good?

Distance learning has come a long way since the days of the mail-based correspondence course. But educators should remember that there is a long tradition of "home study" and "open education" from which they can learn how to most effectively design today's distance education. Today's efforts can benefit enormously from the increased bandwidth and delivery speed provided by our increasingly powerful telecommunications networks. The challenge is to figure out how to best provide excellent instruction, effectively lead meaningful discussion, and fairly evaluate student work, given the opportunities and constraints associated with different distance education technologies. This chapter's scenario asks readers to decide whether a rural school should subscribe to an interactive television service that will provide "live" classroom instruction by satellite or try a Web-based approach that is largely asynchronous.

Chapter 16. Conceptual Connections: Establishing Online Learning Communities

The phenomenal expansion of networking services in the past few years has provided a variety of ways to telecommunicate. The simplest, most common is electronic mail, which is taking its place, alongside voice mail and fax, as a common way for people to communicate efficiently. While e-mail is asynchronous, online "chat" services provide "live" interaction. Computer-mediated communications (CMC) can also include groups. Listservs, newsgroups, and bulletin boards allow for groups to communicate asynchronously, while most chat services allow for group discussion, as well as for one-on-one exchanges. Early approaches to group chat, like MUDs and MOOs, were text based, but a new approach known as The Palace includes a graphic interface, complete with surrealistic landscapes and bizarre "avatars," representing the participants. But how can CMC be effectively used for *educational* purposes? This chapter's scenario asks readers to develop strategies for establishing online virtual learning communities for both teachers and students within a school district.

SECTION 5: FUTURE POSSIBILITIES: VIRTUALLY NO LIMITATIONS

This last section explores some technologies that may become more important in future decades. Chapter 17 addresses the critical issue of what skills a teacher needs to successfully work with technology in the classroom and how to establish a professional development plan for developing these skills. Chapter 18 discusses the potential of virtual reality programming to provide sophisticated forms of instruction. John Dewey once proclaimed experience to be the best teacher and VR may be the best substitute for real experience. Chapter 19 examines the possibility that artificial intelligence may one day play a significant role in the classroom. If so, how will this affect the teacher's role? Finally, Chapter 20 asks how our schools should evolve in the next few decades to most effectively prepare young people for life in the twenty-first century.

Chapter 17. Teacher Training in Technology: The Trials and Tribulations of the Technophobes

One of the critical challenges involved in bringing instructional technology into the classroom is the training of teachers in skills that will enable them to effectively use this equipment. Teachers serve as pivotal "gatekeepers" who will largely determine the extent to which technology is used in their classrooms. Many pieces of hardware have sat idle in the back of classrooms because teachers were not prepared to take advantage of them. But it can be overwhelming for teachers to take on the task of training themselves in technology skills. After all, there is so much to learn! What are the most important skills for a teacher to focus on? This chapter's scenario asks readers to develop a professional development plan that assesses which skills are most critical for them to know before they can teach effectively with technology.

Chapter 18. Is Artificial Intelligence Better Than Authentic Stupidity?

While stupidity can be found nearly everywhere you turn, it is still difficult to find instances of true artificial intelligence (AI). It remains a somewhat futuristic concept. However, what examples do exist today are often described as "expert systems." A program is designed to ask questions of a client. It then checks the answers in a large database of information about the given field. It also uses heuristics to come to diagnostic conclusions and make recommendations, which it provides to the client. Computer programs also guide many complex systems. The Deep Blue computer program even defeated the world's chess champion, Gary Kasparov. Is it conceivable that computers will one day provide intelligent tutoring in schools. This chapter's scenario asks readers to express their opinions as to whether computers will someday be able to replace most of what teachers do today in educating children. If not, what role might AI play in the classroom of the future?

Chapter 19. That's Virtually Impossible! (or Is It?): Virtual Reality in the Classroom

The much publicized virtual reality (VR) is a sophisticated computer application that applies recent advances in computer graphics to the training approach known as "simulation." A simulation attempts to replicate real life by providing vicarious experiences that are as close to their real-world counterparts as possible. It is used to train people, especially for performing in situations where trying the real thing would be difficult, expensive, or downright dangerous. The most famous example is the flight simulator for training pilots. Highly sophisticated computer graphics that react instantaneously to user input can provide effectively realistic simulations. When wired gloves are used, the user can actually manipulate the simulated environment. Add goggles to shut out the real world and the user begins to feel "immersed" in this virtual world. Virtual reality is being used in a variety of fields, including product design, architecture, medicine, chemistry, and, of course, entertainment. Some primitive forms of VR have even reached the public in video arcades. In fact, video games of increasingly higher bit rate might be considered a form of VR. This chapter's scenario asks readers to develop a presentation for other colleagues at a teacher meeting about the potential of using VR in the classroom.

Chapter 20. The Third Millennium School: From Industrial to Information Society

The modern public school and compulsory universal education arose along with the spread of the industrial revolution in the nineteenth century. It reflected the new need for literate populations to work in the new enterprises associated with industrialization. But it also trained whole populations of young people to sit for many hours, working at repetitive tasks, an ideal preparation for a job in the factory upon graduation. The model for schools that has continued right through the end of the twentieth century is a factory model. But the economies of many countries around the world have changed. They are no longer based on manufacturing, which is now done primarily in developing countries. Most jobs in the United States, Europe, and Japan are white collar, not blue collar. Information processing characterizes these economies now. Shouldn't schools in these information societies also change to prepare young people for occupations that primarily involve the processing of information? This chapter's scenario asks readers to develop a plan for the information society school, with an emphasis on what role technology might play in such a school.

From Video to Virtual Reality

TECHNOLOGY AND ITS INSTRUCTIONAL POTENTIAL

Never has technology been more important in the field of education. Technological advances in the second half of the twentieth century have provided unparalleled opportunities for teachers to instruct with great dynamism and effectiveness. Both television and the computer arose as viable new technologies in the wake of World War II. Only a half century later they are transforming how we live our lives and how we learn. As we enter the new millennium, an understanding of these two technologies in all their hybrid forms has become extremely important for educators. One characteristic of excellent twenty-first century teachers will be their ability to efectively use these technologies to advance the education of their pupils

TELEVISION TECHNOLOGIES

Television has come a long way from its beginnings as a black-and-white broadcast medium that could only be viewed "live." Over the years, it has experienced a series of dramatic technological developments. It was given color capability. Videotape was invented, and television footage can now be viewed at one's convenience. Tape is also very much under the control of the user, who can fast-forward, reverse, slow down, or pause the footage. Videodiscs are even more proficient at pausing on a still frame. They also have the advantage of being able to randomly access any video still on a given side of the disc within seconds (with tape there is, of course, a longer wait while the tape shuttles). Both tape and disc formats have evolved over the years. Videotape formats have gotten thinner and cassettes have gotten smaller while retaining the quality of their older, bulkier predecessors. Discs have shrunk from twelve inches to five inches, and these compact disc formats have evolved from the CD-ROM to the much more dynamic Digital Video Disk (DVD). The user-friendliness of television as a medium has improved enormously over the years, and with videotapes and videodiscs, educators can present television footage to their classes in very selective ways. For example, teachers can present only the segments of a video that they want to show, pause on critical still frames, show certain sequences in slow motion, and replay the most important footage if they wish.

Schools of the twenty-first century also will have access to far more television than did the schools of the twentieth century. Television transmission systems have undergone a radical transformation. The old broadcasting tower is still around, but higher-quality results can be obtained in several other ways. Cable can bring a better picture, and cable itself is improving, as its copper coaxial wiring is replaced with optical fiber that can carry more channels and even higher-quality signals. Satellite services can provide enormous numbers of channels with very high quality, and with the newer satellites sending even stronger signals, the latest receiver dishes can be smaller than ever. The increased number of networks associated with this expansion in television signal delivery has resulted in a substantial increase in information-based television footage available for both home and school use. Educators can tune in to the Discovery Channel, the Learning Channel, Arts and Entertainment, USA Network, the Cable News Network, the History Channel, and so on.

Teachers also can now, more easily than ever, use television production as a class activity. The bulky video portapaks of the past have evolved into the miniaturized camcorders of today. Even a child can hand-hold the smallest models. These units also are more durable, because the tubes that registered the visual signal have been replaced by solid-state devices. These "chip" cameras are more sensitive to light, so extra lights are rarely necessary. The automatization of critical camera functions, like exposure and focus, has made it relatively easy to shoot acceptable television footage. Special effects built into cameras— freeze frames, strobe effects, dissolves, wipes, and so on—can liven up the footage. Editing of footage between two video recording units can be done right at school with one of the new, inexpensive editor controllers.

Showing television footage in the classroom has become easier with the availability of the videocassette recorder, as already mentioned. But footage also can be shown more effectively than ever to whole classes because of the larger sets available nowadays. Very clear cathode ray tube sets are now available in widths of more than thirty inches. The new plasma screens, using a variant of liquid crystal technology, can display a very clear signal on a large, flat screen. Projection units have become stronger also, and they can produce even bigger, brighter images for large group viewing.

The video signal itself is clearer these days. New tape formats, like Super-VHS, Hi-8 mm, and the half-inch Betacam, separate the brightness and color signals so as to preserve their clarity. These "component" signals are delivered separately through the multiple pins of an S connector rather than being sent together along the same wire, as they were with the older "composite" approach. The result is a brighter picture with more vivid colors. These formats also preserve many more lines of resolution than did the older videotape formats, resulting in a TV picture with clearer focus and better defined images. But the real quantum leap in signal quality will come with the changeover to an entirely new form of television, known as High-Definition Television (HDTV).

HDTV has more than twice the resolution of the television we are used to.

In fact, it is very close to the clarity of 35-mm film. Its shape will be more like film, longer and shorter than today's TV picture. This upgrade will significantly improve the quality of television, and eventually it will reach the classroom. Unfortunately, this may take some time, because HDTV uses completely different equipment than the older form of television. But by 2006, all broadcast television stations in the U.S. must convert over to HDTV. By the end of the decade, Americans will be watching this improved form of television.

THE DIGITIZATION OF TELEVISION

HDTV represents a major shift in the technology of television, and it reflects an even larger phenomenon in the field of technology. That is the digital revolution, which has migrated from the computer world into every other media format, including text processing, sound reproduction, animation, and so on. Whereas the older form of TV was processed as an analog waveform, HDTV is processed digitally. What is the difference between analog and digital forms of information processing? Analog signals are a continuous waveform, with the amplitude and frequency of the waves determining the characteristics of the information. For example, a loud, high-pitched sound signal would have waves of considerable height (or amplitude) producing its loudness, and many waves (a high frequency) producing its high pitch.

The same signal could be processed digitally. Digital data is either there, or it is not. In a computer, either the electricity is flowing, or it is not. On a magnetic disk, either the surface is magnetized, or it is not. On a laser disc, either the beam reflects, or it does not. This data can be mathematically represented by 1's, for existing data, and by 0's, for nonexistent data.

These binary digits (0 and 1) can be used to indicate any value in the base two counting system. For example, in base two, this number represents a value of three: 11. And this number represents a value of nine: 1001. These numbers can be used to replicate the wave patterns of analog data, so that a given signal can be converted from analog to digital form and back again. Thus our loud, high-pitched sound could be converted into a series of binary digits (0's and 1's) that would encode all the information about the amplitude and frequency of its waveform. This data could be recorded on a compact disc, in digital form. When we play the CD, the data is reconverted back into analog form before being amplified and played on our speakers.

The digitization of television signals has led to several significant developments. Digital editing systems are rapidly replacing the older analog systems. The old method of creating a program involved manually dubbing footage from one videotape recorder to another. But digital systems capture the television footage and allow the professional editor to manipulate it much more flexibly. Special effects are easier to add. When the shots have been ordered to create a program, the footage is exported back to tape. When digital tape is used, the signal is clearer and can be copied with almost no loss of quality.

Digitizing can also reduce the size of the television signal, so it can be sent over telecommunications lines that formerly only handled smaller bandwidth signals, like voice. This compression can be completed by a codec (compressor/decompressor), and the compressed video can be used in conjunction with computer signals. This "desktop video" is being used in distance education systems, allowing teachers and students to see and hear one another in interactive exchanges that require less expensive connections, via phone lines or special ISDN lines (which digitize signals and double the amount of information that a normal phone line can carry). This compressed video has also been part of the information provided on compact discs and on the World Wide Web. Constantly improving compression techniques have led to the development of the Digital Video Disk (DVD), a compact disc which holds several hours of television footage. The movie on DVD is here and already challenging videotape as the public's video medium of choice.

THE COMPUTER REVOLUTION

This discussion of the digital revolution in the field of television brings us full circle to where all the digitization began, in the computer industry. The computer was the first device to digitally process information as a series of binary digits or bits (0's and 1's), rather than as a wave format. And it has been the computer that has most radically transformed our society and that some day may significantly transform our education system. It was the development of the computer chip that led to this digital revolution. This so-called microprocessor "chip" was essentially a set of circuits that could run a computer, miniaturized and pressed on a small piece of silicon. Chips can be found today in nearly every sophisticated piece of electronic equipment.

The chip allowed for the miniaturization of computers. The development of the microcomputer made computing available to the general public and also to teachers in the classroom. The ongoing advances in chip technology have led to the availability of smaller and smaller machines, with faster and faster microprocessors and increasing amounts of random access memory (RAM). Computer capability has also expanded rapidly in terms of magnetic storage devices used to hold data. At first, tapes were used, but disks replaced them because of their faster random access. Hard disk drives have layers of multiple disks sealed in an airtight container. In the past decade, their memory storage capacity has increased from a few megabytes to tens of gigabytes. Likewise, the floppy disk for transporting data has evolved into the Zip disk, with sixty times the storage capacity. Optical discs have also improved. The DVD holds over ten times as much data as the CD-ROM. As machines have become more powerful, their instructional potential has been enhanced. They can run software of greater complexity, with enhanced features and more multimedia resources. For example, classroom microcomputers can already run advanced applications such as virtual reality (VR) and artificial intelligence (AI). Handheld devices will soon be capable of very sophisticated operations.

Computers have played a number of different instructional roles over the past twenty years. When computers first arrived in the schools, in the early eighties, little software was available for them. So programming was a major concern for educators, because this was what you could do with a computer. Programming languages like BASIC, LOGO, and Pascal were taught as part of so-called "computer literacy" programs. Programming forced students to learn a new symbol system. It encouraged them to be creative about developing programs that might do interesting things. It forced them to think with a certain logic, without which they would not be able to get their programs to run. Programming also demanded some problem-solving ability, in that the programs usually needed to be debugged and this required some troubleshooting. The skills associated with programming a computer were fairly high level cognitive abilities and, of course, programming is still widely taught to this day. However, what a novice programmer can accomplish was usually a bit disappointing to those who tried to use the programming. Programming was also somewhat difficult for many students and highly frustrating for those less capable of grasping its principles.

So the predominant use of the new machines began shifting to other kinds of educational endeavors. Programs produced by commercial software companies were distributed across the country, and computer-assisted instruction (CAI) became the next computer fad. This type of software varied in quality, but the best examples showed how effective a computer could be as an instructional device. It could present a well-organized lesson, with appropriate amounts of instruction, drill, and review. Motivation might be enhanced by the inclusion of graphics and sound. It could diagnose a student's skill level. It could provide feedback for students, indicating whether they understood the material. It could provide positive reinforcement for correct responses. It could even respond to how well the student was doing by "branching" to an appropriate sequence that presented easier material to struggling students or more difficult material to those who were doing extremely well. At the end of the lesson, it could evaluate the student's overall performance, by keeping records of how many correct answers the student had entered. It likewise could keep records of how an entire class was doing and even provide recommendations as to what lesson a student should try next.

SOME "KILLER" APPLICATIONS

Even as many classroom microcomputers were running CAI programs, a set of computer applications made their appearance and revolutionized the use of computers. Word processing became the number one use of computers and remains so to this very day. In the field of education, its availability led to the computer laboratory dedicated to improving writing skills. In fact, word processing, along with the development of the spell checker, probably contributed to the movement in the teaching of language arts known as the "whole language" approach. This approach encouraged teachers to begin teaching writing at an early age, while students were learning to read. It encouraged learning to read and write by having students do just that, rather than spending a great deal of time completing exercises to develop skills. There was an emphasis on revising one's writing, which was facilitated by the availability of word processing. There was also a de-emphasis on skills like spelling and grammar. This curricular shift may have been influenced by the availability of spell checkers and, later, by grammar checkers.

The spreadsheet application provided a huge grid upon which computerized calculations could be performed. Changes in the figures could easily be entered, and results were instantaneously provided. The spreadsheet's influence was, of course, far greater in the business world than it has been in education. Nevertheless, its application in the mathematics classroom, along with that of its cousin, the calculator, has been relatively significant. Calculating devices also can be used effectively in any coursework that involves mathematical calculation (such as the physical sciences, for example). They have saved many students from the drudgery of repetitive calculations. They also can save time spent on this fairly low level cognitive task that might be better used to deal with more conceptually challenging mathematics activities, such as problem solving.

The computerized database is another application that has only begun to affect education, but whose ultimate influence on the field may be far greater. Computerized databases allow for storage of data by category. Not only can information be well organized within the database, but it can then be easily retrieved with computerized search techniques. Individual items can be found, and instances that match whole sets of data can be isolated. Students can learn valuable skills when asked to create their own databases and to use them for information retrieval.

Professional databases of information on various topics have the potential to expand opportunities for independent research. Computerized access to these databases, on compact discs or via the World Wide Web, will give pupils in schools access to far more information than they have ever had before. In addition, well-designed indices and sophisticated search engines will help them find the specific material that they are interested in. These expanded learning opportunities may make the aforementioned constructivist approaches more feasible in the classrooms of the future.

Another computer application that has generated some excitement in schools is the multimedia authoring tool. Programs like HyperCard, HyperStudio, Toolbook, Authorware, and Director have enabled teachers and students to create their own instructional programs, without them having to actually know how to program. These authoring languages use straightforward commands (in English), which they convert automatically to computer code. With these applications, even relative novices can create lively interactive lessons that take advantage of graphics, sounds, and even videos.

These authoring tools have eliminated some of the complexity and drudgery associated with programming. Many students have benefited from their efforts to produce these kinds of computer-based materials in that they have learned something about the topic and simultaneously developed some computer skills. However, the process remains rather time-consuming and the results generally remain far less sophisticated than those of professional software developers.

Other computer tools can now assist students who wish to work with publications, with graphic arts, and with television. "Desktop publishing" applications, like PageMaker, provide computerized layout capabilities for text and graphic materials. This software allows users to develop their own professional-looking publications, with multiple columns, headlines, photos, and so on. With today's high quality printers, professional-looking publications can be produced at modest expense.

Photoprocessing software, like Photoshop and PhotoDeluxe, can digitize any still graphic using a scanner to capture the image. The tools provided with these applications can modify an image in almost any conceivable way. Multiple pictures can be combined and arranged in interesting ways. Imaginetive, artistic results can be obtained by users who master the software.

"Desktop video" applications like Premier, Avid, and Media100, developed to edit television programming, can digitize video footage, and its editing tools allow the user to very flexibly place shots in a sequence that can easily be revised by simply dragging them with a mouse. Audio footage can be edited separately, and a variety of audio tools can be used to modify sound in a number of interesting ways. Special visual effects are programmed into the application, and the editor can conveniently select them as transitions between shots. This "nonlinear editing" gives the television producer far more control and flexibility in the editing of the final program than was possible with the old-fashioned analog approach.

COMPUTER NETWORKING AND TELECOMMUNICATIONS

The networking of computers has led to what could be described as a second computer revolution. Gradually, over the past few decades, our homes, schools, and businesses have all been wired so that computers can send information back and forth. Originally, this networking provided connections between a computer and terminals that could be used to access it. As microcomputers began to proliferate, these connections allowed computers to communicate with each other. To send these signals beyond the walls of a facility, the vast telephone network was available. However, the telephone network was designed to process analog signals, used for voice communication, and computer data is digital. So a special piece of equipment was needed to convert the digital signal to analog form, and back again at the other end of the wire, if computers were going to communicate via telecommunications lines. This modulator/demodulator, which was abbreviated as modem, is installed on any computer line connecting to the telephone service. The modem is now a standard built-in feature of any new computer. Older modems could not convert data fast enough to take full advantage of a telephone line's transmission speed, but most of the newer models are able to do this.

Telecommunications connections, both wired and wireless, have multiplied significantly over the course of the past few decades to meet the rising demand for communications services, both analog and digital. The standard phone line remains the basic connection. But for the basic trunk lines and satellite signals, much higher volumes of data are handled and much more robust connections are necessary. For some applications, like the transmission of moving images, a higher rate of transmission is desirable. The amount of data that can be carried along a telecommunications line is called the "bandwidth." Different types of signals have different bandwidth characteristics. While text and voice bandwidth requirements are relatively small, music takes up more bandwidth, still pictures even more, and video's bandwidth requirements are huge. Without sufficient bandwidth available in a connection, a signal will be transmitted very slowly and sometimes will experience degradation. This is why video is now often compressed to reduce its bandwidth before being transmitted.

Telecommunications services now offer several different types of lines with different bandwidth capabilities. The standard telephone line has a bandwidth capacity of 56 kilobytes of information per second (Kbps). An Integrated Services Digital Network (ISDN) line digitizes the signal and doubles the bandwidth to 128 Kbps. A level-one telecommunications connection, abbreviated T1, can carry much more data: 1,500 Kbps or 1.5 megabytes per second (Mbps). Some newer experimental connections can also provide substantial bandwidth. The Digital Service Line (DSL) can receive the equivalent of a T1 connection, at 1.5 Mbps. But it only sends out at the standard 64 Kbps. This Web access strategy allows for downloading information very efficiently off a network, and it assumes that most clients will not often need to send out large signals. Another Internet-oriented service, the cable modem line, uses television cable connections for downloading computer signals at a rapid 10 Mbps. Finally, the most efficient type of connection, the level-three telecommunications line (T3) carries twenty-eight times the bandwidth of a T1 line: 45 Mbps.

Many businesses have added ISDN connections to their regular telephone lines to speed up data transfer. T1 lines are used for many video-based distance education projects. An institution may feed its many smaller lines into a T1 line that connects out to a telecommunications service. Larger institutions may need a T3 connection for this purpose. T3 lines can also carry a full analog television signal. The new cable modem and DSL connections will be used by both business and home clients interested in fast Web access.

Computerized telecommunications connections have expanded significantly in the 1990s and have altered how millions of people exchange information. One good example is the hybrid technology that has arisen for rapid delivery of printed materials. A marriage of the telephone with print duplicating technology, facsimile (fax) services have provided the ability to instantaneously send printed documents over telecommunications lines. Like other electronic forms of communication, this technology has improved the efficiency with which people communicate with one another in every field, including education.

Electronic mail has also provided a fast, inexpensive, convenient way for people to communicate. Like fax, it has helped accelerate the pace of the working world, allowing people in different locations to more efficiently collaborate on projects. It provides an opportunity for teachers to collaborate with colleagues from other schools, in other districts, across the country, or even in other countries. Likewise, students can communicate with their peers in other locations. "Keypals" in different countries can exchange letters much more efficiently electronically than through printed "snail mail" (although aspiring stamp collectors will be disappointed).

Electronic discussion groups can provide interesting information for professionals. There are many educationally oriented listservs and newsgroups to which teachers can subscribe. Some electronic bulletin boards hold postings of relevance to teachers. Not only are there discussions that may be of interest, but also participants often can get specific information that they need from other participants. Teachers need no longer depend on the weekly teacher's meeting for their professional development.

The World Wide Web can provide an enormous amount of information at the touch of a keystroke. Web search engines and extensive indices help users find what they are looking for (although this can still be a struggle). The Web is a research tool of unbelievable magnitude. Websites exist for almost every topic imaginable. The Web has a wide range of material, from little-known facts on obscure topics to entire college curricula to be studied for credit. It is being used extensively in very practical ways, and its commercial applications are only now beginning to be realized. In the field of education, both teachers and students can use it for their own independent investigations. The Web may encourage constructivism in schools, for it provides information for students that they might previously have been unable to obtain. It is especially helpful to those who do not live near a large library.

FUTURE POSSIBILITIES

Some other recent computer developments have exciting potential. One is artificial intelligence (AI), a way of programming the computer to respond as a human being might. One type of AI is the "expert system," a computer program designed to ask a user a set of relevant questions. It keeps track of the responses and then searches a huge database of information about the topic to find out how it should react. It then makes recommendations to the user about how to proceed. In education, AI could be used to support computer-assisted instruction (CAI). This intelligent CAI (ICAI) might tutor students in far more sophisticated ways than is currently possible. For example, it might be able to discern the learning style of a given student and then provide learning materials accordingly.

Another futuristic computer application is virtual reality (VR). This is an advanced form of computer simulation, wherein the user can actually interact with the computer environment, usually with the use of wired gloves and goggles (but bodysuits also have been experimented with). Virtual reality environments seek to accurately reproduce real-world environments. However, VR is also used to design new products and new environments, because they can be tested by users before they are actually developed. Virtual reality applications could provide vicarious experiences for students, which could be both more motivating and more meaningful than simply reading about a phenomenon. Although the costs of these programs is very high at this point, someday we will see VR applications in the schools.

We hope this introduction to the two most significant technologies used in teaching, television and computers, has helped prepare you to work with the scenarios in this book. Many of the aforementioned technological developments will be addressed specifically in upcoming chapters. If there are technical references that you are unfamiliar with, check the reading material in the chapter bibliographies for more information about those topics. This book is meant as only a starting point for you. If you become a teacher, you will need to continue learning about the potential of instructional technologies for the rest of your career.

REFERENCES

Gooden, A., and F. Silverman. 1998. *Computers in the classroom. How teachers and students are using technology to transform learning.* San Francisco, CA: Jossey-Bass.

Heinich, R., M. Molenda, J. Russell, and S. Smaldino. 1999. *Instructional media and technologies for learning.* Englewood Cliffs, NJ: Prentice Hall.

Jonassen, D. 1996. *Computers in the classroom: Mindtools for critical thinking.* Englewood Cliffs, NJ: Prentice Hall.

Kemp, J., and D. Smellie. 1993. *Planning, producing and using instructional technologies.* New York: Addison-Wesley.

Oliver, E. 1994. Video tools for distance education. In *Distance education: Strategies and tools,* edited by B. Willis. Englewood Cliffs, NJ: Educational Technology Publications.

Ravet, S., and M. Layte. 1997. *Technology-based training: A comprehensive guide to choosing, implementing, managing, and developing new technologies in training.* Houston, TX: Gulf Publishing.

Roblyer, M., J. Edwards, and M. Havriluk. 1996. *Integrating educational technology into teaching.* Englewood Cliffs, NJ: Prentice Hall.

Schrum, L., and B. Berenfeld. 1997. *Teaching and learning in the information age: A guide to educational telecommunications.* New York: Allyn & Bacon.

From Conditioning to Constructivism

LEARNING THEORIES AND THEIR IMPACT ON HOW WE TEACH

As we have noted, the last few decades have seen enormous changes in the hardware and software technologies that we have available for education. Television has steadily improved in quality and stands to make a big leap forward with the introduction of HDTV. Computers have increased in power and speed faster than any other technology in history. The software that makes those tools useful has improved as well. Graphical User Interfaces (GUIs) such as Windows, tools like digital nonlinear video editing, and new application programs and multimedia development tools have radically changed what is possible.

Other recent developments have important implications for instructional technology. Over time, our notions of how people learn, and hence how they should be taught, have changed. From behaviorism through cognitive science to today's emphasis on constructivism, we now view teaching and learning very differently from the ways we did a few years ago. To a large extent, what we know and believe about human learning will determine how we use instructional technologies, so we will take a look at that issue here.

BEHAVIORISM

Behaviorism as a theory of psychology and learning became influential early in the twentieth century and reached its pinnacle in the 1950s and 1960s. The theory has its roots in the work of Ivan Pavlov in Russia around the turn of the century. In his famous experiments with dogs, Pavlov showed how an animal could be conditioned to salivate at the prompting of an arbitrary stimulus, such as a bell, if that stimulus were consistently paired with the presentation of food. Gradually, less and less food might be presented along with the ringing of the bell. Finally, food need no longer be offered, and the bell alone could cause the dog to salivate. Pavlov called this process the "conditioned reflex."

One American psychologist, John B. Watson, even tried to use conditioned reflexes as the foundation for *all* behavior, including learning. Watson was the first self-proclaimed "behaviorist," and he formulated the basic principle that we can study only behavior, not mental states or thought processes. However, it quickly became apparent that Pavlovian conditioned reflexes were far too limited to account for any significant portion of what the human brain could do.

Associative learning in animals and human beings was studied extensively in the United States by Edward Thorndike at Columbia University at about the same time that Pavlov was conducting his studies with dogs. He examined how certain types of stimuli affected learning, with a focus on how students might be prompted to learn new material by repeated association with material they already knew. For example, new words could be taught to novice readers by repeatedly pairing the word with a picture of what the word represented. He also examined methods of shaping learning behavior through rewards and punishments. Thorndike coined the phrase "law of effect" to describe how learning could be guided by incentives or disincentives.

Behaviorism's best-known and perhaps most-radical proponent was B. F. Skinner. Skinner, who taught at Harvard University, believed, like his behaviorist predecessors, that whatever psychological processes might be taking place within animals and people, it was possible to study accurately only the observable behavior of organisms and the conditions that produced that behavior. From such studies, Skinner developed an approach he called *operant conditioning*, wherein he modified behavior by altering external conditions, noting the response to those conditions, and encouraging or discouraging that response. These three elements of the learning experience—technically called the discriminative stimulus, the response, and the reinforcing stimulus—make up what Skinner called the *conditioned operant*, which he saw as the basic building block of everything that we (or rats or pigeons) do.

THE IMPACT OF BEHAVIORISM

Although few psychologists or educators are pure behaviorists today, the effects of behaviorism in general linger in much that we do in education. One clear effect that has remained has been our emphasis on writing objectives (learning objectives, behavioral objectives, performance objectives) for all our lessons. Nearly everyone who gets a teaching certificate must learn to write objectives for lessons, and many schools and districts insist on them as well. The idea was originally developed by a protégé of Skinner's, Robert Mager, who made two important points. First, in education, as in other things in life, we need to be very clear about our goals if we are to reach them. Second, we cannot assess how much someone has learned without defining, in observable terms, what learning we are seeking. From these notions, he suggested that we should specify the goals of our instruction in terms of behavioral objectives, which usually consist of three parts: the behavior to be learned, the conditions under which the behavior is to be demonstrated, and the criteria by which to judge the amount of learning. The practice of writing objectives comes directly from behavioral psychology and persists to this day.

Another, more complex legacy of behaviorism was a teaching strategy known as programmed instruction. In this phrase the word *programmed* does not refer to computer programming but to carefully sequencing and developing the instruction itself. Programmed instruction is based on several key principles. First, the instruction is broken down into extremely small steps. If the basic element of all behavior is the conditioned operant, then the way to teach complex behaviors is to teach all the building blocks one at a time. The second key principle is that people learn best by making active responses at each step. Therefore, programmed instruction generally demands that learners make overt responses every few seconds during the instruction. This occurs in tandem with the third key principle: behavior is learned (and recurs) when it is reinforced. Thus, programmed instruction that teaches a complex skill consists of a long series of small steps in which the learner reads some small bit of information, answers a question about it, and gets reinforced for a correct answer, usually by being right.

When it was done well, programmed instruction could be quite effective. When done poorly, as it often was, it was boring and ineffective. Often the steps were *too* small for most people. There was little challenge in answering each question and the pace of instruction was needlessly slow. In addition, there are a limited number of ways to vary reinforcement. How many times can one be told "Good job!" without it losing all meaning? All in all, while there were some excellent and effective instances of programmed instruction, there were also many poor ones, and the technique has not lasted.

Programmed instruction also led to one early example of instructional technology hardware: the teaching machine. Even before the widespread use of computers in education, teaching machines were mechanical devices that presented information and questions, accepted a student response, and informed the learner of the correct answer. These, too, could be effective or ineffective, engaging or boring. Once computers started becoming widespread, teaching machines were superseded by the first instances of computer-assisted instruction (CAI), and the initial large-scale CAI projects were under way by the early 1960s. They were based on behaviorist principles and the techniques associated with programmed instruction.

One problem with both programmed instruction and teaching machines was that they were relatively inflexible. Often, individual learners already knew many of the individual small steps that are a part of any instructional program. However, in a programmed instruction book or a teaching machine that proceeded strictly linearly, there was no opportunity to skip the parts that were already familiar. The idea that occurred to programmers was to make branching programmed instruction. When learners responded to some of the questions, they would be sent to different parts of the program depending on their answers. If their responses were incorrect, they could repeat instruction or be sent to a simpler version of the same section. A series of correct answers could allow them to skip parts of the lesson that they already knew. This turned out to be difficult to implement with just books and teaching machines, but the idea seemed to be terrific. The development of general-purpose computers made it possible.

It was not lost on the behaviorists and instructional programmers that computers could be programmed to present branching programmed instruction. Much of the early CAI was explicitly an attempt to present branching programmed instruction. Early CAI authoring languages and systems were designed to implement this kind of instruction, an influence that has continued to this day. In spite of the increased sophistication of the media that can be presented in CAI programs—video, animation, sound, and so on—the interactions that people have with the programs are often not much more than receiving information, answering simple questions about it, and getting feedback on their responses. If they are lucky, learners might get branched to a different part of the program depending on the answer they give. This instruction comes from the behaviorist tradition and reflects both its strengths and its weaknesses.

Ultimately, as a psychological theory of human behavior, behaviorism did not hold up well. It was clear that while white rats could often be trained to respond in fairly predictable ways, people are more complex. Sometimes they behave as expected, but sometimes they do not. For example, people sometimes spurn incentives to behave in certain ways for philosophical reasons. Even when subjected to physical torment, people have refused to cooperate with those they considered their enemies. Complex thinking processes, like those involved in language, presented special problems for the behaviorist model. In the late 1950s, people started challenging the basic tenets of behaviorism. By the 1970s, behaviorism was being supplanted by cognitive psychology.

COGNITIVE THEORIES

Researchers began to feel constrained by the limitations of behaviorism. Behaviorism was unable to effectively address a critical issue: How do people think? Critics noted that people are more than just the sum total of the behaviors that they engage in. People make plans, remember things, forget things, solve problems, hypothesize, and much more. These aspects of cognition could not be fully understood just by looking at behavior. Psychologists believed they needed to address central cognitive processes like memory, attention, and logical reasoning. Thus, cognitive psychology was born out of the need to understand more about human thought processes.

One major influence on cognitive psychology was the digital computer itself. The behaviorists had argued that people's cognitive processes could not be observed, so they could not be studied scientifically. Yet the computer is a machine that also seems to exhibit cognitive processes. These electronic processes cannot be observed directly either, but they can be studied. In fact, computers offered researchers a way to study human thought processes by modeling them in software. People began to write programs that were intended to mimic human thought processes as a way to develop precise theories of cognition that could be tested.

Cognitive psychology has produced a very general theory of human cognition that varies somewhat from researcher to researcher. This basic conceptualization is generally called the "human information-processing model." The basic idea is that people process information through a series of different systems. There are our sensory systems, like sight, hearing, and so on, which take in stimuli from the environment. Next, an attention and control system helps determine which information is processed and acted on. Much of the information that we deal with is channeled through a limited-capacity system called working (or short-term) memory. This is the real bottleneck in the whole system, since it seems to be able to deal with only a handful of items at a time. Internally, the other major system in human cognitive processing is long-term memory, which holds not only our individual memories but also the concepts and intellectual skills that make it possible for us to think and to learn.

Long-term memory is especially important, of course, since it is where we hold most of what we know. What we know includes our memories of what we have done and what has happened to us. It also includes our knowledge of language, encompassing both word meanings and grammar, as well as basic concepts. Finally, it holds data critical to our performance of specific skills, such as how to ride a bicycle, how to solve quadratic equations, or how to flirt with a stranger. These diverse capabilities are probably stored in long-term memory in different ways, and researchers have distinguished among types of memory, like episodic (memory for events), semantic (memory for meaning), and eidetic (memory for visual images).

The information-processing model implies certain things about how we should teach people of all ages. The goal is to get information and skills entered and consolidated into long-term memory in such a way that the learners can retrieve it when they need it. This is not necessarily easy. For example, to learn something we usually have to pay attention to it, but we can pay attention to only a few things at a time. The more mental effort a task requires, the less likely we are to be able to pay attention to anything else. As teachers, if we do not get a student's attention or if we overload a student with too much to pay attention to, then we reduce the chance that the student will learn anything.

Working memory is similarly limited. It is where we do most of our conscious thinking, but it seems not to be very large, and it takes time and effort to successfully transfer information from working memory to long-term memory. In general, it appears that most of us can hold only about seven discrete items in short-term memory at any one time. This is about the size of an unfamiliar telephone number. Therefore, in instruction we need to ensure that people have the time they need to transfer knowledge to long-term memory. Plus, students need to know that there are strategies, like chunking information meaningfully or using visual imagery, that can make the learning process easier or more effective. Often the effective use of learning strategies is what distinguishes a good learner from a poor one. The process of transferring information to long-term memory is not automatic; learning takes mental work.

Learning involves more than just receiving and storing information, of course. Probably even more important is learning such skills as solving math problems, analyzing interpersonal situations, or writing short stories. Cognitive science points out that people must actively process the information and practice the skills in order to learn. That means that we must find ways to help students link new information and skills to what they already know, put them in context, develop their own perspectives about it, and decide how meaningful this material is to them. We must also ensure that people have the opportunity to perform the new skills—physical and intellectual—that they are learning, especially in meaningful real-world contexts. It is rarely enough just to hear about *how* to do something; we all must also actually *do* it to be proficient. Whereas behaviorists stress the importance of practice in training people to develop certain skills, cognitive psychologists emphasize the need to perform skills in real contexts and to learn strategies, not simply to be trained to engage in specific behaviors.

Various other elements of cognitive science are also relevant to how we teach and hence how we use various technologies in education. For example, artificial intelligence is a branch of cognitive science that attempts to program computers so that they exhibit the key features of intelligent behavior and thought. A variety of approaches to this have been tried, with only partial success. One key method is to program a series of rules into the computer's long-term memory. These rules are of the form "If the following items are in short-term memory, then do this." When hundreds of such rules are present, the behavior of the computer gets quite complex and begins to exhibit some characteristics of intelligence. The most successful of such systems have been limited to very specific fields; for example, some kinds of medical diagnosis, computer system configuration, automotive troubleshooting, and other well-defined areas. In these "expert systems," the rules and data items are specific to each area of expertise. Therefore, the range of problems that most systems can solve is fairly narrow, and they cannot function outside that range.

APPLICATION OF COGNITIVE THEORIES

How else has cognitive psychology affected the field of education? The cognitive psychologist David Ausubel attempted to describe the cognitive structures associated with the learning process. He emphasized the importance of prior knowledge to the learner's ability to understand and remember new material. In introducing a new lesson, Ausubel recommended the use of "advance organizers" that made clear connections between the new information and material that the learner might already be familiar with. To test this approach he conducted an experiment. He taught two similar groups of learners a nearly identical lesson about Buddhism. For one group he provided an advance organizer, the statement that "Buddhism was similar to Christianity in many ways." That group scored significantly higher on a posttest of knowledge about Buddhism. This was evidence that Ausubel's advance organizer approach could be effective.

Ausubel also analyzed the relationships that new material might have to existing knowledge and provided a set of classification schemes. One example might be whether the new information was subordinate, coordinate, or superordinate with respect to material the learner already knew. Subordinate material was more specific, coordinate was equivalent in degree of generality, and superordinate was more general. For example, "shark" might be subordinate to "fish," coordinate with "ray," and superordinate to "Great White Shark." Learners who could classify new facts in this way would be able to develop complex, sophisticated cognitive structures in a given field of knowledge.

So-called schema theorists, like Richard Anderson, followed up on Ausubel's work, calling the cognitive structures "schema." Strong schema are well developed and include a clear set of fundamental concepts as well as specific facts about a given topic. Strong schema allow a learner to quickly grasp new material on a given topic, for he or she can relate effectively to it, know its relationship to similar material, and integrate it with what is already known. Conversely, weak schema make it difficult for learners to grasp new material.

Educators should be concerned with analyzing a learner's schema for a given subject area and then providing material of appropriate complexity. According to schema theorists, *prior knowledge* is critical to comprehension of new material. Schema theory supports holistic approaches to teaching reading, which encourage readers to apply what they already know and to make educated guesses about new words based on their context. It helped spawn the whole language school of teaching language arts, which emphasized language experiences and de-emphasized traditional teaching of phonics to decoding words.

Jean Piaget studied how cognitive structures developed in children. His work identified a series of stages that characterized how a child tended to make sense of the world. According to Piaget, in the first two years of life, in the "sensorimotor" phase, the child establishes a sense of self apart from the rest of the world. In the "preoperational" stage, lasting roughly from ages 3 to 7 years, children begin to establish object permanence but often use simplistic and erroneous cues to determine the size and volume of objects. Certain concepts remain very difficult for them. From about 7 until 11, children move into a stage of "concrete operations" wherein they begin to develop more sophisticated concepts and more accurate, scientific ways of measuring things. Finally, at the stage of "formal thinking" a child develops the ability to think in abstract ways.

Piaget's work had an enormous influence upon educators of the very young. It indicated that until a child reaches a certain age, he or she cannot learn certain types of material. This concept of developmental "readiness" became a critical issue in early childhood education. Introducing certain concepts associated with language and mathematics too soon was simply a waste of time. Despite what the behaviorists may have thought, no amount of practice would move a child from one of Piaget's stages to another. In a sense, when it came to teaching, "timing was everything" (or at least very important!).

The psychologist Robert Gagné took an applied approach, analyzing the cognitive processes associated with learning, and defining the types of learning activities that result in effective learning. He described these as the "Nine Events of Learning." These are

- gaining the learner's attention;
- informing the learner of the objective of the instruction;

- stimulating recall of the prerequisite learning for the objective;
- presenting the stimulus material to the learner;
- providing learning guidance to the learner;
- eliciting the desired performance from the learner;
- providing feedback about the correctness of the performance to the learner;
- assessing the performance; and
- enhancing retention and transfer of the learning.

Cognitive psychology has also been applied to the use of technology in teaching. Intelligent computer-assisted instruction (ICAI) is the instructional application of an expert system. Usually, an ICAI program consists of several different parts that work together. First, there is a piece that knows how to do the task. Second, there is a piece that, over time, learns how the student does the task. Third, there is a piece that compares the two, figuring out what to teach the student. Finally, there is an expert system that knows a variety of teaching strategies. An ICAI program combines these systems to specify how to teach this particular student the necessary information and skills. All the pieces together are able to diagnose where learners have gone wrong (and why) and to plan a way to teach them better.

There are many examples of these systems, some of which have been quite successful. However, most of them have not made it out of the research labs and into actual classroom use. "Buggy" is a program that taught subtraction skills to elementary school children. Through extensive research the authors found that there were a limited number of ways that students could go wrong when they subtract. That is, there were a fairly small number of basic mistakes or "bugs" in their subtraction procedures. Buggy could give the children subtraction problems and, based on their patterns of right and wrong answers, diagnose which bugs they exhibited. It would then teach them ways to debug their subtraction. Several other successful examples exist, including systems to teach geometry, to program in the computer language Lisp, and to diagnose blood infections.

THE CONSTRUCTIVIST APPROACH

Cognitive psychology, like behaviorism before it, is now under attack. One key question continues to be whether human learning and cognition can be understood scientifically. Cognitive scientists have not been able to answer all our questions about human thought and learning. A new interpretation of how people learn, called "constructivism," is challenging both behaviorism and cognitive science, but it is not yet fully developed as a theory. Consequently, there are many varieties of constructivism today. The term constructivism refers to the emphasis on students "constructing" their own sense of the world, their own perspectives on critical issues, their own professionalism in a field, and their own identities as learners. While both behaviorism and cognitive science stressed the role of the *teacher* in the learning process, constructivism emphasizes the importance of the *learner's* initiative in the educational process. It stresses self-discovery, individuality, and independent thinking on the part of the student. The teacher's role shifts from that of an authority who provides information to one of a facilitator, who asks questions, suggests resources, encourages exploration, and learns alongside the students.

The roots of constructivist approaches to education lie primarily in developmental psychology. This approach studies human learning very differently from either behaviorism or cognitive psychology. Developmental psychologists see people neither as entities that merely react to their environments nor as computing machines, but as organisms who develop and grow over time in interactions with their environments. This perspective stresses the importance of each individual's autonomy as a thinker and learner. It also stresses the critical importance of the social context of learning. People learn by interacting with others, testing ideas, and modifying those ideas as necessary. These perspectives are central to most constructivist educational efforts.

Constructivist approaches to learning and teaching have stressed several important principles. One is that the best learning is situated learning; that is, learning where learners solve problems, perform tasks, and learn new material in a context that makes sense to them. Thus, one of the major criticisms that constructivists have of many current educational practices is that much of the learning consists of information and skills that are unconnected to the real world.

Another principle of constructivism is that learners must be supported throughout the learning process using scaffolding. Scaffolding is a process in which a teacher (or even another student) assists a learner in developing a new understanding or a new skill. As the student develops, the supports are removed so that the learner eventually stands on her or his own. Constructivism encourages a kind of apprenticeship approach, wherein novices work directly with an expert, who models effective approaches for them. It also stresses that students not simply mimic a role model, but find their own preferred ways of learning, their own styles, and their own answers.

One example of a constructivist approach to education is the problem-based learning (PBL) technique used in this book. It is important to note that PBL is designed to teach not only problem-solving skills but also the underlying concepts and knowledge in a field. The PBL technique has been widely used in medical education where it is used to teach not only clinical and diagnostic skills but also basic sciences such as physiology. In medical schools, PBL involves giving medical students realistic medical problems to solve from the very start. In general, the students solve the problems in cooperative groups over a span of a week or two. The aim is not simply to teach these students how to deal with real patients. There are several years of medical school, internships, and residencies to accomplish that. Rather, PBL is designed to give students a new way of learning the scientific concepts and processes that they need to know before they ever deal with a patient directly. Clearly the key here is to develop meaningful problems to solve that require learners to acquire the underlying knowledge.

For example, students might, in their first week, be given a problem involving an unconscious patient brought into an emergency room. At first, they would have just a description, but that would be supplemented over time by the results of lab tests, X rays, and so forth. To solve the problem, the group would have to learn what the tests mean, the underlying physiology and anatomy, and much more. In medical schools, the PBL approach has had some success, with students generally learning most of the concepts that they learn in the traditional lectures, integrating their knowledge better, and probably enjoying the process more. PBL has now spread far beyond medical schools to a variety of situations and learners.

There are several key principles in PBL as originally developed. First, the problem is always the first thing to be encountered. No related background material is provided. There is no necessary preparation phase or prior study involved. Second, problems are presented in a realistic context. For example, in medical education students are presented with case studies that look just like real patient cases. Third, students work with the problem at a level appropriate to their current abilities. Similar (or even the same) problems could be used at several different educational levels, with students responding to them with varying degrees of sophistication, depending on their own level of awareness.

Next, the problems are structured in such a way that learners must identify what they need to know in order to solve them and then learn those things. When students do learn those things, they apply them to the process of solving the problem. Usually this is done in groups so that students challenge one another, add to one another's knowledge, and collaborate on the solution they ultimately develop. Finally, at the end of the process, time for reflection must be provided to ensure that students integrate their new knowledge and skills. The result of this process is often better learning that is more accessible to recall later and more readily applied to new situations.

EDUCATIONAL TECHNOLOGIES FACILITATE CONSTRUCTIVISM

Educational technologies can be used to support constructivist approaches. For example, computer networks are being used to have learners communicate about their learning experiences. "Keypals" from different cultural backgrounds can share experiences in a way that helps them develop multicultural perspectives. Classes in different locales can get online to compare the terrain, weather, and wildlife in their respective areas. These experiences can expand awareness about different regions, which is hard to appreciate simply by reading. "Virtual expeditions" conducted on the World Wide Web can stimulate dialogue about the trip between the explorers out in the field and students back in their classrooms. The Internet has provided a powerful new way for students to share experiences, opinions, and information with others at vast distances.

At Vanderbilt University, researchers and educators have developed a complex series of interactive multimedia programs called the Jasper Woodbury series to teach a variety of mathematical skills. Although the series helps ensure that students develop their computational skills, the real goal is to enable individuals and groups to collaborate on complicated real-world problems, during which time they learn to reason mathematically.

Roger Schank, a researcher at Northwestern University, has developed a model of "goal-based scenarios" in which individuals using his interactive multimedia programs are presented with complex problems to solve in a relatively real-world context. For example, someone learning a new language may be placed in a hotel in another country and find it necessary to learn the rudiments of language in order to accomplish goals like sight-seeing or business transactions. Similarly, aspiring business consultants may have a scenario in which they had to improve the performance of a company. In either of these situations, learners get plenty of support, often in the form of videotaped advice from experts.

New technologies can provide the materials to explore, the tools with which to create, and the means with which to communicate. These can facilitate constructivist efforts in the classroom. In the average classroom of the previous century, the resources were so limited that students had to rely heavily on the teacher as a source of information. But in today's classroom, with its access to powerful electronic technologies, information in a variety of media is available and students can explore more effectively on their own. The teacher is freed from playing the proverbial role of "sage on the stage" and can act instead as a "guide on the side."

In many ways, modern constructivist approaches to instruction have taken us back to earlier theories as well as forward to new uses of technology in education. Very early thinkers like John Dewey, Lev Vygotsky, and Jean Piaget advocated many of the practices of constructivism. In the 1960s there was a push toward "discovery learning" in many classrooms, and we can hear echoes of that today. As we begin the new millennium, constructivism has the potential to foster a radically different approach to teaching as well as exciting new uses for technology in the classroom.

Clearly, the theories we hold about learning and cognition are central to how we teach, with or without technology. A great deal of resources, planning, time, and effort must go into developing technology-based instructional materials. Given that, we should try to make them as effective and usable as possible. A behaviorist, however, is likely to develop a very different set of materials from a cognitivist, who will develop something very different from a constructivist. The more we know about these alternatives and the concepts and research that underlie them, the better we can use instructional technologies effectively.

REFERENCES

Aschcraft, M. 1994. *Human memory and cognition.* New York: HarperCollins.

Ausubel, D. 1963. *The psychology of meaningful verbal learning.* New York: Grune & Stratton.

Bandura, A. 1971. *Social learning theory.* New York: General Learning Press.

Bruner, J. 1966. *Toward a theory of instruction.* Cambridge, MA: Harvard University Press.

Duffy, T., and D. Jonassen. 1992. *Constructivism and the technology of instruction: A conversation.* Hillsdale, NJ: Lawrence Erlbaum.

Gagne, R. 1985. *Conditions of learning.* New York: Holt, Rinehart and Winston.

Marshall, H. 1992, April. Four views of learning. Paper presented at the annual meeting of the American Educational Research Association, San Francisco, CA.

Ormrod, J. 1995. *Human learning.* Englewood Cliffs, NJ: Merrill.

Paivio, A. 1986. *Mental representations.* New York: Oxford University Press.

Piaget, J. 1952. *The origins of intelligence in children.* New York: International Universities Press.

Savery, J., and T. Duffy. 1995. Problem based learning: An instructional model and its constructivist framework. *Educational Technology* 5:31–38.

Schank, R. and C. Cleary. 1995. *Engines for Education.* Hillsdale, NJ: Lawrence Erlbaum Associates.

Skinner, B. F. 1938. *The behavior of organisms.* New York: Appleton Century Crofts.

Skinner, B. F. 1968. *The technology of teaching.* New York: Appleton Century Crofts.

Thorndike, E. 1936. Autobiography. In *A history of psychology in autobiography,* vol. 3, edited by C. Murchison. Worcester, MA: Clark University Press.

Watson, J. 1912. Psychology as the behaviorist views it. *Psychological Review* 20:158–177.

Wilson, B., J. Teslow, and R. Osman-Jouchoux. 1995. The impact of constructivism (and postmodernism) on ID fundamentals. Online: ouray.cudenver.edu/~jlteslow/idfund.html.

Curricular Concerns:

STRATEGIES AND SKILLS

The Role of Research

ASKING THE RIGHT QUESTIONS ABOUT EDUCATIONAL TECHNOLOGY

INTRODUCTION

In thinking about preparing curricular materials or lesson plans, teachers constantly ask themselves what might work best. But how are they to know what works best? It is the role of educational research to find out what works best, in what ways it functions most effectively, what types of students most benefit, what subject areas or topics are most suited to this approach, and so on. Unfortunately, finding clear-cut answers to questions like these is seldom simple.

Who should do this research? One important mission of the university system is to foster new knowledge, so it is a significant part of an academic's responsibility to conduct research. Professors from Colleges of Education across the country do a great deal of research. But it also would help if classroom teachers developed their own studies. Teachers may actually be in a better position than university professors to discover what works best with typical public school students because they are right there and they know the classroom environment, the students, the materials, and so on. Studies conducted in classrooms may have more validity in terms of their application to learning in real school settings than studies done under artificial circumstances in nonschool settings. So research conducted by teachers in their own classrooms is to be encouraged.

However, if teachers are to participate in this exploration into how educational practice can be improved, they need to understand research design. They need to know about different approaches to research and which approach is likely to work best for which type of study. One reason why teachers do not often conduct research, besides lack of time and the extra effort involved, is that they are not sure how to go about it. This chapter is designed to inform readers about how to conduct different types of research. It discusses both experimental and descriptive approaches, covering both quantitative and qualitative methods. It also describes the potential of various techniques and discusses some of the potential pitfalls associated with conducting research.

It seemed that the best way to approach this subject was to take an actual research question and explore how one might answer it. One fundamental issue in the field of instructional technology is the role technology can play in improving educational outcomes. In fact, questons regarding the significance of the role played by technology in education have been widely and heatedly debated. Here is an overview of that debate, which focuses on how the answers to these questions might be examined and why researching this issue is no simple task.

Examining a Critical Issue: The Role of Technology in Instruction

In the field of instructional technology, it has long been assumed by many professionals that "mediated messages" might be able to teach students more effectively than a straightforward old-fashioned teacher lecture. After all, the new technologies are capable of moving visuals, sound effects, music, interactive responses, carefully planned sequences, and so on. Shouldn't all of this stimulation and organization lead to instructional effectiveness? And don't students respond to the media with more enthusiasm than they would to the average class assignment? Isn't there a certain power in a mediated message? Why else would companies pay more than a million dollars for advertising time during the Super Bowl? And that doesn't even include the production costs of the commercial itself. Didn't the famous communications guru, Marshall McLuhan, claim that the "medium is the message," implying that the way in which a given medium presented material was more important than the actual content of the message?

For years, instructional technologists conducted studies designed to compare a mediated lesson with a "live" one. Was a radio lecture as instructionally effective as a live one? Was a videoconferenced discussion as effective as a face-to-face meeting? Was a computerized mathematics drill as effective as the same exercise in a book? Over the years, these types of studies became known as "media comparison" studies. And the overwhelming majority of these studies showed that, when content is held relatively constant, there is no statistically significant difference between the mediated message and the live message.

This finding, that the mediated lesson can be just as effective as the original one, was basically "good news" for many instructional technologists, for it supported the ability of mediated formats to successfully capture what went on in a classroom. For many applications of technology, this was just fine. Lessons could be broadcast to students who could not come to a teacher's classroom and those students would learn just as effectively as if they were there. Packaged lessons on videos or computer disks could be mailed to students and they could work on them at their own convenience and still expect to learn just as effectively as they might have learned by attending the class. These findings strongly support today's proliferation of "distance education" projects.

However, these findings were less appealing to instructional technologists who felt that lessons developed for the new sophisticated technologies should be *better* than teacher-led lessons or textbook-based materials. They believed these new dynamic technologies should be more engaging than the average teacher and able to communicate information in more dynamic ways than linear, noninteractive print media. That the new technologies prove superior was also important to instructional technologists because, in many cases, using them made the lessons much more *expensive*. If the costly equipment did not provide an instructional advantage, few educators would want to invest in it.

Over the years a number of researchers had noted that the media comparison studies generally showed no significant difference between lessons that were delivered in different media formats or between mediated lessons and live lessons. Back in the 1960s, both Lumsdaine and Mielke noted this phenomenon. Again in the 1970s, Schramm addressed this issue in his landmark book, *Big Media, Little Media*, as did Levie and Dickie in a book chapter that reviewed the research in the field of instructional technology. But when Richard Clark once again made this point in a 1983 article entitled "Reconsidering the Research on Learning from Media" in the *Review of Educational Research*, it caused a sensation. There was such a strong reaction among instructional technologists that it reverberates even to this day. So much so, that over a decade later, an entire issue of the journal entitled *Educational Technology Research and Development* would be devoted to a discussion of Clark's article.

Why did Clark's article cause such a furor? One reason was probably the timing of his article. It was published at a time when there was a great deal of excitement about new digital technologies. The microcomputer had just recently come upon the scene, and its potential for instruction seemed very significant. Here was a machine that was finally capable of imitating a teacher, in the way it could respond to student input. Even if previous technologies had not proven much better than traditional teaching techniques, surely this dynamic new machine would be able to do so.

Challenges Involved in Researching

Another reason the article received so much attention was that Clark had effectively made a point that many in the field of instructional technology strongly agreed with. He stated that it was the way a lesson was presented, not the medium used, that determined how effective it would be. In other words, how well organized the material was, how clear the objectives were, how relevant the examples were, how clearly the material was explained, whether there were exercises that provided some practice with the material, whether feedback was included for students, and so on, influenced effectiveness. This emphasis upon *instructional design* was seized upon by many instructional technologists, for whom the term "technology" implied technique as much as it did a piece of hardware. These professionals felt that Clark had helped strengthen this aspect of their field.

Another issue here is the difficulties associated with doing legitimate research. How can you prove the effectiveness of a given educational technology or, for that matter, of a given instructional approach? In setting up a media comparison study, a set of artificial circumstances are manipulated to try to isolate a given variable. It is quite difficult to create an experimental design that both controls for all other potentially important variables, yet allows for the key issue to be explored in a way that might truly measure its full potential. Another problem is that studies done in artificial laboratory settings may not be taken seriously by practitioners, who feel that these circumstances do not accurately reflect what goes on in a real classroom.

Yet another serious problem with most experimental studies is that they examine a fairly short, limited learning experience. Seldom does dramatic learning occur as a result of a single lesson or even a few lessons. Nor does that need to happen in our schools. Education is an ongoing experience, and really significant learning may take years. But how many researchers are willing or able to take years to conduct a study? Very few.

Compounding this problem is the insistence of researchers that "significant" findings be defined statistically as those that you are 95 percent certain could not have happened by chance. When teachers read research studies, they should be aware of this fact. What the average person considers significant may not be "significant" to statisticians who analyze the results of educational experiments.

Nevertheless, the concerns of Clark and others have helped instructional technologists face an important issue. How do we ask the right kinds of questions in educational research? How can we appropriately define a media-related variable? For example, it makes little sense to attempt to compare different pieces of hardware. A given technology can be used in a wide variety of ways. It can be used effectively or ineffectively. What is presented on a given piece of technology is much more important than what hardware is used. So to try to make generalizations about different types of hardware makes little sense.

It might make somewhat more sense to compare different pieces of "software." A particular television program or a piece of computer software might be effective or ineffective. However, the problem here is that there will be very little generalizability to your findings. You might be able to recommend a specific title. For example, the computer game "Where in the World Is Carmen Sandiego?" may teach some geography skills, or the television documentary "The Civil War" may teach historical facts. This type of research might help a teacher decide what curriculum materials to use in a given unit. It might even be said to demonstrate the potential of certain approaches to using technology. In the case of "Carmen Sandiego" this might be the use of a simulation game on a computer. With the "Civil War," the approach is the use of firsthand documentary sources of historical information in a television documentary. Demonstrating that these techniques can lead to successful instructional outcomes is helpful for teachers.

But this does not mean that all computerized simulation games or all television documentaries will be instructionally effective. Researchers will still be unable to make the kinds of generalizations about learning with technology that would provide designers of educational materials with specific guidelines. Nor does knowing that a given piece of software can teach geography facts help educators make more general decisions about how to use technology in the classroom.

To discover more meaningful generalizations about educational technologies, a researcher would need to focus on the capabilities provided by technologies. For example, instead of trying to make generalizations about television, a researcher might attempt to determine the effectiveness of using moving visuals for instruction. Rather than examining videotape, the researcher could assess whether learners benefited from being able to review parts of the tape a second time. Instead of attempting to describe the potential of the computer, the researcher might explore the effectiveness of immediate feedback for students on the correctness of their responses. Instead of trying to see if the World Wide Web can be an effective educational tool, a good researcher might narrow the study to an examination of how the hypertext links in a document helped learners pursue their explorations of subject matter.

Even the above-mentioned types of studies would be subject to criticism, of course. For example, it is difficult to explore the variable "moving visuals" per se, since outcomes may depend on the specific visuals shown or on the appropriateness of using visuals to teach that particular type of subject matter. The use of videotape to repeat certain segments will be instructionally significant only if the material demands a reasonably significant amount of repetition, which depends not only on the difficulty of the material but also on the ability of the students attempting to learn it. In examining the effectiveness of feedback, the results will depend on the amount of feedback, the type of feedback, the immediacy of the feedback, and so on. The importance of feedback will, of course, also depend on the difficulty of the material, the prior knowledge of the student, and the aptitude of the student. The significance of using "hypertext" will depend on the number of links, the degree to which the links are directly relevant to the material, and the degree to which the student is able to stay focused upon the topic, despite the potential for going off on a tangent. The one safe statement we can make in the field of educational research is "it depends!"

It is very difficult to design and execute a valid experiment in the classroom, because of the difficulty associated with trying to isolate a particular variable. So many variables are involved in how people learn, and these variables often depend on one another in ways that make them nearly impossible to separate. Even if a given variable actually did operate independently of all others, it would still be difficult to create an experimental situation that could measure it. For, as we have seen, it is very difficult to eliminate the possible influences of other variables in a learning situation.

Guidelines for Good Experimental Design

The best way to set up an experiment is to follow a few basic guidelines. You will want to create different groups, wherein one group is using the media materials that includes the "treatment" that you think may be instructionally effective. This treatment might include any of the aforementioned examples: use of moving visuals, allowing for review, providing feedback, making hyperlinks available, and so on. Another group will experience the same lesson, but without this treatment. This group is called the "control group" and it is used for purposes of comparison with the first group, generally known as the "treatment group." One of the real challenges is to set up a situation wherein everything about the lesson is identical, except for the treatment.

Another challenge is to ensure that there are no differences between the participants in your two groups that might affect the outcome. If you used a lesson about frogs for your study, you would not want to select a class of biology majors and compare them with a class of music majors. In fact, experimenters try to avoid using intact classes as subject groups, since two classes are rarely identical. A better approach is to *randomly* divide an existing class into groups. Students are arbitrarily assigned by chance to the groups, through counting off, choosing items from a container, or using random numbers from a computer. In this way, any differences between students should be equally distributed between the groups. The groups should be equivalent in important ways, such as intelligence, background knowledge, experience, gender mix, and age.

If you still suspect that your groups may differ in their awareness of the subject matter to be dealt with in your lesson, then you can give a pretest that measures their prior knowledge. When the students are then tested after the lesson, those results can be compared with the pretest results. The difference between the scores is the measure used to compare the treatment and control groups. However, if groups have been effectively randomized and there is no reason to suspect differences between them, it is better not to give a pretest, because it reveals what will be asked on the posttest (which is generally identical to the pretest).

The design of a test to measure instructional effectiveness is another challenge for the researcher. The test must be designed to measure the potential impact of the treatment variable. But items need to be selected in such a way that the control group has a legitimate opportunity to correctly answer them. If television footage is used, for example, test questions cannot refer directly to this television clip, if the control group has not seen it.

So a typical educational experiment would proceed like this. The subject groups would be established. If necessary, a pretest would be given. Then the lesson would be taught, with different approaches used for treatment and control groups. A posttest would be administered. Results for the two groups on the posttest would be compared by doing a statistical analysis. In this analysis, the researcher will find out whether the treatment group scored higher and how significant the difference in scores was. Statistical significance is presented as a percentage of the time that the differences in scores might have occurred by chance.

What determines statistical significance the high probability of a result [not] occurring by chance? Several things. First, the obvious factor that you probably already thought of is important: the size of the difference between the two groups. But by itself, this may not be enough. A second factor is how many people are being tested. If you test only a few students, you are unlikely to get statistically significant results. A large number of students can help you find statistically significant results even if the differences are small. A third factor is how similarly the students score on the test. If students, even within the groups, produce scores that are widely divergent, then it will be difficult to find significant results. If the students produce scores that are highly similar to one another, then it will be easier to find significance.

Together, all these factors can make it difficult for a research study to show statistically significant results. The difficulty is deliberate. Researchers want to be highly certain that the results they report are real and not just chance occurrences. Even so, many educational studies can legitimately report statistically significant results.

As noted earlier, media comparison studies usually show no significant differences in student achievement from using different media. This may be because the media in fact have little or no effect. However, there may be other reasons, relating to statistics, for the lack of significance. The difference between the scores might be too small, or the researchers might not have used enough students for the experiment, for example. In addition, perhaps the criterion of less than 5 percent probability is too strict for studies like this. It would be interesting to go back through the literature to see how many findings would have attained significance under a somewhat less stringent standard, like 10 or 15 percent probability.

But carefully done experimental research studies can provide educators with valid, reliable data about the instructional process. Even when there are no statistically significant findings, educators can learn something. Perhaps the study indicates that there are several different ways to get the same results (as most of the media comparison studies have shown). Or perhaps a given approach is not instructionally effective. Although this may disappoint some of its advocates, it is as important to know what does *not* work as it is to know what works.

Descriptive Research

There is an alternative to the experimental research paradigm. One approach that has gained favor in recent years is often known as "qualitative" research, to distinguish it from the "quantitative" data that generally results from an experimental study. It is also known as "descriptive" research, because it attempts to describe student performance in typical learning scenarios, rather than examining specific variables. Some examples of descriptive research are case studies, ethnographies, and histories. The data-gathering techniques most commonly used for descriptive research are observation, surveys, interviews, and analysis of artifacts. Results are not assumed to be widely generalizable, but applicable to a given experience. One strength of this approach is that it examines *real* situations in *real* classrooms, rather than trying to artificially manipulate a set of circumstances for the sake of an experiment.

Observations of learning can be conducted in a variety of ways. The observer might use notes to create a record of what is happening. Or she or he might use an observation instrument that includes the relevant types of behavior that might be involved in the learning experience. Another approach is to record the experiences, either with audiotape or, better still, videotape. Then the tapes can be carefully reviewed, several times if necessary. Sometimes the tapes are transcribed, so that there is also a written record of what transpired.

Observation records are often coded afterward, so that behavioral trends can be established. One advantage of recording the activity on tape is that this coding can be completed very thoroughly afterward. As the researcher reviews the tape, or transcripts of the tape, she or he can more easily categorize behavior into its components. Tape can be rewound for repeated examination and videotape can be played in slow motion so that behavior can be very carefully observed. There are even computerized coding programs that allow researchers to more efficiently label word-processed transcripts with coding that indicates how each piece of behavior can be categorized.

Surveys are an excellent way to obtain ratings on various issues. One common approach is to ask participants to select from a series of choices indicating levels of agreement or disagreement with various statements, generally known as a "Likert scale" (named for the researcher who first used it). Usually five choices are used: strongly agree, agree, neutral, disagree, strongly disagree. These are coded with the numbers 1 through 5, so that a numerical rating can provide a sense of how strongly respondents feel about a topic. When the scoring of all subjects is compiled, an overall reaction to a given statement can be obtained.

Surveys sometimes ask individuals to rank order a set of items to indicate which are most important or most relevant to the issue at hand. Again, numerical values can be assigned to the order in which items are ranked, with the first item being 1, the second being 2, and so on. Overall lists of the critical factors associated with a given issue can be developed, which establish the relative significance of each factor.

Many surveys include open-ended items that allow respondents to fill in their own reactions. This less-structured approach has the advantage of obtaining information that is less determined by the researcher's perspectives about what is important. Since a researcher may omit key issues, include irrelevant material, or even have a bias that influences the study, allowing the participants to express themselves without any interference on the part of the experimenter may provide more valid data.

However, one disadvantage of completion items is that respondents may not express themselves clearly, making it difficult for the researcher to interpret the response. Another potential problem is that individuals express themselves in different ways, sometimes using different expressions for otherwise similar thoughts. The researcher will need to group similar responses together. Sometimes these judgments about how certain statements should be classified can be tricky.

Interviews of participants can provide valuable information that the researcher might not obtain in any other way. A well-developed set of questions can probe an issue in depth and provide perspectives that might never surface through observation alone. The degree to which an interview should be structured depends on a number of factors. If the researcher needs to ask the same questions of all participants in the study, she or he probably should keep the questions consistent. However, sometimes different participants play dissimilar roles or have divergent perspectives on the learning process. In this case, different questions would appropriately be asked of different participants. One obvious example would be that some questions asked of students would certainly differ from questions asked of their teacher.

Generally, it also makes sense for an interviewer to have some questions prepared in advance but to improvise when the occasion demands it. To get really interesting information, an interviewer may need to depart from the original "game plan" and pursue a topic that she or he did not anticipate being raised. For example, if a participant has particularly interesting experiences to relate, the interviewer should help the person tell these stories by prompting him or her with appropriate questions.

Interview questions should also be used to guide a discussion. One challenge for the interviewer is to know when to let the interviewee speak freely and when to break in with questions that help keep the topic on target or which redirect the discussion into more relevant areas. A skilled interviewer can prompt the interviewee in ways that maximize the amount of relevant data provided.

Interviews also can be problematic for the researcher. For example, an enormous amount of information can result from them, which presents its own challenges. In addition, if the responses were tape-recorded, listening to the tapes can be quite time-consuming. Then transcribing them into written documents can be extremely laborious (and even more time-consuming!). Most researchers must go through a process of eliminating some comments that are not really relevant to their study. Categorizing and coding statements can also be a difficult task, especially when the remarks are somewhat ambiguous, obtuse, or complicated. While interview responses can reveal very interesting information about a given area of investigation, they may also be difficult to accurately interpret.

"Artifacts" are physical items that can help researchers better understand what they are studying. Some examples of artifacts are written materials, taped recordings of experiences, and projects constructed of some material. Some of the most important artifacts are those that represent the outcomes of a given learning experience, because an experience can then be evaluated, based on the quality of its outcomes. For example, written reports and creative writing assignments can be read by the researcher and observations about the nature of the learning experience can be based on their content.

In some studies, participants are asked to keep journals, wherein they record their reactions to the learning process. These journal entries can be especially valuable sources of information about the educational experience. Subjects can also be asked to write a paper at the end of their experiences, which reflects on those aspects of their instructional efforts that were most meaningful. Of course, participants can bring their own biases into their descriptions of their experiences. But it is part of the researcher's role to be able to see where a description of events diverges from what was observed or what was described by others.

Ideally the researcher will obtain more than one type of information during the study. For example, a survey might be followed up by interviews. Or observation might be augmented by collecting artifacts for examination. This technique is generally known as "triangulation," named after the technique used in surveying land, whereby distances are accurately determined by measurements taken from three different vantage points. It is a way of verifying data by finding evidence from other sources that corroborates a researcher's conclusions.

The Role of the Researcher

The role the researcher plays in gathering data is an important issue. Unfortunately, when a group of people is under investigation, individuals' behavior is likely to change in some way, however subtly, as a result of being studied. In some studies, the researcher will try to remain as unobtrusive as possible, so as not to affect what is happening. In this way, the experience will be as natural as possible.

Some research facilities have observation rooms with one-way glass, so that researchers can observe their subjects without being seen themselves. Ideally, these individuals will not even realize when they are being scrutinized. Sometimes recording devices are used to capture the experiences, without the presence of the experimenter, who can review the tapes later. If the experimenter does come into the room with the participants, she or he may sit quietly in the back and avoid interacting with anyone, so as to avoid influencing what transpires.

An alternative approach is for the researcher to become a "participant observer." The researcher will interact with subjects and attempt to become part of the group. This technique may further exacerbate the aforementioned problem of the researcher altering the situation she or he is trying to study. However, it may enable the researcher to become an "insider" and thereby obtain information that an "outside" observer would never be able to elicit from participants, because the observer would not be sufficiently trusted. It also may be advantageous for the researcher to try to see the experience from the point of view of the participants, so as to better understand what is happening. An objective researcher may not be able to accurately interpret what is happening within a classroom "culture," if she or he does not understand the basic assumptions involved or the precepts by which the participants' behavior is governed. Only by becoming an insider can the researcher come to fully understand what is happening.

But some qualitative researchers might not necessarily want to take this "ethnographic" approach to researching, where the idea is to explore a "culture" without preconceptions about it. This may be somewhat ambitious. Describing an entire set of circumstances also may be more than some researchers are really interested in. They may have a more specific focus. There may be particular questions or issues that they wish to explore. For example, it might be the role of technology in an instructional unit. The other activities associated with such a unit might be marginally relevant to the role played by technology. But researchers may decide that to describe all of those other activities is too time-consuming a proposition. Furthermore, those descriptions might distract readers from the principal investigation itself. So researchers may embark upon a descriptive study with some specific issues in mind.

Which Type of Research Is Best?

Which is the better approach, experimental (quantitative) or descriptive (qualitative) research? There is no correct answer, of course (although university researchers definitely have their preferences, and they argue incessantly about this issue). Much depends on what you are trying to find out. If you are extremely curious about the potential educational impact of a particular vari-

able associated with the use of intructional technology, then you would probably conduct an experiment where you keep everything constant in your
instructional approach except that variable. But if you are not sure what might
be significant about the use of educational technology, then you would probably conduct some descriptive research, which could explore how students
respond to specific ways of working with the technology. A combination of
approaches could even be used. The overall approach might be descriptive, but
a small experiment could be conducted as part of the larger study to examine
one issue that the researcher has a hypothesis regarding. Or descriptive data
gathering might be used to supplement an experimental study in order to fur-
nish some more specific details about the phenomenon.

Teachers are often so busy with their instructional responsibilities that they
have no time for research. However, teachers are in a unique position in their
day-to-day work to contribute to knowledge in the field. Every day, they
should be trying to see what works with whom under what conditions. Applying this ongoing analysis of classroom learning experience to the design of a
formal study may provide some meaningful results. Research efforts by practitioners may help them improve student performance in their own classes. In
addition, if reported in the research literature, these efforts can potentially provide valuable guidance for other colleagues in the field. Insights into what contributes to successful utilization of instructional technologies would be especially helpful for all of us involved in the field.

RECOMMENDED READING

Clark, R. 1983. Reconsidering the research on learning from media. *Review of Education-
al Research* 53 (4): 445–459.
Pepper, S., and R. Hare. 1999. Establishing research-based knowledge in teacher educa-
tion. Paper presented at the American Educational Research Association, Montreal,
Province of Quebec, Canada, ERIC, ED 429969.
Weiss, J. 1994. Keeping up with the research. *Technology & Learning* 14 (2): 30–31, 34.

OTHER REFERENCES

Fowler, F. 1993. *Survey research methods.* Newbury Park: Sage.
Jonassen, D., ed. 1996. *Handbook of research for educational communications and technology.
A project of the Association for Educational Communications and Technology (AECT).*
New York: Simon & Schuster Macmillan, ERIC, ED 407934.
Kerlinger, F. 1986. *Foundations of behavioral research.* New York: Harcourt Brace
Jovanovich.
Levie, W., and K. Dickie. 1973. The analysis and application of media. In *The second
handbook of research on teaching,* edited by R. Travers. Chicago: Rand McNally.
Lumsdaine, A. 1963. Instruments and media of instruction. In *Handbook of research on
teaching,* edited by N. Gage. Chicago: Rand McNally.

Mielke, K. 1968. Questioning the questions of ETV research. *Educational Broadcasting Review* 2: 6–15.

Office of Educational Research and Improvement. 1997. *Envisioning an educational research, development, and dissemination system. Final report.* Washington, DC, ERIC, ED 411324.

Schnorr, D., and D. Painter. 1999. Partnering the university field experience research model with action research. Paper presented at the American Association of Colleges for Teacher Education, Washington, DC, ERIC, ED 428058.

Schramm, W. 1977. *Big media, little media.* Beverly Hills, CA: Sage.

Threlkeld, R., and K. Brzoska. 1994. Research in distance education. In *Distance education: Strategies and tools,* edited by B. Willis. Englewood Cliffs, NJ: Educational Technology Publications.

SCENARIO

You are a district technology coordinator working with an elementary school that has just set up a new language arts computer laboratory. Unfortunately, considerable controversy surrounded the funding of this lab. A number of teachers in this school questioned the degree to which computers could effectively facilitate the development of language arts skills and were disappointed that a significant percentage of the school's limited resources were spent on the lab. One group of teachers wanted to expand the school library instead, so that its holdings would be substantially increased. They argued that a wider selection of appropriate reading materials would improve reading and writing skills more significantly than would the availability of computers. Another group of teachers, which was smaller but quite adamant, felt that the money might have been used to replace the wooden floor of the gym, which is extremely worn in many spots, with some pieces of it even starting to pry loose, creating potentially hazardous conditions for gym classes and sporting events.

Concerned about the controversy, the principal of this school would like you to investigate the potential effectiveness of using computers to develop language arts skills. He secretly hopes that your results will support his decision to create the lab, but he also realizes that one should look into this issue without prior bias. He specifically tells you that he hopes you can assess this situation "as objectively as possible." But he is willing to generously provide further funding for software to be used in the lab and will indicate to his teachers that they are expected to bring their classes to work in the lab on a weekly basis. He will also announce at the next teachers' meeting that the staff should cooperate with you in any way you request, since your study has a high priority. This might include structuring class sessions in such a way as to test certain questions that you, as a researcher, might have. This cooperation might also include tolerating your presence in the lab during class sessions, completing survey materials, or responding to interview questions, during free periods.

How would you design a study (or set of studies) that might clarify whether computers can play a meaningful instructional role in language arts? List those aspects of computerized instruction that might make a difference. What kinds of *capabilities* might a computer laboratory provide that would facilitate communication skills? What kinds of *activities*, unique to the technology-rich environment of the lab, might occur that would enhance the quality of a language arts curriculum? Also list the *outcomes* that you might focus on as indicators of the effectiveness of computerized language arts instruction. In your discussion, try to carefully distinguish among *issues* associated with hardware, with software, with instructional approach, with content items, and so on.

ISSUES INQUIRY

1. How do you define a "medium" (or "technology") as an experimental variable? In so-called media comparison studies, experimenters tried to compare mediated lessons with "live" lessons. Or they would compare two different media delivering the same information (computer vs. book, for example). Why is this issue problematic?

2. How can you isolate the effects of a medium from other variables, such as the teacher, the student, the programming used, the subject matter, and the type of student?

3. Do you think that past technologies may not have made a difference in instructional outcomes, but future ones may be so much more powerful and sophisticated that they *may* make a difference?

4. What would you list as critical issues in the study requested by the principal in this chapter's scenario? Is it difficult to select certain issues to the exclusion of others? Or would you, as a researcher, perhaps not select issues and instead examine experiences without preconceptions?

5. Describe your own perspectives on the two different types of research, experimental and descriptive. Do you have a preference? Why?

6. How do you feel about educational research? Should teachers spend their valuable time reading the research literature? Should teachers try to conduct their own studies in the classroom and contribute to the research literature? Why or why not?

CHAPTER 2

Surviving the Information Explosion

RESEARCHING ON THE WORLD WIDE WEB

INTRODUCTION

The number of websites on the Internet has skyrocketed in the past few years. Companies list theirs in TV ads. Individuals announce major life events on them. Schools post lunch menus every week. There is an enormous amount of information on the Web, so much that no one is quite sure just how much there is. Web "search engines" have automatically indexed tens or even hundreds of millions of pages, and they are still growing rapidly. One recent prediction is that there will be a billion pages on the Web in the next few years.

All of this makes the Web an incredible resource. Not only are there vast quantities of information available with lively pictures, sounds, and videos, but there are websites that are highly interactive, allowing you to play games, take tests, learn skills, and communicate with other people. No library could hope to duplicate the sheer volume of the Web, no matter how big their collections. If you need to learn something, if you want to be entertained, even if you want to read a book, you will probably be able to find it on the Web.

All this information is usually accessible within seconds, but there is more material available than anyone can deal with or even comprehend. Therefore, finding what you want can be hard, sometimes harder than in a library, because the materials are not as well organized or indexed. Finally, many of those billion pages are junk, with unreliable, irrelevant, or inaccurate information. Let's look at these problems in more detail and then discuss what teachers can do to make good use of the Web in spite of them.

First, the sheer size of the Web is an obstacle. That's not necessarily a problem unique to the Web, since a well-stocked university library can also be massive and overwhelming when you first enter. Certainly, no one can read everything in even a small-town public library. The real difference lies in the fact that it is increasingly difficult to find just what you want on the Web. Your local library—school, town, university—may not have every book, every magazine, every journal, every document that pertains to your interests, but you can quickly find out what they do have and where it is. By looking in the catalog at titles, authors, and abstracts you can narrow down the list to the ones that seem most relevant. Usually, if they are on the shelves and not checked out, you can scan through what's available until you find what you need or something close.

Search Engines

The Web is not like that yet. If you rely on just your own efforts, browsing from one likely site to another, then you may never have the time to find the best material. To help solve this problem, a variety of sites and search engines have been developed to help people find interesting and relevant sites. Search engines like Yahoo!, Alta Vista, Excite, and Lycos have approached the problem in different ways, although nowadays most of them incorporate elements of the others.

The basic strategy is to have computer "robots" do the indexing. They can do it faster than people can, so they can reach a much larger proportion of the pages out there. The problem is that computerized search engines are not as discriminating as people. They can't tell whether a site has good or poor information. All they can do is ask whether they have indexed that page before and, if not, to do so. Some search engines only look at page titles and other information contained in a page's "header." Others index every meaningful word on the page, to make a vast database of words and where they appear on the Web. All this is done automatically by computer programs, without human intervention.

An alternative strategy is used by Yahoo!, which pioneered the development of Web indices. These vast indices are maintained and expanded by staff hired to search the Web and select sites to be included. This has the advantage of having real people screen the sites before they are added. Even though the standards are not very high, the procedure does eliminate many poor sites that simply don't have much to offer. People often are able to make better judgments more quickly about the value of a site than a computer can. A drawback is that it takes a lot of time and effort to accomplish this. The company must have individuals constantly combing the Web for good sites and removing links to those that have changed or disappeared. Even so, Yahoo! has probably not screened more than 1 or 2 percent of the total number of sites on the Web.

Obviously, with a huge database of key words and associated websites, it can be a daunting task to find relevant material even with the aid of a search engine. For example, when we searched for the word *education* on Alta Vista, it found 25,524,328 pages that had that word on them (your results may vary!). Obviously, this did not do us much good, since we cannot browse through that many pages, and many were likely to be worthless to us, anyway. Clearly, we need ways to narrow down the search.

Most search engines give you ways of doing that. For example, most of them allow you to combine search terms to look for only those pages that have two or more key words in them at the same time. For example, when we went back to Alta Vista and asked it to search for pages that had both the word *education* and the word *technology*, it found 4,808,586 pages that contained both terms. This is still not usable, but at least it's less than 20 percent of the original number. When we went back again and added the word *distance* to the search, it cut the number to 408,082, which we hope includes just about everything out there dealing with educational technology in distance learning. By continuing to add terms we could eventually get down to a number that we can actually look at and consider. At the same time, we have to hope that we haven't narrowed the search *too* much and cut out things that could be important to us.

Some search engines allow the user to use the connecting term "near." It functions much like "and" but is more discriminating. It will find only sites in which the two terms connected by "near" are within a certain number of words of each other in the website text (maybe ten or twenty words away). This strategy will produce fewer sites and probably more relevant sites, since the proximity of terms increases the likelihood that they are related. For example, if you are looking for information about the Kent State shootings in 1970, entering

"Kent State" near "shootings" might help you find instances in which these terms are paired.

Another strategy used by many search engines is the ability to "weight" one of your terms. This is a way of indicating to the search engine which term is most important to you. In the example of the Kent State shootings search, the researcher might want to weight "Kent State" more heavily, since it is the more specific term (*shootings* is a more general word, which might refer to basketball, photography, cinema, hunting, etc.). In Excite, for example, users can apply an exponential power to a term to indicate how heavily they wish to weight it. Cubing a term places greater emphasis on it than simply squaring it. This weighting helps the search engine rank the relevance of the sites it finds. It will list the ones with the most instances of the term "Kent State" at the top of the listings it provides, when the search has been completed.

Some search engines allow you to "refine" the search by viewing a list of terms that appear in a high percentage of the documents it found in response to your original request. You can then go through that list and tell the search engine to include certain terms and to exclude others. When you click on "Search" again, the engine then uses both of those elements to narrow the search further. In general, with any search like this your aim is to narrow it sufficiently to get a list of "hits" that is small enough to browse through on your own. Sometimes you can tell quickly, as you scroll through the first few pages of results, whether you have done it well and are getting pages that have the information you need.

How to Take Advantage of the Vast Resources on the Web

Search engines and indices are useful tools, especially for experienced researchers who know what they are looking for. A lot of good material is available, and with some time and effort we can often find what we need. However, education is more than just supplying information to people. The younger the learners, the more they may need direction. Few would suggest that the best way to educate elementary school students is to give them a library card and let them loose. Libraries are tremendous resources, but learners need goals, guidance, activities, and assistance in order to learn successfully.

The most fundamental problem with researching on the World Wide Web is its sheer size. As discussed previously, so much information can be accessed that it is difficult to find what you are interested in. In fact, there is often so much information on any given *topic* that you conduct a search for that it is difficult to choose which sources to further investigate. Students who hope to use the Web for research purposes will need to learn effective search techniques. Selecting *appropriate* terms is the first important skill. *Combining* a number of related terms is a critical approach, since it is the most effective way to reduce your search items to a manageable number. Choosing the right terms to combine also helps you find the sources that are truly on target in terms of topic. Sometimes more sophisticated Web search skills will help narrow the search, like weighting the importance of certain terms, excluding specific material with a "not" command, or aggregating a series of terms into a compound word or phrase. When a long list of Web pages is provided by the engine, the student needs to be skilled at skimming through and isolating those that seem most promising. Good Web navigation skills allow young researchers to efficiently locate the most relevant sites, and the use of bookmarks will help them store those sites for future reference. Without good search skills, the research process on the Web can be very time-consuming and tedious.

A second problem with the information on the Web is its credibility. Most books, magazines, academic journals, and newspapers go through an editorial process. The idea is to publish only significant material that can be checked and verified. Since publishing a book or periodical can be an expensive proposition and readers have many other choices for obtaining their information, reputable publishers have powerful incentives to make sure that what they publish is accurate and interesting to its potential readers. No such constraints exist on most of the Web. Publishing materials there is inexpensive and easy. Many of us who get on the Internet have an account that includes some disk space to publish Web pages. A very large number of us take advantage of this. Others pay a little extra money for the right to develop a whole website. Usually no one is around to edit or verify the information on any of these sites.

Consequently, it can be difficult to know whether specific information found on the Web will be accurate, up-to-date, socially redeeming, and so on. Although the same can be said for almost any other medium, the problem is acute on the Web. This situation is also especially difficult in the case of school-children surfing the Web, who may be unable to make those distinctions. This seems to impose a couple of obligations on teachers. First, they need to be the initial line of defense, screening sites and guiding students toward the ones that have the high-quality, credible, and usable information that they might need. Second, teachers must teach students how to assess the credibility of the information that they find.

This can be done by helping students learn to identify the source of the information, evaluate its credibility, relate it to things they know from other sources, consider the purpose of the site, and so forth. This critical analysis of Web material can be tricky. Sites that look wonderful may not have worthwhile information, while important scholarly papers may be presented as text-only sites, with little visual appeal. Teachers will have performed a major service for their students if they can teach them these analytical skills. Such skills will be useful for a long time to come.

Another challenge for teachers is to use the Web in educationally meaning-ful ways. Many lesson plans are available for teachers that include the Web. They can be found in books, magazines, and even on the Web itself. However, many such lessons use this tremendous resource in essentially trivial ways. The World Wide Web is a good source of information, but just supplying informa-tion is not enough. Teachers must add the context, the goals, the tasks, and the assessment tools that students need for genuine learning. Teachers need good learning plans that make good use of the Web and that also challenge students to critically assess what they find on the Web.

The Web shouldn't be used simply because it is there. Often, other sources of information are easier and faster to use. For example, a good almanac might supply basic facts in a minute or two without the bother of going online. On the other hand, the Web might supply information and experiences that cannot be found in your school library, either because the Web information is more up-to-date or because the library cannot purchase everything. It is important for teachers to find uses for the Web that cannot readily be duplicated by other media.

Some characteristics of the Web as an information resource are special. For example, it can have more current material than most other information sources. In addition, once you find good information on one site, you can often follow the hyperlinks to other sites with more related material. Finally, it would be prohibitively expensive for most schools to stock the range of multimedia resources that can be found on the Web. Lesson plans that include Web-based information and searches should make use of these Web features.

Lessons using the Web should involve the students in much more than simply looking up isolated bits of information (the classic Web scavenger hunt). It is not that learners do not need information. It is that they can learn it best within a problem-solving context or as part of accomplishing a meaningful task. If a lesson calls for students to solve a problem requiring information that they can only find on the Web, then they are likely to use this technology effectively. For example, many sites on the Web contain up-to-date data on environmental issues like water pollution. Many also will contain excellent hyperlinks to other good environmental resources on the Web. Printed data on water pollution might not be as compelling or current. A good lesson might require students to gather such information, summarize key points, graph any quantitative data, and draw conclusions about trends. This could be followed by a discussion of possible reasons for the indicated results, with suggestions for further research to test the hypotheses.

Such assignments demand far more from students than a Web scavenger hunt that asks them to find three examples of water pollution in the United States. Not all learning is created equal. Some learning is more significant, deeper, and more complex than other types of learning. As educators, we should be pushing students to think more deeply rather than just scratching the surface. Educational thinkers have categorized types of learning that differ in various ways. One obvious difference might be that found between learning physical skills like dribbling a basketball, social skills like mingling at a cocktail party, and cognitive skills like performing long division.

Levels of Cognitive Skills

More subtle distinctions can be made among types of cognitive skills, and these are important because they are what we are most concerned with in education. Probably the most famous instance of classifying cognitive skills can be found in Bloom's taxonomy. He established six ascending levels of thinking: Knowledge, Comprehension, Application, Analysis, Synthesis, and Evaluation.

Knowledge is the lowest level of cognition, and it involves merely remembering factual material. Although knowledge is important, it may not be significant in and of itself. That is, knowledge is valuable mainly insofar as you can use it to think in more profound ways. Knowledge gains its importance primarily because it may underlie the other five types of cognition. Thus, when we give students lessons that involve memorization of facts, we should be sure not to stop there. We need to take them to other levels as well. When we assess whether someone has gained knowledge, we usually do so by having them recite facts, list them, identify the correct response, and so on. For example, we might ask students whose three laws of motion underlie much of classical physics (Sir Isaac Newton).

The second level, Comprehension, takes us another step. Certainly, we have all known people who can spout facts without convincing us that they really understand what they are talking about. At the Comprehension level, we are checking for understanding. We might do this by asking students to paraphrase a theory rather than simply recite it. For example, we could ask them to explain what Newton's third law of motion means. Certainly this is more valuable than just knowing disconnected facts, like Newton's birthplace, the date of his death, or how old he was when he "discovered" gravity.

Application is the third level of cognition in Bloom's taxonomy. At this level, learners can take what they already know and use it in some way. For example, Newton's third law states that $F = ma$, which means force equals mass times acceleration. It is relatively easy for most of us to memorize the formula and its verbal equivalent (Knowledge). It is a bit more difficult for many of us to describe in our own words what it means (Comprehension). Even harder is to use the formula to solve a real-world physics problem (Application). Clearly, to assess students' ability to apply what they know, we need to assign tasks that require them to actually solve problems, complete challenging projects, and so on.

Next in Bloom's taxonomy is Analysis. This skill is more complex still and involves taking an object, a process, or a situation and breaking it down into its constituent elements. For example, faced with a new piece of hardware, an electronics engineer might study its design to figure out what it does and how it works. A scientist can analyze a chemical by literally breaking it into its elements. A historian might analyze the causes of the American Revolution by examining specific aspects of the historical experience. This is not a skill that comes automatically when you know, comprehend, and apply a topic. It takes a student a step beyond those levels of learning. Some of the thinking processes involved in an analysis might include deduction, induction, generalization, specification, comparison, and prediction. When Sir Isaac Newton formulated his third law of motion, he had to analyze which factors most affected objects in motion, and he came up with mass and acceleration as the two that contributed to the force imparted by moving objects.

The next level, Synthesis, is the mirror image of Analysis. Instead of breaking things down into their constituent elements, with Synthesis we are building them back up. Synthesis is the ability to put elements back together to form new ideas, new theories, or new creations. Often it is a design process. An architect might examine the various needs, opportunities, and constraints of a situation and address them in the design of a building that has never been seen before. Or a teacher takes ideas from several different sources to create a lesson that grabs students' attention and makes that day's work special. Newton was able to synthesize what was known about the force with which objects move into a formula that established the relationship between the critical variables ($F = ma$).

Finally, the sixth level of Bloom's taxonomy, Evaluation, involves intelligent critiquing of a product, a process, or a theory. It may rely upon any of the first five types of cognition. To make reasoned and accurate judgments, one may need to have knowledge, comprehend the situation, be able to apply skills and knowledge, analyze the situation, and synthesize your ideas. Otherwise, the evaluation is likely to be ill-informed and mere opinion. By Evaluation, Bloom meant an assessment by an expert, not the uninformed opinion of a novice. For example, Einstein evaluated Newton's formulations about the universe and knew that his laws did not fully explain all phenomena. Einstein's theory of relativity was developed to explain aspects of physics that Newton's laws did not account for.

Why are we telling you all this? We believe that good teaching requires us to push students further up through the progression represented by Bloom's taxonomy of educational objectives. Merely teaching facts and Knowledge isn't enough. Comprehension is better, but moving from there to Application is even better. As students progress, they should acquire skills in Analysis, Synthesis, and Evaluation as well. Similarly, if the vast array of instructional technologies that we now have at our disposal, including the World Wide Web, are used primarily for fact finding, then we have not made good use of them. However, if we incorporate the use of these technologies into lessons that require higher levels of thinking, then we can improve instruction considerably.

To summarize, there is little doubt that the Web can be a tremendous source of educational materials and experiences. But we all know that it is not enough for us merely to point students to a networked computer and tell them to find important information. Students deserve well-constructed lesson plans, engaging them in important tasks that could benefit from the use of Web resources. When the Web is harnessed to a powerful teaching strategy, it can have a major effect on the teaching and learning process and on the achievement of students.

RECOMMENDED READING

Ellsworth, J. 1997. Curricular integration of the World Wide Web. *TechTrends* 42 (2): 32–34.

Hackbarth, S. 1997. Integrating Web-based learning activities into school curriculums. *Educational Technology* 37: 59–71.

Oliver, K. M. (1997). Getting online with K–12 Internet projects. *TechTrends* 42: 33–40.

Rakes, G. 1996. Using the Internet as a tool in a resource-based learning environment. *Educational Technology:* 52–56.

Smith, R. A. 1998. Weaving a Web of research skills. *Learning and Leading with Technology* 25 (8): 60–63.

OTHER REFERENCES

Athenia Associates. 1998. Search engines: How software agents and search engines work. Online: www.webreference.com/content/search/how.html.

Dabbagh, N. 1998. Web based instruction—practical applications. *Educational Media International* 35 (3): 149–230.

Harasim, L., S. Hiltz, L. Teles, and M. Turoff. 1995. *Learning networks: A field guide to teaching and learning online.* Cambridge, MA: MIT Press.

Kirsanov, D. 1997. HTML unleashed: Strategies for indexing and search engines. Online: www.webreference.com/dlab/books/html-pre/43-0.html.

Pedram, M. 1999. Introduction to search engines. Kansas city public library. Online: www.kcpl.lib.mo.us/search/srchengines.htm.

Shenk, D. 1997. *Data smog: Surviving the information glut.* New York: HarperCollins.

Shiran, T. 1997. Search engine glossary. Online: www.searchengine.watch.com/facts/glossary.html.

Webster, K., and K. Paul. 1996. Beyond surfing: Tools and techniques for searching the Web. Online: maji.com/~mmelick/it96jan.htm.

SCENARIO

It is late summer. You are sitting comfortably, thinking about nothing in particular, when suddenly a thought pops into your head. When you recover from the novelty, you pay attention to it: School starts soon! What are you going to do? Will you be ready? Well, yes, in some ways you are prepared, but there is a complication. Immediately after school finished last spring, contractors started working on installing computer network connections, extra electrical lines, and, gasp, computers in every classroom, including yours.

You still haven't heard how many computers you will get, but it will be at least three, and maybe more. They will all have Internet connections. Before the end of school, your school administrators explained to everyone how the project was going to work. The construction and installation were expected to be completed before the new school year started, and you certainly haven't heard anything different all summer. The Internet connection will be run through a service called "Bess," which will not allow student and teacher access to objectionable sites. Bess will also supply a large number of links that have already been screened by teachers and certified as having high-quality, credible information. You plan to add to that list of links by searching the Web regularly for other worthwhile sites.

You realize that now you had better start thinking carefully about how you are going to use these new resources. Even though Bess will screen sites and keep your students from getting into too much trouble on the Internet (your fingers are crossed!), you don't want them just surfing the Net from site to site aimlessly, even if the places they find do have "redeeming social value." You want to give them some research tasks that have real meaning for them and that take full advantage of this new technology.

Your first idea is to look around for what other people have done. You find books with sample lesson plans that require Internet resources, and you find many websites with even more suggestions. Overall, though, you are disappointed. You find some interesting ideas, but most of them are neither engaging nor educational. They send students in search of trivial facts on the Web. Even then, there is not much real searching going on, because the lesson plans supply two or three sites that are guaranteed to contain the information. Yawn! Why not just give students some time with an almanac or other reference book and save all that money spent on the technology? Besides, the educational value of looking up random facts is not very high.

No, this doesn't really do it for you. You want to think of some ways of using the Web that really get students' attention, that force them to think, that ask them to critique websites and use the information they find in meaningful ways. Apparently, you will have to create these lesson plans yourself.

Choose a topic in biology: environmental issues, population growth, endangered species, evolutionary studies, or anything you find interesting. Write a lesson plan for this topic, using whatever format you usually use for lesson plans.

The plan should have several characteristics. First, it should demand higher-level problem-solving skills, not just fact retrieval. Obviously, finding facts on an issue can be important for solving problems about it, but the final goal should encompass more sophisticated mental processing. Second, the lesson should require extensive use of the Web as a source for information not easily found anywhere else. It should insist that students analyze the information they find on the Web, critique that material (and the websites themselves), and then synthesize their overall findings into a final project or paper.

ISSUES INQUIRY

1. A good lesson plan should suggest meaningful tasks for the students to complete, along with intellectual goals to strive for. What kinds of tasks can you give students to help them move through the six levels of Bloom's taxonomy: Knowledge, Comprehension, Application, Analysis, Synthesis, and Evaluation?

2. Describe some features of the World Wide Web that are not true of printed materials. How can you best encourage students to take advantage of these Web capabilities in their research efforts?

3. Describe some websites with which you are familiar that most effectively take advantage of the capabilities of the World Wide Web. Discuss some specific ways in which these websites are so outstanding.

4. Discuss how you would orient students to the use of Web search engines. What features of search engines would you focus upon? Do you have a preference for any particular search engine? What makes it usable and effective for you?

5. How would you teach students to intelligently critique websites? What aspects of a site are most important: content? appearance? use of special Web capabilities?

CHAPTER 3

Deconstructing Constructivism

THE PARADOX OF PLANNING
UNSTRUCTURED UNITS

INTRODUCTION

In the introductory chapter "From Conditioning to Constructivism," we presented an overview of how learning theories have changed over the decades and of how our perspectives on learning can affect our use of instructional technology. It is now time to take a closer look at those issues, especially as they relate to the most current theories.

One of the current buzzwords in educational circles is *constructivism*. As we noted in the earlier chapter, constructivism at this point is not really a complete theory of learning. In addition, there is not just one constructivist point of view. Instead, a number of perspectives on learning and understanding can be called constructivist. Thus, constructivism is more a *philosophy* of learning that holds a few major guidelines as central to the process. Some of these ideas are old, and others are new. Some are well established, and others require more testing and research. All in all, it is clear that teaching in a constructivist fashion can be very different from teaching in a more traditional one. The ways technology is used in this approach vary as well.

The key to understanding constructivism lies in the belief that people learn by actively trying to make sense of information and experiences. That is, learners do not passively receive knowledge from others, or even passively observe the world. They *construct* knowledge through their interactions with people and their activities in the physical world. In education, according to this view, information is not just transmitted from teacher to student. Instead, learners seek out information that is relevant to them and incorporate it into their existing understanding of the world. Therefore, good teaching does not involve simply telling people facts or conveying information. It means setting up conditions that support and encourage individuals in developing their own concepts and comprehension. More direct instructional approaches do not, according to many constructivists, result in truly deep and lasting learning.

In addition to this basic idea, constructivists tend to agree on a few key points. First, knowledge depends on the situation and the context. What we know in one setting may not generalize well to other settings. Thus, for most constructivists, it is important that we ground our learning and teaching in specific situations as well. Not only do we learn purely abstract concepts poorly, but our motivation is lower until we understand how information fits into a broader context. A second general principle shared by many constructivists is that learning is inherently a social activity. In particular, given the central importance of language and communication to human beings, to learn effectively we must test our ideas against those of other people: arguing, explaining, collaborating, and discussing. The constructivist approaches to learning and teaching discussed in the following section tend to flow from these basic ideas and others like them.

Constructivist Approaches to Teaching

There is no simple set of constructivist teaching strategies that we can list for you. Many of those working in the field start from a set of first principles like those just outlined. From these principles and an interest in helping learners grow, they develop materials and activities that provide relevant learning opportunities. What they develop can be reading lists, interactive multimedia programs, hypermediated materials, laboratory exercises, communications systems for encouraging people to collaborate, videos, or a variety of different experiences. You can be sure of one thing—whatever is developed will include active experiences for the students and a requirement that they think hard about what they are doing. Let's look at some specific teaching strategies that might be used in a constructivist curriculum or lesson.

First is the requirement for active learning. Although few behaviorists (or any other "ists" in education for that matter) would argue with the idea that learners should be active rather than passive, constructivists put a special emphasis on certain kinds of activities. These should be experiences that are personally meaningful to the learners, that require significant amounts of work to master, and that are not especially "canned" to produce a given result. For example, most science teaching includes significant work in the lab. However, a constructivist would argue that lab experiments should be real ones that have some importance for the learners. They should not be the pseudo-experiments that you find in some lab manuals where a learner simply follows step-by-step instructions to obtain a predetermined result. In addition, the teacher, acting more as a facilitator and a colearner, should be open to exploring new paths that might open up as the lab session progresses. Such intellectual detours are, for the constructivist, the central point of the learning, not a distraction from it.

Many of the teaching/learning activities developed by constructivists bear a resemblance to earlier "discovery learning" approaches. However, there are a few differences. First, some of the discovery learning programs were simply ways to teach predetermined content, which would not be a part of a constructivist lesson. Second, constructivists would be more likely to focus on the processes of learning and inquiry than on the content of the instruction.

A famous Russian psychologist, Lev Vygotsky, has become very influential in constructivist circles. He studied child development and learning and formulated a principle of learning he called the "zone of proximal development." What he meant by this was that at any given time, children are primed to learn and develop in certain ways, if appropriately assisted by an adult. In applying this principle, it is the teacher's role to discover where learners are right now and then to support and guide them in solving problems and developing further. The goals are to help learners to internalize the new developmental level and to become more independent and responsible in their own problem solving and learning.

For example, you are probably planning to become a teacher. If you haven't already, then at some point you will spend some time in a classroom as a student teacher. You may be nervous about this prospect, since you may not be certain that you have all the skills you need to control the class, teach successfully, respond appropriately to individual students, and so forth. In a sense, you are right, because you do not have all the skills of an experienced teacher. However, you are in your zone of proximal development for taking your next step as a teacher. A good supervisor will observe you carefully as you encounter this new situation. He or she will see what you do well and what you are struggling with. At just the time when you are best able to benefit from advice, the supervisor may provide a suggestion or a new teaching tip.

If one principle of constructivism is to identify the moments when people are most ready to learn and take advantage of them, then a second and closely related principle is to support learners as they solve problems and learn new material. Often called "scaffolding," this principle can be compared to building a wall. While the wall is being built, there is a period of time when it may not be self-supporting. Scaffolds are erected to prevent the wall from falling until it is complete and can stand on its own. In a similar way, one of the key roles of the teacher is to support students as they construct meaning from the information and their experiences. The skilled teacher gradually withdraws such learning scaffolds as the students become able to support their own ongoing knowledge and learning.

For example, if you were to teach a group how to use a multimedia authoring program such as HyperStudio, the overall goal would probably be to have the learners develop a set of skills such that they could produce their own multimedia programs without help from you. At the beginning, however, few of them could do that on their own. You might first work with them to help them define a meaningful project to complete. Then, as they worked on projects of their own choosing, you would provide the scaffolding by observing what they are doing, reminding them of key commands in the HyperStudio program, suggesting the use of features that would enhance their work, and so on. Over time, you would provide less and less support as the students worked more and more on their own.

Getting Situated

Another important principle for constructivist teaching is called "situated learning." This stems directly from the idea that all learning is inherently intertwined with its context. One constructivist criticism of the way that education is normally conducted in schools and universities is that it is too abstract. Students are frequently expected to learn facts, concepts, and skills divorced from any real context. They are drilled in arithmetic without applying the skills to problems that mean anything to them. They learn abstract principles of economics without addressing any real economic problems. They are expected to memorize historical dates and names without context. Science is presented as a set of facts rather than as an ongoing process of thought.

It is not that current teaching practices do not use examples, "word problems," and other devices. It is that the overall approach is turned around the wrong way. Students learn the isolated basics and then are expected to apply them to artificial problems. The constructivists argue that a better approach is to ground all learning as much as possible in tasks, activities, and problems that are meaningful to the student. If it is important that we learn facts, then we will learn them most effectively while engaged in meaningful tasks. To see what this means consider something that you are "expert" in, whether it is sports statistics, popular movies, or anything else. If you are well versed in the area, then clearly you know many facts and concepts related to it. How did you learn them, by sitting down and tediously memorizing them? Of course not. You picked them up as you went along, pursuing your interest for its own sake. As you learned more and more about your area of expertise you undoubtedly have found it easier to learn more. In addition, your understanding of the area has deepened and become richer. All this happened not because you drilled yourself in the basics but because you were engaged in activities that were important to you. The learning then came naturally. Constructivists, through the use of situated learning, hope to extend such experiences more widely, even all the way to school-like subjects.

That is what is meant by situated learning. It is learning that is located or situated in a real-world context and that is meaningful to the lives of the learners. One example of this approach can be found in the Jasper Woodbury programs produced at Vanderbilt University. Named after the character who introduces the problems and helps guide the learners, these interactive multimedia productions are aimed at teaching mathematics through its application to meaningful problems. For instance, one of the programs in the series teaches basic data analysis and statistics to elementary and middle school students by having them work through problems in ecology while collecting and analyzing data. Another program has students plan overseas trips to help them learn about geography and culture.

Another major principle of constructivism is its emphasis on collaborative and cooperative approaches to learning. As mentioned earlier, constructivists note that much authentic learning is done socially. That is, we learn by expressing our ideas to other people, testing them, and getting feedback. We couldn't communicate even at a basic level if that were not so, because even the basic meanings of words depend on social agreement. Some radical constructivists even speak of the "social construction" of reality itself, or at least our understanding of reality. Thus, discussion with other students at about the same level is a key part of constructivist teaching and learning. It is here that we can find out whether our understanding of concepts holds up under scrutiny. Discussion with other students and an instructor is a minimum requirement for much of constructivist learning.

However, just having students "discuss" a topic may be minimally effective. Discussions without a goal can be useful, but they may also be sterile. Thus, many constructivist activities stress cooperative and collaborative problem solving and learning. By working with others to define a problem, for example, and then finding ways together to solve it, learners naturally engage in many of the social aspects of good learning. They test their ideas against those of others. They discuss and argue, and eventually they may come to a shared and deeper understanding of the subject.

Successful Constructivist Projects

How do these basic (and sometimes vague) principles translate into actual teaching? This can be a tough question. It is one thing to theorize about scaffolding and situated learning, but quite another to put them into practice. First, let's look at some existing learning systems that have been developed from a constructivist perspective. This might give you some idea of how others have accomplished the task of translating theory into practice. Then we will discuss the planning process for doing it yourself. Even though some of our examples involve large and complicated multimedia projects, you can do good constructivist teaching on a smaller scale without that kind of technology.

One enduring constructivist approach to learning is exemplified by this book. Problem-based learning (PBL) was originally developed as a teaching method in medical schools. Realizing that the traditional way of teaching basic science to medical students was neither motivating nor especially effective, the originators of PBL sought another approach. No one doubts that basic sciences—anatomy, physiology, biochemistry, and others—are of vital importance to medical students. However, most medical students hope to become doctors, not researchers. Two years of lectures and tests on scientific concepts rarely seem to meet the intellectual and emotional needs of the students. By presenting beginning medical students with actual patient cases (maybe sometimes altered a bit for pedagogical purposes), PBL flips around the learning process.

Here's how it works: A group of perhaps a dozen students are given a description of a patient case. Since they are unlikely, even as a group, to possess the knowledge they need to understand it, they must figure out what they do not know and how to learn it. Under the guidance of a faculty facilitator, the groups may divide up the work of discovering basic concepts, asking questions, narrowing down possible diagnoses, and so on. In doing so, they are forced to grapple with the relevant scientific knowledge, learn the central concepts, and develop their problem-solving skills. Two years of such intense effort using this approach seems to work. On objective examinations, students who learn in medical school through PBL seem to learn as much as students taught in more traditional ways, and they enjoy it more.

The basic concepts of PBL have been applied to a variety of other fields, including law, business, geography, economics, various sciences, and many others. In addition, PBL has been used not only in postgraduate professional education, but also in undergraduate settings and high schools. We are especially pleased with the results of the method in our graduate courses in instructional technology. The students like it, too, if their evaluations of the courses are any indication.

Other good examples of a constructivist approach to learning can be found in the work of Roger Schank at Northwestern University. He has developed an approach to teaching, called goal-directed scenarios, in which students are given realistic and motivating situations to deal with. He uses interactive multimedia computer programs to implement this approach but notes that it does not require technology. Given a low enough student/teacher ratio, it could be done in the classroom without technology. His team has developed programs for professional education as well as for college, high school, and elementary school. In the course of solving problems within these scenarios, the students can learn a variety of concepts and skills.

In one multimedia program, newly hired consultants for a large business consulting firm are put into the position of having to help a client company solve its financial, personnel, and manufacturing problems. In doing this they "meet" with people (such as their boss) when a video clip pops up and the person speaks to them. Frequently, the learner will be asked to make a decision about an employee, an investment, or some other key topic, which they enter into the computer. Each decision has an outcome determined by the computer program that may emerge gradually. The learner can "keep score" of progress through the program by looking at feedback about the company's current finances, employee morale, and so forth. It is a complex program, with elements of games, simulations, and virtual reality. It also appears to be an effective teaching tool. The consulting company spent a lot of money developing the program but has more than recouped its investment through increased learning and lowered costs.

Another program developed at Northwestern is for much younger children. Drawing on the fact that kids like to look at movies, the group put together a gamelike program in which students get to see movie clips as they travel around the United States (although they do their traveling entirely on the computer screen). The catch is that in order to travel they are forced to learn some geography. The approach is similar to that taken in the well-known Carmen Sandiego computer games.

Several times in this book we have mentioned the Jasper Woodbury series developed at Vanderbilt University. Let's take a moment to describe them more fully. The series includes twelve "adventures" that are designed to teach mathematical thinking processes to children in the fifth grade and up. Another goal is to help students make connections to other disciplines such as science and social studies. The adventures do this by having students work through complex problems (usually involving fifteen steps or more) guided by a character named Jasper Woodbury. These problems in science, social studies, and other areas are likely to involve the student in collecting and analyzing data, performing calculations, drawing conclusions, and applying what they have learned to the next steps. We mentioned the ecology and trip planning problems earlier. Others include business planning, architectural design, and tool design. The programs in the series can be used in a variety of ways and by a variety of students. They can support individual investigations by students as well as group problem solving.

Planning Your Constructivist Lessons

Assuming that you want to teach in a constructivist manner, you still face the necessity of having the information and materials available that students might need, of guiding students toward meaningful questions to address and problems to solve, of facilitating their progress toward their goals, and of helping assess whether they have attained them. All this takes planning and preparation.

At this point in your education, you are probably already familiar with lesson plans and how to do them. However, as you know, most lesson plans are much too "instructivist" to fit well into the approach outlined in this chapter.

That is, they lay out the goals of the lesson (the teacher's or curriculum's goals, not the students'), they prescribe a set of activities and information, and they may even describe how students will be assessed. All this seems antithetical to a constructivist point of view.

Another system of instructional planning seems even less likely to meet the needs of the constructivist classroom teacher. Instructional design is a systematic method for analyzing, designing, developing, implementing, and evaluating instruction, from individual lessons to large-scale multimedia projects. As such, it has been used successfully in a variety of settings. However, most teachers find it far too time-consuming to practice day-to-day during the school year. In addition, most instructional design models seem to encourage, if not demand, highly instructivist teaching. All in all, these formal instructional design techniques may not be easy for most teachers to use in creating constructivist units.

What is needed is an approach that you as a working teacher could use to plan your own constructivist lessons. It may seem to be paradoxical to write about planning constructivist lessons, but it still must be done. Real teachers cannot always follow all the suggestions of the current theories. They still have a curriculum to teach, and they do not have unlimited time to spend on a specific topic or lesson. They must have at least some control over their classrooms (if only for appearances' sake!), and administrators and parents want to see grades and other indications of students' progress. Constructivists may talk about putting students in charge of their own learning, of pursuing individual interests wherever they may lead, and so forth, but some compromises are probably needed right now to implement a significant part of that theory.

One discussion of how to plan constructivist-style units is found in a book by Roger Schank entitled *Engines of Education*. In this book he advocates radical changes in how we teach, and he describes some of his efforts. Schank believes that his approach using goal-based scenarios can be applied widely to a variety of settings. This teaching/learning strategy does not necessarily depend on using computers and other technologies, since it could be implemented with handouts and other low-tech materials. The more significant problem is that current student/teacher ratios do not allow teachers to work intensively with individuals and small groups. Therefore, interactive multimedia can often make this type of teaching possible.

Schank lays out a set of steps for developing goal-based scenarios. Their purpose is to ensure that you end up with a scenario that, when worked through by an individual or group of students, will result in a higher level of skills than before. There are two key criteria for judging such a scenario. First, is it interesting to the students? Second, does it require them to learn and use the appropriate skills? Schank lists six major steps:

1. Identify a set of target skills.
2. Develop one or more "missions" that require the target skills.
3. Choose a focus.
4. Create a cover story for the mission.

5. Plan the operations.
6. Build learning environments to support the target skills.

Let's look briefly at each of these points. Identifying target skills is a problem for people who teach almost anything. Although it can be relatively easy to lay out a set of facts and concepts that people "should" know, it can be more difficult to explain why they should know them and what they should do with them. For example, in studying history, is the point really to know a set of names, locations, and dates? Or is it to be able to analyze historical situations, develop and defend coherent explanations of historical events, relate current situations to their historical roots, and so forth? Are science courses supposed to teach the current theories and facts, to develop abilities to reason scientifically, or to prepare one to become a scientist? Similar questions can be asked of most disciplines that one might study. At any rate, a key step in preparing to teach by any method is to decide what you want the students to get out of the learning.

The "mission" of a goal-based scenario defines what the student will try to achieve during it. In an economic scenario, the mission might be to start a business at the microeconomic level or to run the Federal Reserve at the macroeconomic level. In some scenarios, there might be a variety of missions for students to choose from. In learning statistics, one might choose an ecology scenario where data are to be analyzed to save an endangered species, or one might instead select a baseball scenario in which one uses statistics to help recruit the best possible team. Again, the key here is to develop a mission or set of missions that will be enjoyable and meaningful to the students.

In the third step, one chooses a focus for the scenario. Schank suggests several possibilities:

- Designing a process or object
- Controlling a system
- Discovering new information and concepts
- Explaining an event or situation

In addition, a scenario could have multiple foci. Basically, the focus of the scenario determines the actual set of tasks that one will have to perform in order to complete the mission.

Next, one develops the "cover story" for the scenario, according to Schank. Like the scenarios in this book, the cover story explains the context of the mission and tasks. It sets the stage in a relatively realistic way, putting you into the situation where problems will arise for you to solve. The consultant visiting a business is one cover story. Another might be a traveler arriving at the airport in Madrid and needing to use Spanish to find a hotel, a restaurant, and popular tourist attractions. Of course, the scenarios in this book concentrate on educational settings, but with different students you would want to match the cover stories with the audiences.

The fifth step involves planning the operations of the scenario. These are the specific steps that the student must take while completing the tasks, including the resources they will need and so forth. For example, in a PBL unit in medical school, the group might not get all the information about a patient at one time. Instead, they will get the results of lab tests only after a certain amount of time has passed and only if they have requested them. Similarly, an economic simulation would show the results of a decision to raise interest rates only after some period of time had passed. In any lesson like this, the set of interactions and their results need to be planned out, at least at a general level.

Finally, the last step in creating a goal-based scenario is to develop the learning environment. This means gathering the materials that the students will need (or references to them), preparing handouts or other ways of communicating the mission and cover story to the students, outlining what kinds of tools are available, laying out any rules that must be followed, and so forth. In developing an interactive multimedia program from all this, there are the final steps of programming the computer, testing it, and so on. In a simpler situation, you need to have the materials ready and be prepared to work with students and groups as they complete the tasks.

All this sounds like a lot of work, and it is. But you should realize that a good constructivist-style lesson, including a goal-based scenario, will be a long and complex one for the students as well. You are trying to develop meaningful goals and missions for the students to achieve. These goals should require them to learn and use a variety of skills, perhaps in more than one discipline. Therefore, a good lesson will probably take students many days or even weeks to complete, depending on how much time they have. Although you may write a typical lesson plan quite quickly, the activities usually are over quickly as well. In contrast, a goal-based scenario or PBL problem will keep you and the class busy for a long time while teaching much more in the process.

RECOMMENDED READING

Cennamo, K. 1996. A "Layers of Negotiation" model for designing constructivist learning materials. *Educational Technology* 36 (4): 39–48.

Duffy, T. M., and D. H. Jonassen. 1992. Constructivism: New implications for instructional technology. In *Constructivism and the technology of instruction: A conversation*, edited by T. M. Duffy and D. H. Jonassen. Hillsdale, NJ: Lawrence Erlbaum.

Roblyer, M. 1996. The constructivist/objectivist debate: Implications for instructional technology research. *Learning and Leading with Technology* 24 (2): 12–16.

OTHER REFERENCES

Albanese, M., and S. Mitchell. 1993. Problem based learning: A review of the literature on its outcomes and implementation issues. *Academic Medicine* 68: 52–81.

Brooks, J., and M. Brooks. 1990. *In search of understanding: The case for constructivist classrooms*. Alexandria, VA: Association for Supervision and Curriculum Development.

Bruner, J. 1986. *Actual minds, possible worlds.* Cambridge, MA: Harvard University Press.

Cifuentes, L. 1997. From sages to guides: A professional development study. *Journal of Technology and Teacher Education* 5 (1): 67–77.

Fosnot, C. T. 1996. *Constructivism: Theory, perspectives, and practice.* New York: Teachers College Press.

Gruender, D. 1996. Constructivism and learning: A philosophical appraisal. *Educational Technology* 36 (3): 21–29.

Lueddeke, G. 1999. Toward a constructivist framework for guiding change and innovation in higher education. *The Journal of Higher Education* 70 (3): 235–260.

Marlowe, B., and M. Page. 1998. *Creating and sustaining the constructivist classroom.* Thousand Oaks, CA: Corwin Press.

Murphy, E. 1997. Constructivist learning theory. Online: http://www.stemnet.nf.ca/~elmurphy/emurphy/cle2b.html.

Oliver, K. 1997. *Realizing the potential of scaffolded instruction in situated learning environments: Lessons from a formative evaluation.* ERIC, ED 413310.

Savery, J., and T. Duffy. 1995. Problem based learning: An instructional model and its constructivist framework. *Educational Technology* 35 (5): 31–38.

Schank, R. C., and C. Cleary. 1995. *Engines for education.* Hillsdale, NJ: Lawrence Erlbaum.

Wilson, B. G., ed. 1998. *Constructivist learning environments: Case studies in instructional design.* Englewood Cliffs, NJ: Educational Technology Publications.

SCENARIO

Your school district has decided to revamp its science curriculum in all grades. Your principal, Mr. Jones, is about to receive his doctorate from a nearby university and he is excited about the discussions in which he has participated regarding an approach to instruction known as constructivism. Constructivists emphasize student-centered learning, feeling it is very important that pupils be allowed to explore topics on their own and come to their own conclusions about important issues they will face in their adult lives. He now wants his staff to develop effective instructional materials based on this constructivist learning approach.

Jones has assigned teams of people from various backgrounds to work on this effort. This team will not necessarily be responsible for doing all the work of designing and developing the materials. But it will be responsible for specifying the process that the district will follow. You are part of the team responsible for the fourth-grade science curriculum.

The key point is that the materials that are ultimately developed must be based on constructivist principles (not to be confused with constructivist "principals" like Jones!). Rather than following the usual didactic instructional models, the materials must provide students the opportunities and support they need to "construct" their own internal understanding of the material in the curriculum.

Your team has decided that a key issue will be to describe the curricular planning process that the district will follow in developing these materials. You have a limited amount of money, time, and other resources to expend on this project, and it is vitally important that everyone working on it have an understanding of the procedures the various individuals and groups will follow.

In response to Mr. Jones's request, you need to clarify your own professional perspectives about the constructivist approach to learning. Is this a valid way of learning? Would you prefer it to the traditional time-honored teacher-led approach? If you feel it has merit, what types of instruction might be best served by this approach? How extensively should it be attempted in a school curriculum?

Finally, you need to explain how a teacher can plan constructivist lessons for teaching a fourth-grade science unit on insects. This may be a challenge, since the actual activities may mostly be determined by the individual students themselves. If the unit plan is too structured, it probably will not allow the learner to work as independently as constructivists would recommend. But if some structure is needed, how can it be designed to permit (or even encourage) a considerable degree of student initiative?

ISSUES INQUIRY

1. What do you think about constructivism as an approach? Will such a potentially unstructured strategy work?

2. What is the most effective way to plan class activities that give students more freedom (and more responsibility) to learn?

3. From your experience, do you believe that constructivist teaching methods are appropriate for all students? Or might some students benefit more from those methods while others do better with more instructivist methods? How would you characterize the types of students in each group?

4. Do some subjects lend themselves to more constructivist methods than others? If so, describe them. Why do you think this is so?

5. Perhaps we do not have to choose either constructivist or instructivist teaching methods. Perhaps instead we should see teaching strategies as lying on a continuum between the two extremes. If this is so, then maybe different strategies are most appropriate for different situations, subject matters, and audiences. Discuss this possibility and how you might put it into practice.

6. Perhaps even more difficult than reconciling the idea of "planning" with that of "constructivism" is the problem of reconciling the fact that states and districts have prescribed curricula. How can you plan lessons that teach a given curriculum and still use genuinely constructivist methods?

7. You have spent years in various educational institutions (although hopefully were never "institutionalized"!). As a student, did you ever have a teacher who used constructivist teaching methods? How did those experiences differ from more traditional ones? Which did you think were most successful? Which were more enjoyable?

CHAPTER 4

How Can Technology Facilitate Constructivist Units?

INTRODUCTION

Constructivism is an instructional approach which, over the course of the past decade, has gained considerable support in academic circles and that also appears to be impacting more and more K–12 classrooms. Its tenets are essentially to encourage pupils to initiate their own learning experiences, with an emphasis on their being able to "construct" their own set of mental representations topics, and issues. Before working with this chapter, it would be helpful to read about constructivism in the preceding chapter, "Deconstructing Constructivism: The Paradox of Planning Unstructured Units," and the introductory chapter entitled "From Conditioning to Constructivism: Learning Theories and Their Impact on How We Teach." Many constructivists stress the significance of how reality is socially constructed, arguing that children's perceptions of the world depend heavily on the views of significant others around them, like parents, siblings, friends, and teachers. Some of these influences—for example, ethnocentrism, racism, sexism, militarism, and fundamentalism—are considered questionable by many constructivists (given *their* constructions of reality!). They feel it is important that schools encourage pupils to think for themselves, and if they are to do so, they need opportunities to explore on their own.

Unfortunately, in some educational settings it is difficult for students to explore on their own because of insufficient resources. The information sources in most classrooms are fairly limited. The library is generally the best place for students to do their research, but many school libraries are small and their collections certainly do not include information on all possible topics. The local public library collection may also be inadequate in many subject areas. For small schools in small towns available materials may be quite limited. Many schools in poor urban neighborhoods may also have inadequate, dated library collections. Even in well-financed suburban schools, students may find that doing a report on Kosovo is difficult because little information is available within the school, beyond a short encyclopedia entry and an atlas, which may still show the united Yugoslavia of 1989. Without sufficient resources, how can students be expected to investigate effectively on their own? It is obviously very difficult to implement a constructivist curriculum in an information-poor learning environment. This problem can be overcome to a significant degree, by the availability of new communications technologies.

Information Access Through Communications Technologies

Technology can provide a vast array of alternative information sources and thereby compensate for a paucity of information within the school building. In fact, it may be no coincidence that the constructivist movement has grown at a time when advances in technology have provided so many new resources for students. This book is filled with examples of how different types of technologies can facilitate educational efforts. But in this chapter, we examine these technologies from a unique perspective. How can they help teachers and students really open up the educational process, freeing them to explore and discover?

Perhaps the most obvious way in which this can happen is for students to get online and access the countless resources available on the World Wide Web (see Chapter 2, "Surviving the Information Explosion: Researching on the World Wide Web"). What a tremendous opportunity for them to explore? Some worry that there are too many questionable websites that children might log onto with material that is inaccurate, biased, inflammatory, or offensive. Others worry that it is such an unstructured information environment that undisciplined learners can become overwhelmed, confused, or directionless. But with appropriate guidance, pupils should be able to pursue their own interests and obtain a great deal of information on almost any issue. Furthermore, nearly every perspective on a given topic will likely be available somewhere on the Web. So students can examine the various sides of a subject by accessing different websites. Such an experience would be truly "constructivist."

In addition to being the world's largest repository of information, the Internet also has enormous potential as a communications medium (see Chapter 16, "Conceptual Connections: Establishing Online Learning Communities"). Online exchanges with co-learners, teachers, and subject area experts can really enhance a learning experience. Special websites, like Ask An Expert (www.askanexpert.org), provide lists of experts in a wide variety of subject areas whom students can contact to ask questions and request information. Listservs, newsgroups, and chat sessions online can provide opportunities for group discussions on a myriad of different topics.

The sharing of ideas is a process that constructivists encourage, since it is through multiple perspectives that young learners can best examine topics and reach their own conclusions. If constructivists are right about how reality is largely socially constructed, then interaction with others is an extremely important part of one's education. The Internet can provide wonderful opportunities for young people to expand their social contacts and thereby be exposed to new ideas. Communicating with people from other cultures can be an especially interesting experience, since their perspectives are likely to be quite different. The Internet is a global medium, and it offers many potentially stimulating international contacts via keypal relationships, chats, or listserv exchanges (see Chapter 10, "It Takes a Global Village: Multicultural Studies Through Telecommunications").

Although it can be very exciting to make online connections to the vast stores of information and the human resources on the Web, not every school can provide sufficient time online for each student. So packaged sources of information are also important. Optical discs hold enormous amounts of text, as well as multimedia files, so that one small disc can provide a wealth of information. Multimedia encyclopedias on CD-ROM are a good example, as are digital atlases. There are also many excellent compact discs and 12-inch videodiscs filled with a great deal of archival material that students can use for their research projects: North American birds, NASA photographs of the solar system, the National Gallery of Art collection, and so on. A reasonably extensive collection of optical discs can provide as much information as whole library aisles. Now that the compact disc format has evolved from CD-ROM to DVD, each little disc will hold over ten times as much material (see Chapter 14, "Digital Developments: Television's Technological Transformation"). Those digital encyclopedias will become much more extensive, with more entries, longer articles, and many more multimedia files to engage children with the sights and sounds of our world. No longer will library size be such a significant issue for schools.

Other media formats can also play a dynamic role in the constructivist classroom. While DVD videoplayers are becoming more widely available, videotape is still the dominant television medium. Having videos available for student viewing also can facilitate research efforts. Television programs can provide information in special ways, showing students things that would not be as clear from simply reading about them. Television demonstrations and dramatizations can bring a topic to life. Viewing television programming is motivational. A good video library can help stimulate students in their efforts to find out about a wide variety of topics.

Creative Projects with Technology

But research is only one facet of a constructivist classroom. An equally important aspect can be opportunities for students to communicate what they have learned. In attempting to teach others, students can deepen their own understanding. Expressing what they have learned may also help pupils define their own individual perspectives about the topic. Here is where technology can play a unique role. For it is through technology that students can apply their imagination to create dynamic media projects that go beyond the written or oral report.

For example, developing a PowerPoint presentation complete with pictures, sounds, and maybe even video segments can help motivate students to do their best work, especially if they will be required to show these presentations to the rest of the group. Working with computer equipment, video cameras, and audio recording equipment in developing these kinds of presentations can be quite engaging for pupils. The World Wide Web can provide pictures and sounds for such presentations. Students can also shoot pictures in books with a digital still camera. They can record their own sounds with mike and audiotape player. They might even shoot video clips of dynamic demonstrations or relevant roleplaying. Digitized pictures and sounds can then be captured by PowerPoint and integrated into the presentation. With audiovisual elements incorporated into colorful text screens, such a presentation is likely to be far livelier than an oral report and will also probably be more effective at getting the rest of the class interested in the subject matter.

Another approach might be to use authoring software such as HyperStudio. Authored programs, like PowerPoint files, can include multimedia materials with animated text on colored backgrounds. But they can be more sophisticated than PowerPoint, which is essentially a linear application. With an authoring system students can create a hypertext-based, nonlinear tutorial. Links can be established to other parts of the program, thereby providing many choices for users to pursue. Such a lesson can be a dynamic learning experience for other pupils in the class. In addition, developing a hyperlinked, multimedia tutorial can be a challenging assignment, from which the student can learn a great deal, both about the topic and about the authoring application. Students with some advanced computer skills may wish to work with more-sophisticated authoring applications than HyperStudio, such as Director, Toolbook, or Authorware.

Developing a Web page is yet another creative opportunity for students to present, material that they have been studying. Software packages like PageMill, FrontPage and Dreamweaver can help pupils create their own Web pages. These Web page development applications are relatively user-friendly, allowing the user to create a multimedia, hyperlinked learning environment, much like an authored program. A Web page can easily link the user to other worthwhile sites on the Web (authored files are also now capable of this, but not as conveniently or efficiently). Another significant advantage to creating a Website is, of course, its potential accessibility to millions via the Internet. If a teacher can find space on a server for student Web pages, they can be viewed by classmates, friends, and family. Privacy and safety become issues, but students need not include phone numbers or addresses that might subject them to unwanted solicitation. Some student Web pages may ultimately be appreciated by many other people around the world who are interested in their subject matter.

Producing a short television program is another excellent way for students to involve the rest of the class in what they are studying. For example, pupils might produce a dramatization that re-creates an historical incident, literary episode, or moment of scientific discovery. Working with video can be very motivating for students, and they may investigate a subject more thoroughly if they are trying to write a script. Television production can also facilitate the development of a variety of skills, for it demands imagination, research, writing ability, organization, social sensitivity, and of course some technical knowhow. Many of these kinds of productions will need to be shot sequentially in camera, because no editing equipment is available. With editing capabilities, students can shoot raw footage and then carefully sequence it later with the editor. Two recorders (or camcorders) can serve as a primitive editing system. An inexpensive editor can be connected between the two VCRs to facilitate the editing process. Now there are inexpensive digital editing software packages like Avid's, which allow for editing television footage in a computer. With an editor, students can develop more-polished productions.

The constructivist approach stresses the importance of pupils developing their own unique ways of expressing what they have learned. What better way to practice constructivism than to have students create their own projects. The creative process also will help them more fully develop their own thinking about the topic. In addition, reactions of others to their production will help them evaluate whether their understanding of the material is thorough and whether their perspectives on the topic are reasonable. Finally, teachers need to realize that technology can provide many different opportunities for students to create interesting projects that help them share what they learned with their classmates.

A Sample Unit: Ancient Egypt

Imagine you are a teacher interested in developing a unit in a constructivist way. How would you start? And how might you use technology to do so? Let's see how this might be done, using the often-taught topic of Ancient Egypt as an example. One way to begin might be to have the class divide the main topic into subtopics of interest to individuals or pairs of students. Subtopics can be established in a number of possible ways. One might be to look at aspects of Egyptian life: hieroglyphics, architecture, art, politics, war, religion, the status of women, everyday life, slavery and so on. Another approach would be to examine different historical periods: the ancient kingdom, the middle kingdom, the New Kingdom, Nubian dynasties, Greek conquest and Roman rule. Still another might be to report on famous personalities like Tutankhamen, Akhenaton, Tutmose III, Ramses II, Hapshepsut, Nefertiti, Cleopatra, Ptolemy, and Cheops.

An important issue with constructivist units is how much freedom to give your students in selecting their own topic of study. Really radical constructivists might not even like the concept of having a unit in the first place, since it pre-determines the choice of material to study. But given the prescribed nature of most public school curricula, few teachers feel they can give their students freedom to study anything they want. Somewhat radical constructivists would probably say that there should be freedom of topic choice within the boundaries of the unit itself. In this case, students would be free to explore anything as long as their investigations have something to do with Ancient Egypt. Many teachers prefer to structure student choices somewhat, because this allows for comprehensive coverage of many important topics and avoids duplication of topics. If these research projects are eventually going to be reported back to the whole class, these issues matter. As a teacher, you might not want to skip discussion of the hieroglyphic writing system just because nobody showed an interest in it. Neither would you want four class reports on mummification because it was such a popular topic. Another concern is that some children would have difficulty coming up with their own topic or might not have a preference even if you presented them with alternatives. So teachers invariably suggest topics to students, even when they are trying to be constructivist.

How can technology help these students explore this cryptic ancient culture? What kinds of media materials might be of assistance in this unit? Ancient Egypt is a topic about which a great deal has been written. Some interesting books are available, and many of these should have pictures of the famous monuments, the wall paintings, the sarcophagi, the death masks, the canopic jars holding the vital organs of the deceased . . . (we better stop here!). Students should probably start in the school library or the public library. The teacher might check out books and bring them to class for students to use. The challenge is usually to find materials for every student's report. Invariably a few of the topics prove difficult to research because information about them is scarce. But this is where technology can be used to supplement printed resources.

The World Wide Web seems to have something on nearly every conceivable topic. If you cannot find it on the Web, better broaden your topic or pick another one. Students having trouble finding print resources can get online and use a Web search engine to find relevant material. If they find Web searches somewhat overwhelming, some students might just begin looking in fairly obvious places for information, like the home page of the Egyptian government tourist office or at the website of a museum with a good Egyptian collection, like the Metropolitan Museum of Art in New York City or the Louvre in Paris. More advanced students might want to try accessing a historical or archaeological database through its Web access. One tricky aspect of students searching indiscriminately for Ancient Egypt on the Web is that some strange cults may be preoccupied with things Egyptian (like Seth, their god of evil, or the burial rituals), and they might wind up on some weird Websites.

An exciting way to learn about Egypt might be to get online with some other students who are studying the subject. Teachers can find out about potential online exchanges on a wide variety of topics by visiting big educational Web clearinghouses, like GlobalSchoolNet (www.gsn.org). Maybe there are listserv discussion groups about the Ancient Egyptians or a class that wants to show your pupils their papier mâché pyramids via desktop video, using CU-SeeMe software. Better yet might be an exchange with a class in an Egyptian school to converse, hopefully in English, with children who have not only actually visited the pyramids, but whose ancestors built them! Kidlink (www.kidlink.org) is a good website on which to look for student exchanges overseas. A number of websites specialize in helping educators contact specialists in various topic areas. An online experience with an Egyptologist could be very exciting for the class.

There might even be an online field trip headed to Egypt, which you could sign up for. These experiences allow students to follow a team that travels to Egypt, exploring the ruins, meeting the locals, taking photographs, keeping diaries, and so on. These travelers use satellite uplinks to post Web materials daily about their adventures for classes back in the United States to view. So students can engage in a kind of "virtual field trip" to an interesting site. Previous such expeditions are archived on the websites of the organization that sponsored them, so Web surfers can still read the journals, see the photos, and check out the maps showing where the travelers went. Two Web-based organizations that oversee such online travel are AdventureOnline (adventureonline.com) and Globalearn (www.globalearn.org).

Ancient Egypt has been addressed on many compact discs. Multimedia encyclopedias will have detailed entries on the topic that should include photographs of famous monuments like the Great Pyramid, the Sphinx, and the Temple of Karnak. National Geographic has had many articles about Egyptian antiquities, which are available on the organization's set of archival CDs. One of National Geograhic's most interesting cover stories described the colossal job of moving a set of four seventy-five-foot-high statues of the Pharaoh Ramses II at Abu Simbel. They were cut into blocks and then reassembled one hundred miles downriver of the Aswan Dam, whose giant reservoir would have otherwise submerged the monument. The photography in this article was spectacular. Other commercial CDs will provide material about Ancient Egypt because this is a topic often addressed in school curricula. There is surely one that displays the collection of exquisite treasures found in the tomb of the boy pharaoh Tutankhamen, which became more famous than ever when the collection toured a series of museums in the United States back in the late 1970s. In fact, the Egyptian collections of many of the world's premier museums can be found on their CDs and Websites. Some of the better Egyptian collections are at the British Museum, the Louvre, and the Metropolitan Museum of Art.

Many television documentaries also have been made about exploration of the ruins of Egypt and what has been learned about its ancient society. Film footage was taken of the most famous archaeological dig of all time, the one that uncovered the tomb of King Tutankhamen in 1922. Consequently, the opening of the tomb and removal of the treasures can be seen in documentaries about Ancient Egypt. A few years ago, a major PBS series that retraced the conquests of Alexander the Great took viewers to Egypt, where Alexander founded the great city that still bears his name, Alexandria. Some television programs about Egypt may be of a less reputable, unscientific nature, given all the New Age mystery that surrounds this ancient culture. They may suggest, for instance, that extraterrestrials built the Great Pyramid or that the Sphinx guards some esoteric knowledge left for humankind by a superior race from the lost continent of Atlantis. Here is where a teacher needs to decide whether indulging in this kind of speculation is an acceptable way to heighten the pupils' interest levels.

Another interesting way for students to examine Ancient Egypt might be to analyze how it is portrayed in the popular culture. There have been several films about Cleopatra, beginning in the silent era and including the extravagant Elizabeth Taylor production of the early 1960s. Mummies have appeared consistently in the horror genre, and The Mummy was a box office hit in 1999. Several biblical extravaganzas have depicted Ancient Egypt enslaving the Israelites, including the famous Ten Commandments. Even Disney has ventured back to ancient Thebes, with its animated feature about Moses. A worthwhile class exercise might be to discuss some of the inaccuracies associated with these films and to compare the image of this ancient society we have been given by Hollywood with the conclusions archaeologists have reached.

Deconstructing Pop Culture Images

Media studies lend themselves to constructivist units because they represent one of the primary reasons why our "reality" is socially constructed. The popular culture conveys a certain image of a phenomenon, which may have very little to do with what a scientist might say about it. This image may be a perpetuation of misconceptions once supported by experts but now discredited. But a more likely explanation is that Hollywood has concocted an exaggerated version of ancient practices to make for a more entertaining production. This film version may appeal to the public's imagination in some way and then become ingrained in the popular consciousness.

For example, many Egyptologists say that the society's preoccupation with death rituals was not morbid, but reflected the very optimistic view that there was a happy afterlife. So Egyptian culture was positive and healthy, not dark and forbidding. But this perspective would not be especially welcomed by the producers of horror movies about mummies, which depend for their success upon our long-standing revulsion about this way of preserving the dead and play upon our mental images of a shadowy Ancient Egypt characterized by frightful burial rituals in dark, dusty tombs.

Studying an ancient society can lend itself to constructivist approaches in part because we have had to intellectually "construct" what we know about these people. Much of it is conjecture. Some of our assumptions are based on very little data and may need to be questioned periodically. Just pointing this out to students can serve as an important lesson. They should question what they learn and need to realize that some of what they are exposed to may be speculative, distorted, or simply inaccurate.

An interesting exercise might be to discuss the following scenario (oh no, another one!). Suppose a nuclear holocaust occurs within the next fifty years that destroys civilization as we know it. But the human race rebuilds, and five centuries from now a group of future archaeologists find artifacts from the United States that date back to our century. These items include some remains of buildings and some videotapes. What impression might these future historians get of our society from such limited data? It might be fun for students to discuss how impressions might vary depending on what type of building the historians uncovered. Certainly finding pieces of the Lincoln Memorial might give a different impression than finding remnants of the Empire State Building or of a McDonald's. What about the videos? Would it be *Schindler's List, Star Wars,* or a Marx Brothers movie? What conclusions might these future archaeologists draw from this circumstantial evidence that fell into their hands largely by chance? Is this fictitious scenario not similar to what we must try to do today to reconstruct what Ancient Egyptian society was like?

Constructivist principles not only can guide a school unit, but also could be the topic of one. For if teachers want their students to appreciate how relative people's perceptions can be and to examine how such different perspectives are formed, then direct discussion about these issues is appropriate. Using technology to provide examples from the popular culture is an excellent way to approach this kind of lesson. Analyzing how movies, television shows, and rock songs affect our perceptions about different topics can be fascinating for young people. Examining some Web pages with extreme views can even be a valuable experience, for they demonstrate how different people's perceptions can be. The effects of the modern media make for an interesting unit, especially if examined from a constructivist perspective.

Constructivist approaches depend on the availability of sufficient amounts of information for students to explore. Different sources of information with varying accounts can help pupils truly appreciate how reality may be socially constructed. Technology-based resources can provide a wealth of information with a wide variety of views on a given topic. It is a potentially powerful tool for constructivist teachers who want students to discover things for themselves and to reach their own conclusions.

RECOMMENDED READING

Dede, C. 1995. The evolution of constructivist learning environments: Immersion in distributed virtual worlds. *Educational Technology* 35 (5): 46–52.

Hirtle, J. 1996. Constructing a collaborative classroom. *Learning and Leading with Technology* 23 (8): 27–30.

Jonassen, D. 1995. Supporting communities of learners with technology: A vision for integrating technology with learning in schools. *Educational Technology* 35 (4): 60–63.

OTHER REFERENCES

Boyer, B., and P. Semrau. 1996. A constructivist approach to social studies: Integrating technology. *Social Studies and the Young Learner* 7 (3): 14–16.

Greening, T. 1998. Building the constructivist toolbox: An exploration of cognitive technologies. *Educational Technology* 38 (2): 23–35.

Lebow, D. 1995. Constructivist values and emerging technologies: Transforming classrooms into learning environments. *Proceedings of the 1995 Annual National Convention of the Association for Educational Communications and Technology,* Anaheim, CA, ERIC, ED 383318.

McDonald, H., and L. Ingvarson. 1997. Technology: A catalyst for educational change. *Journal of Curriculum Studies* 29 (5): 513–527.

Means, B., and K. Olson. 1995, April. Technology's role within constructivist classrooms. Paper presented at the annual meeting of the American Educational Research Association, San Francisco, CA, ERIC, ED 383283.

Nicaise, M., and D. Barnes. 1996. The union of technology, constructivism, and teacher education. *Journal of Teacher Education* 47 (3): 205–212.

Salomon, G. 1998. Technology's promises and dangers in a psychological and educational context. *Theory into Practice* 37 (1): 4–10.

Silverman, B. 1995. Computer supported collaborative learning. *Computers and Education* 25 (3): 81–91.

White, C. 1996. Merging technology and constructivism in teacher education. *Teacher Education and Practice* 12 (1): 62–70.

Wilson, B. 1999. How technology aids constructivism in the social studies classroom. *The Social Studies* 90 (1): 28–33.

Wolffe, R., and D. McMullen. 1996. The constructivist connection: Linking theory, best practice, and technology. *Journal of Computing in Teacher Education* 12 (2): 25–28.

SCENARIO

You have been teaching sixth grade for nine years. You enjoy your work but are beginning to get tired of the same routine. You fear that the "teacher burnout" you have heard about for years may be catching up with you. The inevitable whining of certain students is starting to grate on your nerves, misguided parental concerns seem a bit more irritating, and the paperwork is more tedious than ever.

Although you already have your master's degree, to refresh yourself you have again started taking courses at a local university. This strategy seems to be helping to reinvigorate you. After being with children all day, it is nice to interact with adults for a change. In one of these courses, the educational philosophy of constructivism has been discussed as a way of revitalizing classroom instruction. In the other course, the instructor is enthusiastic about technology, and he recommends that students be encouraged to use new technologies to explore topics on their own. The courses are interesting, and some of the ideas appeal to you. You begin thinking seriously about making your classroom more constructivist.

However, you are apprehensive about changing your approach to teaching. In theory, you have always thought students should have choices about what they want to learn. You also have always felt that one of the most important parts of your job is to build students' self-confidence in their own ability to research a topic, synthesize what they have learned, and communicate it effectively to others. But in the past, when students worked on their own projects, the effort always seemed problematic right from the start. Some pupils could not figure out what they were interested in and, even when they finally decided on a topic, were not very motivated to search for research materials. Another difficulty has been *finding* materials on their topic. Often a given topic had to be abandoned because materials on it were scarce. You feel that one of the serious challenges associated with the constructivist approach is to provide enough interesting material for kids to learn on their own.

Then you start to consider your other instructor's recommendations. In the past, she mainly relied on library books and encyclopedias for student reports. What about using technology to expand the range of materials available for student research? Also, what about encouraging students to present what they learn with technology, rather than just having them write the usual reports? You begin considering how to take advantage of whatever technology-based resources you can find.

Your class contains three Macintosh computers, which sit in the back of the room. One is connected to an inkjet printer. You have a CD-ROM encyclopedia, an electronic atlas, and several other CDs with archival material on a variety of topics. The school has a computer lab with twenty computers that are networked to a laser printer and to the World Wide Web. The presentation software package PowerPoint is available on these machines and the teacher station is connected to a projector that displays the computer's output to the entire class. The Web page development software Front Page is also available on each machine as is the authoring software HyperStudio. The lab also has a scanner for digitizing pictures.

The school has subscribed to the "Channel One" newscast project, so a television is permanently mounted in your classroom. You can obtain a videocassette recorder from the audiovisual center adjacent to the library, along with projectors for film or slides. The school has a tape library with about seventy titles and still has some old filmstrips and about twenty 16-mm films on an assortment of topics. But there is a regional resource center that lends media materials to participating schools, and its collection is far more extensive. Cameras for shooting photographs and video camcorders are also available for students to use, under teacher supervision.

You decide to try the constructivist approach for a two-month period, with a special emphasis on using technology, both for researching and for presenting the findings to the class in a dynamic way. How can you most effectively use technology to strengthen your constructivist unit? Describe a variety of different approaches to using technology that might help make your experiment with constructivism a success.

ISSUES INQUIRY

1. Do you think that advances in communications technologies have played an important supporting role in the constructivist movement, providing enhanced access to information that facilitates student research efforts?

2. How significant are the opportunities provided by technology for students to share what they have learned and thereby validate their "constructions of reality"? In what way can technology-based projects foster students' intellectual growth?

3. Can you think of an example of the pop culture "reconstructing" a phenomenon for the public? Describe how it has been distorted in the popular imagination by its portrayal in films, television, shows, songs, and so on.

4. Technology can provide a "learning environment" of its own. Commercial television often creates a sanitized world of danger, intrigue, and romance in which beautiful people usually find happy endings. The Web can be more counterculture, with unusual characters of all kinds posting their bizarre websites and interacting in obtuse ways online. Motion pictures can be more daring than television in exploring forbidden themes, but they generally are quite mainstream. The big blockbuster movies are invariably family entertainment. Genres in the music industry represent every subculture, from honkies (country music) to headbangers (heavy metal) to hearthrobs (pop mush). If the constructivists are right about reality being "socially constructed," how does technology convey and reinforce its own versions of reality, which much of the public comes to accept as fact.

Difficult Decisions

CRUCIAL YET COMPLICATED

TV or Not TV? That Is the Question

COMMERCIALIZATION OF THE CLASSROOM

INTRODUCTION

In the early 1990s, a relatively radical proposal, called "Channel One," was advanced by a successful young entrepreneur named Chris Whittle. He approached the educational establishment with an offer to provide television equipment throughout the entire building of any secondary school that signed up for his project. He further promised a twelve-minute newscast for teenagers, to be broadcast every day, as well as scores of educational programs that had previously aired on the Public Broadcasting Service. He also promised television programs designed for teacher development, to be shown at staff meetings. Yet this would not cost the schools a single cent.

How could this be? Whittle's scheme was to pay the bills for all this with revenue collected from advertisers. The twelve-minute newscast would contain two minutes of commercials. Whittle had more than enough companies willing to pay for the costs of the project. Commercial advertising time can be extremely expensive (for example, a thirty-second spot during the Super Bowl now costs more than 1 million dollars). Advertisers of products that appeal to teens were eager to gain access to the huge group of adolescents attending the nation's secondary schools. Apparently the money generated from advertising fees would be more than sufficient to cover the costs of the equipment, the production of the newscast, and the rights to the PBS programming. The advertisers would be happy. The schools would be happy. Whittle, especially, would be happy.

Opposition to the Channel One Project

But educators responded to this proposal with a number of concerns. They objected to this intrusion of commercialism into the classroom. School was a place for learning, not for selling. It would be inappropriate for time during the school day to be allotted for this type of business activity. That time had already been paid for by the taxpayers and should not be given over to any outside enterprise. Many also feared that students would remember the advertisements better than they remembered the news stories. They argued that the production value of the ads was going to be much higher than that of the news segments, and the ads' clever gimmickry and slick techniques would have students talking about the "cool commercials," rather than about the "boring news."

Many felt quite strongly that the school, as guardian of its students' welfare (sometimes legally described as "in loco parentis"), should not allow its charges to be exposed to the manipulative messages of advertisers. There was some concern about what types of products would be sold. There was a concern that the school might be perceived as sanctioning certain types of sales. Some worried about the "captive" nature of the school audience. Students would not have a choice to turn the channel or to leave the room. There were misgivings about the impressionable nature of the audience. Adolescents do not always show good judgment. For example, they can be especially susceptible to peer pressure. Teenagers might be expected to respond to advertising appeals which claim that all their peers are buying something. After all, wasn't one of Whittle's advertisers Nike, the company that pioneered the need among young athletes for the sneaker that sold in triple digits?

Even if ultimately students seldom purchased items advertised on Channel One, many felt that simply having commercials in the classroom sent the wrong message to teenagers. This legitimized the materialistic values of our society. It condoned the sales techniques used to sell merchandise, which some educators found questionable. It emphasized how the medium of television, despite all its educational potential, has been largely co-opted by show business and commerce.

There also were concerns about the Channel One newscast. Many feared it would be a waste of the students' time. If the programming were poorly produced, students would ignore it. Even if they wanted to watch, the viewing environment, during homeroom or lunch would probably be somewhat distracting and not especially conducive to learning. There were no guarantees that a teacher would follow up the newscast with discussion. Even when teachers were interested in doing so, there might not be time during a homeroom period. Without some teacher follow-up, students were unlikely to benefit very much. Critics felt that very little learning would take place as a result of watching the newscast.

Others were more worried about the students' being exposed to a particular perspective about public affairs. Only certain types of stories might be selected for coverage. The coverage might assume a particular slant, perhaps that of the Whittle Corporation, a corporation with its own message to "sell." If impressionable young people were going to see newscasts every day, they might well be influenced by them over time. It would be difficult for parents and teachers to monitor the content of these newscasts. It would be even more difficult for them to influence how they were designed. The public is generally willing to entrust their children to teachers who were certified in institutions of higher learning. But why should it trust the executives of a company whose principal concern was not to educate young people, but to make money?

Chris Whittle's proposal was met with an outpouring of outrage on the part of many educators. Articles were published that labeled him a devilish figure, claiming that the Channel One Project would be a "Faustian bargain" for the schools. Schools would be literally "selling out" their students in exchange for television equipment and some programming to show on it. The debate over Channel One focused on this trade-off.

The Potential Advantages of Subscribing to Channel One

Although few educators were enthused about showing commercials in the classroom, many found Whittle's offer appealing, because they wished that their schools had more technology. Channel One gave the average-sized secondary school about $60,000 worth of television equipment. Every classroom would have a television set. These televisions would be cabled to a schoolwide network. At the "head end" of this cabling would be a control center that could send programming to every set. This control unit would have several videocassette recorders to record and play tapes. It was also connected to a receiver dish on the roof of the school, which would capture programming transmitted by satellite from the Whittle Corporation.

This schoolwide television system would be used to show the Channel One newscast and the other educational programs Whittle provided. But it could also potentially show all kinds of programming. A videocassette recorder could be connected to any classroom TV to show a video. If the school subscribed to cable television, teachers could show programming on any of the information-based cable networks, like the Discovery Channel, the Learning Channel, Arts and Entertainment, the Cable News Network, or the Public Broadcasting Service. Student television productions could be presented in a classroom, or to the entire school. Special events at the school could be telecast to every classroom. The Channel One Project would transform the television capability of every school that subscribed.

Many educators also felt that a newscast expressly designed for adolescents was a good idea. They witnessed how oblivious many young people were about current events. They were disappointed in how little teenagers knew about important news stories. To expose them to ten minutes of news each day might be a good idea. If the newscast was expressly designed to hold their attention, all the better. Postnewscast discussions could further strengthen a growing awareness about current events. Perhaps students might be prompted to read about some news stories, after finding out about them on the Channel One broadcast.

The Channel One newscast was not entirely filled with news either. Only the first five minutes of it were actually devoted to the news events of the previous day. The last half was dedicated to a feature story, which might be on any topic and would last a full week. Many science and social studies topics were explored on these weekly features. The topics were often those of particular interest to teens. In this way, Channel One attempted to provide more variety in its programming. It also served as an opportunity to cover a topic in more depth than was possible during the opening part of the program, when a number of different news items needed to be covered.

Some even felt that the commercials might provide an educational opportunity. Teachers concerned about any negative impact associated with advertising could discuss how advertisers attempt to influence audience perceptions and behavior. The persuasive techniques used in Channel One commercials could be analyzed in class discussions. Channel One might help students become more aware of how people are manipulated by advertising. Other "critical viewing" skills might also be discussed.

So this project was debated, both pro and con, for months after its inception. Whittle attempted to reassure the schools in several ways. He established a "blue ribbon" panel of educators to screen his newscasts for content and coverage. He banned any advertising that might be considered controversial, including ads for cigarettes, alcohol, or birth control products. He made it clear that school officials had control over whether a given newscast would be shown to students. The newscast was transmitted at night and automatically taped by a videocassette recorder in each school. A school representative could then watch the program the next morning before showing it to students, to make sure that there was no objectionable material on it. If there was, it need not be shown that day.

The Nationwide Proliferation of Channel One Schools

Whittle also addressed his critics who opposed the commercialization of the classroom. He pointed out that for years schools had allowed advertising within their walls. School libraries held periodicals filled with advertising. Posters, pamphlets, and packets, emblazoned with various corporate logos, have regularly been mailed by various companies to the schools (McDonald's on nutrition, Exxon on environmental issues, Adidas on fitness, Apple on computer literacy, and many others). These materials can often be seen on school bulletin boards, and they have been distributed to students for years. Whittle himself had sent printed materials to schools that were sponsored by corporations. It was how he got the idea for Channel One in the first place. Commercials entered the classroom a long time ago. Why the objection now?

However, several states, including the two most populous states of California and New York, banned the project from its schools. This raised an interesting legal question about school governance, because individual schools and districts within those states signed up for Channel One anyway, claiming that the principle of "local control" of schools superseded the authority of the state's education office. The California cases went to court. It was decided ultimately that the schools would be permitted to continue subscribing to Channel One, but the state had the right to withhold its funding for those schools.

For the most part, Channel One was a great success. Throughout the rest of the country, thousands of secondary schools subscribed to the project. The project became profitable in a very short period of time. Within a few years, twelve thousand schools had signed up. In some states, like Michigan, Ohio, and Texas, over half of the secondary schools throughout the state had subscribed. One estimate claimed that, by the late 1990s, over 40 percent of the nation's secondary school students were viewing Channel One.

Research into the Effects of the Channel One Project

During the early stages of the project, researchers attempted to determine the effects that Channel One had on its clientele. A number of studies investigated how much teenagers had learned about current events from the program. They compared the results of current events quizzes taken in Channel One schools with the same quizzes taken by students of the same age and background in non–Channel One schools. Results showed that the Channel One watchers did slightly better, but generally no better than ten percentage points higher. These gains were less than spectacular, but they were gains.

Educators debated whether these results supported the project or not. Some felt that it was unrealistic to expect dramatic learning gains from an activity that took up only ten minutes of the school day. They argued that *no* activity engaged in for ten minutes of the school day would have resulted in learning gains of more than 10 percent on a test of specific items. Others felt that the small gains proved that the program had little instructional impact. For them, these minor improvements in current events awareness did not justify the time devoted to the Channel One broadcasts. For many critics, these benefits were not significant enough to justify the school's exposing the students to commercials.

Other research studies explored student and teacher reactions to the newscasts. For the most part, students responded favorably to the broadcast. They said they usually watched it. Most felt that it was interesting. Most felt that they learned something from it. Furthermore, few claimed that the commercials were their favorite part. Even fewer indicated that they had purchased items as a result of watching a commercial on Channel One.

To the surprise of some, the teachers were generally even more positive about Channel One than the students. The vast majority felt that the newscasts were effectively done. They perceived the information provided as unbiased, important, and delivered in a manner that would hold the attention of teenagers. They did not strongly object to the commercials, and a strong majority indicated that they were willing to allow commercials in their classroom in exchange for the equipment and the newscast.

Another survey indicated that in some schools the Channel One project had in fact led to a transformation of how television was used throughout the building. Many Channel One schools had seen their own student-produced newscasts spring up. These school-related efforts were broadcast throughout the building, right after the Channel One newscast concluded. Media specialists in some Channel One–equipped schools reported that they were using a great deal of the educational programming that Whittle had provided, in addition to the newscast. They also reported increased use of cable programming (CNN, in particular, was shown when there were very dramatic events occurring). Special events and schoolwide functions were shown on the school's television system (like the principal's address to the parents on school visitation night). Student activities using television were also apparently facilitated by the availability of Whittle's schoolwide television network.

Ironically, Chris Whittle himself ultimately lost control of Channel One, as his company foundered. Despite its success, he overspent on other ventures, like his highly publicized Edison Project, designed to develop a technology-based "school of the future." Whittle wound up in tax trouble with federal authorities, and his company was dissolved. However, Channel One was purchased by the K-III publishing firm, which is best known for its Weekly Reader publication. It continues to broadcast the newscast to thousands of schools under its new management, and the number of Channel One subscribers appears to still be growing.

The broadcast appears to be neither the powerful learning tool that Whittle claimed it was, nor the advertising coup of the decade. It seems to be a modest instructional success and a somewhat successful advertising venture. In fact, some of Whittle's companies dropped their ads, but others have taken their place. Many educators feel that the newscast could be more effectively used to further expand adolescents' awareness of current events. However, this depends largely on teachers making the programs relevant to teenagers and encouraging students to pursue topics that they find interesting. Like any effort to educate, good materials are a necessary prerequisite for learning, but for really strong results, it takes good teaching.

Commercialism in the Schools

Although the Channel One experience is clearly the most expensive, high-profile instance of advertising in the nation's public schools, it is far from an isolated phenomenon. Advertisements are appearing in greater numbers each year in our classrooms in various forms: leaflets, booklets, posters, book jackets, signs, and so on. They appear not only on school athletic scoreboards, but on bulletin boards and in the school cafeteria. Many schools have licensed their food services to commercial fast-food enterprises. The vast majority of schools provide machines that sell commercial soft drinks, candy, and so on. Companies develop curriculum materials that feature their brand name prominently. McDonald's has units on nutrition and Microsoft has educational materials about computers. Some companies specialize in assisting corporations market their logos in schools. One example is Cover Concepts, which sells advertising space on slick book covers.

In addition, a digital version of the Channel One Project has come into the classroom. ZapMe! Corporation provides free computer equipment and Internet access for schools, which must use each computer at least four hours per day. Of course, the interface has been layered with advertising strips like the ones normally seen on the World Wide Web, for which ZapMe! receives corporate advertising dollars.

Finally, marketing companies have been allowed into schools to do their research on what appeals to young people with "focus groups" of students. In exchange, the company contributes in some way financially to the school, often by providing much needed equipment for laboratories or gyms. Corporations pay these marketing companies for this information to help them target young consumers.

Is school the place for all this commercialism? Many think the trade-offs are worth it. But others feel that it distracts students from school's principal mission to educate young people. One thing is certain. It's a phenomenon that continues to grow.

RECOMMENDED READING

Celano, D., and S. Neuman. 1995. Channel One: Time for a TV break. *Phi Delta Kappan* 76 (6): 444–446.

Greenberg, B., and J. Brand. 1993/4. Channel One: But what about the advertising? *Educational Leadership* 51 (4): 56–58.

Labi, N. 1999. Classrooms for sale. *Time*, 19 April, 44–45.

Rank, H. 1993/94. Channel One: Asking the wrong questions. *Educational Leadership* 51 (4): 52–55.

Tiene, D. 1993. Channel One: Good or bad news for our schools? *Educational Leadership* 50 (8): 46–51.

Tiene, D., and E. Whitmore. 1995. Beyond the Channel One newscast: How schools are using their schoolwide television networks. *Educational Technology* 35 (3): 38–42.

OTHER REFERENCES

Cheatham, B., and A. Cohen. 1989. Channel One forges ahead despite complaints about ads. *School Library Journal* 35: 9–10.

Ehman, L. 1991. Using Channel One in social studies classrooms: A first look. Paper presented at the National Council for the Social Studies conference, Washington, DC.

Johnston, J. 1995. The dilemma of teaching and selling. *Phi Delta Kappan* 76 (6): 437–442.

Johnston, J., E. Brzezinski, and E. Andeman. 1994. *Taking the measure of Channel One: A three year perspective.* Ann Arbor, MI: University of Michigan, Institute for Social Research.

Knupfer, N. 1994. Channel One: Reactions of students, teachers, and parents. In *Watching Channel One: The convergence of students, technology, and private business,* edited by A. Devany. Albany, NY: State University of New York Press.

Knupfer, N., and P. Hayes. 1994. The effects of Channel One broadcasts on students' knowledge of current events. In *Watching Channel One: The convergence of students, technology, and private business,* edited by A. Devany. Albany, NY: State University of New York Press.

Rist, M. 1991. Whittling away at public education. *The Executive Educator* 13 (9): 22–28.

Rudinow, J. 1990. Channel One whittles away at education. *Educational Leadership* 47 (4): 70–73.

Streitfield, D. 1992. Low marks for Channel One study casts doubt on TV program's effectiveness in schools. *The Washington Post,* 1 May, C5.

Tate, C. 1989. Opinion: On Chris Whittle's school-news scheme. *Columbia Journalism Review* 28: 52.

Tiene, D., and E. Whitmore. 1995. TV or not TV? That is the question: A study of the effects of Channel One. *Social Education* 59 (3): 159–164.

Wartella, P. 1995. The commercialization of youth: Channel One in context. *Phi Delta Kappan* 76 (6): 448–451.

Whitmore, E., and D. Tiene. 1994. Viewing Channel One: Awareness of current events by teenagers. *Mass Communications Review* 21: 67–75.

SCENARIO

An aggressive telecommunications firm called Bigbucks Broadcasting has come up with a proposal for the secondary schools throughout your state. For each school that agrees to be part of its program, it will equip the entire building for television reception. This package includes a satellite dish, a control unit to route all signals, cable wiring throughout the building, a television set in each room, and several videocassette recorders. But that's not all! For what good is equipment without anything to show on it?

This proposal also includes a daily twelve-minute informational program for young people entitled "Teen TV," which will address news items and issues important to adolescents. Some of this material will cover the same types of stories generally found on commercial news programs, but targeted to a teenage audience. Other stories will report on show business, sports, fashion, etc., in a segment called "Pop Goes the Culture." Each Friday, "Teen TV" will conclude with a three- to five-minute feature called, "Making a Difference," which will report on an innovative, worthwhile project initiated by an American adolescent.

Bigbucks Broadcasting has also worked out a deal with the Edutainment Channel and will provide programming that has appeared on that network, free of charge, over the satellite system. The school can tape these programs, and teachers can show them, without copyright restrictions, for a period of one school year.

How could all this be free? Well, of course, there is a "catch." Two of the twelve minutes of programming will be devoted to commercials. Advertising money will cover the costs of the equipment and the programming. Certain types of ads will not be aired, including those for cigarettes, alcoholic beverages, and birth control products. Otherwise, the same ads that are being aired on commercial television will be broadcast into the classroom on "Teen TV."

The decision to subscribe to "Teen TV" is not an individual teacher's decision. If the school opts for the service, all classrooms in the building will be required to show the programming. Consequently, there is a great deal of discussion about whether your middle school should subscribe. Opinions vary.

The school media specialist is definitely in favor of subscribing. She has told you that she feels it is a great deal and has all kinds of ideas about how to help teachers take advantage of television as an instructional tool. The principal also seems to favor the idea, although he is waiting to see how the entire staff reacts. Some staff members feel that it would be nice for students to show greater awareness of current events and hope that "Teen TV" will help inform them. They feel that a news program that is specifically designed for teenagers may heighten their interest level in current events

On the other hand, there are a few teachers who strongly oppose what they call the "commercialization of the classroom." They argue that impressionable young people in a captive situation should not be exposed to the manipulative messages of advertisers. Some worry that the news program will convey a particular perspective about the stories and thereby bias the students in a certain way. Others object to the fact that it may interrupt the students' work, if shown in homeroom or study hall.

Because this decision as to whether or not to contract for "Teen TV" is somewhat controversial, it is on the agenda for the next school board meeting. This meeting is open to the public and a sizable crowd is expected to attend. The merits and drawbacks of the "Teen TV" proposal will be debated at the microphone set up for feedback from the community.

Your principal is concerned that he be fully prepared to address any issues that are raised at the school board meeting. He has asked you to prepare a list of "Pros" and a list of "Cons" regarding "Teen TV" for him to use as a set of notes during the meeting. You will need to make two thorough lists of all potential arguments. He has also asked you, and the rest of the staff, to state your own perspectives in a brief memorandum to him, by the end of the week, so he can see how his staff feels about "Teen TV." Finally, he has requested some specific ideas from those who support participation in this project as to how the equipment provided by Bigbucks might be used to benefit the educational mission of the school (besides the viewing of the "Teen TV" newscast, of course).

ISSUES INQUIRY

1. If you were a school principal, would you recommend "Teen TV" for your school? Why or why not?

2. If you were a school media specialist, how might you take advantage of the television equipment that your school received from Bigbucks Broadcasting? What kinds of activities would you encourage teachers to get involved in that utilize television as an instructional medium?

3. If you were a classroom teacher, how might you follow up the "Teen TV" broadcasts to further inform the students in your homeroom period about current events? What kinds of activities might students pursue, on their own, that could complement the viewing of "Teen TV"?

4. Would you use the commercials shown during "Teen TV" to discuss some advertising techniques of persuasion used by advertisers to convince viewers to buy their products? Describe how some of these techniques work.

5. Do you think that small learning gains from a television program like "Teen TV" are enough to justify its use? Or might the showing of this type of program be justified on other grounds? If so, what other benefits might result from the use of such a newscast?

6. How do you feel about corporate sponsorship of educational materials in the classroom, which includes promotion of the company name (and perhaps even of company products)? Under what conditions might this practice be acceptable? What are the advantages and disadvantages of using these types of materials in the classroom?

CHAPTER 6

Is a Computer's Place in the Lab or in the Classroom?

INTRODUCTION

It is always exciting when a school receives its shipment of brand-new comput-ers. The boxes are opened, and the pristine plastic hardware looks so clean and "hi-tech." Connecting the wiring and watching the screen light up for the first time, to the accompaniment of a high-pitched chimelike sound, can be an inspiring moment for any technology coordinator. But now the inevitable ques-tion arises: Where do we put these machines?

In actuality, most schools probably have determined the answer to this question long before the equipment arrives at the building. Hopefully they did so with a reasonable amount of deliberation, because the location of the hard-ware is a critical decision that will significantly influence who has access to the equipment, when it can be used, and how it will be used. Furthermore, this may not be an easy decision to make. There are good arguments to be made for placing ten or twenty machines in a computer laboratory. But there are also sound reasons for taking those ten or twenty computers and distributing them to ten or twenty classrooms, so that each room in the building has at least one computer. In fact, because both strategies have merit, schools may compromise, placing some computers in a laboratory and giving the rest to individual class-room teachers. It might only place computers in classrooms where teachers have expressed an interest in having them. Another strategy is to place com-puters on movable carts, so that they can be taken to classrooms when teachers need them.

Advantages of a Computer Laboratory

Placing all the computers in a computer lab has some logistical advantages. For example, security is simplified. Only room has to be made secure, not a score of different rooms. A school might be able to afford special locks or even an alarm system for one room, but not for ten or twenty. Special hardware, like scanners and color printers, can be made accessible to everyone in the building when placed in a lab, rather than in an individual teacher's room. This hardware can also be used more conveniently and efficiently if it is placed in the same room with multiple machines. For example, a scanner can be used by an entire class of students simultaneously working on multimedia projects. Or a printer can provide hard copy of the stories produced by a creative writing class held in the lab.

The distribution of software on disks can be more easily supervised in a lab. Disks can be more conveniently disseminated in a lab, and they can be monitored more easily than can disks that are disseminated throughout the entire building. A piece of software can be shared more easily by students with-in the lab than by students throughout the building. Computer software appli-cations can also be more economically purchased in multiple disk sets, or "lab packs," or with site licenses that allow for multiple users off a network. Buying single titles for individual machines around a school building can be a more expensive proposition. There may also be needless duplication of titles, if software purchase is not monitored carefully on a buildingwide basis.

There are also advantages to networking computers these days. Not only can a machine gain access to file server software over a network, but it can also be connected to the Internet with all its resources and potential for communications. Networking may be a much simpler issue for computers in a lab, for a network can be much less expensively established in a single room than throughout an entire building. Aggregating a school's machines in a lab will make it more likely that each machine will have Internet access via a networked connection. The access times of lab computers will also probably be faster than they would be for machines in individual classrooms because of the length of the wiring it would take to connect some classrooms to the main network hub. If done properly, a lab's connection to the main trunk line could be short and telecommunications correspondingly quick.

Another potential advantage associated with setting up a computer laboratory is that enough machines will be available to allow everybody in a class to use them at once. Ideally, each student will work on his or her own machine. Even if two or three students share each machine, they can still learn a great deal. This low student-to-computer ratio helps maximize student learning in a lab. In a regular classroom with one or two computers, the student-to-computer ratio is likely to be on the order of fifteen to one, or worse.

A lab is likely to have special equipment to project what the teacher is demonstrating on his or her machine. This projection device, whether a video projector, a liquid crystal display unit sitting on an overhead projector, or just a large television set, can help facilitate full class instruction. With most computer applications, it is much easier to learn by directly observing or by actually doing than it is to learn by listening to a teacher describe what is to be done, without benefit of seeing his or her screen. It is unlikely that such projection systems will be available in individual classrooms, making it harder for teachers to adequately demonstrate what can be done with the machine.

Teaching in a Lab

In a lab, teachers would be able to conduct a class wherein everyone can be involved simultaneously in learning on a computer. The lesson might consist of a whole group activity in which the teacher shows the class how to work with an application or runs a piece of software for the group. At times, it might involve students working individually to learn a particular computer application, like word processing, use of a database, or a Web page development tool. Or the lesson might be one where students work individually on their own projects, using the machines to find resource material, to write reports, to communicate via e-mail, or to create multimedia presentations with software applications.

Working in a computer lab may be problematic for a classroom teacher who lacks computer expertise. Teaching students how to work with a relatively sophisticated application may be too difficult for many teachers. But often teachers can effectively supervise their students working with relatively simple applications, like word processing, Web browsing, or running computer-assisted instruction. The more computer literate the students are, the easier this would be for the instructor. The more computer literate the instructor, the more he or she will be able to accomplish in the lab.

Another possibility is that a computer specialist might be available at the school to teach lessons in the lab. The classroom teacher would then be relieved of the basic responsibility of conducting lessons in the lab. This might literally be a relief for teachers who have little computer background. In addition, these teachers could benefit from these lessons by learning computer skills alongside their students. Or they could help the computer instructor by working with individual students during the lesson, which might also enhance their own computer literacy.

Not all teachers feel entirely comfortable supervising their class in a computer lab because of the technical difficulties or student questions that might arise. But in some ways, this scenario is preferable to the classroom situation where only one or two computers must be shared by the entire class. Scheduling the equipment can be a challenge. Giving everyone equal time on the machines is another concern, especially because spending time on a computer appeals to most students. Planning appropriate computer activities for individual students, or small groups, is yet another responsibility. Supervising student work on these computers while teaching the rest of the class can also be problematic. Some students will become involved in inappropriate activities, like playing noneducational games or exploring websites for "mature" audiences only. Others will need assistance to use the machine effectively. Many teachers would prefer to bring their class to a lab than deal with the responsibility of having a computer or two in their own classrooms.

Potential of Computers in Classrooms

What would be the advantages of placing a few computers in each classroom rather than locating them all in a lab? The most important potential advantage is that the teacher and the students would have constant access to the machine. In theory, they would be able to use it with any lesson, and computer-based activity might thereby become a more important part of the curriculum. Computerized activities might become more fully integrated into the students' daily classwork. Word processing would be available to help the students produce more professional papers. Database material could be accessed on CD-ROMs and the Web. Mathematics software could supplement instruction. Computer graphics and multimedia authoring tools might provide wonderful opportunities for children to be creative.

However, is it not possible for the computer lab to serve a similar function? The class can certainly bring its work to a computer lab and use the machines to work on units in which they are already involved. But some argue that lab access is too restricted in most schools for these sessions to significantly affect what goes on in the classroom. The time allowed in the lab is not sufficient for students to rely on a computer to assist them with their work on a consistent basis. When students need to explore the Web or word process their papers, they may not be able to get in the lab to do so, especially if it is heavily scheduled with classes.

Having some computers in the classroom also gives the teacher more flexibility in using the machines with individual students. The teacher can provide access to students who might most benefit from the experience. Software can help individuals with particular learning difficulties or challenge others who are bored because they already understood the material some time ago. Most teachers aim their lessons to students of average ability to maximize the number who will benefit from them. But this strategy does not always succeed for the faster and slower students. Computerized lessons can sometimes provide material at appropriate levels for either the learning disabled or the gifted.

A computer can also enliven a classroom with multimedia experiences. Most digital data enhances its text with pictures, sounds, and videos. Such materials generally help enhance levels of attention and motivation. These materials also can provide more concrete experiences for students than the usual text. Even simple pictures and sounds can provide a sense of what a phenomenon is like. And sophisticated computer programs can do much more, by simulating real experiences. With applications known as virtual reality, the user can actually interact with the simulated environment. The famous educator John Dewey of Columbia Teachers College said experience is the best teacher. Technology can provide a more *experientially based* set of learning activities in the classroom. Having it available consistently for this purpose in the classroom can be advantageous.

Curriculum Integration of Computers

Another way in which the computer can help individualize instruction is to engage the particular interests of students. An enormous amount of information is available on compact discs and via the World Wide Web. Computerized search tools can help students efficiently and effectively zero in on what they are looking for. Alert teachers can help students find computerized material on topics of interest to them and thereby more effectively involve them in their schoolwork. They can provide CDs or Web addresses that will help individual students delve deeper into a topic. While these activities can also go on in a lab, there will be far more opportunities for these searches if the computer is available in the classroom on an ongoing basis.

The computer can serve as a vehicle on the "information superhighway." It is a powerful teaching resource and connecting to it can open up the classroom to a wealth of important, interesting material, if the students look hard enough for it. To have to go to a lab in another part of the building to take advantage of these opportunities can be awkward. Having some networked computers right in the classroom can allow for a great deal of independent learning.

Providing students with opportunities to explore on their own is important. The earlier chapter on learning theories described an instructional approach called constructivism, which supports this type of independent investigation. Constructivists believe that young people learn most effectively when they have thought carefully about a topic. If they are allowed to come to conclusions on their own, this is the most powerful form of learning. They will not only remember what they have learned but may incorporate it in their perceptual schema or adopt it into their value system. If access to databases, the Web, and other online sources of information can allow students to "construct" knowledge, then it is all the more imperative that some computers be available in classrooms on a permanent basis.

Placing computers in individual classrooms may also encourage more teachers and students to develop an interest in working with these machines. Its constant presence in the room as a resource may help remind teachers of its educational potential, or even place some pressure upon them to take advantage of it. There will likely be some students with computer experience who can provide some positive role modeling in how to use the machine effectively. Seeing the computer's potential may encourage less-experienced students and teachers to work with it.

Availability should also enhance computer "literacy," if it encourages more extensive utilization. Ongoing practice with applications will develop skills. Observing others work with more sophisticated functions can help raise levels of competence with the machine. It is an interesting question whether computer literacy can best be enhanced in the lab or the classroom. The lab is probably preferable for teaching formal lessons in the use of computer applications. But students may be better able to learn informally from one another on machines that are available in the back of their own classroom, since they are available all the time, not just occasionally.

Hopefully this enhancement of computer literacy will also include the teacher. Teachers can grow in their awareness of how computers can assist in the educational process as they watch their students work with them. They can develop skills with the equipment as they deal with it on a daily basis. Sometimes a "sink or swim" situation results in the most accelerated learning. In having to "deal with" a set of computers in their room, many teachers will rise to the challenge.

Computer Placement in Different Types of Schools

The computer placement decision is not a simple one. Advantages and disadvantages are associated with any strategy taken. In fact, the best answer to the question of where to place new computers is probably, "It depends." Many issues may influence the computer placement issue, including the type of school, the hardware, connectivity, availability of expertise in computing, and so on.

The decision may depend on what kind of school is involved. For example, would an approach that seems appropriate for an elementary school be equally appropriate for a secondary school? These two levels of schooling have a number of important differences, including learner maturity, scheduling, and specialization of coursework.

The higher maturity level of secondary students makes them better candidates for independent work on a computer. Some might question the degree to which very young children in the early grades are really "ready" to take advantage of a computer. But it is somewhat difficult to say how this factor might influence computer building placement. Perhaps young children should receive some basic training in a lab situation that would enable them to work more proficiently on a computer by themselves. Others might argue that having a computer in the classroom on a permanent basis will more effectively raise the computer literacy of young children, because of the daily exposure and ongoing demonstration of how a computer can be used.

Secondary schools, of course, have a departmentalized administrative structure, wherein each subject is taught in a separate class period. Elementary schools generally use a "homeroom" model, where the students stay with the same teacher all day. The homeroom approach allows for greater flexibility at the elementary level in the planning of learning activities. An elementary school teacher can rotate students' computer time throughout an entire day, while a secondary school teacher has only fifty minutes a day to do this. So independent computer work may be more easily arranged in an elementary school classroom than in a secondary classroom. Lengthy computer-based activities, like certain simulations, may be easier to run in an elementary school classroom, given the availability of the students for the entire day. In a secondary classroom, lengthy activities would have to be interrupted and continued during another class period.

Placing computers in individual classrooms might also be problematic at the secondary level because teachers are not necessarily assigned to a given room. What if computers are left in a room that is unoccupied part of the school day? While unsupervised, those machines could be underutilized, abused, vandalized, or even stolen. If the school is located in a high crime area, it might not be wise to operate under this arrangement.

The more specialized and sophisticated nature of course materials at the secondary level may also affect computer placement decisions. Certain subject areas may be better suited for computer use and thereby may be given higher priority for access to school computers. Many secondary schools have special computer labs for mathematics or for science. Rarely does one find a special "social studies computer lab," probably because fewer software titles for this subject area are available and perhaps because only a minority of teachers in this discipline have a strong interest in the computer as an instructional tool.

The decision to allocate separate labs for separate subject areas use may also be affected by the school's size. Secondary schools are often much larger than elementary schools, so having several labs is a way to achieve comparable student-computer ratios. The number of students engaged in mathematics instruction, for example, during a given period of the day at a large high school may well outnumber the total enrollment of an elementary school within that same district.

Most elementary school teachers teach all (or most) of the curricular subjects in their homerooms. This situation may provide them with more opportunities to use the computer than their counterparts at the secondary level. If so, having a computer or two available in the classroom at all times may be a better strategy for computer use at the elementary level. Since the elementary curriculum can encompass almost any topic, the computer software available at the school might be used more heavily. The constraints associated with using computer materials in the elementary school will probably be more likely related to age or skill level. This situation is perhaps most obvious on the Web, where the vast majority of materials have been developed for users who read at an adult level, making Web use challenging for elementary school students, especially in the lowest grade levels.

Other Factors Influencing Computer Location

The amount of hardware a school already owns also will affect where its computers will be placed. With enough machines, a school can both establish a lab and place computers within individual classrooms. But sometimes adding new computers to an existing hardware collection has its own challenges. A school's new computers may not be easily integrated with its previously purchased equipment, either because the platforms differ (Windows versus Macintosh) or the operating capability is very different (Pentiums versus 386s). Combining significantly different types of machines in the same lab can be problematic. Software that runs on some machines may not run on others. Some machines may have functionality that others do not. Students can become frustrated when different machines in the lab do not respond consistently.

The wiring situation at the school may affect computer placement decisions. Many schools are not fully wired. Since having online access adds considerable functionality to a computer, this capability needs to be evaluated when placing computers. If only the lab has Internet access, this is a strong reason for placing most of the school's computers there. On the other hand, if all classrooms throughout the building have been wired for network capability, this helps justify placement of computers in individual rooms. Thus, schools at different levels of technological sophistication should approach the placement of new computers in different ways.

Staffing issues also may influence how computers are to be placed throughout the building. The most basic issue is probably simply supervision. A computer lab may not be as productive a facility if staff is not available to supervise it. Students may need assistance, for example, in working with the equipment, using software, or accessing a printer. The advisability of establishing a lab also may depend on the availability of faculty members qualified to teach computer classes. Bringing entire classes into a lab may not work out well if the instruction provided there is not effectively delivered. Along with establishing a lab, schools should consider allocating funds for a computer instructor, if the lab is to function at maximum effectiveness.

Staff attitudes about computers might affect hardware placement decisions. If the majority of teachers in a building are uncomfortable with having computers placed in their rooms, it will be far more difficult to effectively implement that strategy. If there is a mixed response from staff to placing computers in classrooms, the appropriate approach might be to place machines only in rooms where teachers have indicated an interest in using them. Of course, the degree of overall faculty "computer literacy" will significantly affect the degree of success with which computers are used throughout the school building, regardless of how computers are placed.

Likewise, the students' computer literacy will influence how the machines are used in a school. In some schools, many students have a higher computer skill level than their teachers. In these situations, student (and parent) demand for technology may be high. Placement of machines also may be affected by levels of student sophistication on computers. For example, with students who can work independently on a computer, there may be less concern about providing ongoing staff supervision in a lab. Providing lab instruction also may be a less important issue.

Some educators feel that until teachers and students are comfortable with computers, it makes little sense to place a machine in their classroom. This can be a waste of resources, especially if the machines sit idle throughout most of the school day. Others who feel computer literacy is very important might argue that the need for exposure to computers is even more imperative when school levels of computer literacy are very low. Computer literacy levels may influence hardware placement strategy. If the level is relatively low, then computers may first be placed in a laboratory used for formal training of both students and teachers in basic computer skills. Once an adequate level of computer literacy is achieved, then machines could be made more available in classrooms, so that students can take advantage of them. However, some may feel that having a computer available in the classroom is the more effective way to build computer skills. Its ongoing presence may generate an interest in learning about it and allows for ongoing practice with the machine.

Before attempting to determine where to locate its new computers, any school should assess its own unique situation to determine what factors will impact the potential utilization of these machines. The extent to which the school is wired, the availability of space for a lab, the percentage of teachers with computer expertise, the availability of a computer specialist, faculty attitudes about technology, overall student computer literacy levels, and many other issues will affect how computers can be used most effectively in the building. Any well-conceived policy for computer placement should consider all these factors and weigh which issues are most significant. Only then should school personnel proceed to place computers throughout the school building.

RECOMMENDED READING

Fraundorf, M. C. 1997. Distributed computers and labs: The best of both worlds. *Learning and Leading with Technology* 27 (7): 50–53.

Roos. G. 1996. Classroom or computer room: Where should the computers be placed? Online: www.wcape.school.za/wced/edit/compclss.htm.

Salomon, G. 1990. The computer lab: A bad idea now sanctified. *Educational Technology* 30 (10): 50–52.

Schofield, J. 1995. The classroom and the lab as contrasting learning environments. In *Computers and classroom culture*, edited by J. Schofield. New York: Cambridge University Press.

OTHER REFERENCES

Cowles, J., J. Larabee, and S. Hothem. 1986, February. Computer laboratory management: Making effective use of your computers. Paper presented at the Ohio State Department of Education Computer Fair, Columbus, OH.

Dublin, P. 1994. *Integrating computers in your classroom: Early childhood.* New York: HarperCollins, ERIC, ED 380181.

November, A. 1997. Magic links: Changing the focus of technology planning. *Learning and Leading with Technology* 24 (8): 54–56.

Sandholtz, J., C. Ringstaff, and D. Dwyer. 1990, April. Teaching in high-tech environments: Classroom management revisited. Paper presented at the annual meeting of the American Educational Research Association, Boston, MA.

Switzer, A. 1995. Computer education on a tight budget? Think "Lending Library." *Teaching PreK–8* 26 (2): 64–65.

Shade, D. 1996. Are You Ready to Teach Young Children in the 21st Century? *Early Childhood Education Journal* 24 (1): 43–44.

Zollman, A., and J. Wyrick. 1988. *Teacher assessment of elementary schools' computer laboratories.* Report prepared for the Fayette County Public Schools, Kentucky.

SCENARIO

At the beginning of the school year, you were asked by your principal, Dr. Watson, to join the Technology Committee at Simply Elementary. The committee will make a variety of decisions associated with how to best utilize the technology resources in the building. Twenty new microcomputers were ordered at the end of last year, and the committee's first big decision will be where in the building to place these machines.

The committee's chair is the District Technology Specialist, Mr. Holmes, who has strong opinions about how computers can best be utilized in elementary schools. He feels that the school should have a computer lab, filled with these twenty machines. There is, in fact, a room available in the school that could be used as a lab. It is a former classroom that became vacant years ago, when local demographics led to a drop in enrollment at Simply Elementary. The room would need to have more electrical outlets installed, along with the proper wiring to network these machines. It could also use some new tables to place these computers on.

But the room is centrally located within the building, conveniently accessible to all classrooms and only two doors down from the school library, so that classwork in both facilities could be easily coordinated. The room is large enough that it also could hold several file cabinets for the school's software collection. The principal seems to agree with the technology specialist's proposal to create a laboratory, and he has already suggested, at a recent teachers' meeting, the possibility that this room may soon become the new computer lab.

However, a number of your colleagues on the committee feel differently. Yesterday, Miss Moriarity, a young teacher with a strong interest in technology, spoke with you over lunch about her hopes that she will have a computer, or two, in her own classroom. She feels that the computer will provide all kinds of exciting new learning opportunities for her class. She also feels that having it available in the room throughout the school day will be far preferable to having to take her class to a lab, which will probably be scheduled by other classes much of the time.

Mrs. Baker, another committee member, also very much wants a computer. She plans to use it herself, to prepare materials for the class and keep her records. She also is lobbying for a liquid crystal display unit on an overhead projector, so that she can display computer software on a large screen, for the entire class. She especially likes programs from Tom Snyder Productions, which are specifically designed for group activities, rather than individual work.

However, many other teachers throughout the school have quite vocally expressed their preference that the computers be housed in a laboratory. Some of these teachers are technology enthusiasts who feel that having a small number of computers in their classroom restricts computer use to a few at a time, and this approach to using computers is too limited. They would prefer to have sessions in a lab where the entire class can use computers at the same time. Specific lessons can be taught to develop computer proficiency, or the computers can be used for class projects.

Other teachers in the building might be classified as "technophobic." Most of these teachers simply are not sure how they would include computerized activities as part of their everyday schedule. They view the prospect of having a computer in their classroom as an added complication, rather than an exciting opportunity. These teachers would prefer to bring the whole class to a laboratory, where the librarian, Mrs. Baskerville, promises to provide training in how to use various computer applications. In this way, each child will have an opportunity to work on a machine either alone or with a partner. The teacher would assist on an individual basis, but could rely on the expertise of Mrs. Baskerville to oversee the lesson. She has taken several computer courses as part of her certification as a "media specialist."

Many teachers are not sure where they stand on this issue. Some have suggested a compromise position, wherein most of the computers would be placed in the laboratory and some would be placed on movable carts. Then teachers who wanted a computer in their own room could request one, much as they might request other pieces of media equipment.

A meeting of the Technology Committee is scheduled for next week. All committee members need to submit a short "position paper" by the end of the week, indicating their perspectives on where the computers should be placed in the building. You therefore need to formulate your thoughts on this issue, and develop this paper, within the next few days. Describe where you think these twenty computers should be placed and discuss your rationale for this plan.

ISSUES INQUIRY

1. In formulating your proposal for how the computers should be placed, along with the potential advantages, be sure to think about what the possible *disadvantages* may be in a given strategy. What do you gain and what do you lose?

2. Rarely is any one given approach equally effective under all circumstances. Intelligent policy decisions generally take the specific circumstances into account. Analyze which aspects of the situation at Simply Elementary are likely to most significantly affect where the computers should be located. When not specified in the scenario, discuss how different possible conditions at the school might necessitate different approaches.

3. Does the decision depend largely on how many computers a school already possesses? Does it make sense to first create a lab and only then to begin placing computers in classrooms? Why would this approach make sense? Why not?

4. Usually the computer placement decision is only the first step in establishing a dynamic program for school computer utilization. What other decisions associated with setting up a school computer program might be very important?

5. What policies might accompany your decision about computer location, to ensure that the computers are ultimately used to best advantage? For example, what policies might be established for use of a laboratory, in terms of appropriate computer use, sharing of machines, access to printers, use of a scanner, and so on?

6. How would you help a teacher who has no clue about how to use her new classroom computer? Would giving it to another more competent, enthusiastic colleague be a reasonable option, despite whatever regulations might officially prohibit this action?

7. Does the classroom placement approach work well in elementary school classrooms, but not so well in secondary schools? Why or why not?

8. What are the advantages and disadvantages of portable computers? Is this a viable substitution for a computer right in the room? Can flexibility in providing machines be achieved without too many hassles (scheduling, delivering, maintaining, etc.)?

CHAPTER 7

Replacing Books with "Notebooks"

HARD COPY VERSUS SOFTWARE

INTRODUCTION

Not long ago, headlines around the country proclaimed that the chairman of the Texas State Board of Education was proposing the state stop buying textbooks and lease laptop computers for all students instead. As you might imagine, the ensuing debate has been fierce and long-lasting. Texas has not yet followed through on the plan, but the proposal served to focus public attention on the multimillion dollar issue of how significant a role new communications technologies should play in the schools of the twenty-first century.

Of course, in some ways the Texas proposal was a logical extension of what has been happening in schools during the past few years. School districts nationwide are scrambling to keep up with rapid advances in technology. Schools are buying and installing scores of computers for their labs and classrooms. They are purchasing thousands of dollars worth of software for their students and teachers. Districts are rapidly wiring all school buildings with computer networks that connect to the Internet. For more than a decade there have been demonstration and research projects in which students and teachers have been given computers for long periods of time. However, the Texas proposal was the first to suggest that computerization of educational resources be tried on such a large scale. Then again, as any Texan will tell you, everything's bigger in Texas.

Can Schools Afford It?

This proposal raises questions about how instructional technology might be adopted wholesale by schools on a widespread basis. All kinds of different issues are involved: financial, educational, social, logistical, and so on. Jack Christie, the chair of the Texas school board, has made two major arguments in favor of his proposal, one based on financial considerations and the other from an educational perspective.

First, let's look at the financial situation. According to news reports, Texas, which buys school textbooks on a statewide basis, is likely to spend about $1.8 billion on textbooks over the next six years. Even so, they have a difficult time keeping these books current, in terms of both the information provided and the teaching strategies suggested. A recent study indicated that Texas spends about $30 per student per year on technology and about $450 per student per year on books.

Clearly, $30 a year is not enough to buy a computer for a student. That is why the proposal is to replace *books* with laptop computers. Apparently there are computer companies willing to lease computers to the state for about $500 a student a year. After some period of time, the state would own the computers. These computers would be loaded with basic software, including word processing; a Web browser; and so on. Thus, if we are just talking about the hardware, the cost per pupil for renting laptops is similar to the cost of purchasing textbooks.

But what about the costs of the digital versions of the textbook materials? How will their costs compare with those of comparable printed materials? One direct comparison we can already make is between digital and hard copy forms of the standard encyclopedia. Although a complete set of the *Encyclopaedia Bri-*

tannica in book form can cost hundreds or thousands of dollars, a two CD-ROM set with the same material can be had for under $150. Other reference material can be similarly discounted when it is provided in CD form. This cost disparity between electronic text and printed text is likely to increase in the coming years, for economic trends favor electronic text. With the paper shortage, the cost of bound hard copy materials continues to increase. On the other hand, costs for the amount of information you can store in microchips and on magnetic disk drives continues to plummet, as the capacity of these digital storage devices grows exponentially each year (see the discussion of "Moore's Law" in the introductory chapter entitled "From Video to Virtual Reality: Technology and Its Instructional Potential"). Consequently, we should witness an ongoing shift from hard copy print to digital storage of text.

Furthermore, new developments in optical disc technology have provided the potential to carry far more digital information on compact disc than previously possible, at potentially even lower prices per page of text. The Digital Video Disk (DVD) compact disc format stores about twelve times as much data as a CD-ROM (and may have largely replaced it by the time you read this). The costs of text on DVD will be cheaper than the already economical expense of text on CD-ROM. DVD will allow enormous quantities of text information to be stored on a single disk. One DVD disk will hold many textbooks. It could easily provide all of the reading material that children have today in all of their textbooks assigned for courses at several grade levels and still have room for related audio and video materials, which printed texts are incapable of providing.

Many publishing companies, including textbook publishers, are coming to see that they are in the business of selling information, not books. They are already beginning to market this information more extensively in new media formats. Many large publishers provide supplementary materials for important texts on compact disc or videotape. As already mentioned, entire encyclopedias have been available for some time on CD, and more books are likely to appear in this format, as portable computers with CD players become more widely available. In addition, publishers are starting to work out arrangements whereby institutions and individuals can buy just the information they want and need over the World Wide Web. Both the buyers and the sellers then save because the information can be downloaded directly without incurring the cost of printing, binding, and so on.

All in all, even though the details are not yet clear, the idea of replacing textbooks with computers could ultimately work from a financial standpoint, especially given the rate at which the costs of digital storage of information continues to drop each year. The main problem with going to computerized text is that even if the cost of providing information in digital form is much cheaper than providing it on hard copy, the cost of the equipment it takes to access that digital information remains a significant additional expense. The costs of microcomputer processors and memory chips is dropping rapidly, however, so the digital "reader" of the future may be quite reasonably priced. Nevertheless, it may be many years before the costs of providing digital text actually become comparable to those of printed texts.

The Book As an Instructional Medium

The next question is whether there are pedagogical advantages to shifting from books to digital text. Even if digital information is more expensive, if it is more instructionally effective, the additional cost might be justified. Digital text might still be more *cost-effective*, in terms of educational gains. Let's examine this critical issue, by comparing the advantages and disadvantages associated with the use of both textbooks and the new digital information sources.

It is important to recognize that, although the textbook has been the key educational medium for quite a long time, it is not necessarily the best one. Hundreds of years ago, when colleges and universities first came into being, the primary means of transferring information from professor to student was the lecture, not the textbook. The reason for this was not because all professors were spellbinding public speakers. The problem was that books were simply too expensive for most students. The lecture was much more cost-effective. But after the invention of movable type in the fifteenth century, books became less expensive, and ordinary people could own and read them. Nowadays, we take them for granted, with cheap paperbacks available in supermarkets, book superstores, and airport shops. In literate societies, books are everywhere, and they are cheap enough, even at current textbook prices, to be easily usable as a primary source of information for instruction. Even so, the advent of the ubiquitous textbook is a relatively recent development.

Books, even textbooks, have some distinct advantages as instructional technologies. They are inexpensive in comparison to other media materials, including computer software titles and video programming. They do not require expensive and vulnerable equipment for operation. Books can contain large amounts of high-quality information, which includes not just the text itself but full-color graphics and photographs that have higher resolution and better color fidelity than almost anything you will see in a video or on a computer screen. They are highly portable devices and can be used almost anywhere with enough light to read by. In general, the type and background of the pages are easy on the eyes, and in fact some research indicates that people can read significantly faster from the printed page than from a computer screen. Books allow for random search, especially when carefully indexed. Accessing digital material can involve equipment-related delays: the computer may need to be turned on, it may take some time to locate the particular file, and so on. Books can be used at the learner's own pace. They are time-consuming and expensive to copy on one's own, which publishers like, since this tends to limit illegal copying. Books can survive at least some environments that electronic equipment would fail in, but at the same time, since books are inexpensive compared with pieces of electronic equipment, they are easy to replace if they are damaged. All in all, books are a pretty good deal.

However, books have disadvantages, too. In many fields, as the information changes rapidly, it is difficult for textbook publishers to produce up-to-date editions quickly enough to avoid obsolescence. Even if they do, school districts may not be able to afford to replace their versions with the new editions very often. We have recently seen books in use in schools that did not include information about critical events such as the first moon landing or the collapse of the Soviet Union. Also, in spite of the large amounts of text, graphics, and photographs possible in books (and in spite of its potentially high quality), books cannot present moving visuals or interact well with students. Those characteristics have to be supplied by other media. It is much easier to quickly find specific material using a computerized search of electronic text than it is to flip through the pages of a book. Add to that the fact that the cost of books is rising while the cost of electronic media is falling, and we see that books are rapidly losing some of their advantages.

Advantages of Electronic Text

Let's examine in more detail the advantages that electronic text might provide. Computerized searches of electronic text allow students to research topics more efficiently and effectively than is possible with hard copy text. While the table of contents and an index can help readers find material in a book, these research aids are quite limited compared with the advanced search techniques available with most electronic text. Researchers can find all instances of a given word or phrase in an electronic text. They can find material on a given topic in electronic texts that have been classified according to topic. In addition, searches can be refined by combining several topics with descriptors like "and" or "near," which only find instances within the body of information that include all of the terms entered. Thus, users can conduct relatively sophisticated searches that zero in on precisely the information they are looking for.

To make electronic text fully searchable in these ways, specialists must classify material and label it with subject descriptors. This process will increase the costs of electronic text. Producers of electronic textbook materials will need to decide whether these costs are justified by the added functionality provided. Certainly, most libraries have moved to electronic catalogs. Major databases, such as the ERIC database of educational materials, are searchable in this way. Electronic encyclopedias also provide computerized search capabilities. As students learn the skills of searching for and evaluating online information, they will find it easier, faster, more complete, and more accurate to do so. These skills are important for today's professionals, and schools that hope to best prepare their students for the workplace may want to consider this significant advantage of electronic text over printed material.

Electronic materials have another potentially significant advantage over printed materials. They can provide audio and video materials, which may significantly enliven the educational experience. In addition to being motivational for the student, these digital multimedia resources can enhance instruction in ways that textbooks will never be capable of. Audio resources can help teach music, drama, foreign language, and other subjects where the spoken word or music is important. Video clips can enhance instruction in most all subject areas by providing demonstrations, dramatizations, historical experiences, and other visual displays.

Incorporating these multimedia resources into electronic educational materials can be expensive, however. Although some of this material is available for free in what is known as the "public domain," in most cases available audiovisual material is copyrighted, and the rights to it can be quite expensive. An alternative approach is to produce new materials, but this can also become costly. Publishers who wish to enhance electronic educational materials with multimedia clips will need to decide how much of this material they can afford and whether these multimedia resources will significantly enhance the sales potential of the work.

Another potential advantage of electronic materials are the links that can be programmed to take the reader to related materials. So-called hypertext, or hypermedia in the case of multimedia resources, can automatically transfer students elsewhere in the work, if they wish to connect to other resources on that topic. The hypermediated learning environment allows learners to explore topics easily and efficiently. If the links are sensibly conceived, the student can benefit significantly by being linked to additional worthwhile information on a topic.

Some costs are associated with programming hyperlinks into text materials. Incorporating hyperlinks may raise the costs of these materials somewhat. But the other potential disadvantage of adding hyperlinks is that students may follow them blindly and fail to learn the material on the pages where they started. The relatively unstructured learning experience of moving from link to link may not be as educationally sound as following a structured, organized linear set of materials that moves from simple to more complex topics in a given subject area. Weaker students, in particular, may fail to learn effectively in a hypertext environment, since they may choose their links unwisely, fail to return from where they linked to, and have difficulty making sense of the material if it is not carefully structured for them.

In Texas, another argument in favor of the "laptops for textbooks" proposal has been the issue of keeping educational materials current. No state or district can afford to replace all their textbooks every year or even every few years. Over time, the books become outdated. History textbooks sometimes name the wrong person as president, provide erroneous maps, or fail to mention important current events. Science texts do not include the latest research in key areas. Math books fail to reflect the most current approaches to teaching that subject. When this happens, eventually the only choice is to replace the entire book, even though much of it might still be accurate.

Electronic information is more easily and inexpensively modified than printed text. This is especially true for material online. Thus, students would have access to the most recent news stories, as well as extensive background information in their social studies classes. Math students might receive problem sets based on the latest research on teaching math. Science students not only can see the latest research from the universities but also can be actively involved in gathering and analyzing data as well. In timeliness, there is no contest.

Compact Discs or Networking?

As previously mentioned, right now electronic materials can be distributed to students who have their own laptop computers in two basic ways. Students can be given a compact disc containing all the information needed for a particular course of study (or for all the subjects taken in a given school year). The other distribution system is online. Students can connect their laptops to course materials at a website and download what they need when they need it.

Instructionally there should be only minor differences between the two distribution systems. Both support digital materials that are easily searchable, hyperlinked, and contain multimedia resources. Memory-intensive multimedia resources like video might be more efficiently run off a CD, especially if the student's Web connection is slow. On the other hand, hyperlinks on an online system might more easily connect to the vast resources of the World Wide Web. But even these generalizations depend on various factors. A robust Web connection, like a cable modem, might provide efficient access to video clips. Hypertext material on a compact disc can be programmed to access websites and will readily do so if the computer running the CD is connected to the Web.

Which of these two approaches is more reliable? Having a CD might more effectively guarantee ongoing access to information, anywhere and anytime. An online system depends upon the availability and reliability of connections. Few schools have a Web connection for each student right now, nor will they in the immediate future. Furthermore, not all students have Internet connections available at home. Low-income students, in particular, might suffer if text information were available to them only online, since their homes are less likely to have the necessary connections.

One solution to these networking limitations is to download network-provided materials onto high-density magnetic storage devices: hard drives, Zip drives, Jaz drives, and so on. Then the material is both permanent and portable. Children can take their text material home with them on their laptop machines (plus whatever drive was necessary). Some materials might even be printed out on paper, if need be (as in cases where student computers were lost or inoperable for a time). In fact, the "compact disc versus online delivery" debate might eventually become less meaningful, when schools have their own recordable CD units and can make their own copies. Online sources of information could easily and inexpensively be downloaded and made available on CDs.

Which of these two delivery systems, CD or online, would be less expensive? Again, it is difficult to say. Compact discs involve the costs of pressing the discs and shipping them. With online materials, however, one has to factor into the overall equation the costs associated with establishing and maintaining the networks needed to access the information and leasing the servers used to store it. With either approach, the most significant costs would not be delivery-related charges but would be associated with the development of the materials themselves, their marketing, company profits, and so on.

Access to Other Electronic Resources

Of course, if students are given their own computers, they might take advantage of other resources apart from textbook materials. Students might obtain and view on their machines scores of commercial CDs containing information on various topics, including the aforementioned CD-ROM encyclopedias. Another potential source of information is the vast amount of information on the Web for free, which students could also access, assuming adequate networking capability.

This ability to get on the information superhighway is another potentially huge advantage that the computer "notebooks for textbooks" plan might provide. The World Wide Web is fast becoming a huge repository of information—some of it good, a lot of it half-baked at best. Nobody knows just how big the Web is any more. It has been growing too fast and changes too quickly for that. But millions of pages exist, far more than any of us can ever possibly examine. Chances are, no matter what topics you are interested in, or are assigned to study, you will be able to find something about them on the World Wide Web.

Many educational administrators see the availability of all this free information on the Web as an opportunity to keep the costs of educational materials down. But few would suggest that the information on the Web be allowed to replace textbook materials, since information must be appropriately selected, organized, sequenced, and written with the target audience in mind. Although much of the information in a given textbook would probably be available somewhere on the Web, it would probably be in a variety of different locations and it would be too difficult for students to track down on their own, in an appropriate sequence.

In fact, the potential of the Web may be limited by the difficulty of finding high-quality relevant material amid the huge glut of information. It is easy for young people to lose their focus as they "surf the Web." Web use in schools may also be constrained by concerns that students will be accessing material that is inappropriate for minors. Filtering systems are available, but they often operate ineffectively, inadvertently screening out many inoffensive and worthwhile sites.

The vast resources of the World Wide Web might best be provided for students by teachers or curriculum specialists within a district who could develop units that take advantage of Web-based materials. Although the Web materials would be available for free, this process would incur some potentially significant costs associated with the time spent by professional educators to find these materials and organize them into units. Well-planned use of Web resources could enhance a school's curriculum in exciting ways. The material could be current and engaging in ways that textbooks seldom are. Chapter 2, "Surviving the Information Explosion: Researching on the World Wide Web," suggests some ways for teachers to effectively use Web resources.

Providing laptops instead of textbooks could also afford other significant educational benefits for school districts. If adequate networking capability were available, students and teachers could take advantage of the enormous instructional potential of computerized telecommunications: e-mail, listservs, electronic bulletin boards, and online projects. Communicating and collaborating with others can enhance educational experiences. Information about a topic can be shared. Resources can be pooled. Related experiences can be discussed. The perspectives of others from different cultures can be appreciated through real exchanges. Chapter 16, "Conceptual Connections: Establishing Online Learning Communities," describes these opportunities for networking in more detail.

Mere Replacement or Significant Shift?

To the extent that either traditional or new publishing companies work to provide CDs and websites that can replace textbooks, we still have to ask some key questions about them. Are they just the same old wine in new bottles? Do they add anything new and effective? Are they cost-effective? Using new media to deliver the same content in the same way will not result in any better or different learning. Instead, we need to look at what the new media do especially well and take full advantage of those characteristics. Digital resources can have more up-to-date information; can provide animation, sound, and video; and are capable of interactive features like self-graded tests or online discussions with other students. But can these capabilities significantly improve learning, and will those gains be significant enough to justify any additional costs? Or would student learning be just as extensive with well-written, effectively illustrated, up-to-date books? We are just beginning to see some answers to these questions. The research is difficult to do well and sometimes seems to support the preconceptions of whoever is paying for it. However, over time, these answers will become central to the debate.

Also critical to this debate will be the role played by the new digital technologies. The equipment is rapidly becoming more portable, more powerful, and less expensive per byte of information stored and processed. The palm-sized digital assistant is already widely used in the business world. Tiny, portable, inexpensive digital devices may soon become the medium of choice in education. In the near future, school districts may begin to use their textbook budgets to order these kinds of devices. The proposed Texas plan to buy laptops for schools may become a cost-effective proposition sooner than we thought possible.

RECOMMENDED READING

Kerin, J., and C. Frank. 1995. Beyond the textbook: Learner-powered multimedia. *Technos* 4 (4): 22–25.

Rockman, S., and M. Chessler. 1998, December. Laptop use shows increases in student learning. *Connection*. Online:
www.microsoft.com/education/k12/articles/spedec98.htm.

Texas schools may go to laptops. 1997, November. Online: CNET News.com, www.news.com/News/Item/0,4,16630,00.html.

OTHER REFERENCES

Albion, P. 1998. Challenging the unquestioning rush towards adopting laptop programs in schools. Online: www.qsite.edu.au/conference/qsite98/albion/albion.html.

Berry, D. 1997. Using electronic texts in the classroom. *Multimedia Schools* 4 (1): 22–27.

Conail-Engel, I. 1994. The school textbook—Can we now throw it away? *Educational Media International* 31 (4): 250–252.

Healey, T. 1999. Notebook programs pave the way to student-centered learning. *T.H.E. Journal* 26 (9): 14–17.

Hopkins, M., and J. Ittelson. 1994. Electronic publishing and core curricula. *Educational Technology* 34 (7): 21–22.

Larson, T. 1995. Making an interactive calculus textbook. *Journal of Interactive Instruction Development* 7 (3): 20–24.

Levy, M. 1997. Reading and writing linear and nonlinear texts: A comparison of technologies. *On-Call* 11 (2): 39–45.

Lyall, S. 1994. Are these books or what? CD-ROM and the literary industry. *Technos* 3 (4): 20–23.

Matthew, K. 1997. A comparison of the influence of interactive CD-ROM storybooks and traditional print storybooks on reading comprehension. *Journal of Research in Computing in Education* 29 (3): 263–275.

O'Keefe, S. 1995. Electric texts. *Internet World* 6 (10): 56–58.

Satran, A. 1994. New media educational products: The "digitizing straw into gold" fallacy. *Educational Technology* 34 (7): 23–25.

Siegel, M. A., and G. Sousa. 1994. Inventing the virtual textbook: Changing the nature of schooling. *Educational Technology* 34 (7): 49–54.

Wright, A. 1993. Futures of the book: A preliminary history. *Educational Resources*, ERIC, ED 375830.

SCENARIO

Your state has begun to explore the idea of replacing textbooks with portable laptop computers for all students. Since your school district is one of the most technologically advanced in the state, it is likely to be one of the first to experiment with this idea. Needless to say, the proposal is controversial, and few politicians are going to back it without gathering a lot of information and garnering a lot of support. So far, as a beginning fifth-grade teacher, you are unsure about where you stand on the issue. You haven't had much time yet to explore it in depth, but from what you've heard, both sides have made some interesting points.

Your principal is an avid supporter of instructional technology and more knowledgeable in this field than most school administrators. Today, he asked you to serve on a districtwide committee to examine this proposal and its implications. Most districts are setting up such committees, which will report on up the line to the state capital. You have been asked because your principal wants both experienced and beginning teachers on the committee (and you are definitely early in your career!). He has told you that your job is to keep an open mind, to not be too bound by tradition, and to examine the evidence as objectively as possible.

The first meeting of the committee is next week. You tried to explain to the principal that you really didn't know much about it, but he seemed unconcerned. He suggested some basic readings, and he said that your job was to provide the perspective of a beginning teacher and to think about how you might take advantage of this change in your classroom. This won't be easy. You will need to think about both the curriculum and the applications of technology. The principal suggests that you start by gathering information to understand the pros and cons. The decision won't be made for some time, so you need to do some work.

First, your job is to put together all of the pros and cons you can think of for the proposal: Should we use the textbook budget to buy computers instead? What software will be needed? What will we gain by doing this? What will we lose?

Your second job is to decide which side of the issue you stand on and write a brief for that position. (A "brief" is lawyer lingo for a document that lays out the facts in a case and makes the best argument for your side.) In this brief, make the best case you can for your point of view. You should also anticipate the major arguments on the other side and try to refute them.

ISSUES INQUIRY

1. Do you feel that the "laptops for textbooks" proposal has any merit? Why or why not? What are the key issues in this debate?

2. Describe several ways in which electronic text materials differ from printed text materials. Discuss the degree to which these features may (or may not) be instructionally advantageous.

3. Electronic text might be provided to schools in several ways. Compact discs could be distributed. The material could be made available online. Perhaps a combination of approaches might be most appropriate. Discuss how you feel digital information might most effectively be delivered to schools.

4. One very dynamic use of student laptops might be online. Discuss some of the potential instructional benefits of the World Wide Web. As a teacher, would you consider having students use Web materials instead of their textbooks or only as a supplement to their textbooks?

5. If each pupil had a portable "digital assistant" to use in school, how significantly would this change the educational experience? How radically might this equipment change the ways students learn, the ways teachers teach, and the way the curriculum is structured?

CHAPTER 8

Is Educational Technology Sometimes Just Too Expensive?

INTRODUCTION

It is probably impossible to get into any serious discussion of education today without the issue of costs raising its ugly head. Some individuals will point at rising costs and falling or steady test scores to show that increasing the amount of money spent on education will not improve the situation. Others will point to teacher salaries relative to those of other professionals to argue for allocating more money to schools. Still more arguments will arise over how to spend the money that schools do receive: more teachers, higher salaries, technology, textbooks, media materials, special educational opportunities, or many other possibilities.

This is not the place to debate most of those issues. They are complex and often seem to generate far more heat than light when addressed by politicians and special interest groups on all sides. After all, this is a book about instructional technology, so this chapter focuses on just one piece of this jigsaw puzzle. Two key questions here are how to determine the costs of educational technology and whether these investments are worth it. Possible factors that affect our answers to these questions include the setting (school, district, community, etc.), the learner population and their needs, the types of hardware and software involved, how those technologies are used, and the sophistication of the teachers.

Central to any discussion of costs, of course, is the fact that schools have limited budgets. Governments, school districts, school boards, and individual school administrators are always forced to weigh the benefits of different uses of the limited funds available. Some of these expenses are optional, while others are not. Frequently, hardware purchases and technical support are seen as expendable in times of tight budgets. Legislatures and voters are unlikely to approve endless tax hikes or bond issues for raising more money.

In this chapter we review the types of costs incurred when using educational technology. We then discuss the types of benefits that might be realized from using it. Not all of these benefits are easily measured or readily converted into dollar amounts, which can make it more difficult to compare different uses for the limited funds that schools have. Finally, we discuss how one might decide among competing technologies and materials.

Cost Categories

As several chapters in this book illustrate, educational technology consists of far more than just the basic hardware. Hardware needs software before it is useful for much of anything, including instruction. This software might include computer programs, videos, and various other prerecorded media. In addition, there are other materials costs, infrastructure costs, and personnel costs that accompany the use of most educational technologies. Some of these costs may be covered by the regular school operating budget, but others are likely to require critical decisions by those allocating the funds.

Among the most important and typical costs of educational technology are the following:

- *Hardware.* This category includes computers, peripheral devices such as scanners and printers, VCRs and monitors, video and digital cameras, and so forth.
- *Software.* This group includes a variety of programs that run on the computers, VCRs, and other hardware. Without good software, hardware is largely useless. Many investments in hardware have been wasted because there was insufficient or instructionally ineffective software.
- *Infrastructure.* This can be a very large category depending on the circumstances. It can include the computer networks used to link the hardware, the furniture on which to put it, and even the electrical connections to keep it running.
- *Maintenance.* Sometimes those responsible for budgeting will not realize at first that just buying the equipment is not enough. It will not keep running forever, especially in a rigorous school environment. Even well-behaved kids are not easy on equipment. Over time, computer mice will disappear, hard drives will crash, and video cameras will need to be cleaned and serviced.
- *Personnel.* Although school administrations like to think that their teachers deal effectively with technology all on their own, they usually discover otherwise. Most schools or districts require a technology coordinator (maybe more than one!) to order new hardware and software, to teach the students and teachers how to use the technology, to keep it maintained, to upgrade software as needed, and to perform a variety of other tasks.
- *Materials.* This category includes computer diskettes, videotapes, cables, and many other incidental expenses that can add up quickly over time. Educators who fail to budget for such costs will be caught short fairly quickly.
- *Training.* One common mistake in educational technology (and one that has occurred repeatedly in the history of the field) is that institutions will spend a great deal of money on the hardware but not support it well. As we are seeing currently with the infusion of networked computers into the system, a major part of that support is training the teachers and students to make good use of the equipment and software. Without this, the technology may not be used at all, let alone used effectively. For years, expensive computers have gathered dust in the backs of classrooms because nobody taught the teachers how to use them or how to teach with them.
- *Services and Utilities.* It costs money to run computers and other equipment. At the very least, someone has to pay the electric bill. Other services might include paying the telephone company for connections into the school buildings as well as the cost of an Internet services provider to connect you to the Net.

Clearly, every situation is unique, but these major categories do seem to cover the kinds of costs any school system will face when using educational technologies. The allocations to the various expenses will change from school to school, but not the basic types of expenses. A new school being built today will probably have computer network cabling included as part of the construction costs, which is cheaper than adding such wiring to an old building. Many older schools are now discovering that they must perform expensive upgrades to their electrical wiring just to use the computers they purchase. A district that has been steadily encouraging its teachers to upgrade their technology skills probably has spread that cost over several years, in contrast to the district that suddenly wants everyone to become "technologically literate" this school year. Even so, many costs must be budgeted for every year, so you and your administrators should not think that once you have bought the machines, the expenses are completed.

Until recently, many school districts have tended to think of hardware purchases in much the same way as buildings: as "capital expenses" that are made once and do not have to be repeated for a long time to come. This classification obscures the fact that computers and VCRs do not last nearly as long as buildings. Hardware might better be thought of more as an "operating expense," which must be addressed on an ongoing basis. The computer and television industries are changing rapidly and better models are introduced almost every day. Camcorders today are now digital, so that the analog models of a few years ago are literally old technology that is incompatible with the new. Most personal computers are obsolete in about three years. They can still be used for some tasks, but there will be software that no longer runs well on them, if it runs at all. Add to that the fact that maintenance costs will start to climb as equipment ages, especially in a school setting, and it is clear that computers need to be replaced regularly. In our experience, four years is too long, so a replacement schedule of once every three years seems about right. Better to build into the budget replacing one-third of the computers every year than to try to find the money to replace them all at once every three years. One possible downside of this plan, of course, could be the increased technical support caused by having several different models of computers available in the same location.

Estimating Cost

How can you use these categories in estimating costs for new technologies? First, next to each one, list the types of costs that are included for the project you have in mind. For example, if you want to estimate the cost of adding five computers to your classroom, the first cost is buying the hardware itself. Remember that this is the cost for *all* the hardware, so do not forget to include monitors, printers, and other key ingredients, if they are not included in the base price.

Other costs might be easy or difficult to estimate. Nowadays computers often come with software, but it is not always high quality or fully functional. In addition, most schools want to standardize on specific programs. You can expect to keep adding software on an ongoing basis. New instructional software might appear on the market after the initial installation. And do not forget the fact that computer software probably has to be upgraded frequently, so upgrades should be in the budget, too. Other types of materials may also be in the budget, such as instructional videos.

Infrastructure costs may or may not be important in your situation. Perhaps your school already has the necessary electrical and communications cables installed. On the other hand, if you are bringing new computers into your classroom, you should consider the problem of furniture. Are desks or tables available? Will you need extra chairs? How about the printer and scanner; where will they go? With this expensive equipment, there will be security concerns. Digital cameras are marvelous devices, so marvelous that others will want them, too. Do you have the cabinets (with locks!) that you need to keep such equipment safe?

In the initial excitement of getting new equipment, setting it up, and trying it out, we often forget about maintenance costs. Most of today's technology is remarkably reliable, but things still go wrong. In a school environment, the problems are especially frequent. The equipment may be used far more heavily than it was designed for. Keyboards may have liquids spilled on them. Cables that are frequently plugged and unplugged may eventually fail. Disk drives will inevitably crash. A technology budget has to include money to replace and repair as needed.

Personnel costs can be difficult to gauge, since many educators seem to perform multiple job functions. Is there someone at your school to take care of the equipment, run the lab, or perform other tasks? If so, what percentage of his or her time will be devoted to these activities, rather than to other duties? Even where technology support is handled by classroom teachers, these responsibilities incur expenses that should be estimated. The "opportunity cost" is whatever this faculty member had to give up to take on the technology responsibilities. This is a real cost to the institution. Finally, it is always important to estimate personnel costs as including not only the direct salaries of those involved but also any benefits such as insurance and pensions.

Along with personnel costs come the costs associated with training. Whether your school relies on in-service presentations, contracts out for workshops, or reimburses teachers for taking university courses and obtaining advanced degrees, they all cost money. If the training is done well, these expenses could be money well spent for your school district (see Chapter 17, "Teacher Training in Technology: The Trials and Tribulations of the Technophobes"). Nevertheless, any calculation of the costs of educational technology must include them. Without good training both in how to use the technology and in how to integrate it with teaching, teachers are unlikely to use it to its full potential. If that happens, the expenses may indeed have been more wasteful than useful.

Materials, services, and utilities comprise a miscellaneous group of potential expenses that can still make or break the implementation of instructional technology in education. We cannot really imagine teaching well without paper, pencils, chalk, and so forth in a traditional classroom. In the same way, it will be difficult to do well in a technology-based classroom without diskettes,

Zip disks, printer paper, blank videotapes, reliable electricity and Internet connections, and so forth.

So, Is It All Worth It?

It is difficult to put dollar figures on the types of costs listed in the preceding section. They depend too heavily on your specific circumstances and the vagaries of the marketplace. But we can see that implementing technology in education can be quite expensive. In the past few years the federal government, state governments, and local school boards across the country have spent literally billions of dollars on computers, on wiring schools to the Internet, and on other educational technologies. The question that inevitably arises is, "Is it all worth it?"

To determine the worth of expenditures like these, it is necessary to consider not just the money and other resources going into the system, but also the benefits coming out. In business and government, this is usually called "cost-benefit analysis," and it can be difficult to do objectively and accurately. Sometimes it is relatively straightforward to estimate the basic cost of the technology, even with all the preceding factors cited. However, it can get more complicated. Accountants will want to depreciate the value of purchases over time, so that the cost of a building that may last thirty years is correctly valued as years go by. It may be complicated to identify the precise source of utility costs and to predict such costs in the future. In addition, the funds for technology purchases may come from a variety of sources: federal and state governments, local school boards, grants, or others. This may affect the decision, as some money might be "earmarked" for specific types of expenditures.

Benefits can be especially difficult to identify, measure, and anticipate for the future. Businesses can sometimes use measurements such as sales or productivity, but how do we measure the benefits of education at different levels? Even when we identify specific benefits, we may not be able to measure them in dollars and cents the way we did costs, so whether the technology was "worth it" may still require a judgment call.

Even so, most people believe that education confers very important benefits on both individuals and society. We often "sell" the utility of education by referring to the jobs that you can hold and the income you can earn, if only you complete high school, college, or graduate school. Public schooling is based on the premise that everyone benefits—through a healthier economy and better citizens—if children are educated. At the same time, we have various ways of measuring the success of schools and students. Standardized tests are often used to track long-term trends in the effectiveness of education. Many states now have proficiency tests that are used not only to check on individual youngsters but also to serve as "report cards" for the schools as a whole. But it is problematic to connect the use of specific technologies to improved test scores or other measurements. Converting educational benefits to some common measurement (such as money) that allows easy comparisons is equally uncertain.

One simple way of classifying the potential benefits of educational technology is to look at the *effectiveness, efficiency,* and *appeal* of the resulting instruction. These three categories allow us to compare different approaches to teaching and learning. In combination with the cost data discussed previously, they can help us to determine which of our projects and uses of technology are indeed "worth it."

Effectiveness refers to whether the students actually learned anything important. Although conceptually simple, this judgment can be difficult to make accurately and consistently. We could give simple tests or other assessments of student learning, like the ones used every day in schools. If students do well, then we usually attribute their success to the instruction we provided. To get more reliable and valid data, we might give tests both before and after the students use the technology to see whether they improved. Nowadays, many would not trust the tests we made ourselves, so perhaps we would want to see what effect our new instructional technologies had on proficiency tests or other standardized measurements. It can be difficult to identify the effects of technology-based instruction on global test scores, which reflect the impact of the entire educational experience. Such improvements may or may not have actually taken place, and they may not be attributable to the use of technology. However we attempt to measure it, effectiveness is one of the most important benefits we can hope to see from the use of educational technology. If all the money, time, and effort we spend on technology in schools does not help students learn more and better, then it does seem pointless.

Along with effectiveness, we can also look at the *efficiency* of the instruction resulting from the use of technology. Suppose you had two ways of teaching about dinosaurs to fourth graders. One was based on traditional paper-and-teacher techniques, like lectures, books, handouts, and so forth. The other used a variety of high-tech devices like CD-ROMs and the Internet. Perhaps you used each program with different youngsters and found that children learned about the same amount of information and concepts about dinosaurs using either one. Would you then conclude that it did not matter which one you chose?

Probably not, because you would still want to look at the costs of each program in money, time, and other resources. One program might be much more expensive. One of them might take much longer in terms of both student and teacher time. In general, if two ways of teaching result in similar learning outcomes, we probably want to choose the one that is more efficient, that is, that uses our resources better. Money is just one important resource. The other major one is time. If our class spends twice as long as necessary learning about dinosaurs, then that is time that they cannot spend learning about something else. Educators may not always like to admit it, but efficiency can be important for them, as well as for businesses.

Often we tout the use of technology in education by pointing to its *appeal* for students. We note how much students seem to enjoy working on computers and shooting videotapes. Therefore, we are often tempted to say that technology is "worth it" simply because it is appealing to many students. We also may assume that students who are drawn into the instructional setting and activities by the technology will necessarily learn more than they would using only printed materials.

However, very little evidence exists to back up this assumption over the long term. Unfortunately, this argument has been made with every new educational technology from radio, through films and television, to the latest in interactive multimedia delivered over the World Wide Web. Certainly, all of these technologies are appealing to people. We all listen to the radio, go to movies, watch television, and work and play on computers on our own time, a sure sign that we like doing those things. The key questions are whether that appeal lasts very long, whether it transfers into educational settings, and whether it results in learning gains.

Might the appeal of new technologies be due mainly to their newness? A "novelty effect" has been acknowledged in educational technology circles for quite some time. Basically, this means that new technologies can be very appealing to people at first due merely to their freshness. However, over time, they lose their novelty as still newer gadgetry comes along and diverts people's attention. We can see the novelty effect at work in many areas of our lives. The first video games were novel at the time, but few gamers play Pong and Pac-man any more. The newer games have better graphics, sounds, actions, and so forth that bring people back. Over time, they will lose their novelty as well, and game designers will have to find new ways to attract customers. The few games whose popularity lasts longer than average usually have something beyond novelty to recommend them, such as appealing characters or a special challenge for the players.

So it is with instructional technology and especially computers. On the one hand, computers and their software programs are becoming so powerful and so versatile that perhaps new applications will always keep the medium fresh. On the other hand, given the history of media and technology, educators should not count on the novelty effect. The days are coming to an end when we can count on youngsters to remain interested in instruction just because it happens to involve a computer. We need to build in a deeper appeal than just novelty to keep students interested.

Besides, just keeping students interested does not guarantee learning. Are they interested in the right things? Or is their attention drawn to flashy but irrelevant animations rather than to learning materials with substance? Do they enjoy the colors and sounds they encounter without actually reading and absorbing the content? Anyone who has watched a teenager "surf" the Web knows that it is possible for someone to bounce from page to page without spending nearly enough time on any one to learn from it. Children (and adults!) often race through cable TV channels in the same way using the remote control. Clearly, surfing is an appealing activity without necessarily being an educational one. Therefore, when we try to measure the benefits of educational technology, just looking at its appeal to students is not enough. We need to include effectiveness as well.

Estimating the actual benefits of using educational technology may require sophisticated research and evaluation strategies. Researchers in universities and other institutions are working on this. However, the best studies often take years to complete, and the results still may be tentative. One way to bolster the case for the benefits of technology, then, is to cite studies whose results support the instructional effectiveness of using technology. Bear in mind that it will probably not be possible to translate those benefits into the language of dollars and cents. In addition, you should remember that the technology in and of itself is not the critical issue. Usually, technology can be shown to result in learning gains only when it is used effectively. Always make the educational use of the technology the focus, not the technology itself.

So, to buy or not to buy? That is the question. To a certain extent teachers no longer have the option *not* to use technology, given the expectations of students, parents, and administrators. Video, audio, and computers are ubiquitous in our culture and proliferating in the schools as well. Rather than focusing on how much technology is needed, it might be better to discuss how to use technology. If the technologies are present and the additional costs of using them in instruction are small, then clearly a wide variety of uses could be cost-effective. On the other hand, if you are making or assisting in the decision to purchase new technologies, then it would be a good idea to estimate their true costs, possibly including all of the categories just listed. Since the dollar estimate that results is likely to be large, you should also take a close look at the potential benefits. Check the research literature and talk with colleagues to see if good evidence exists to support your strategy for using technology. Has it worked effectively in other places?

To summarize, knowing whether educational technology is worth it may not be an easy task. We have to look at costs first, since they often limit what we can do. There is no point to pricing a new technology if we know that our school will never be willing to budget for it. But expenses should be considered in light of potential benefits. In our personal lives we all face expensive purchasing decisions. When we buy a new car, a computer, or other costly goods, we do so because we think that the benefits to us will outweigh that expense. Many schools are now deciding to spend scarce funds for technology. Their expectations are that the educational benefits will eventually justify the costs. Gradually, we also hope that ongoing research will clarify how we can get the "biggest bang for the buck" out of educational technology.

To conclude on a positive note, we can never fully predict all the possible future benefits from using technology in education. The creative talents of those involved in hardware and software design have often outpaced the ability of institutions to predict the uses and benefits of the technology. In 1908, who would have assumed that the tedium of typing would evolve into the convenience of word processing? In 1990, who would have assumed that millions of schoolchildren would use the Internet to enhance their learning? Who knows what artificial intelligence and virtual reality may bring in the next decade. There may be benefits to using instructional technologies that we have not even thought of yet.

RECOMMENDED READING

Dede, C. 1998. Rethinking how to invest in technology. *Educational Leadership* 55 (3): 12–16.

Melmed, A. 1995. The costs and effectiveness of educational technology. *Proceedings of a Workshop for the Critical Technologies Institute.* Santa Monica, CA: Rand Corporation, ERIC, ED 392409

OTHER REFERENCES

Baker, E., and H. O'Neil, eds. 1994. *Technology assessment in education and training.* Hillsdale, NJ: Lawrence Erlbaum.

Doughty, P. 1978. Cost-effectiveness analysis and instructional technology: A review of conceptual issues and selected references. ERIC, ED 179249.

Keltner, B., and R. Ross. 1996. *The cost of school-based educational technology programs.* Santa Monica, CA: Rand.

Lent, R. 1979. A model for applying cost-effectiveness analysis to decisions involving the use of instructional technology. *Journal of Instructional Development* 3 (1): 26–33.

Levin, H. 1983. *Cost effectiveness: A primer.* London: Sage.

Monk, D., and J. King. 1993. Cost analysis as a tool for educational reform. In *Reforming education: The emerging systematic approach*, edited by S. L. Jacobsen and R. Berne. Thousand Oaks, CA: Corwin.

Otto, S., and J. Pusack. 1988. Calculating the cost of instructional technology: An administrator's primer. *ADFL Bulletin* 19 (3): 18–22.

Stecher, B. 1987. Estimating the cost of computer education. In *Planning and evaluating computer education programs*, edited by R. E. Bennett. Toronto: Merrill Publishing.

SCENARIO

You are a second-grade teacher in Muhammed Ali Elementary, an inner-city school in one of the poorest areas of Detroit. The school is in need of many repairs. The paint is peeling, floor tile is coming up, and windows are cracked. A window in the teachers' rest room has a round hole wide enough to allow the wind to whistle through it and the chill to creep in during the dead of winter. Some say it is a bullet hole.

There is another such hole in one of the library's windows. The book collection is small, dated, and little used. The district's library budget has been cut back, year after year, and few new titles have been purchased over the past few years. Most of the pictures in these books are of successful white people, even though the population of the school is over 90 percent African American.

There is a computer lab, obtained with some special federal funding earmarked specifically for equipment purchase. It has ten machines, but they are not networked. One problem you hear is that the school's electricity is somewhat unreliable and one of the computers has never worked properly after a particularly severe outage last summer. There is a small software collection, which consists mainly of floppies and a few CD-ROMs.

The school's principal, Mrs. Williams, has secured a three thousand dollar grant for school resources with a local foundation. At an administrators' conference, she recently worked out two possible arrangements for spending these funds. One is with Scholastic Books, to provide the school with a new "multicultural package," which includes about two hundred fifty new children's books that address minority group themes and include characters with children of color. The other deal was very different. For the same three thousand dollars, Apple Computer has agreed to sell the school three new computers, with an inkjet printer and their primary school software package of compact discs, which includes an electronic encyclopedia and a picture atlas. Mrs. Williams tells you that she would like you to be on a committee she is forming to decide how the grant should be spent. She is excited about the possibility of improving the computer lab with these new machines but wonders if the school library should be a higher priority.

At lunch, you discuss the two options with some of your colleagues. Mr. West says that the computers would make the school look like it has moved into the twenty-first century and would give students the kinds of opportunities for developing some computer skills. "These underpriviledged children should have the same opportunities with technology that the suburban kids get," he says, with conviction. Your colleague, Miss Miller, who has also been teaching second grade for a number of years, has a different perspective. She says she would ask for the books, feeling that it is more important to have a better collection of reading materials, so that the children can select their own books during their quiet reading time. She also feels that some shiny new books relevant to these students would help motivate them to read.

This conversation unsettles you somewhat. While you remain convinced that students might benefit from work on a computer, you are not so sure that the benefits will justify the cost of this equipment, especially when you think about how many books your students would have available for the same price. Since second grade is a particularly critical time in the development of reading skills, this could be a very meaningful acquisition. But is computer literacy just as important?

Do you opt for the computers or the books? Discuss what factors most significantly influenced your decision. Is computer literacy as basic a skill for students today as literacy? Then discuss your perspectives on the cost-effectiveness of instructional technology, in general. Are some types of technology potentially more cost-effective than others? How can the high costs of sophisticated instructional technologies be justified?

ISSUES INQUIRY

1. Have you had some experiences with instructional technology wherein you questioned whether it was worth the price tag? Describe some of these experiences and discuss why you felt that way.

2. Is the principle problem associated with the cost-effectiveness of instructional media mostly related to cost or to effectiveness?

3. How might the costs of instructional technology be reduced? Have corporations shortchanged the schools by not providing low-cost models of computers, videocassette recorders, televisions, and so on?

4. How might the effectiveness of instructional technologies be enhanced so that they are worth what was paid for them? How might instructional efficiency be improved? How might technology be used more extensively so that the impact or cost per student is enhanced?

5. Have you experienced hardware being purchased so that the school's image is maintained as one that is up-to-date? Has this "public relations" function been a higher priority than the instructional purpose for which this equipment should be used?

6. What is the best way to invest money in technology?

   Option A: Buy as many inexpensive pieces of equipment as possible.
   Option B: Buy higher-quality pieces of equipment, even if it means you will have fewer of them.
   Option C: Buy mostly inexpensive equipment, but include in your purchase some expensive equipment setups where more sophisticated work is possible.

7. What should be sacrificed to pay for school or office technology? Should teacher/trainer salary allocations be used for this purpose? Could fewer teachers function more effectively if they have more technology to assist them (automation in education)?

8. Rarely is cost-effectiveness examined. It is complex and somewhat costly to do properly. Should schools put some time, effort, and money into determining the cost-effectiveness of their technology investments? How can the costs of cost-effectiveness studies be justified?

Social Issues

RIGHTS AND RESPONSIBILITIES

Internet Indiscretions

THE LIMITS OF FREE EXPRESSION IN CYBERSPACE

INTRODUCTION

Freedom of speech and freedom of the press are two of the cornerstones of the American political system. They are enshrined in the Bill of Rights, and battles have been fought over their meaning, scope, and limits for over two centuries. One problem has been that the framers of the Constitution could not possibly

137

anticipate all the different communications technologies that would be developed after they codified our freedoms. In the late eighteenth century, who could have imagined that we would send voices, music, and pictures invisibly through the air? If you had suggested that there would be satellites orbiting the earth and allowing people to talk instantly between continents, you might have been thought mad. Freedom of speech and of the press meant very specific things to the framers of the Constitution. Speech meant just that: talking to individuals or groups within range of your voice. The "press" referred to printed material produced by actual printing presses.

Telephones, radios, televisions, and computers have all raised new questions about how we define freedom of speech and of the press. How much freedom is allowed on these media? How much control can government exercise over them, especially when the government regulates the airwaves and frequencies used by broadcasters? Although there have been court battles (and physical battles, too) over freedom for newspapers and other print publishers, many of the issues have been settled in this area. There is not much that print publishers cannot print legally, from political opinions to secret government documents to pornography. Even libel against specific people can be very difficult to prove against a publisher.

The situation is somewhat different with electronic media, although the United States remains one of the world's freest countries. The government has been more likely to try to regulate and control what is broadcast on radio and television than what is printed. Many of the regulations and laws have been upheld by courts. For example, there have been "equal time" laws in which broadcasters have been forced to air different sides of issues. There are controls on advertising on television and radio, as when the government banned the broadcast of cigarette advertising years ago. Such regulations have been blocked by the Constitution when people tried to apply them to print media, but they are allowed with other forms of "the press" because of government's control over broadcasting frequencies and licenses.

What About Standards for the Internet?

Now we have the Internet and the World Wide Web, which present new challenges for freedom of speech and of the press. Before the Internet, it could be difficult to publish information to a wide audience. Printing presses, radio and TV transmitters, and distribution systems for books are all expensive and difficult to obtain access to. Editors and producers often screen what is distributed. Now, however, people are using the Internet to overcome those barriers. Although not everyone has access to the Web yet, large and rapidly increasing numbers of people do. Cost of access is dropping, and often people can use schools, libraries, and other sites to get online for free.

If you want to publish your own materials, you can often find space on the World Wide Web for free or as part of an inexpensive commercial package that includes e-mail and other services. When you publish material this way, it is immediately available to the hundreds of millions of people worldwide who have access to the Web. And you don't need to deal with those pesky fact checkers and editors, either. It might turn out to be difficult for people to find your information, but at least it is available to them. The information that you or I put up, as well as that presented by millions of other people, may be right or wrong, offensive or inoffensive, important or trivial. For the most part, no one is checking.

The situation on the Internet, then, stands in stark contrast to the situation at newspapers, magazines, broadcast television, book publishers, and so on. Instead of having professional reporters, editors, and others screen information for us, we have to do it ourselves. We have to sift through lists of websites, comparing what we find with what we already know and what we need. Sometimes we find exactly what we want. Sometimes we find potentially good information, but we can't figure out if the information is reliable. Sometimes we accidentally run across information that is blatant and offensive.

The size of both the Web and its potential audience may be a problem as well. Although electronic copying machines have made a form of print publishing widely available, few people can afford to disseminate such materials very widely. In contrast, any Web server is equally accessible throughout the world, regardless of its size or location. Thus, for a few dollars a month, people can put their opinions, facts, or pornographic musings online where people can access it literally as easily as they can link to CNN or Newsweek. Popular sites may receive tens of thousands or even millions of visitors a day. Among the most popular are those that supply pornographic text and images.

Naturally one of the major concerns these days from parents through schools and all the way to the U.S. Congress is this pornography on the Internet. Few people are comfortable with granting children free access to pornographic materials on the Internet or anywhere else. The question, of course, is how to stop it. We will look at some of the possibilities later in this chapter. However, the problem of what is on the Internet, whether it should be allowed, and what to do about it go far beyond just sexually explicit material. There are issues about websites that explain how to make bombs or commit other illegal and destructive acts. There are concerns about hate speech and hate groups and whether they should be allowed free rein to publicize their views. And there are many other gray areas where matters of opinion and taste may determine one's reactions to the information and graphics one finds online.

Educational Examples

Here's an example from the field of education. Most schools, even at the high school level, have some restrictions on what their students can say or write on school property or in school publications. Even at the college or university level there have been attempts in recent years to restrict certain kinds of "hate speech," offensive articles in school-supported newspapers, or other controversial communications. In the K–12 schools, these restrictions may be upheld by courts because the individuals speaking and writing are minors, and the school is held to have an interest in maintaining order and setting standards for behavior. In higher education the restrictions have often been struck down by courts as unwarranted constraints on free speech and a free press.

Therefore, high schools might be able to restrict student criticism of teachers and administrators in the school paper, for example. They also have some control over how students dress, what they say to one another, whether they may pass out leaflets at school, and so forth. In general, however, these standards apply only at school or related activities (such as field trips). When the student leaves the school grounds, the responsibility and authority of school officials end. Presumably, students could publish their own student newspaper out of a private house but could be prevented from distributing it at the local school.

Recently a new pattern has begun to emerge. Instead of publishing newspapers, students are publishing Web pages. And some of these Web pages are getting teachers very upset. Often the pages that are creating the greatest consternation among school authorities are the ones that directly criticize teachers, principals, and schools. There have been several court cases recently in which school officials have suspended students for creating such Web pages. Although no one doubts that the schools have the right to control the content of their own Web pages and Web servers, these student-generated pages were actually placed on independent servers, such as those run by many Internet services providers (ISPs). They had no connection to the school.

The question that arises is obvious. Although no one likes to be criticized, does the school's right to control some student speech, writing, and activity at the school itself really extend beyond the school and beyond school hours? So far the courts have said no. If a student makes assertions on a Web page that are actually libelous, of course, a teacher could sue the student in question or, in the case of minors, the student's parents.

Major Controversy at Northwestern University

There is even more controversial and perhaps more potentially dangerous information that could be posted on the World Wide Web. One issue that has generated much controversy on and off the Net is the Holocaust—the mass murder of Jews by the Nazis during World War II. Some countries, such as Germany and Canada, have laws against making certain kinds of statements about the Holocaust, including the suggestion that it did not actually occur. The United States has no such laws, of course, since they would quickly be declared unconstitutional by the courts.

But the United States does have many people who feel very passionately about the Holocaust and other issues. Posting material on the Web or elsewhere that is historically inaccurate (for example, that the Holocaust did not occur) as well as painful to millions strikes many people as not only unwise but downright wrong. Some work hard to get the material removed, if not by the government (which would violate the letter of the law), then by the Webmaster or whoever controls the Web server in question (would this then violate the spirit of free speech?).

An example is found in a recent case at Northwestern University. An engineering professor there, Arthur R. Butz, wrote a book in 1976, entitled *The Hoax of the Twentieth Century.* In it he made a historical argument, which was far outside his area of expertise in engineering, that the Holocaust did not actually occur. Twenty years after the publication of his book he used the free Web server space provided by Northwestern University to summarize some of the same arguments, reference his book, and link to other information along the same lines (http://pubweb.nwu.edu/~abutz/). It is not an extensive website, and there is no directly racist or anti-Semitic material or commercial advertisements for his book or anything else. The major objections to it have to be that it makes historical claims that are not shared by the vast majority of historians, that are not supported by most of the historical evidence available, and that are offensive to large numbers of people.

Overall, Northwestern University has taken the position that Butz is following the guidelines for putting material on its Web server. The administration is careful to distance themselves from the content of his pages while defending his right within an academic setting to voice them. He is a tenured professor, he makes a clear distinction between his engineering expertise and his historical efforts, and he does not bring his views about the Holocaust into the classroom (where the university would have a legitimate complaint because it is not relevant to the engineering curriculum). Therefore, they tolerate him and, as one news story has it, wait for him to retire.

Interestingly, another engineering faculty member maintains that he was sanctioned by the university for opposing Butz's views. Sheldon L. Epstein was an adjunct engineering professor at the university who protested the fact that Northwestern had, in his view, provided a forum for the Butz's offensive and inaccurate views. Epstein did bring Holocaust issues into his engineering classes. The university maintained that he deviated from his syllabus by doing so, and it failed to renew his contract the next year. Epstein believes that he was punished for speaking out, but the university denies it. He also has placed his views on the World Wide Web (http://metalab.unc.edu/team/history/controversy/candor00.html).

What Can People Place on the Web?

So the question becomes at all levels, What can people put on the World Wide Web? When is it legitimate to "censor" people, either through governmental decrees or private actions? The U.S. Congress continues to pass laws to keep sexually explicit materials off the Net and out of the easy reach of minors. As of this writing, however, there is no shortage of such material available. Beyond that, there are also plenty of sites that contain information many of us find horrifying, such as step-by-step instructions on how to build a powerful bomb like the one that blew up the Federal Building in Oklahoma City. Many people believe that such information should be censored.

More difficult cases involve material that is not necessarily overtly dangerous but that still offends people, such as personal criticisms or denial of the deliberate mass murder that took place in Nazi Germany. Criticism is a part of life. None of us can expect to be liked and respected by everyone. Is it automatically disruptive of something like a school environment? Similarly, the Holocaust is clearly a legitimate area for serious historical research. There are many ongoing questions about what happened, why, how, and so forth. In addition, historical scholarship, like any research, may be done well or poorly and is always subject to revision, challenge, and new evidence. When, if ever, does historical research become so poor or so biased that it no longer qualifies as legitimate research?

As already discussed, there is a difference between taking governmental action to prevent or punish the publication of certain material and taking private action to ensure that it does not appear in *your* newspaper or on *your* Web server. For example, our Constitution prevents the government in most instances from preventing the publication of specific material in a newspaper or from demanding that the newspaper publish certain articles. On the other hand, the editors of the *New York Times* are not required to publish everything that comes across their desks. They select stories using many criteria such as newsworthiness, quality of writing, solidity of the evidence presented, and so forth. Few people question their right to exercise editorial control. Certainly, it is not usually considered "censorship" of the stories that are not published for various reasons.

Similarly, if a private company runs a Web server, few people would object to their controlling what appears on it. There is no reason for General Motors' employees to put up material either for or against the reality of the Holocaust, and few would object to GM's removing any such material that it found. The situation gets a little trickier if the private company is running Web servers for hire. In this case, though, the situation is usually handled by a contract between the Web server company and the individuals, groups, or organizations that use their services. If the company wants to restrict the kind of content that can be displayed, then it can write the restrictions into the contract, and the other parties don't have to sign if they don't want to.

Acceptable Use Policies

This approach is similar to how many schools, districts, colleges, and universities handle the situation as well. Most such organizations now have "acceptable use policies (AUPs)" that govern how students and others can use their computing and networking facilities. An AUP may cover many areas and usually serves as an informal contract between the organization and the person (student, faculty, staff) who signs it. In addition to specifying what kinds of material can and cannot be posted, an AUP might cover what sites or kinds of sites a student is allowed to visit. Once the student has accepted the AUP, if he or she violates the terms of the policy by, say, going to a pornographic site, then the penalties have already been spelled out.

Universities are likely to use AUPs somewhat differently. They are less likely to try to restrict what students and faculty see on the Web than to spell out what they may place there, since many universities offer free Web space to students, faculty, and staff. Northwestern University, for example, does have a prohibition against using university Web servers for commercial activities. University AUPs seldom prohibit personal opinions, however, since that would contradict the long tradition in this country of academic freedom at the university level.

Academic freedom is a tradition that goes beyond the First Amendment to the U.S. Constitution and affects most private and public institutions of higher education. Professors have had a long history of defending their rights to say and study virtually whatever they want within academe. Often even when an institution might arguably be within its rights to restrict speech or publication using its facilities, issues of academic freedom will prevent it from doing so. Although this tradition has not always been applied uniformly, it is nevertheless a powerful force in most colleges and universities.

When developing an AUP for an educational institution, you need to be careful to take into account a variety of concerns. These include legal issues, the traditions of a particular institution, the age and status of the students, and many others. An AUP might cover a large number of areas, including

- commercial use of Web server space;
- what sites people may view or use;
- use of computers, software, and networks for activities unrelated to the mission of the institution;
- the content of Web pages and other material stored on the computers;
- the penalties for breaking the policies;
- procedures for applying or appealing the penalties; and
- the use of e-mail and other facilities for personal reasons.

Usually the content of an AUP will be the result of a long process of negotiation among different interest groups at an organization. This is especially true at an educational institution, because of the strong sense of self-governance and independence often found among the faculty. Officials high in the organization might have an interest in protecting it from lawsuits and criticism. On the other hand, individual instructors and students might press for the greatest possible freedom of expression. Technical staff charged with running the computer systems and networks might want to minimize the time they need to spend as watchdogs, so certain AUP stipulations will address potentially disruptive circumstances.

Spamming

Pornography and controversial opinions are not the only ways that individuals might misuse Internet access. As noted, universities often restrict the commercial use of their Web servers. E-mail can be misused as well. If you wanted to send out a mass mailing through the Postal Service, it would cost you a great deal of money and time. These expenses, believe it or not, provide a natural restriction on the amount of printed "junk mail" that you receive. If the companies were not profiting from their mailings, you would not get so many catalogs.

E-mail is different. "Spamming" is the practice of sending out large numbers of e-mail messages about such topics as the latest pyramid scam to get rich quick or the attractions of a specific website. Spamming is easy, quick, completely automated, and inexpensive for the sender. However, it can impose costs on ISPs as well as on those who receive a great deal of it. It clogs up networks and e-mail in-boxes. And it is a nuisance to most of us. Often AUPs will prohibit it.

Spamming may also create issues about freedom of expression similar to those raised about radio and television broadcasts. Normally, nobody can force someone to go to a website. You might get to an offensive one by mistake, but a simple mouse click will usually send you somewhere else. However, e-mail is closer to what is sometimes called a "push" technology (like broadcasting). That is, the sender is in control over whether the spam ends up in your in-box, in contrast to the Web where you decide whether to "pull" a page to your computer by clicking a link. Some people argue that no one has the right to force us to accept material that we do not want. However, e-mail may be a special case, because you can still delete a message even before you have read any more than the subject of the message.

Increasingly, individuals, organizations, and companies are proposing restrictions on spam, even though it is often the case that one person's information is another's spam and vice versa. If you are in the market for a low-cost computer, the advertisement that just appeared in your in-box may contain exactly the facts you need. If you are waiting for an important message from home, the same ad is a distraction and a nuisance. No one has worked out ways to resolve these dilemmas yet.

Filtering the Internet

Many schools have taken another path to what is sometimes called "safe computing." It is possible to have the computers and servers themselves block access to objectionable sites and communications. For example, America Online lets its subscribers filter out spam, although sometimes the filters will remove material that you are interested in as well. Many commercial e-mail programs allow you to create your own filters to automatically send advertisements to the trash can. When you use these filters to avoid e-mail from specific people (an ex-boyfriend or girlfriend, perhaps?), they are called "Bozo Filters." Similarly, a variety of commercially available pieces of software can filter out websites before students even have a chance to visit them. At the time of publication, some of the more popular filtering titles were CyberPatrol, Cybersitter, and Net Nanny.

A Web filter can operate in several different ways or use a combination of methods. One way is to search for key words in a site and block any that use objectionable language. This may work moderately well for many of the basic curse words that you might want to keep away from elementary school children, but it has serious disadvantages. Does the word *breast* automatically signal a pornographic site or might it be contained in a site on cancer that could add to a high schooler's research paper? Does the word *Nazi* mean that the site in question is maintained by an extremist group, or is it instead a legitimate historical resource? Computer programs are not necessarily good at making these kinds of distinctions.

A second way that a filtering program can work is by allowing students access only to a set of approved sites. This means that responsible human beings have visited the sites and decided that they are inoffensive and have some potential educational value. The company that produces the software may hire the people who make these decisions, or teachers may submit sites for inclusion on the approved list. Clearly, people can make more subtle and effective distinctions among sites than software can. This system has its trade-offs, however. By denying students access to any sites that are not on the list, the filter can all but ensure that students do not view objectionable material. But the Web is a huge resource and the company and the teachers may be able to review only a small fraction of the available sites. Inevitably, students may lose the opportunity to use valuable resources simply because they are not on the list.

A complementary method for filtering is to maintain a list of forbidden sites. Again, this list could be created and maintained by either the school or the software company. This has the advantage of leaving the rest of the Web (the millions of sites not on the list) open to the students. However, the problem of scale still exists: People can review only so many sites. There will always be many that contain objectionable material that no one discovers until a child visits at exactly the wrong time. The new sites that appear regularly can also present problems. With either of these latter methods, the software company will provide regular updates of the approved or forbidden lists.

The various programs and services that filter material for schools and other institutions can be an extreme way of solving some of the problems discussed here. They can be so extreme that, for example, the courts seem to be leaning in the direction of forbidding public libraries from using them because of the restrictions on free speech that they impose. There are less drastic ways of dealing with the issues.

The first way, of course, is to maintain adult supervision over student access to the Internet. Even with filtering software, there is no real substitute for a responsible adult. To assist teachers in this supervisory role, teachers, schools, and districts can maintain their own growing lists of good educational websites. Alternatively, a variety of websites are available, maintained by reputable organizations, that provide extensive links to good sites in all content areas. Often these organizations rate the sites, either overall or for different grade levels.

"Seals of approval" from these watchdog groups can be seen on many websites. Two of the most reputable are RSAC and SafeSurf. RSAC, the Recreational Software Advisory Council, was formed by a consortium of software production companies to monitor their own products. SafeSurf, on the other hand, is a parent-based watchdog organization that was founded to protect children from offensive material on the Web. Teachers who hope to maintain close supervision over their students should become aware of these organizations and their standards for approval of Web material (which are displayed on each of their websites).

There is no single simple answer to the questions raised by these issues of freedom of speech and of the press as they relate to the Internet. Policies and practices will vary, depending on the level of education (elementary, secondary, or university), the type of institution (public or private), the traditions and culture of the organization, and the laws in force. The elements involved are complex: technological, legal, sociological, and so on. And you can be sure that these issues will change over time, as the technology and culture changes around us.

RECOMMENDED READING

Frazier, M. 1995. Caution: Students on board the Internet. *Educational Leadership* 53 (2): 26–27.

Mason, L. 1995. The elephant and the net cruiser: Regulating communication on the net. *Information Technology and Libraries* 14 (4): 236–239.

Nordgren, S. 1995. On Northwestern Website, professor argues that Holocaust didn't happen. *The Philadelphia Inquirer,* 16 January.

Resnick, P. 1997 March. Filtering information on the Internet. *Scientific American,* 62–64. Online: www.w3.org/pub/www/pics.

OTHER REFERENCES

American Library Association. 1997, July 2. Resolution on the use of Internet filters. Online: www.ala.org/alaorg/oif/filt_res.html.

Fletcher, B. 1996. WWW resources for discussion on acceptable use policies. *Communication: Journalism Education Today* 29 (3): 14–15.

Lindroth, L. 1998. How to improve online safety. *Teaching PreK–8* 28 (7): 20–21.

Marcroft, T. 1998. Safety first: Managing the Internet in school. *T.H.E. Journal* 26 (5): 71–73.

O'Donnell, V. 1986. The pornography controversy: Issues, effects research, and First Amendment rights. Paper presented at the Speech Communication Association, Chicago, IL, ERIC, ED 279051.

Solomon, G. 1998. Child safety on the Internet: An analysis of recent thinking. *Journal of Online Learning* 9 (2): 17–19.

Wallace, J. 1997, November 9. Purchase of blocking software by public libraries is unconstitutional. *The Ethical Spectacle.* Online: www.spectacle.org/library.html.

SCENARIO

You are the Webmaster for an urban community college. You have worked hard to make the World Wide Web a central part of the marketing, administrative, and instructional efforts of your college, and you are proud of the progress you have made. The college's Web presence is growing, and the look and feel of the site are attractive and professional. Increasing numbers of students are coming to the college at least in part because of the website. Once there, they are increasingly likely to use it to access instructional materials of many kinds.

As part of this, you have been encouraging professors to put course materials and instruction on the Web, but you can't offer them much assistance in doing so. You also haven't monitored the professors' activities, not wanting to become a default WebCop. Now that you have begun to offer students small amounts of disk space for their Web pages, you don't much want to police them either. You have always assumed that everyone would be responsible, but now you are not so sure.

Recently a student group contacted you about the website of one professor and demanded that it be removed. The professor in question teaches radiographic technology to prospective x-ray technicians, but he has used his Web space for something else entirely. He has supplied extensive material about the Nazi Holocaust, arguing that it never happened and that it should be called the "Hoaxocaust." He has also linked to a surprising number of other sites that make the same claim. Suddenly you are reminded of a case at Northwestern University, and you begin to wish that you were not in the middle of this. The student group is outraged, demanding that these Web pages be removed. The historians on the faculty who have looked at this material at your request say that it is nonsense. The professor refuses to remove it, arguing that there is no policy that covers it and that his right to academic freedom trumps everything else.

So far, the damage to the college's Web image and reputation appears minimal. Since the Web is largely a "pull" medium in which one must actively request any information, most people have never even seen these pages. As publicity about the incident grows, though, that is changing. You have made sure that there are no links from official college pages to this material, and the professor has removed anything from his pages that identifies the college (although the Web address does provide a way of identifying your institution).

When you talked with him, however, the professor did indicate that he has bigger plans. He hinted that he intends to "spam" the newsgroups and electronic mailing lists using his college account. This will allow him to send his views, for free, to tens of thousands of new people, maybe more. And it appears that he is also investigating the use of more-sophisticated "push" technologies, like the programs that automatically send out material to thousands at regular intervals. To make matters worse, you have received inquiries on the site from places like Canada and Germany, where it is a crime under at least some circumstances to state that the Holocaust did not happen.

You have prevailed on the president of the college to start taking some responsibility for this issue. She has convened an ad hoc committee of faculty, administrators, and students to look into it. Unfortunately, this group wants to start their investigation with a report about the situation from the college Webmaster (namely you). Write such a report, making recommendations about what to do about the existing website, what to do about the professor's plans, and what should go into a collegewide acceptable use policy for the Internet. Justify each of your recommendations as succinctly as possible.

ISSUES INQUIRY

1. What standards of acceptability should apply to Web content? If "socially redeeming" content justifies otherwise questionable material, how can we define this term? Is the professor in question making a contribution to our historical knowledge? Was the movie *Deep Throat* legitimate art (or legitimate entertainment!)?

2. Should an individual be allowed to use *institutional* resources to say things that many at that institution would object to? Should an organization have to supply bandwidth and drive space for material like this? Is this a different issue from whether or not an individual can use his or her *own* computer account to communicate a potentially offensive message? Can an individual realistically make a Web page available without involving some kind of organization (at least an ISP)? Does it matter whether the organization involved is a private or public institution?

3. Can an institution ban any type of material it wants on a Web page? Some court rulings, like *Pickering v. Board of Education of Will County*, have said public facilities cannot forbid statements of criticism against themselves. Other rulings, like *R.A.V. v. St. Paul*, have said that universities cannot forbid statements simply because many members of the institution disagree with them. If an institution can legitimately forbid certain types of expression on its server, *who* should determine how far those restrictions go: only top decision makers, a consensus attained at a meeting, a referendum, and so on?

4. Should it matter whether or not this professor "spams" his information out to others? Does the medium matter in terms of whether it has "push" or "pull" characteristics? Should there be more stringent standards for push technologies, like radio and television, than for pull technologies, like books and Web pages?

5. Some past court rulings about questionable material and free speech used "local standards" of acceptability as a guideline. What offended the vast majority in a given locale was deemed unacceptable, especially if it had no "redeeming social value." But how can "local" standards be applied to a global medium like the Internet? What is considered "pornographic" in Alabama may not apply in California. If a "Hoaxocaust" Web page is deemed acceptable in the United States, what about in Germany or Israel, where more intense sensitivities on this topic may exist?

6. Should material that might be deemed inappropriate for certain groups (minors, for example) be banned entirely from the Web, even if it is acceptable for adults? Does this not infringe upon the rights of those adults who wish to view this type of material?

7. Should Internet filtering software be used to block certain websites, even if it may prevent access to many worthwhile websites (the software just screened out the site on the basis of a word that might potentially be used in an offensive way)?

8. If labels on websites or ratings systems for software filters are used, *who* decides how sites should be labeled or rated and *on what basis*? Can companies be reasonably expected to appropriately evaluate their own products, for example? If we rely on labeling or rating for the Web, can this approach ever hope to cover a sizable percentage of the existing sites? Or is it doomed to be representative of only a small minority of websites?

CHAPTER 10

It Takes a Global Village

MULTICULTURAL STUDIES THROUGH TELECOMMUNICATIONS

INTRODUCTION

The famous media theorist Marshall McLuhan coined the term "global village" over three decades ago to describe how telecommunications could transcend the vast distances across our planet and acquaint us more intimately with some faraway places than we were with towns ten miles up the road. In the 1960s, the Space Age ushered in a new era of global awareness. The moonshots helped us look back and literally see our own planet hanging in the blackness of space for the first time. Those gas-burning engines that propelled the space shots also helped modernize the airplane. Jet air travel allowed thousands to visit exotic locales around the world and made business far more international. The term "shrinking planet" was used to describe how the rest of the world became a more accessible, familiar place.

The Space Age also spawned the satellite, which revolutionized global telecommunications. The television in the living room was beaming footage of foreign leaders, lively overseas festivals, horrible disasters that killed thousands, poverty-stricken conditions in the Third World, and so on. Radios blared an increasingly international pop music, featuring overseas acts like the Beatles, Brasil66, and Bob Marley. International telephone service was extended and improved tremendously.

So extensive and efficient was the world's telecommunications infrastructure by the 1960s that McLuhan argued it had transformed the planet's awareness of itself. Americans could see instantaneously what was happening in places like Ireland, Israel, and India. They became more familiar with names like Belfast, the West Bank, and Kashmir than with towns in nearby counties. They idolized the Beatles and purchased Volkswagen Beetles. They discovered the taco and Thai food. French and Italian designers set the pace in fashion. The globalization of American culture was accelerating.

McLuhan's observations extended to how media shape our consciousness. In a global village, Americans could no longer be so parochial in their perspectives. Even if it was mostly "mediated," their exposure to the rest of the world was more extensive, immediate, and intimate than ever before. On a daily basis, people were forced to acknowledge a variety of different cultures in parts of the world that they had never seen.

Globalization of the American lifestyle has continued apace over the past few decades as the telecommunications industry has continued to advance, with telephone service expanding everywhere, radio and television signals proliferating throughout the world, and most recently with the computerized networking of the planet. If McLuhan were still alive today, he would no doubt be fascinated with the Internet and its potential ramifications. He would probably be pleased to see that his characterization of the planet as a global village has become more appropriate than ever.

How can educators address this accelerating globalization of our society? How can they effectively raise international awareness? How can they interest young people in other cultures that they may never have heard of? One potentially engaging approach is to use technology to bring intercultural educational units to life. Film and television can show pupils what other societies are like in ways that books cannot. Digital multimedia resources on compact disc allow students to explore information sources about other cultures in dynamic ways. The Internet may provide the most exciting opportunity of all. For it is a truly international medium that extends to nearly every corner of the planet. The Internet has provided fast, reliable, and inexpensive connections to literally millions of people, who represent many different cultures. This chapter describes how intercultural educational experiences can be facilitated in dynamic ways through the use of communications technologies.

Why Is Intercultural Awareness Important?

In the nineties, the field of education in the United States has witnessed a growing emphasis on "multiculturalism." In a heterogeneous society like the United States, one critical concern is that people from different racial and ethnic backgrounds be able to coexist and collaborate in positive ways. Although not as blatant a phenomenon as it once was, racism remains a serious nationwide problem. An awareness of different cultural perspectives is taught in schools, in the hope that the populace can come to appreciate rather than deprecate its diversity. Tolerance and appreciation of ethnic differences has been encouraged to help mitigate the ethnocentric tendencies of many young Americans.

The focus in many schools may be on the specific minority groups with a significant presence in the United States. But the larger multicultural mission is to expand awareness about the variety of cultures to be found throughout the world. Complementing the multiculturalism movement is a growing interest in international studies. Appreciating the impact of culture need not stop at our shores, but can be extended all over the globe. One reason for developing international perspectives is the global role played by the United States. As the world's superpower, this country has unavoidably inherited some degree of responsibility for resolving national conflicts, combating terrorism, and encouraging economic development.

In addition, American business became increasingly international in the second half of the twentieth century. Many large American firms now do business all over the world and have subsidiary divisions in different countries. The biggest of these "multinational corporations" are represented on every continent and in nearly every country. Thus, our economy is now a global one, with events in other parts of the world affecting the financial fortunes of every American. An understanding of the societies with which we do business has become very important for our own welfare.

Another global phenomenon that has mushroomed in the past few decades is tourism. More Americans than ever are traveling overseas and their appreciation of what they see depends on their having some knowledge of the countries they visit. How these travelers interact with foreigners will ultimately influence how others perceive this country. Unfortunately, the "Ugly

American" has been a global stereotype. It describes tourists from the U.S. who are generally upset when people from other societies fail to cater to them and who chauvinistically enumerate the ways in which these foreign practices are inferior to the "American way." This persistent image of us abroad can best be dispelled by travelers from the United States with a greater awareness and sensitivity to the cultures they are visiting.

For a variety of political, economic, and social reasons, the schools need to prepare young Americans for dealing with people from other countries. Some of our young people will ultimately enter the foreign service, assume overseas military posts, work for international assistance organizations, or be involved in humanitarian efforts in poorer parts of the world. Many will work for multinational corporations and be called upon to interact with their counterparts in foreign offices, to travel to other countries on business, or perhaps to work overseas for an extended period of time. Finally, large numbers of them will tour various regions of the world, will purchase foreign products to bring home, and will have opportunities to interact directly with people from other lands.

Incorporating Intercultural Experiences into the Curriculum

An appreciation of other cultures has long been part of the social studies curriculum, as well as an important component of foreign language study. Sometimes it also arises in the literature read in language arts courses. One standard activity is to have students study a different culture directly, by reading about various aspects of a given society: its history, language, customs, religion, holidays, and so on. This approach can be highly informational, but it may not give students a true feeling for the culture.

Another approach is to expose the class to cultural artifacts, like artwork, literature, music, dress, and food. Students can sense the culture in a more immediate way than just reading about it. This exposure to ways in which the culture expresses itself can be both enlightening and engaging. Trips to museums, concerts, or festivals can help bring the special qualities of another culture to life. Bringing artifacts into the classroom can help students experience aspects of another culture more intimately.

Having visitors from a different society come into the classroom to talk about it can be an even more interesting experience, especially if they are able to express what their culture means to them and how it has influenced their family, friends, and others from their ethnic group. This kind of testimonial can give students an even more intimate sense of what another culture is like and why its perspectives may differ from mainstream American culture.

A potentially even more intense experience can be having students from another country enrolled at the school or in the class. Many high schools have foreign exchange programs that bring in students from overseas. There will be opportunities to observe and interact with these individuals over an extended period of time. These experiences can be very interesting and enlightening.

One of the best ways to immerse oneself in a cultural experience is to study the language of another country. Differences in language can help expose subtle differences in culture. Also, language courses invariably incorporate aspects of culture into the lessons. Is there a French course that doesn't include the landmarks of Paris in its practice dialogues? Spanish courses often cover the geography and customs of Latin America. Italian courses may provide background on ancient Roman architecture and Renaissance art. Of course, proficiency in a language can provide many opportunities to learn more directly about societies in which it is spoken, including reading documents in that language, interacting with foreign nationals in their native tongue, and perhaps eventually living abroad on one's own.

Some schools are enterprising enough to sponsor trips overseas. Travel will, of course, allow students to experience another culture on a firsthand basis. There is probably no better way to enhance your understanding of another society than actually going there. But travel requires blocks of free time, calls for some planning, and often can be quite expensive. Students who have an opportunity to travel are fortunate. Such trips are generally rare occurrences, even for those with the financial resources to cover the costs.

In lieu of real travel, schools can take advantage of technology to convey what a trip to a foreign country might be like. Films and videos of real footage from other lands can provide a vicarious experience of that culture. Compact discs and websites with many pictures and sounds can also communicate some sense of what being in another country is like. The Internet can provide what is sometimes termed "virtual travel," where the class can follow online the travels of a group of adventurers in an interesting part of the world, who telecommunicate back their photos, videos, journals, postcards, and so on. Technology offers many opportunities for students to experience other cultures from the confines of their classrooms.

Culture Through the Lens

One of the best ways for students to obtain glimpses at other cultures is through film and video. It is important to read about other societies, but reading will not easily give pupils a sense of what sights and sounds they might encounter in another culture. Documentaries about other cultures can be quite interesting and illuminating for young people, conveying the appearance of the people, the sound of the language, the look of the villages, the noise of the marketplace, the types of clothing, the kinds of foods, and so on. Documentaries can show typical daily activities as well as special events like lively festivals. Filmed interview footage allows people to communicate what is unique about their culture. Film can make a unit on a foreign culture come alive.

While generally not as valuable as documentaries, entertainment-oriented films also can teach pupils a great deal about foreign countries. Movies produced in other countries can show the look of the society, as might a documentary. Especially when written and directed by nationals from that country, foreign films may communicate important messages about life in that society. Analyzing the perspectives of different characters may help students appreciate what is valued in this particular culture. Plot twists may also reflect how expectations for behavior differ in other lands. Cultural indicators abound in some foreign film genres, like India's Hindi musical dramas and Japan's samurai films.

Even if the film or television show is a Hollywood production, there may be a great deal to learn, especially if an effort has been made to accurately portray how people live overseas. Accurate historical portrayals can be very helpful in providing background about a country. Unfortunately, the standard Hollywood approach is to distort the facts in favor of creating an entertaining story. Characters are often caricatures, and stereotyping is common. Often the bad guys are foreigners. In many movies, significant roles for nonwhite characters were played by white performers, and the negative stereotyping of other races has been flagrant.

How the United States has addressed its own racial issues is another interesting theme to examine in light of the movies produced during a given era. One of the first major Hollywood film directors, D. W. Griffith, was a southerner, and his epic silent film *Birth of a Nation* tells the story of how the Klu Klux Klan helped saved the American South after the Civil War from the recently freed African Americans and Northern "carpetbaggers." By the 1960s, Hollywood was addressing the issue of race relations in a way that was more respectful of African Americans, with movies like *Guess Who's Coming to Dinner?* and *In the Heat of the Night*. In the 1990s, Hollywood has come full circle with films like *Dances With Wolves*, in which the standard "good guys versus bad guys" formula has been turned upside down. It was the Native Americans who were the sympathetic group from whose perspective the story is told, and whites are the ruthless villains.

Film analysis can be a dynamic way of stimulating class discussions about cultural bias, cross-cultural confusion, and stereotyping. Let's take the classic British film *Lawrence of Arabia* and think about what questions teachers might ask their pupils about the different groups portrayed, after they have seen the movie. First they might want to compare the depiction of the various Arabian ethnic groups, the Turks, and the British. Does the film take the British point of view, or does it successfully convey the perspective of the Arabs? What stereotypes of each group may have been perpetuated? What were the most interesting cross-cultural experiences in the film? To what degree was T. E. Lawrence's identity crisis related to his effort to simultaneously negotiate several very different cultures? Finally, what can this film teach us about the British Empire, the Ottoman Empire, World War I, the birth of the modern Arab states, and so on?

Television, of course, can also provide a wealth of material about other cultures, minority groups, and racial conflict. Today's expanded television offerings on cable can bring some very dynamic programming about other societies into the classroom. Many classrooms are now equipped with television sets and more and more have access to cable programming (see Chapter 5, "TV or Not TV? That Is the Question: Commercialization of the Classroom"). Many excellent programs about other countries and cultures are available on information-based cable channels like Discovery, the Learning Channel, the History Channel, Arts and Entertainment, and so on. In addition, the news networks, like the Cable News Network, Fox News Channel, and MSNBC News, can provide live coverage of dramatic events happening overseas. Sometimes, as it did during the Gulf War in Iraq, this coverage can involve students in the international scene in a very compelling way. Television also has the advantage of being up-to-the-minute, a quality important to today's "with-it" young audiences.

Television programs and movies can effectively immerse students in a cultural experience for an hour or two. This may be the best way to get students to actually feel a sense of what it might be like to visit another country. It may help them identify with being a member of a different culture. But the potential weakness of the film or television experience is that it is non-interactive. This is one important reason to conduct some class discussion after the show (especially when the program appears to be biased or inaccurate). It also is a good reason to explore other more interactive educational materials that can give pupils more control over the instructional experience.

Culture on Compact Disc

Computerized resources can provide this interactive capability that allows students to more actively examine aspects of other cultures. Multimedia materials related to a society are available to students at the click of a mouse. Video clips, still pictures, and sounds can all enliven a lesson, and they can be programmed to appear when a student wishes to see certain aspects of a culture. Compact discs are available that package material about a given society, such as modern Italy, ancient Egypt, Native American tribes of the Northwest Coast, and so on. These CDs can serve as museum-like archival resources, displaying the "artifacts" of a given society.

These computerized resources have another feature that allows for student discovery: the hyperlinked connections between related types of material. Students can click on these pieces of hypertext to move quickly to material in which they are most interested. This control over the experience can help develop learning skills, and it also tends to be motivating. These digital materials also often allow users to find specific information using computerized searches. Students interested in the games played by different cultures may be able to find that material on a CD by quickly using "game" as a search term. Pupils can *actively* explore various aspects of a given culture.

Sometimes video clips of experts on the CD can provide explanations about what the user is viewing. This approach can provide interesting information and help learners make connections that otherwise would not be apparent. Such prerecorded video "guides" may also suggest potentially fruitful ways to explore material on the disc or even lead a tour around its contents. Such guidance may be important to students who lack the ability to navigate through the materials in a purposeful way. The characters in these video clips also can challenge pupils to think more deeply about the customs of this foreign society, getting them to analyze why this culture has evolved in its own unique way and what some of its strengths and weaknesses might be.

Video materials depicting scenes in other societies have already been discussed as an excellent way of communicating how different other cultures can be. The problem with digitized video on CD-ROMs has been its poor quality. Fortunately, the new compact disc, the Digital Video Disk (DVD), can potentially hold over ten times as much information as a CD-ROM. With improved video compression techniques, television footage on DVD approaches the quality of full-screen, full-motion analog television. These technical breakthroughs allow for the inclusion of much higher quality video and longer television segments within the hyperlinked, interactive materials provided on a DVD compact disc. DVD combines the audiovisual dynamism of television with the interactivity of the computer and will be able to provide the schools with some very powerful media materials about other cultures. Video-based "virtual tours" of interesting buildings, urban districts, or remote regions of other lands will be available on DVD. Imagine exploring a computerized version of the old district of Jerusalem and interacting with digital members of the population. Such simulated cross-cultural experiences could be quite interesting.

Culture on the World Wide Web

The World Wide Web was appropriately named, for it has become a truly global medium. As such, the Web contains enormous amounts of information about other cultures. Much of it has been posted by members of those societies. Some of this material will be in the language of that society, but a great deal of it will be in English. The real challenge is sorting through it to find the most interesting, relevant material. Another challenge, especially for young learners, will be making sense of it and understanding the cultural context within which new information can be integrated.

Thousands of websites provide information about other cultures. Some are sponsored by governments. Some have been developed by the tourist industry. Others are museum sites. In addition to these general resources, there are websites that focus on unique cultural phenomena. For example, there are websites about festivities overseas, like Carnival, Octoberfest, or the summer solstice at Stonehenge. There are websites established by dissident cultural groups, like the Kurds, Palestinians, and Tamils. You can find all sorts of culture-specific practices that are relatively obscure in the United States. For example, a Web search on "Ichibana," the Japanese art of flower arranging, will probably turn up several sites specifically devoted to this practice, as might a search for the sport of Thai kick boxing.

Some of the most exciting websites available for learning about other societies are those dedicated to "virtual travel." Examples of websites that provide these experiences are AdventureOnline (adventureonline.com), Globalearn (www.globalearn.org), the Jason Project (www.jasonproject.org), and Global Schoolnet (www.gsn.org), a huge clearinghouse of online activities that includes access to these online expeditions. This phenomenon takes advantage of the World Wide Web in a very dynamic way. Here is how it works.

A group of adventurers sets out to an interesting part of the world with a general itinerary and the intention of exploring interesting aspects of the society and natural setting that they travel through. They are generally led by someone experienced in overland travel, include a mechanic or technician, for equipment repair, and bring some experts in topics appropriate to the locale. For example, on the Mayaquest expedition to the Yucatan, there was an anthropologist who specialized in Mayan culture and a biologist with expertise in the flora and fauna of the rain forest. This team proceeds to travel around, collecting information and recording experiences as they go. They take photos and shoot videos. They keep journals. They send letters back home. They complete reports about their observations. This data is uplinked back to the United States with a portable satellite dish, and it is placed on the home server for the expedition where it can be accessed on the Web.

While the expedition is going on, thousands of students across the country can follow what is happening online. If their school has paid a fee that allows them to participate in the expedition experience, they can actually send messages to the adventurers, who receive them via satellite. Students can ask particular participants questions about the expedition. During Mayaquest, the biologist would probably answer a question about indigenous monkeys, and the anthropologist would respond to a question about Mayan hieroglyphics. Some questions might be in response to the travelers' journal entries of a more personal nature about encounters with the ancestors of the Maya. While only a fraction of the hundreds of questions could be answered, this process provides a degree of participation in the experience that has successfully engaged thousands of pupils.

For schools that have not subscribed as participants in the adventure, the website can be accessed, but without the connections necessary for interacting with the team. In addition, the collected data from past expeditions are available for free viewing on the Web. Each of the previously named virtual travel sites has already conducted numerous expeditions to various exotic locales around the world, and the final site for each contains megabytes of interesting text, audio, still pictures, and videos. Logging on to one of these sites might be a good way to begin a classroom unit about another culture.

Electronic Exchanges with Other Cultures

In addition to being an enormous source of information about cultures around the world, the Internet provides an excellent means of establishing personal contacts with people overseas (see Chapter 16, "Conceptual Connections: Establishing Online Learning Communities"). Electronic mail provides an efficient, inexpensive way to keep in touch with others at great distances. The modern version of the pen pal is the "keypal." Several large-scale online clear-inghouses on the Web are designed to provide opportunities for students to connect with their peers overseas. The most extensive is probably Kidlink (www.kidlink.org), but others are E-pals (www.epals.com) and Intercultural E-mail Classroom Connections, IECC (www.stolaf.edu/network/iecc).

Most of these online experiences are free. When one first logs on, there are sometimes some preliminaries, which clarify what the site is for and what the spirit of this experience should be like. Kidlink is for those under the age of 16, who type in their agreement with statements about the need for harmonious relationships between the different peoples of the world. Then the user can navigate around the site to explore the possibilities. Attempts to establish meaningful contact may or may not be fruitful at first, but the number of opportunities is so extensive that persistent online participants should eventu-ally be able to contact someone who is interested in responding back.

Kids can connect in a variety of ways. Kidlink includes keypals, a Kidcafe for online chat, listservs, and even a Village Cafe for adults whose children are involved. Keypals can connect by means of a huge database of participants, which users can examine and then proceed to initiate contacts. Many of the par-ticipants speak other languages, so this could be an opportunity to develop lan-guage skills and interact with someone from another culture in a more authen-tic way.

Keypals are one-to-one experiences, but there are also opportunities for groups to communicate. IECC's site includes a huge database of classes that wish to connect, with suggestions for what the basis of the exchange might be. Classes can use the online addresses of classes overseas to exchange experi-ences with another group. Perhaps they will work on a project together or con-verse about what life is like in their respective countries. Here is where cultural awareness can evolve as students in each of the classes discuss their interests, their families, their schools, their holidays, and so on. Sometimes these exchanges involve more than two classes, and some large-scale global online projects can involve tens or even hundreds of classrooms around the world. For example, Kidlink has an international calendar project wherein young people from all over the world collaborate online to create a calendar that includes hol-idays from many different cultures. This multicultural calendar has served as a topic of conversation for Kidlink keypals and participants in Kidlink's online discussion groups.

Another common form of international exchange on the Internet is the asynchronous group discussion on either a listserv or a newsgroup. Kidlink has many of these on a variety of different topics that young people are interested in: for example, the environment, technology, space exploration, and the role of the United Nations. Anyone can sign on to a listserv and then receive the e-mail messages sent to it by other participants. Newsgroups can be accessed upon which other participants have posted messages. Some of these newsgroups address controversial issues, and some are for special-interest groups. The Kidlink electronic discussion groups are designed to air opinions from young people of different cultural backgrounds. As such, students around the world can gain insights into how culture may influence one's perspectives and can work toward intercultural understanding, even with groups very different from their own.

The aforementioned "Kidcafe" at Kidlink is an online chat service open to all. Chat is, of course, a "live" synchronous electronic discussion, unlike e-mail-based "message" exchanges, which are asynchronous. Children can join in the various conversations in the different rooms of the cafe. Speaking of chat services, there are also opportunities to interact with foreigners on more general services, like IRC (Internet Relay Chat) or The Palace. IRC (light.lightlink.com) has a Kidclub for young people to address issues of global significance, like poverty, hunger, pollution, endangered species, and so on.

Beyond Text: Graphic Interfaces and Video-Based Exchanges

The Palace (www.thepalace.com) is an increasingly popular piece of chat-based software that provides a graphic interface. Participants meet in colorful, sometimes surreal settings created with computer graphics. You can see computer graphic representations of other participants, as well as read the text of their conversations. An individual's icon or "avatar" may or may not depict him or her in any realistic way. In fact, these avatars can be fairly outrageous, and their conversations may be equally provocative. So for younger students, visiting the KidsTown palace site would be more appropriate, because it is designed for children and is supervised by adults. Most of the exchanges on these large-scale chat sites will be in English, but other languages are in evidence, and contact with overseas participants is possible.

Finally, Internet-based television exchanges allow students from different countries to actually see and hear one another live. The software used in the vast majority of these compressed video projects is called CU-SeeMe (www.wpine.com). With a camera and microphone hooked to a computer and the CU-SeeMe software, two classes connect across the Internet. The quality of the picture and sound can be weak because of the limited bandwidth of the system (or its smallest "pipe") or the limited processing power of the computers involved. For several years only black and white was possible, but now color is supported. To connect, one site needs to address the other site's computer using its Internet Protocol (IP) number. Up to twelve sites can participate simultaneously, using a "reflector" site established on a server and some more-sophisticated software called Meeting Point.

These exchanges allow students from different cultures to interact in more personalized ways than text-based systems. The audiovisual experience is exciting, much closer to actually going overseas. A large database of schools and projects using CU-SeeMe connections, along with other types of online exchanges, can be found on the huge nonprofit educational clearinghouse called Global Schoolnet (www.gsn.org).

Compression techniques for video are rapidly improving, so that other videoconferencing technologies may provide opportunities for intercultural exchanges. Although somewhat expensive for schools at this point, as the technology advances and the prices drop, it may soon be financially feasible for schools to use more robust means of telecommunications for two-way video exchanges than the Internet. Someday satellite-based videoconferences with very clear signals may be more common between schools in different countries.

Making Connections

These overseas electronic connections, both individual and group based, are widely available for teachers. Through global Web clearinghouses like Kidlink, E-pals, and Global Schoolnet, teachers can find keypals and online discussions with overseas colleagues. Teachers who hope to effectively develop and deliver units about other cultures may learn some techniques from an international listserv about multiculturalism, for example. They may be able to connect online with an academic expert in intercultural education. They may want to become "key colleagues" with other teachers who have an interest in international studies and want to share ideas. These exchanges may include teachers in other countries, who can provide their own unique perspectives and may agree to involve their classes in online exchanges or projects. The opportunities with the Internet in this area are nearly endless.

The new technologies provide innumerable exciting opportunities to transcend the distances between countries and to explore the great variety of cultures around the world. It is up to today's teachers to involve their students in the exciting world of international studies. It is, first, a way to add some fascinating material to the curriculum. It is also a way to help young people address the ever-increasing globalization of American culture. Finally, it also should help pupils communicate more effectively with their peers of backgrounds different from their own.

Hillary Clinton once wrote that "it takes a village," rather than just the nuclear family, to properly socialize and educate young people. That concept should be extended to encompass our ever-shrinking world, so that today's youth can bring a more cosmopolitan, multicultural perspective to everything they do, wherever they happen to live in our global village.

RECOMMENDED READING

Cummins, J., and D. Sayers. 1996. Multicultural education and technology: Promise and pitfalls. *Multicultural Education* 3 (3): 4–10.
Kontos, G., and A. Mizell. 1997. Global village classroom: The changing roles of teachers and students through technology. *TechTrends* 42 (5): 17–22.

Roblyer, M. 1996. Technology and multicultural education: The "uneasy alliance." *Educational Technology* 36 (3): 5–12.

OTHER REFERENCES

Appelbaum, P., and E. Enomoto. 1995. Computer-mediated communication for a multicultural experience. *Educational Technology* 35 (6): 49–58.

Cebrian de la Serna, M. 1995. Television: A one-way bridge between cultures? Objectives for a curriculum on television. *Educational Media International* 32 (2): 69–74.

Cummins, J., and D. Sayers. 1995. *Brave new schools: Challenging cultural illiteracy through global learning networks.* New York: St. Martin's Press.

Cushner, K., A. McClelland, and P. Safford. 1980. The classroom as a global community. In *Human diversity in education: An integrative approach,* 3rd ed. New York: McGraw-Hill.

Fabris, M. 1993. Using multimedia in the multicultural classroom. *Journal of Educational Technology Systems* 21 (2): 163–71.

Garcia, J. 1993. Reconceptualizing multicultural education: Understanding diversity through technology in the information age. *Teacher Educator* 29 (1): 32–42.

Hawkins, J. 1995. Technology for tolerance. *Teaching Tolerance* 4 (1): 16–21.

Heath, I. 1996. The social studies video project: A holistic approach for teaching linguistically and culturally diverse students. *Social Studies* 87 (3): 106–112.

James, J. 1993. Integrating technologies in global studies. *Media and Methods* 29 (3): 22–24.

McLuhan, M. 1964. *Understanding media: The extensions of man.* New York: McGraw-Hill.

SCENARIO

As a new junior high school social studies teacher, you have found that it is very difficult to get teenagers to take other cultures seriously or to generate an interest in the history of non-Western parts of the world. Were you this immature when you were 13? It's hard to believe (but it's also hard to remember!). Anyway, your descriptions of foreign customs have often been met with reactions like "How weird!" or "That's not fair." In fact, your department chair has unfortunately heard some rumblings about this negativity on the part of your students. He has asked for you to come talk with him next week and to bring some sample lesson plans along.

But last week one of your colleagues mentioned how excited some of her students were about having received electronic mail from overseas "keypals" (the modern version of "pen pals"). These letters from teenagers in Asia had told some interesting stories that included culture-specific references. They also asked some interesting questions about life in the United States. Your colleague said she was able to stimulate some meaningful class discussions based on these letters. This direct contact with other teenagers seemed to prompt some degree of interest in life outside the United States.

You realize that technology might help you generate more excitement about your social studies units. The speed and convenience of electronic mail could help expedite the exchange of letters with foreign students. In addition, that global repository of information, the World Wide Web, could serve as an excellent vehicle for exploration of other lands. You sit at your computer after school and conduct a few Web searches using Excite. Although many of the foreign Web pages were in other languages, there seemed to be a great deal in English about countries all over the world. The travel industry's Web pages, in and of themselves, could serve as starting points for students interested in specific places.

You also realize that another major resource for conveying a sense of what life might be like in another country is television (and film). Actual footage from another country can involve students in ways that a textbook will never be able to, by showing the sights and sounds of exotic locales. This includes not only documentary footage, but movies designed primarily to entertain. What better way to interest a class in African colonialism than to show *Out of Africa*? And this kind of material is available for a dollar or two at the local video store.

You decide that your social studies units can be enriched significantly by using technology-based resources. You also realize that it would be smart if you include some media-based activities in the lesson plans that you need to show to your department chair next week. Develop a lesson plan for a unit on a foreign country, which extensively incorporates the use of technology to enrich and enliven the classroom experience.

ISSUES INQUIRY

1. Discuss your own feelings about the importance of teaching about different cultures in the classroom. Is it inevitable that people will egocentrically value their own ethnic group or race above all others, so that teaching "multicultural" values can only accomplish so much? How critical is it that young people develop an appreciation of human diversity?

2. Discuss how film and television segments can provide unique contributions to a unit about another country or a different cultural group. What properties of these media make them advantageous ways to introduce units about faraway places or different subcultures? What kinds of discussion questions should a teacher ask at the conclusion of the program to get pupils thinking about what they have just seen?

3. Discuss how films and television programs have distorted the American public's perceptions of this country's minority groups. Give examples of how certain groups have been stereotyped and identify instances of these portrayals in specific programs, if you can.

4. With its huge repository of material about other countries, the World Wide Web has the potential to stimulate student interest in multicultural issues. What interesting assignments might be prompted by pupil visits to websites about other cultures? Can

you think of any creative activities that might follow up the exploration of foreign websites?

5. The Internet has opened up a whole new world of opportunities for interesting cross-cultural communications. Explore some of these online opportunities and discuss which computer-mediated approaches you feel might be most appropriate to use in a classroom: keypals, listservs, newsgroups, chat, The Palace, CU-SeeMe, and so on. What are some of the advantages and disadvantages of each system?

6. How might you prepare students in your class to initiate communications with other students from overseas? What kinds of questions might they ask these foreign students? How might they most effectively describe their own culture to foreigners? How can they be sensitized to cultural differences that may become apparent during the exchange?

CHAPTER 11

Coming to Conclusions About Inclusion

WHAT ROLE FOR ASSISTIVE TECHNOLOGIES?

INTRODUCTION

It can be a challenging task for an educator to work with a student who has disabilities. But it can be an even more challenging assignment to work with a special needs student while simultaneously teaching a full class of other children. Today, with the policies of "inclusion" established by a series of federal laws, many teachers have students with disabilities in their classes. Since the education of these students was often exclusionary and inadequate in the past, there is now an effort to provide more for those with disabilities.

How can the well-intentioned policy of inclusion be effectively implemented, and is it realistic? Is it fair to expect so much of the classroom teacher? Is it fair to the rest of the class, if the teacher must spend a great deal of time working with a special needs student? Is it a good system for the student with a disability, more helpful than being in a special class? These issues have been widely debated since "mainstreaming" began about twenty-five years ago.

Some Background About Educating Students with Disabilities

Until the latter part of the twentieth century, students with disabilities were rarely dealt with in the schools. Doctors and school administrators encouraged parents to send these children to institutions. Some schools did make provisions for "handicapped" or "retarded" students, as they were called in those days. A school district with sufficient resources might have special classes for these students. But it was not until 1975, with the passing of the federal Education of All Handicapped Children Act, that schools were required by law to make provisions for special students.

This landmark statute mandated that every student, regardless of the type of disability, be given equal educational opportunities. In some cases, special education classes were established, with teachers trained in this specialization. Students with less severe disabilities might be "mainstreamed" into regular classes for part of the day or sometimes for the entire day. Special education programs at universities grew, producing certified professionals to assist these students in obtaining an education and living productive lives.

The 1975 law required that each special needs student have an Individualized Education Program (IEP) developed by a team of professionals. An IEP team includes the classroom teacher, a special education teacher, a school administrator, the parents, and relevant therapists, including an assistive technologies specialist, if needed. This plan clarifies how the student will be assisted in obtaining a "free and appropriate education (FAPE)." It sets reasonable objectives, specific to the nature of the disability. It specifies the need for certain types of assistive devices. It indicates whether such devices are also needed at home. It clarifies who might be assigned to give this student special assistance. Once written, the IEP serves as a kind of "contract" between the student's family and the educational professionals involved. Breaches of this contract may be addressed with school administrators and might eventually wind up in court, if satisfactory arrangements cannot be worked out for all parties concerned.

The Education of All Handicapped Children Act also included provisions that stressed how achieving FAPE for special needs students would mean placing them in regular classes with their nondisabled peers. The rationale behind so-called mainstreaming was to give disabled students an educational experience that was, as much as possible, just like everyone else's their age. There would be opportunities in regular classes that special needs students could benefit from. Their self-concepts might be improved if they felt more like everyone else. Attitudes about the disabled might not be as negative or condescending if the two groups interacted more with each other. There seemed to be a number of good reasons for inclusion.

Although mainstreaming was somewhat controversial, the movement to provide meaningful assistance to special students in schools grew throughout the eighties. In 1990, the U.S. Congress passed the Individuals with Disabilities in Education Act (IDEA), which strengthened the legal position of children with disabilities, and their families, in their efforts to obtain a good education. This bill mandated that schools provide appropriate assistive devices for students with disabilities regardless of the cost, as determined by the individual's IEP.

The IDEA strengthened the concept of "least restrictive environment (LRE)," which stressed the need for students with disabilities to be with their nondisabled peers in school. The law also encouraged the practice of inclusion, which was a continuation and expansion of the mainstreaming approach. Through the eighties, mainstreaming often had been carried out in superficial ways. Students with disabilities were sometimes only mainstreamed into special classes, like art, music, and physical education, but not into core curricular classes like mathematics, science, English, and social studies. The term "inclusion" implied that students with disabilities should be placed into regular classrooms for all subject areas.

But inclusion met with opposition from many classroom teachers, who did not feel that they were prepared to deal with students whose problems were relatively severe. This seemed an additional burden added to an already stressful job. Another concern of teachers was the amount of time that might be diverted from teaching the whole class. Could they address the needs of a disabled student and simultaneously supervise the activities of twenty or thirty other young learners? Inclusion was considered a controversial plan by many educators. These issues are still being debated today.

Physical Disabilities Encountered in the Classroom

Students can bring a wide variety of disabilities into the school setting. Some are genetic, some are a result of natural causes, and some have unknown causes. Of the genetic disabilities, many are present at birth, but some appear later in life. The most commonly acquired causes of disability are due to injury or disease. Classification systems differ, but three basic types of disabilities are motor, sensory, and cognitive. Motor impairments limit movement in any part of the body and generally involve a malfunctioning of motor nerves or muscles. The primary sensory disabilities are visual and hearing impairments. Cognitive disabilities affect the ability to think and process information. All types of disabilities can range from mild to severe in their impact.

Motor disorders impair the movement of part of an individual's body. The two principal causes are disease and injury. They can be caused by dysfunctions of the nervous, muscular, skeletal, or endocrine systems. Paralysis may be localized or more general. The most debilitating situations can involve paraplegia, with paralysis of limbs or even quadriplegia affecting all four limbs.

Nerve-related diseases, such as multiple sclerosis or polio, can lead to progressive general paralysis. The most common neurological disorder is cerebral palsy, wherein a brain lesion or abnormality debilitates motor functioning. Another common nervous disorder is spina bifida, wherein birth defects in the vertebrae affect the spinal cord, causing paralysis in the lower part of the body. Epilepsy is another nerve-related disorder whose convulsions can render an individual physically incapable of functioning for periods of time.

The most common muscular disorder is muscular dystrophy, wherein the muscles gradually degenerate, leading to paralysis and sometimes death. Osteogenesis imperfecta is a rare skeletal disease marked by extremely brittle bones. With cystic fibrosis, the endocrine system secretes a thick mucus that can clog the lungs and block the action of the digestive system. Growth is inhibited, and life expectancy is only about thirty years.

Injuries are another major cause of physical disabilities. Severe damage to limbs or other parts of the body can permanently paralyze them. Head injuries are a common cause of disabilities, both motor and cognitive. They can result in either temporary or permanent loss of brain function, and the consequences can be either mild or severe. Often the part of the body or cognitive function affected depends on the specific area of the brain that was injured, since brain function is specialized by region. Some injuries would lead to motor dysfunction or paralysis. An injury to the occipital lobe might cause blindness, since this is the area where sight is processed. Despite brain specialization, neurologists have documented cases of other sectors taking on some of the functions of an injured region and, over time, restoring some functionality, especially at younger ages.

Sensory Impairment: Blindness and Deafness

Sensory disabilities affect the individual's ability to perceive the world around them through one or more of their sensory channels. There are some very unusual instances of individuals with brain disorders that prevent them from kinesthetically feeling certain sensations. For example, there are rare cases in which pain cannot be felt, so that the person has to be careful not to inadvertently hurt themselves. But most sensory disabilities involve the primary sense organs, the eyes or the ears.

Blindness can be total, but many "legally blind" people can see shapes or very small "tunnels" of the world. Legal blindness usually is defined as having worse than 20/200 eyesight *after* attempts at correction. 20/200 means that the individual can see at 20 feet what someone with normal vision can see at 200 feet, ten times the distance. Another issue in visual impairment is the width of the field of vision. A normal field of vision is 180 degrees. Some visually impaired individuals can only see in a small range, having a kind of "tunnel" vision. Others cannot see straight ahead and have clearer peripheral vision. A visual field smaller than 20 degrees, whether it is central or peripheral, is considered legal blindness.

Eye diseases, like cataracts, glaucoma, retinitis pigmentosa, or macular degeneration, can lead to serious visual impairment. A cataract is cloudiness of the lens within the eye, which can significantly block light and blur vision. Fortunately, new surgical techniques can remove the clouded lens and replace it with an artificial one. Glaucoma is excess pressure on the eyeball, usually due to a disturbance of the fluid that fills the eye. It can gradually destroy the optic nerve and cause severe visual impairment. Retinitis pigmentosa is an inherited disease wherein the retina gradually degenerates, resulting in loss of both night and peripheral vision. Macular degeneration involves the gradual deterioration of the central area of the retina. Its effect is the opposite of retinitis pigmentosa, in that the central vision is lost, while the peripheral is retained. Another problem with retinas is that they can detach from the back of the eye. Fortunately, in many cases, surgeons can often reattach a loose retina.

Deafness is rarely total, and many who are considered deaf can hear some sounds and feel the vibrations of loud sounds. Few teachers will have students in their classes with severe hearing loss. Ear infections are one of the most common causes of hearing loss, especially in infants and students in the primary grades. Meningitis, encephalitis, and other infections with high fevers can cause damage to the auditory nerve. Contraction of rubella (German measles) by pregnant women can cause deafness in newborns, as can a premature birth or other pregnancy complications. Some deafness appears to be inherited, since about 30 percent of deaf children have some deaf relatives. Teachers should be aware that chronic ear infections and hearing loss can significantly impact children's early learning, especially their language development. Periodic hearing tests for children are especially important for this reason.

Cognitive Disabilities Faced by Young Learners

Individuals may face a wide variety of cognitive disabilities, including, in descending order of severity, mental retardation, learning disabilities, and communication disorders. Mental retardation is generally characterized by lower general mental functioning and is measured by performance on the standardized Intelligence Quotient Test. An average IQ Test score is 100, and an IQ below 70 is generally considered mentally retarded. Degrees of retardation are also usually measured by IQ, with 55–70 being considered "mild" and 25–50 described as "moderate" to "severe". An IQ below 25 is labeled as "profound" retardation.

What causes mental retardation? Some cases are associated with genetic syndromes, like Down's and fragile X, wherein there is some inherited chromosomal damage. Other cases are associated with prenatal metabolic malfunctions such as phenylketonuria and Tay-Sachs disease. Sometimes the brain does not form properly, as with anencephaly or hydrocephalus. Other prenatal causes of retardation can be illness during pregnancy, fetal alcohol syndrome, and drug addiction. Retardation also can result from serious brain damage sustained in an injury.

Learning disabilities are less severe than mental retardation, but nevertheless still generally involve some cerebral dysfunction. These problems can take many forms, and there is no one clear definition of "learning disabled." Some of the difficulties are with memory, either short term or long term. Others are problems with processing information. Some cognitive disabilities relate to use of language, like difficulty reading (dyslexia) or writing.

Attention deficit disorder (ADD) and hyperactivity are two conditions often associated with learning disabled students. Attention deficit refers to the inability to concentrate on a task for an extended time. Students with attention deficit syndrome rarely complete their assignments. Instead, they are easily distracted and tend to get up and move about the room, rather than remaining focused and in their seats. This hyperactivity, which generally accompanies ADD, can be quite disruptive to a classroom.

Communications disorders interfere with individuals' ability to express themselves. Mild disorders might involve difficulties articulating clearly, conditions like lisps and stuttering. Serious disorders involve difficulties like aphasia, a term used to describe difficulties in decoding language. Aphasic individuals may use picture-based communications systems because of their inability to process language, which seems to be too abstract for them. Aphasia is sometimes a result of head injuries.

These disorders often impact one another, leading to multiple disabilities. Nervous system trauma can cause both motor impairment and cognitive dysfunction. Many visually and hearing impaired individuals have learning disabilities. A number of diseases and conditions can result in concurrent motor, sensory, and cognitive impairments. Communications disorders often accompany other disabilities.

The term "syndrome" is used to describe a typical set of characteristics that accompany a given disorder. With syndromes like Down's, children will face deficiencies in both their physical and mental development. With Usher's syndrome, deafness is accompanied by visual impairment due to retinitis pigmentosa. Determining the variety of different problems an individual must cope with is one of the challenges that teachers and IEP teams face. Determining the severity of each disability is another challenge. And figuring out what devices might best assist the person in overcoming the disorder may be the most challenging task of all.

Assistive Devices for the Physically Impaired

Assistive devices can help people with disabilities cope with various aspects of their lives. Some enable them to move around more effectively. Others help them use their hands more fully. Some devices improve vision or hearing. A special class of assistive device enables those with disabilities to learn more effectively.

What kinds of devices can help individuals with different types of disorders use technology? For those with motor impairments, several methods can be used to activate a computer and input information. Those using wheelchairs usually find it difficult to get close enough to the machine, because wheelchairs can take up space that separates the individual from the computer. Also, tables may be the wrong height for the wheelchair. So techniques for positioning and propping may be necessary. Pillows may help, or the person may need a special brace. Wheelchairs that elevate and tilt can also help position the person to work with a computer. Special tables have been designed to allow for better accessibility.

If individuals have difficulty using their arms or hands, then accessing a computer in the usual way, with a keyboard and mouse-driven cursor, may not be possible. Special "switching" devices are available, so that physically impaired people can input data into a computer. The person might press a lever or move a joystick. Another method might be to use a "head switch," wherein a pointer strapped to the face is used to press keys. Different switches and sticks have been designed to be activated by different parts of the body, including the mouth, eyes, or even the tongue. Individuals can now interact with a computer by means of eye blinks, directed laser beams, or even puffs of breath. Touch screen input may be helpful to some students, allowing them to select icons onscreen more easily than using a mouse, roller ball, or scratchpad. Light pens can also be used to select onscreen items.

If the person's motor disability prevents them from accurately selecting and pressing specific keys, then other devices may help. Special pads or braces may be needed to prop up the user's arms, so the fingers are positioned to effectively strike the keys. Enlarged keys on oversized keyboards can help. A key guard can be placed over the keyboard, with holes in it to help direct the fingers right onto the keys, so they strike them accurately. Extrasensitive keys may remove some of the strain of keyboarding. Remote control keyboards and mouse-type devices are available for those whose access to the machine is limited. Touch tablets with easily activated membrane surfaces can be used as alternatives to the standard keyboard and/or the mouse.

Assistive software also can help eliminate some of the struggling associated with using a keyboard. Software can be programmed to provide "macros," which allow for commands that normally require multiple keys, such as control or option key commands, to be selected with a single key. "Word prediction" software can attempt to complete a word based on the first few letters. Like a spell checker, it rapidly searches its huge database of words to select those that begin in the same way. When it guesses correctly, it saves some typing. Certain software programs will present letters onscreen, so that the user can input lettering by scrolling through the alphabet and then activating a switch when the desired letter appears. Some of these systems are automatic, with the letters scrolling by onscreen without any need for user control until the time comes to select a given letter.

An alternative approach is to bypass keyboarding altogether with voice-activated systems. These systems have improved considerably in the past few years. It has become common to be asked by an automated phone system to say a given menu choice, instead of pressing a telephone key. Some of the better voice recognition programs are now able to take reasonably accurate dictation, although the process can still be slow and letter-by-letter correction of difficult-to-decipher words is still necessary at times. Many systems also take some time to be "trained" to recognize an individual's pronunciation, and they may not work well with another person's voice. The prices for such programs have dropped in the past few years. Inexpensive versions can be purchased for as little as one or two hundred dollars. This may still be expensive for low-income individuals, but these programs used to cost much more and financial assistance is sometimes available through a variety of organizations. In fact, as computers become more powerful and sophisticated, voice recognition may ultimately replace typing as the primary form of inputting information. This trend will certainly help persons with physical disabilities work with technology.

Overcoming Sensory Impairments with Technology

Some special devices also are available for those with sensory disabilities. For the visually impaired, one can use very large letter sizes, like 36 or 48 point, generally available with most fonts. Special software can magnify text even more for those with severe visual impairments. Large colorful onscreen icons may help some who have trouble reading text. But icon-driven systems can be problematic for those with visual impairments.

Ironically, in many ways the older computer operating systems based on keyboard commands could be easier for blind persons to work with, if users memorized the keys for basic commands, knew the location of items on the keyboard, and kept their hands properly positioned on the home keys. The newer icon-driven approach to running software can be difficult for them to operate, since reading the icons off the screen may be challenging for them. More-sophisticated user interfaces are not necessarily improvements for everyone!

Some visually impaired individuals can read Braille, the internationally standardized kinesthetic reading system of raised dots that represent the letters of the alphabet. There is software that can convert electronic text to Braille and drive a Braille printer to produce hard copy that can be read by a visually impaired individual. This efficient way to produce Braille documents will help provide more written materials for the blind.

But if a written copy is not necessary, another approach for the visually impaired might be to bypass vision altogether and use sound. There are two types of computerized speech, synthesized and digitized. With synthesized speech, the computer is manufacturing words out of "noises" that represent the basic speech sounds (phonemes). Digitized speech, on the other hand, is a recording of the actual voice, only saved in digital form rather than in analog form as it would be on an audiotape or videotape.

Synthesized speech will never be as accurate as digitized speech. It usually sounds rather robotic, because it is difficult to program with a natural sounding cadence and proper inflections. Another significant challenge is to adjust to the many nonphonetic pronunciations in the English language. But there is one important advantage to using synthesized speech rather than digitized speech. A computer can read electronic text aloud for the user with synthesized speech software, phonetically sounding out the words as it goes. This can be an excellent accommodation for those with visual impairments. They can hear a reading of any text that is inputted into a computer, including any text they themselves enter.

Digitized speech can also be helpful for the visually impaired. While audio files can take up much more memory space than electronic text, with today's huge hard drives and fast processors, computers can record and play back a great deal of digitized sound. Directions can be provided within programs in audio form. Information can be provided in audio file formats rather than text file formats. One major advantage of digital speech is the ease with which it can be modified. In the future, the visually impaired probably will use digital and synthesized speech far more often rather than relying on text that they must struggle to read.

Students with hearing loss, on the other hand, will rely more on printed text material to communicate. For a while, much of this text will still be inputted by keyboard. Today, telecommunications techniques allow the deaf to communicate much more efficiently than in the past, with teletypewriter (TTY) devices that allow text to be sent across telephone lines. Compact units that include keyboards and a place to insert the phone have been developed. Each state now has a relay system for TTY users that relies on operators to help type text for the deaf and to talk with hearing people they want to phone, so that the hearing impaired can contact anyone by phone, using their TTYs. Recent developments include devices to be used with cellular telephones and pagers.

With e-mail and fax, electronic communications to and from the hearing impaired can be sent as text, thereby avoiding the aural issue altogether. Keyboard-based electronic "chat" systems allow deaf people to communicate live with others. E-mail provides written exchanges in asynchronous form. On listservs, deaf people can exchange ideas and socialize. Some of these listservs or newsgroups are expressly for deaf people.

As computers improve, they will be better able to convert from voice to text or even into sign language, using video clips. The aforementioned voice recognition systems can convert spoken comments to onscreen text, which the deaf can then read. Synthesized speech programs will provide voice from text. As computerized devices become increasingly miniaturized, hard-of-hearing people will be able to carry special palm-sized voice-to-text (and text-to-voice) converters around with them to help them communicate. These units will have preprogrammed phrases and common words that can be called up with a single key. They will eventually be far more automatic and efficient than using pencil and notepad.

Deaf people will continue to benefit from ongoing improvements in audio amplification, transmission, and miniaturization. Hearing aids are becoming smaller and more powerful. Chip-controlled units can respond more effectively to differences in volume and can set specific frequency ranges to amplify, depending on the type of hearing loss. Wireless microphones that pick up sound and transmit their electronic signal to a playback device are becoming more durable, powerful, and lightweight. They can be used by the hearing impaired in group situations, to hear a speaker at a distance.

Television captioning also has become more widespread, with the legal mandating in 1993 of closed-caption decoding capability on all new television sets. All public broadcasting programming and many commercial broadcasts embed closed captioning in their transmissions, allowing the deaf to better appreciate the programming. Many commercial videos for rent are also closed captioned. As one of our society's most important sources of information, education, and entertainment, the television set is now more accessible to the hearing impaired.

Software and the Learning Disabled

Technology can help those with learning disabilities in a variety of ways. First, most children enjoy working with computers, so just the opportunity to work on the machine can be motivating. Computer work also can be private, so students who are struggling are not exposed to the scrutiny of their peers, which might be embarrassing. The computer is tireless and will continue patiently working with a student for a long time (even one who repeatedly makes the same mistakes!).

The computer can be motivating, providing lively graphics, sounds, and videos to involve students who may be difficult to engage because of their learning difficulties and their general frustration with schoolwork. These multimedia materials also can be used effectively to communicate material in concrete ways, providing relevant pictorial material or giving demonstrations with video. Clear visual examples can be very important for the learning disabled, especially if they have difficulty processing text or conceptualizing abstract ideas.

Other computer capabilities can be used to assist instructionally. For example, computers can provide digitized speech to help weak readers comprehend text material. Or synthesized speech can provide feedback for students about their writing efforts. Spell checkers can be effective instructional tools for students with learning disabilities. Identifying spelling mistakes and suggesting possible spellings can be very helpful to students whose spelling is weak.

Repeated exposure to the correct spellings may also help students learn them. Grammar checkers may also provide useful guidance.

Software designed for drill-and-practice can be very helpful for children with learning disabilities, for they generally need more exposure to the material than the average student. Repeatedly practicing a process can help them master it. Good drill programs will include clear feedback and appropriate reinforcement. By providing compliments and lively graphics or sounds when students get the right answer, the program can motivate and help pupils build confidence.

Software that remediates may be even better. It can provide hints for the correct answer or, better yet, explanations when the student has made a mistake. Programs can also branch, taking students either back to easier material or ahead to more challenging problems, depending on their performance. For those with learning disabilities, it may be necessary to backtrack for more practice or review. In the future, artificial intelligence techniques will be used in software, so that the program may be better able to adjust to individual learners and may "learn" by working with them how best to present material for them.

The novelty of working with a computer may help motivate the student with a learning disability. Also, computers are capable of providing some interesting new approaches to learning that may help involve the user. Simulations and virtual reality programming can place pupils in an environment they can explore. Not only are these programs very engaging, but learning through a simulated experience can be an effective approach for a student who is struggling. Many of the best computer programs are games, which also can be quite motivating. Slower students might find it hard to compete with their peers. But with many computer games, the competition is more with one's *own* previous performances. The objective is to improve one's score over the last time. Many students with learning disabilities like video games, and playing educationally-based computer games can be highly motivating.

At the moment, few software titles are expressly targeted for the learning disabled. But many programs operate at various levels of difficulty. Sometimes the "beginner" segments can be used effectively by students with learning disabilities. Slower students may enjoy working with software designed for younger children, but its approaches may seem too babyish, and if their peers see them using it, they may be embarrassed. Teachers may need to do some legwork in identifying and obtaining appropriate software titles for their pupils with learning disabilities, but the effort can be well worth it.

Developing the Individualized Education Program

How can those with disabilities be most effectively empowered to learn? As already mentioned, the process established by law is to bring together a team of specialists to develop an Individualized Education Program (IEP). Including the appropriate parties is important, and at a minimum the meetings should include the classroom teacher, a special education teacher, a school administrator, and the parents. If assistive technology is a consideration, a specialist who knows what devices are appropriate and available should be brought in.

The first stage in the IEP is an assessment, to determine the nature of the pupil's disabilities and to analyze how they might be addressed. Tests might need to be conducted as part of this process. Examination of school records may be helpful. It can be important to interview the student, parents, and previous teachers. The information gathered in this assessment is then used to develop the actual plan.

The elements of the IEP were clearly outlined by IDEA in 1990. First, there must be a statement of the child's ability levels and past academic performance. Goals must be established for the student to achieve by the end of the school year. Specific intermediate objectives must be listed, which will facilitate the attainment of the aforementioned general goals. Specific educational services that will be important in allowing the student to progress must be identified. These could include the use of technology and assistive devices, as well as any plans to provide special tutoring or training. A timetable should be developed for the implementation of the plan. If the child is to be included in regular classes, the plan for how this can best be accomplished should be described. Whatever the educational placement, a justification for it must be articulated. The individuals involved in the IEP's implementation must be listed and their roles clearly defined. Finally, an evaluation plan must be developed to monitor the student's progress.

A student's IEP must be reviewed and possibly revised at least once each year. A parent must consent to the plan and be given a copy of it. It serves as a kind of contract with which to proceed, engaging all involved parties to work together with a common overall strategy for helping the child. It encourages the collection of data to best inform the decisions that are made. The IEP also can provide a degree of accountability, in that goals and objectives should be clearly stated and evaluation planned to assess whether they are met.

In terms of recommending how technology might be used to help the child, the IEP process is where specific types of devices may be stipulated. Determinations may be made regarding exactly which type of device is needed or how it might need to be customized for the individual child's circumstances. Estimates may be established as to what devices might cost. Whether the student needs this equipment at home, as well as at school, should be decided. Once all parties have agreed to the terms of the IEP, the school must obtain the recommended assistive technology. If the school does not comply, the parents can take legal action.

Approaches to Selecting Devices and Applications

Since there are a very large number of different devices on the market, the first challenge is to define precisely what type of device would be best for the disabled student. This recommendation should be clearly stated in the IEP and will include physical and cognitive specifications for such a device, according to the student's needs and learning profile. The next step is to explore all the different possible models and brands that might be appropriate. While price is a consideration, the school district is bound by the terms of the IEP to provide funds to cover the purchase of this equipment. Once a device has been purchased, it may be necessary to adapt it to the student's specific needs. A special technician may be needed, if this is the case. Then the student may need to be trained to use the device. For this a specialist may be brought in, or the company may provide some training in the use of its equipment. Some training for the teacher or the parents in the use of the device may also be important, especially since they will probably be the ones who will need to help the student use it on an ongoing basis.

Educators can look for various types of assistive devices or special software in a number of places. Books published in the special education field provide lists of equipment and vendors, and catalogs also are available. The World Wide Web has many sites for the disabled with extensive listings, links to other sites, and scores of products represented. Some conventions for special education professionals include exhibits where this equipment is available for close examination and hands-on experimentation.

There are several problematic aspects of purchasing assistive devices. One is that the technology changes rapidly, so it is difficult to keep up with the latest systems and their capabilities. Nobody wants to purchase antiquated equipment, but that may happen if buyers fail to do their research. Another problem is cost. Many of these systems are very expensive. These costs can deprive schools of other purchases that they might have wanted to make. Another issue is the question of whether the device or software will work as promised. Many of these systems are new and in the experimental stages of their development, so not all of the potential "bugs" have been worked out. Maintenance for very specialized systems also can be a problem, for parts can be difficult to obtain and few technicians may be available with the expertise to complete the repair.

Finally, there is no guarantee that the student will take advantage of the technology. Sometimes students find the devices uncomfortable or user-unfriendly. Under some circumstances, the device proves unsuccessful in assisting the student because it was not the most appropriate selection to begin with. In other cases, poorly motivated users fail to maximize the potential of an assistive device.

Despite the many challenges associated with the selection process, assistive technology can make a huge difference for certain individuals. When the process is competently carried out and the student responds well to it, then the educators involved have every right to feel proud of their efforts. This is truly technology that makes a difference.

RECOMMENDED READING

Barry, J., and B. Wise. 1996. Fueling inclusion through technology. *School Administrator* 53 (4): 24–27.

Brett, A. 1997. Assistive and adaptive technology—Supporting competence and independence in young children with disabilities. *Dimensions of Early Childhood* 25 (3): 14–15, 18–20.

Howell, R. 1996. Technological aids for inclusive classrooms. *Theory into Practice* 35 (1): 58–65.

OTHER REFERENCES

Chambers, A. 1997. *Has technology been considered? A guide for IEP teams.* Reston, VA: Council of Administrators of Special Education and Technology and Media Division of the Council for Exceptional Children.

Cook, A., and S. Hussey. 1995. *Assistive technologies: Principles and practice.* St. Louis, MO: Mosby.

Flippo, K., K. Inge, and M. Barcus, eds. 1995. *Assistive technology: A resource for school, work, and community.* Baltimore, MD: Paul Brookes.

Gray, D., L. Quatrano, and M. Liberman, eds. 1998. *Designing and using assistive technology: The human perspective.* Baltimore, MD: Paul Brookes.

Heward, W. 1996. *Exceptional children: An introduction to special education.* Columbus, OH: Merrill.

Kautzman, A. 1998. Virtuous, virtual access: Making Web pages accessible to people with disabilities. *Searcher* 6 (6): 42–49.

Margolis, L., and S. Goodman. 1999. Assistive technology services for students: What are these? Online: www.ucpa.org/html/innovative/atfsc_index.html.

National School Boards Association. 1996. *Technology for students with disabilities: A decision maker's resource guide.* Alexandria, VA, ERIC, ED 411659.

Newroe, K. 1997. *Telecommunication technologies to deliver assistive technology services.* Washington, DC: Association for the Advancement of Rehabilitation Technology, ERIC, ED 342180.

Schulz-Hamsa, I. 1998, March. Inclusion and technology: A marriage of convenience for educational leaders. *Proceedings of the Society for Information Technology & Teacher Education International Conference.* Washington, DC, ERIC, ED 421123.

Winter, S. 1997. SMART planning for inclusion. *Childhood Education* 73 (4): 212–218.

SCENARIO

You are in your second year of teaching fifth grade in a suburban school district. You are finally feeling confident about your entry into the profession. The class is responding well to assignments, and some of the discipline problems you faced in your first year have eased. You still hope to individualize your instruction more effectively, so that you can help all of your students reach their potential.

You are approached by your principal, Mrs. Marx, one morning about what she describes as a "special assignment." A fifth grader with disabilities, named Louise, has moved into the district, and you will be asked to take this student into your class.

This girl is in a wheelchair as a result of an auto accident that her family was in two years ago. Neither of her legs can support her weight, and one of her arms has lost fine motor control. She cannot type or write with that hand. In that accident, she also sustained some brain damage, so that she also has a learning disability. She needs clear instructions, sometimes repeated several times, and she has some memory difficulties. Her vision also was impaired significantly by these injuries. Although she is not legally blind, Louise cannot read the standard print size in most books.

The principal is aware of your interest in individualizing instruction, and she feels that the inclusion of this student in your class is the best course of action. She knows that this will be a challenge, but it is one that she hopes you will be willing to take on. What can you say?

Two days later, when you first meet Louise, you are struck by the sad look in her brown eyes. You experience a sudden, strong sense of sorrow about what has happened to her. You sincerely hope that you can help her in some way. You notice almost immediately that she is drawn to the two computers in the back of your room. She stares back in that direction and asks twice, in a soft voice, about software titles that sound like they are for younger children.

You decide that probably she will want to work with a computer, and that this might be a good way to have her work on her skills. Your first challenge is giving her full access to one of the machines. Within her wheelchair, Louise cannot really reach the keyboard or see the screen very clearly. But another problem is that you have very little software that would be at her cognitive level, since she is approximately two years behind in her reading skills and more than three years behind in mathematics.

Unfortunately, you do not know very much about specialized "assistive" hardware or software. You also are worried about how time-consuming and complicated any effort to investigate this area might be. You call the district technology coordinator, and he is not especially helpful. He says he is overwhelmed right now in his efforts to network the high school's computer laboratories. A special education specialist comes to the school once a week to provide advice, but she does not seem to have much sophistication with technology.

You speak with Mrs. Marx, and she agrees that it is important for Louise to have computer access. She says funding is available at the district level for technology that could be used for Louise's assistive devices and maybe also for some software. Unfortunately, you suspect that an expensive assistive technology solution for her might preclude your obtaining the new computer you requested for your classroom next year. The district's budget was determined prior to Louise's move into the district. Assistive devices can be expensive, and the budget is tight.

You are unsure where to begin in helping Louise. How can you determine what special devices she needs and what specialized software might help her work with a computer? How can she be trained with this equipment? Finally, how can you best help her improve her basic language skills? You read her student file, which has some confusing medical terminology in it. There is a set of reports from doctors and psychologists that identify her problems. But you do not fully understand some of this language, and these specialists seem to offer few recommendations that relate to a classroom setting. You feel overwhelmed.

In addition, you are concerned about spending too much of your time and energy working with Louise, since you cannot neglect the other twenty-three students in your classroom. How much attention should you devote just to Louise, when the rest of the class also needs your assistance? What conclusions do you come to regarding the amount of time classroom teachers should spend addressing the needs of a special student, when this takes time away from working with the rest of the class? You wonder if laws requiring the inclusion of students with disabilities in regular classrooms are a good idea.

You are required to help develop an Individualized Education Program (IEP) for Louise that outlines what will be done to help her succeed in school and that specifically addresses her disabilities. Describe the process associated with creating this IEP and what its recommendations might be regarding how Louise might be assisted by technology. What specific measures might be taken to help her work with computers? Then discuss how you feel about the challenges posed by having a disabled child in your classroom, concluding with an opinion about the advisability of inclusion as a strategy.

ISSUES INQUIRY

1. Identify the issues surrounding the appropriateness of including a given student with disabilities in a particular classroom. Some of these concerns will relate to the disabled individual. Other considerations will involve the nature of the classroom situation into which this student will be placed.

2. Describe some specific circumstances under which you would *not* recommend that a student be included in a regular classroom. Then describe the kinds of situations wherein inclusion might work out well.

3. What are the potential primary benefits of inclusion for the disabled student? What, on the other hand, are the potentially disadvantageous by-products of inclusion for the person with a disability?

4. What are the potential primary benefits of including a disabled student in a classroom for the rest of the students in that class? What, on the other hand, are the potential disadvantages of inclusion for the classmates of a person with a disability?

5. Should the regulations legislating inclusion be extended, left just as they are, be more restricted to certain cases, or revoked altogether? Defend your opinion with some solid reasons.

CHAPTER 12

Fair Use

COPYRIGHT OR COPYWRONG?

INTRODUCTION

The copyright conundrum is one of the more controversial, difficult issues surrounding the educational use of media materials, because it involves two legitimate sets of rights that come into direct conflict. On the one hand, there is the right of someone who creates a product to profit from it. On the other hand, there is the right and the responsibility that an educator has to use appropriate materials for teaching purposes. The fact that most schools constantly face budget shortages makes this a very real problem for many teachers, since the school may not be able to afford all the materials that teachers want to use with their lessons.

How does copyright work? Any material published before copyright was officially established as federal law in 1910 is unprotected by copyright. The legal term generally used to describe such material, which anyone can use without restrictions, is that it is in the "public domain." Some material, like government documents and media productions, is automatically considered within the public domain. Government materials were produced using public funds, so the public has the right to them. Copies of the Copyright Law of 1976, for example, would be available from the Library of Congress and could be copied for use in a class. Likewise, NASA video footage from space missions is copyright free.

But most material published since 1910 has been copyrighted. Copyright provides legal protection to owners for the length of their lives plus another fifty years. This protection covers creative productions in a variety of different formats: printed materials, music, television, and computer software. It extends to any original material, whether it is classified as fiction or nonfiction. It gives the person or institution that owns it the right to determine whether others can use the material or not. It also allows the copyright holder to determine levels of compensation for the work from those who wish to use it. One reason for the half-century extension of copyright past the author's death is to ensure appropriate guardianship of the work, but it is also designed to provide compensation for the work to his or her heirs.

However, a high percentage of the copyrights held do not belong to those who created the materials, but to the companies that offered them contracts for its distribution and sale: book publishers, motion picture companies, television networks, and so on. This book belongs to McGraw-Hill, not to the authors. Copyright exists, to some degree, to protect the work's originators against inappropriate use of their material. But it exists mainly to protect the commercial interests of corporations. The creators receive royalties, a percentage of the overall profits. With texts like this one, the writers will typically split 10 or 15 percent of wholesale profits.

Following the copyright statutes is often a straightforward matter. Few would argue that the school should not pay for the new book *Insects: Friends or Foes?*, which will be placed in the school library and made available for students to use for many years. To Xerox the entire book instead would constitute a clear infringement of the publisher's copyright protection.

But should the school be expected to buy this book when a teacher wants simply to show four photos of ants from it during one of her lessons about the rain forest? Here the amount of use is far less significant, so many would argue that the amount of compensation that a book company deserves also should be considerably lower than the cost of the entire book. In fact, the value of using only four photos is probably not worth anyone attempting to calculate or collect. Furthermore, the copyright on the photographs may not be held by the book publisher, but by four different photographers whose various whereabouts may be difficult and time-consuming to determine.

So the issue of fair compensation can become quite problematic when use of those materials is limited and that utilization is for socially redeeming, noncommercial purposes, like educating young people. This issue has been labeled by the legislative and judicial system as the question of "fair use." The doctrine of fair use was most clearly established by Congress in passing the Copyright Act of 1976 and in a set of Classroom Guidelines subsequently negotiated by representatives of the publishing industry and the education profession. In a series of cases, the American judicial system has determined that some circumstances justify this fair use of materials for educational purposes without compensation for the producers of those materials.

What Constitutes Fair Use?

So what factors might determine whether a given situation falls under the doctrine of fair use? First, the material must be used strictly for educational purposes. Second, only a limited amount of the overall work can be used. The general guideline is that if less than 10 percent of the overall work is used, it is considered fair use. Another issue is whether the most essential or unique part of the work is being used; if it is not, this is less likely to be a copyright infringement. Finally, the degree to which a work's use may deprive the copyright holder of potential remuneration will affect whether its use is considered fair and an exception to copyright.

For example, if some college instructors want to use some of the material from this book, they might be allowed to use about two and a half chapters' worth, which would represent about 10 percent of the twenty-four chapters. But the issue of essentiality might also come into play. Since the twenty chapters with *scenarios* could be considered the critical part of this work, a court might consider 10 percent of the work as precisely two chapters and no more. In addition, a court would probably forbid any use of *all the scenarios* from this book without compensation to the publisher, despite the fact that the actual number of pages devoted to the scenarios themselves constitutes less than 10 percent of the whole book. Why? Again the issue of essentiality is the key. The scenarios themselves are the most essential part of this work and to use all that critical material, despite its relative brevity compared with the rest of the book, would most likely be considered an infringement of copyright (hint: so don't try it!).

The nature of the work is another consideration in copyright cases. Fictional work has been more thoroughly protected by the courts than nonfiction, since it is more likely to truly originate with the creator. Nonfiction work is often based on previous work that the authors have researched, and therefore it is usually not considered as original as a creative piece of writing, composing, or producing.

How the instructor uses the work is also a factor in determining whether fair use applies. Spontaneity is sometimes an issue, in that educators may use materials without prior permission from the holder of copyright, if to wait for it would result in the loss of a "teachable moment." "Cumulative effect" also is considered. If teachers use the same material over and over, it is more subject to copyright infringement than if they only use it only once or twice. There is a clear logic here in that, even if only small amounts of the work are used, when they are used *many times*, then the amount of overall use is more substantial and subsequently some compensation for the material might be in order.

Compensation is a critical issue in any copyright case. Of course, the user cannot profit from presenting material that has been created and copyrighted by someone else. But the courts have taken this issue one step further. The use of copyrighted material without compensation cannot in any significant way deprive the producers of revenues that they might otherwise have received. When an instructor provides significant amounts of Xeroxed material from a book that allows students to complete assignments without purchasing that book, this may well be a copyright infringement because this practice can serve in lieu of having students purchase the book, thereby depriving the publisher and authors of compensation that otherwise could be theirs. The national copying chain Kinkos lost a major lawsuit over just this issue, the copying of classroom materials that were copyright protected.

Questions of Interpretation

Unfortunately, many of these guidelines are open to interpretation. How is 10 percent to be estimated? What will the frame of reference be? For example, in anthologies, which print only part of a work, how can this standard be applied? Does 10 percent apply to only the particular excerpt? Or does it apply to the whole anthology? Or to the entire work from which the excerpt was taken? Another ambiguous case is that of installments, which provide the overall work one piece at a time. What about chapters in books that are edited, so that a given author may only be responsible for a single chapter? Does the chapter, rather than the whole book, become the frame of reference for applying the 10 percent standard? When a book is part of a larger series, like a trilogy, is the book or the entire series the frame of reference?

Some of the same questions might be applied to other media formats. If a single episode in a television series is used, is that episode the frame of reference or does the body of work refer to the entire season or the entire airtime consumed by this show since its inception? If a piece of software includes six different activities, is the frame of reference any one of those activities or the entire set of six?

Some of these issues about whether a significant amount of the work was used may depend on how the material was initially copyrighted. It may be specified by legal contract. However, in other cases it may be up to the courts to interpret these matters.

What about the condition that the material be used specifically for educational purposes? How is "educational" to be defined? How can it be distinguished from "informational"? Need it be part of a formal curriculum? Does whether school credits are given help determine whether an activity is educational or informational? Can learning by browsing on the Web or by watching public television be considered educational, even if those activities had nothing to do with any schoolwork? How does fair use apply to informal learning experiences?

Can a product created mainly to entertain have educational elements? Does it have to be used in an educational way? The novel *Emma* was written mainly to entertain, but it is used in many literature courses. How about the movie made of *Emma*? Can it be considered educational? What about the *Mad Magazine* parody of the movie *Emma*? On a different track, could *Animal House* be used for educational purposes? If so, need it be in a course on American cinema or could it be used in a course on higher education?

Does the setting determine whether this material is educational or not? Is talking about the weather only educational in science class? Conversely, is a discussion of recent election results in a science class considered "noneducational" since it did not relate to the science curriculum in any way? Or are election results an educationally relevant topic, as long as they are being discussed within the confines of the school, because the school has a social studies curriculum and an expressed interest in developing "citizenship," which is clearly stated in its mission statement?

To be educational, must this material be used in a classroom? Would material used as part of "on-the-job" training be considered educational? Or if profits are simultaneously being made, does this nullify the principle of fair use, because the nonprofit condition is not met?

To what degree does *not charging* for the presentation of materials exempt an individual from copyright infringement? For example, can a man invite a group of his friends to his house for a free showing of a taped copy of a pay-per-view championship fight that took place the night before? Or is his doing this possibly depriving the cable television company of revenues from members of his group who otherwise might have paid to see the fight?

The answers to most of the preceding questions about fair use and copyright infringements would depend on how the copyright laws have been interpreted by the legal system. This is one reason why it is sometimes hard for educators to know for certain when they are infringing upon copyright laws. Teachers are too busy to research the legal nuances of copyright law. They are not lawyers. Even if they did develop a background in this area, there have been so many different interpretations of the law that it might still be difficult to say whether a given set of circumstances would be considered fair use or not. With several different factors involved, each of which is difficult to define precisely, how can one predict how a judge would rule?

Permission or Paying Can Be Problematic

In fact, the ambiguity associated with copyright has probably contributed to teachers assuming that a great deal of material is fair game. Since most teachers do not want to be restricted in what materials they can use, ignorance may be bliss. They have no incentive to learn about copyright, because that information might discourage them and interfere with their resourcefulness in finding worthwhile teaching materials. Many instructors probably feel that the educational and nonprofit aspects of the fair use doctrine are the most critical issues. If they are using materials for a socially beneficial purpose and not benefiting monetarily from it, why should they worry about it? What does it matter what percentage of the material they use?

The financial aspects of the copyright issue are critical. Covering the cost of educational materials can be difficult. School budgets are usually limited in terms of how much money teachers have to spend on materials for their classes. It is not often possible for teachers to purchase enough copies for their entire class. Often it's a case of using the material under infringement of copyright or not using it at all. Some teachers are willing to use their own salary to purchase materials, but many teachers cannot afford to do this or feel that this goes beyond what should be expected of them.

In lieu of purchase, instructors can try to obtain permission for classroom use from the creator of the material. However, this can be a time-consuming process without any guarantee of success. The teacher may have to research who holds the copyright, as well as how to contact them. A formal letter describing the intended use must be written. Then there is a wait for the reply or, worse, no reply at all. Sometimes it is nearly impossible to find exactly who has the copyright or where they are located. Even when a teacher does receive a response to this kind of request, it is sometimes a refusal. Many of these are impersonal form letters from big publishing companies. Teachers are generally too busy to take the time and trouble to pursue permission from copyright holders, especially when the chances of success are by no means assured.

One of the authors of this text had an experience with copyright during the production of a television program that exemplifies what a struggle obtaining permission can be. He wanted to use some footage from a twenty-five-year-old film about the famous shooting incident at Kent State University. He tried to locate the film company listed in the credits, but without success. He then contacted a staff member at the university's audiovisual services department to see if he knew where the disposition of copyright on this film stood. He was given information about another film company that years ago had supposedly purchased the rights to the film. There was a New York City telephone number listed with this information, so he called it. A message machine came on that sounded like the phone was in a private residence. He left a message, but never heard back. So how was he to get the permission he sought? It is possible that this copyright was no longer in force, if the film companies who had owned it no longer existed. But would he be breaking the law if he used some footage from a film whose copyright he could not determine? Could the copyright still belong to an individual or to that individual's heirs? The experience convinced this author that dealing with copyright permission was no simple matter!

With the temptations to use copyrighted material sometimes difficult to resist and the costs in actual money or time associated with purchase or permission, many teachers do opt for breaking the copyright regulations. This happens daily (perhaps hourly?) in classrooms across the United States. Some teachers copy whole sections from books. Others show dubbed copies of television programs, without paying any rental fees. Many use pirated software on their computers.

The Question of Enforcement

How is copyright infringement enforced? Where are the "Copyright Police"? In fact, no formal mechanism to enforce copyright standards exists. Administrators may give lip service to the importance of observing copyright restrictions, but rarely will they hassle their teachers about infringements, because the teachers' most likely response would be to complain that the school should have purchased the material in the first place. As guardians of their schools' limited budgets, principals are then placed in an awkward position.

Media specialists and school librarians often know more about copyright than anyone else in their schools. But while they may report copyright infringements to higher administration, they do not have the authority to actually enforce standards of fair use. Sometimes, like teachers, these specialists may philosophically be more in sympathy with children benefiting from educational opportunities than they care about giant multinational corporations making sufficient profits from them.

The truth is that rarely will any other adult know what transpires in a teacher's classroom. If copyrights are being violated, it is unlikely that an administrator, other teacher, or parent will ever find out about it. And if they did, it is unlikely that they will care. *They* do not know what constitutes fair use either, and probably do not think very much about it. So teachers are generally in a position to use whatever materials they can obtain, without concerning themselves with copyright issues. The likelihood of getting caught is infinitesimal.

The only parties in whose interest it is to enforce copyright standards in the schools are the producers of educational materials. And these producers usually do not have the time to spend monitoring whether schools are copying their materials. So copyright is generally unenforceable. Right now you may be reading a Xeroxed copy of this page, rather than reading it in the book itself.

One significant copyright issue for teachers is whether they know what constitutes fair use. Many remain unaware of how it has been defined by law. Some probably assume, for example, that they can excerpt more than 10 percent of a work without infringing copyright. Maybe they imagine the percentage is closer to 20 or even 50. Others may not be aware of the issue of uniqueness, that is, how critical the particular excerpt is to the overall work. Even the issue of denied compensation may not have been thoroughly considered by some.

But another important issue can be how teachers *feel* about copyright issues. Do they acknowledge that their responsibilities to teach most effectively should be constrained by the producers' rights to compensation? Or do they justify violations of copyright as a necessary transgression for a good cause; that is, their efforts to provide their students with worthwhile materials that the school will not otherwise pay for. Their concern for their student's education may outweigh their concern that others be paid for their efforts to create and disseminate these materials. Philosophically, probably few teachers want to break any laws. But the dynamics of this situation tend to favor helping the students they know well and are responsible for, rather than honoring the rights of strangers, who are unlikely to show up demanding compensation.

New Technologies Raise New Questions About Copyright

Fair use has always been difficult to apply consistently. But during the past few decades, its application has become even more complicated and confusing, as new types of media and means of instructional delivery are developed. It is difficult enough to apply standards of fair use to printed materials used in conventional classrooms. How do you apply these same standards to the use of digitized materials available on a website for use in Web-based instruction that thousands can use, if they pay the fees? Or how does fair use apply to a broadcast of *Men in Black* that a teacher taped on his home VCR and now wants to show in his classroom, ostensibly to supplement a social studies book chapter entitled "Multiculturalism and the Acceptance of Other Types of People"?

One problem with the new media products is the ease with which they can be copied. Tapes of audio or television programming are easily dubbed. Software can be pirated with copy programs or downloaded off the Web for free. MP3 software has facilitated widespread pirating and playing of audio clips via the Web. For generations, "bootleg" audiotapes of concerts, both live and on the air, have circulated and often sold well.

Another problem with these media materials is that they are often expensive. While teachers and schools might consider actually purchasing an item if it were more reasonably priced, in many cases the price is beyond what they can afford to pay. So the alternative approach, to copy it for free, becomes the only viable option. Because expensive materials can be pirated so easily and inexpensively, the temptation to do so is difficult to resist, and many teachers find these kinds of opportunities irresistible. Tape libraries in classrooms can be built this way. Software collections can be augmented.

To address some of these issues, guidelines specifically for media materials have been established. The Guidelines for Off-Air Recording of Broadcast Programming were adopted by Congress in 1979. They stipulate that recordings of commercial television transmissions can be shown for instructional purposes in a classroom if they are used within ten days of the broadcast. They can be kept for examination by the teacher for another forty-five days, after which they must be erased. If the programming is considered "instructional," rather than mainly for purposes of entertainment, recordings can be used for teaching purposes for one year and then must be erased.

Guidelines for the use of computer software have not been so clearly delineated by statute. The creators of computer programming have long hoped that traditional standards of copyright would apply to computer code and that they would be able to dictate the conditions under which their products could be copied. But their efforts to do so have not always been very successful. For example, software producers usually insisted that purchasing one program meant that it would only be used on a single machine, at least at a given time. They tried to prevent purchasers from loading software from a single disk into multiple machines, in an attempt to force multiple purchases.

Unfortunately, this approach was very hard to enforce and many teachers disregarded it. Limited school budgets did not often allow for multiple purchases. In addition, it was difficult to teach computer skills to a class when there was only one copy of the application. Although some software was coded with copy protection, many titles could be duplicated quite easily with copy software. The temptation to simply copy a single title several times was too great for many teachers.

For many years, educational software suffered from a vicious cycle that retarded the growth of the industry. High prices for titles encouraged piracy, which limited profits, which meant companies kept prices high, which encouraged piracy, and so on. A lower-profit, higher-volume approach by software producers might have improved the situation, but rarely was this strategy adopted. Unfortunately the situation led to many educators simply disregarding the copyright laws.

More-sophisticated methods of preventing copying have been developed over the years. Better copy protection algorithms have been developed. Digital timers that disable software after a given number of days allow users to preview it, but not keep it. Counters that know how many machines are accessing a given application off a server can prevent its use in more machines than the user has contracted for. However, each of these systems can still be beaten by a reasonably resourceful user. For example, if the timer has run out on a trial copy, another trial copy can be downloaded off the Web. A network-controlled counter can be overriden by downloading a copy onto an extra machine's hard drive, then simply taking that machine off-line and using the application locally.

Online Issues: Are Hyperlinks a Copyright Violation?

To address some of these problems associated with software copyright, the U.S. Information Infrastructure Task Force (IITF) conducted a review of the copyright laws in 1994. The IITF's report, generally known as the White Paper, concluded that there was no need for a new law addressing copyright, but only for some changes in the existing law, mainly to clarify how the new digital technologies were to be addressed. For example, it indicated that copyright protection traditionally associated with "distribution" of a creator's work also applies to *online* dissemination, so that disseminating an electronic copy would be considered the equivalent of distributing a hard copy version of the work. This interpretation is consistent with previous copyright standards.

Given the ease with which information can be distributed online, in the future there may be less actual purchase of materials for permanent ownership and more *use* of material on a temporary basis. For example, researchers may not purchase books but may instead pay to examine them online. A system of automated fee structures for copyrighted materials may be used to provide differentiated levels of access, based on time elapsed, number of screens navigated, or some other set of criteria.

Such a system might change today's fair use scenario, wherein using more than 10 percent of a work makes an educator liable for the entire cost of that work. Users might also be able to purchase only the parts of the work that they are interested in, for fees adjusted to reflect that percentage. A teacher who wanted to use four photographs from the book *Insects: Friends or Foes?* could do so at modest cost. This solution might work well for both of the parties involved in such transactions. The creator of the material would receive some compensation, and the users would pay only for what they actually wanted.

The IITF White Paper addressed these possibilities with several proposals. One was to eliminate the fair use exemption with electronic materials in favor of a fee structure. Another provision stated that it should be a violation of copyright law to tamper with copyright protection programming used to limit access and manage fees. Finally, to enforce these standards, the IITF proposed placing the responsibility for overseeing appropriate use on Internet Service Providers like America Online. Another controversial clause defined hyperlinks to other copyrighted material as a potential infringement of copyright law. Web page developers might thereby be liable for creating any hypertext links that took the user to a copyright-sensitive document.

The White Paper recommendations have not as yet been enacted into law by the U.S. Congress. They have been criticized by many educators as too restrictive and a threat to the long-standing fair use standards. The public debate will continue for some time over how to deal with the issues that new technologies have raised about copyright.

Distance Education and Copyright: Issues of Scale

Another copyright issue raised by technology is related to some of the new instructional delivery systems that allow educational materials to be used across vast distances by huge numbers of potential clients. Televised instruction can cover enormous geographical areas. National "Universities of the Air" broadcast educational programming throughout entire countries. For example, China's Television University is available to whatever percentage of its billion people have a television set. The Internet is a medium that is available to millions who have the connections to log on. Material posted on the World Wide Web can receive thousands of "hits" per day.

Why do these new systems of educational delivery with their large numbers of potential users raise new sensitivities about copyright law? One reason is the potential amount of lost reimbursement that could be involved in a copyright infringement. A major publishing house or software producer is unlikely to waste time investigating copyright infringement in a single self-contained classroom because the amount of potential profit involved is so small. Not so with these large-scale distance education (DE) systems. Even if the reimbursement per user is modest, the numbers can be so large that the potential profit may be significant. So these new delivery systems have become the focal point for an ongoing controversy about copyright and how it can be applied to specific forms of distance learning.

The enormous numbers of students sometimes involved in large-scale DE projects may affect future interpretation of the "cumulative effect" clause of the Copyright Act of 1976. This issue has generally been applied to questions of repeated use. But it could also be applied to the issue of *how many* users are involved. The cumulative effect on sales of a work may be much greater if thousands, rather than a few dozen, are using the material.

In addition, enforcement of copyright law may be more feasible with DE than it has been in a self-contained classroom. Distance education projects are far more open to scrutiny because of their public nature. Educational telecasts can be tracked and monitored. Web-based instructional systems can keep track of which addressees have logged on to them. Those checking for violations of fair use can monitor these efforts far more easily than they could check up on activities behind the closed door of a self-contained classroom.

A number of companies that produce educational materials have publicly announced their intentions to press charges against DE projects that fail to compensate them adequately for their materials. The debate over how these fees should be determined is already well under way. Naturally the corporations involved want reimbursement for each instance where a student uses the material. But it can be difficult to determine appropriate levels of reimbursement for materials used in many DE projects. Payment of fees may be relatively straightforward if only *one* major text is involved, but it can become quite complicated if the course includes materials from many different sources, each of which is subject to some fee because of its copyright protection.

Producers of instructional materials for DE projects may also find that their work is sometimes being used without compensation. In many of these projects, people can use the materials without paying tuition, if they are not interested in obtaining academic credit. When a Public Broadcasting Service station broadcasts a television series as part of an accredited college course, there will be people watching and learning who do not actually register for the course. The same situation can apply to course materials on the World Wide Web that users who do not sign up for course credit can access for free.

Future Issues

Advancing technology has complicated some other issues related to course development and delivery, which will need to be addressed in the near future. One involves the use of supplementary "reference" materials. It is a commonplace practice for college instructors to put some supplementary material "on reserve" in the library, for students who wish to pursue the topic in greater depth. With these nonrequired, supplementary materials, many educators feel that making one copy available for the class should only require that one copy be purchased, despite the fact that many students may use it.

While this way of operating is common in college courses, should similar principles apply to Web-based course materials? In this case, is it fair for the instructor to place supplementary materials online and available for thousands to read for free? Might not this free availability potentially limit sales? Again, a practice that on a small scale is not especially controversial can become a legitimate bone of contention when the global reach and huge utilization levels of the Internet come into play. One solution is to password protect the materials to restrict levels of use, but not many college instructors have the Web sophistication to establish such protection.

In a similar vein, the networked automation of library services has raised some copyright questions. Many college instructors can now easily obtain books and articles from throughout their state via interlibrary loan by ordering them online with a click of the mouse. In some library systems, Xeroxed copies of materials are made for clients and mailed directly to their offices. Does this efficient access to materials reduce the likelihood that individual users and other libraries will need to purchase these materials? Why buy any printed material, when it is probably available somewhere in the state library system? Does this process infringe the copyright clause protecting creators against loss of potential income?

There are also some interesting issues to be settled regarding "intellectual property" rights to profitable DE ventures. Who owns the copyright, the instructor or the institution? Technology has further complicated these questions. For instance, if the university uses taped footage of an instructor's lectures in subsequent semesters of a television-based course without the videotaped instructor getting paid for teaching the course, is this fair? A Web-based course might raise similar questions if, for example, the university collects tuition for use of a Web course after the instructor who created the site has left the institution. If the institution wants these rights, then it will probably need to include provisions in its contract with faculty that establish its claim. Such a contract clause might indicate what kind of reimbursement, if any, will be provided to faculty who develop such courseware.

So how will these new technologies ultimately affect copyright law? The Copyright Act of 1976 was worded in a way that may not apply to DE. It said fair use applied "in the course of face-to-face teaching activities." Can videoconferenced classrooms be defined as "face-to-face" because teachers can literally see the faces of their students and vice versa? Where does this leave asynchronous forms of DE, where teachers may seldom interact directly with their students, and they may never actually "see" one another's faces?

Can the old standards be applied to these new circumstances, or is there a need for new interpretations of the fair use doctrine, perhaps even for an additional set of guidelines legislated by the Congress? Will the definition of fair use be broadened or narrowed? Many issues have not yet been resolved. Because the financial stakes have been raised, copyright has become more controversial than ever, with the introduction of newer, more-sophisticated technologies.

RECOMMENDED READING

Dagley, D., and J. Lan. 1999. An analysis of copyright-related legal cases and decisions: Implications to designing Internet-based learning activities. *Educational Technology Review* 11: 19–24.

Elkin-Koren, N. 1995. The challenges of technological change to copyright law: Copyright reform and social change in cyberspace. *Science Communication* 17 (2): 186–200.

Switzer, J., and R. Switzer. 1994. Copyright question: Using audiovisual works in a satellite-delivered program. *T.H.E. Journal* 21 (10): 76–79.

OTHER REFERENCES

Bender, I. 1993. A matter of respect: Copyright law and new technologies. *Technos* 2 (3): 24–26.

Bielefield, A., and L. Cheeseman. 1997. *Technology and copyright law: A guidebook for the library, research, and teaching professions.* New York: Neal-Schuman Publishers, ERIC, ED 403919.

Botterbusch, H. 1996. *Copyright in the age of technology.* Bloomington, IN: Phi Delta Kappa.

Dalziel, C. 1996. Copyright, fair use, and the information superhighway. *Community College Journal* 67 (1): 23–27.

Eisenschitz, T., and P. Turner. 1997. Rights and responsibilities in the Digital Age: Problems with stronger copyright in an information society. *Journal of Information Science* 23 (3): 209–223.

Kamp, S. 1998. How does "fair use" apply to software being used in schools? *Technology Connection* 5 (1): 19.

Lan, J., and D. Dagley. 1999. Teaching via the Internet: A brief review of copyright law and legal issues. *Educational Technology Review* 11: 19–24.

Roberts, K. 1996. Fair use of technology. *Science Scope* 20 (1): 40–41.

Taylor, C. (Producer). 1996. *Copyright, the Internet, multimedia and the law.* [Video] (Available from Chip Taylor Communications, Derry, NH).

Wand, P. 1995. Commentary: Technological change, intellectual property, and academic libraries: An outline of the issues. *Science Communication* 17 (2): 233–239.

Weiner, R. 1997. Copyright in a digital age: Practical guidance for information professionals in the midst of legal uncertainty. *Online* 21 (3): 97–102.

What's fair? 1994, June. *A Report on the proceedings of the national conference on Educational fair access and the new media.* Washington, DC, ERIC, ED 398903.

SCENARIO

As a sixth-grade teacher at an urban school, you have tried your best to find interesting material to supplement the rather dry textbook that your school uses to teach social studies. You are about to teach a unit on Africa, which potentially might be of interest to your largely African American class. However, the text covers Africa in a manner that you fear will be rather uninspiring for your students, especially since you yourself had trouble reading it without yawning repeatedly. Part of the problem is the bland, simplified, overly optimistic manner in which it is written. The chapter entitled "Africa: Land of Many Riches" opens with these gripping words: "Africa is the second largest continent. It has many natural resources." The text proceeds to focus on topics like the cash crop of Uganda, with a full explanation about the differences between a plantain and a banana (they are "cousins" in the world of fruit, as far as you can determine). There is an emphasis on facts about the geography, the cities, the leaders, the names of some political parties, and so on. There are also a number of dates, generally the year in which each country achieved its independence, the year in which it may have held its last election, and perhaps a year in which it was visited by the pope or some monarch from Europe. Some of the information is out of date. For example, many of the leaders listed are no longer in power.

What is missing is any real sense of the human drama that has played itself out in Africa: the continuing importance of tribal identities, the legacy of the slave trade, the mixed blessing of European colonialism, the AIDS epidemic, and so on. Because the text is several years old, also missing are any references to events that your students may have seen in the news, like the election of Nelson Mandela in South Africa, the Hutu genocide of Tutsis in Rwanda, or the collapse of Mobutu's quarter-century-long tyranny over Zaire. You feel that there are many aspects of the African experience that your students might find interesting, but they do not seem well represented in your social studies text, *Our World and Its Many Cultures*.

Your own interest in Africa was sparked by some of the major films you have seen; for example, *Cry Freedom, Out of Africa*, and *Amistad*. You decide that one strategy for engaging your class in the subject matter would be to rent some of these films on video and play them in class. You also notice that several programs about Africa are scheduled on educational channels this month. PBS has a program on the impact of modernization in Kenya on the Masai tribe. Discovery has a special on the Zulus' role in South African politics. The Learning Channel has a show on the impact of British colonialism in Nigeria. You set your videocassette recorder accordingly.

Two weeks later, your plan to enrich the African unit with videocassettes gets off to a tremendous start with the showing of *The Ghost and the Darkness*, the fact-based film about the man-eating lions of Tsavo who disrupted the building of the trans-Kenyan railway by the British. Particularly interesting to your class was the arrival of a group of Masai warriors who are brought in to help hunt down the lions. You feel your strategy is working so far. However, when you later speak with the school librarian about reserving the VCR again for next Monday, she acts a bit annoyed. She says that about half an hour ago she overheard some of your students discussing *The Ghost and the Darkness*. This is not a film that the school has the rights to show, she explains. She then asks what you plan to show next. You mention the PBS special that you taped at home last year, entitled *Clash of Cultures: The Masai in Kenya*. She explains that the school has a contract with the local PBS station for programming, with rules about copying that must be carefully observed. So you ask if she happened to have made a copy of this program and she doesn't think so.

You decide to proceed with your original game plan: to show the class your own taped copy of the show on the Masai tribe. But when next Monday arrives, there is no VCR in your room. When you ask the librarian about this, she says that she has discovered that the school no longer has the right to use that program since it was originally broadcast over a year ago. You are annoyed, since you planned to show the program that afternoon and to pass out Xeroxed copies of some 1930s photographs of Masai rituals, which you printed from your compact disc collection of *National Geographic* magazines. With some irritation, you describe your lesson plans and how they will be disrupted if you do not get to show the program. But her response is that she is not sure that you have the rights to show the *National Geographic* photos, since the school does not own a copy of that issue of the magazine.

Now you are really annoyed. At lunch, you go home and return with your own VCR. The lesson goes extremely well. After the Masai program ends, the students ask questions for about twenty minutes. They react with great interest to the old photos showing a lion hunt, a ritual dance by adolescent males, female earlobe decoration, and so on. You feel that your media strategy has been quite successful so far in engaging the class in a study of Africa. Some students even seemed to have read the assignments in the text, since several were able to identify African bananas as "plantains" when you showed them photos of a Masai feast.

But the next morning, you receive a message from the principal's secretary asking you to come speak with her about some concerns expressed by the school librarian. You immediately realize that this meeting will be about your supposed infringement of copyright. You hope that your presentation of these materials for educational purposes was legal and plan to argue that this is a case of what is legally termed "fair use." You did not show the entire Masai program or even all of the photos in the *National Geographic* article, so you used only selected segments of the materials. You have not materially benefited from their showing (in fact, you paid for the video rental of *The Ghost and the Darkness*!).

You doubt that your activities have affected the sale of any of these materials, except perhaps future rentals of *The Ghost and the Darkness* by your students (although you suspect that they might be *more* likely to rent it now that you showed it than they ever would have on their own). You feel that the school has paid to use PBS programming and its contract with the local station should cover your use of that program. Even though the school has not purchased a copy of the *National Geographic* issue on the Masai, *you* paid for your National Geographic CD. You should have the right to show photos from it, even if they were shown in a format other than the one you purchased.

Write a memorandum to your principal Mrs. Weston that deals with the copyright issues associated with your use of these materials. If you feel that at least some of this constitutes fair use, explain why. If you have some second thoughts about using some of the material, discuss your perspectives on the issue and describe how you would deal differently with using these kinds of materials in the future. Conclude the memo with your thoughts about the "spirit of fair use."

ISSUES INQUIRY

1. Can you think of situations where you might want to use copies of materials and the applicability of copyright law is unclear? Discuss the issues involved in each case, in attempting to apply the fair use principles in assessing its copyright status.

2. As a future educator, how do you feel about the fair use doctrine established in 1976 for printed materials? Should it be more liberal (allowing more than 10 percent of a work to be copied, for example) or not?

3. How do you feel about the 1979 statute that prohibits the videotaped use of commercial television programs ten days after the program was originally broadcast? What about the one year time frame for educational programs?

4. What are your feelings about the copyright-protection-assured software producers who want to be paid for the number of machines on which their programming is being used? Is this fair, or should a teacher be able to load a program on multiple machines without additional cost, once a single copy has been purchased?

5. Can you think of any ways in which copyright laws might be more effectively enforced? How can this be done without constraining the teaching process or establishing an irritating form of surveillance?

6. Do you feel that copyright laws should apply different standards to *distance education* classes than those which have been established for the self-contained classroom? Why or why not?

New Opportunities

ENGAGING OR ENRAGING?

CHAPTER 13

Is Hypermedia Worth the Hype?

INTRODUCTION

"Hypertext" and "hypermedia" are terms that refer to ways of linking electronic resources together so that a user can simply click on a highlighted item and the cursor will automatically shift to another item, which should have some conceptual connection with the first item. Nowadays, everyone learns about hypertext from using compact discs and exploring the World Wide Web. True to its "hyper" prefix, which means "better," hypertext has some advantages, especially when meaningful links are established. But is hypertext always helpful for learners? This chapter explores the issues raised by the increasing availability of hypermediated materials.

A Hyperattenuated History of Hypermedia

Like so many technical advances, hypertext was a concept long before it became a reality. Around the same time that the first huge mainframe computers were being developed, as World War II came to an end, a high-level government adviser named Vannever Bush wrote a report about the possibility of text that could be linked directly to other text, skipping over other material or switching to an entirely different document. Such connections might make it easier for readers or researchers to move quickly to material that might be of interest to them. He argued that such techniques might make information processing more efficient and effective.

A few decades later, Ted Nelson at Brown University was able to develop an early form of hypertext with a program he called Xanadu. Text materials in Xanadu could be accessed in nonlinear fashion because links had been programmed to take the user directly to another part of the document. By the mid-1980s, object-oriented computer "authoring" systems like HyperCard and Toolbook were being developed, which provided opportunities for users to establish direct links between screens regardless of the order in which those screens were placed in the program. These links allowed for nonlinear movement through material. Links established between words became known as "hypertext." When links were developed that connected to or from nontext materials, like a picture, sound, or video clip, the term "hypermedia" was often used, rather than hypertext.

By the early nineties, hypertext was being used in many pieces of educational software. Hyperlinks were used in menus to send users directly to whatever information they were most interested in. Hypertext was also sometimes included within paragraphs of material, to provide quick connections to another topic or to provide the definition of a term, in the glossary. One example of the effective use of hypertext could be found in the electronic encyclopedia. First Groliers', and then other encyclopedia companies, produced "multimedia encyclopedias" on compact disc, whose entries included hypertext links to related material. Some of these links connected to multimedia resources (pictures, sounds, videos), and many of us probably first experienced a hypermedia link with one of these electronic encyclopedias.

Other database-oriented CDs also began to appear at this time, which provided hyperlinked information about a given topic. Electronic field guides for different types of animals became available with ways to find specific species using hypertext. Museums produced CDs that displayed their collections, and they used hyperlinks to allow efficient navigation between similar types of items. An electronic version of the book *How Things Work* became quite popular, partially because of its dynamic hypermedia links to animated demonstrations.

By the early nineties, the hypermediated environment of the World Wide Web developed by Timothy Berniers-Lee had appeared on the Internet, and it rapidly became a huge source of information, accessible to growing numbers. In the Web environment it was easy to link materials. Most Web pages would have numerous links to other pages within the same site and sometimes links that took the user to other websites altogether. The Web has made hyperlinked information something that most of us take for granted.

How Hypermedia Helps

In well-designed electronic documents, hyperlinks are readily available to move from menus to different sections, back and forth between pages, back to the last menu, to a glossary, and between pages within the document. But these types of links only replicate what could always be done with printed materials. Readers of printed books can use a table of contents or an index to quickly find the material they want. They can flip forward and backward between pages. They can quickly look up items in a glossary. From within a given passage, they can reference material on other pages, if they are given the page number(s) where it is to be found.

In some ways, hyperlinks are just a way of making electronic text as user-friendly as printed text has always been. The ability to link automatically is important in an electronic document, since only a small portion of the material may appear onscreen at any given time and scrolling linearly through electronic documents can take longer than flipping through pages of printed material.

But is there anything advantageous about linking text and multimedia resources within an electronic document that supersedes what can be done with printed books? There is likely to be less effort involved in clicking a mouse than thumbing through printed pages. Since the hypertext link happens automatically upon selection, it involves less struggle than scanning a printed page for related material. Another advantage is certainly the speed with which the reader is taken to the material, which is almost always quicker than flipping through printed pages (assuming fast computer access times to the hypertext materials). But a more significant advantage may be the speed with which readers can access material in *other* electronic documents. While readers can go to other sources of printed text to continue their pursuit of information, this is often far more cumbersome and time-consuming than simply linking to another Web page or linking to another source on the same CD.

For it is not only the *speed* of access that can make hypertext effective in an electronic learning environment, but also its *size*. Many electronic sources of information are extensive. A CD can hold an enormous amount of text; an entire encyclopedia, for example. The World Wide Web is a huge body of electronic text, extensively linked by hypertext connections. The availability of so much material at the click of a mouse has made the hyperlink an important feature of these new electronic environments.

It is certainly fun to be able to move quickly throughout a hypermediated environment and access lively resources so quickly and easily. But what are the potential *educational* implications of a nonlinear, hypermediated environment? It is an environment that gives the learner more freedom to move about at will. It is less restrictive, but is this necessarily always advantageous? Don't instructors sometimes want to focus learners on specific materials in a specific sequence? Doesn't providing hyperlinks potentially disrupt that effort to deliberately structure an educational experience, by allowing students to move through materials in a random sequence that may have little coherence to it? A hypermedia environment is not necessarily unstructured, but it is structured differently from a traditional linear one. It provides a multiplicity of potential learning paths, rather than just one.

Linking and Associative Learning

Hyperlinked material is often referred to as "nonlinear," in that users need not follow the linear process of proceeding through the material from start to finish, as you might normally read a book. In a nonlinear environment, there is considerable flexibility in how users can move around the document. This is a major advantage for those who know what they are looking for. Students can conveniently explore related material and move quickly to other information that is of interest to them. This easy movement through material may be more efficient than the linear approach of the traditional book, where students may need to search through a great deal of material before coming to the critical material they seek.

Hypertext also may allow students to explore materials more "naturally," the way they think, through associations made between one concept and the next. Could the hypermedia environment be more conducive to this type of learning than materials limited to the conventional linear format? Vannever Bush's landmark article about the possibility of hypertext was entitled "As We May Think," which illustrates that one initial impetus for linked text was to provide opportunities for learning by association.

In fact, many learning theorists, like the famous behaviorist Edward Thorndike, have stressed the importance of "associative learning." People may most effectively learn new material through mental associations they make to material they already know. Only when the appropriate intellectual "connections" are made will learners properly conceptualize the material. If learners are unable to relate to a topic, they are unlikely to even remember what they have read. Why not assist in this associative process by literally making the connections through hypertext?

The cognitive learning theorists also have emphasized the importance of making connections to prior knowledge encoded in our cognitive "schema." Learning theorist David Ausubel's concept of the "advance organizer" has addressed this issue. He advised instructors to plan introductory material for any unit that made a connection to material the students should previously have encountered, so that they would be able to immediately relate to it. This material would serve as a way of providing an orientation, or organizing principle, in advance of the rest of the lesson; hence, the name advance organizer. The guiding principle was that associations made between prior knowledge and new material would facilitate learning. There is an extensive literature dating back many decades that supports the significance of associations in the learning process.

If associative learning is indeed so important, then hyperlinked learning environments may prove instructionally advantageous, because the embedded links may help even slower learners to connect effectively to related material. The speed with which this occurs in an electronic environment is an important factor, since some learners are easily distracted or may lack motivation. Any delays involved in finding related material may discourage them from pursuing it. But with highlighted hypertext, learners can be guided automatically to interesting, related material. A thoughtfully designed nonlinear document with appropriately identified links can show a student how certain ideas and topics are related to one another, serving as a potentially effective teaching tool. Guided by links, the user may come to see how meaningful connections between concepts can be made.

Hypermedia and Constructivism

Other learning theorists, like Jerome Bruner, have stressed the importance of "discovery learning." He felt that the most important thinking processes are those that involve some originality. Simply being told about certain principles in science is not as intellectually stimulating for students as having them attempt to discover these principles for themselves. Bruner believed that telling students too much is a mistake. Setting up situations where students can learn on their own is a more effective instructional approach, if you want students to learn to think rather than just learn to comprehend or memorize.

The constructivists also feel very strongly about this issue. When students explore on their own, they can learn how to learn. They may be motivated to explore topics in more depth. They can better personalize their knowledge, making it more meaningful for themselves. Students also tend to remember better what they have explored on their own because of their involvement in the learning process. They take "ownership" of what they have learned on their own. It is theirs, rather than just a set of facts they have stored somewhere in their brains.

If discovery learning and its pedagogical stepchild constructivism are valid approaches to educating young people, then nonlinear learning environments may be instructionally advantageous. Extensive electronic sources of information with many links may best facilitate such student-initiated efforts. They allow for more learner control of the educational experience than does a linear environment in which the learner is guided step-by-step. Linked materials provide more opportunities to explore. Pupils are free to decide which links to pursue and to chart their own paths through the material. Thus, the learning experience can become uniquely theirs.

The availability of so much hypermedia on the Web and on CDs in today's classrooms has probably helped the constructivist movement. Technology is providing access to the information "explosion." Children's efforts to research on their own are no longer limited by the size of the school's library collection or the degree to which that collection has materials on a given topic. Turning students loose to do their own research is an approach far more likely to succeed in today's schools, if pupils have access to the vast resources of the Internet, electronic encyclopedias, archival material on CDs, videotape collections, and so on.

Hopefully, gone are the days when the encyclopedia was the only source of information in the school about a given topic. Learning can be a more thoughtful, challenging experience when there is so much material to choose from and when these materials have so many different possible learning paths connected by hyperlinks. As they encounter hyperlinks, pupils are forced to think about the material as they decide whether to link or not. Having so many sources and paths available may also encourage more personalized forms of learning and individualized expression of what they have learned, for when there is more material available than they can incorporate in their report, students may be forced to synthesize what they have discovered, summarizing it in their own words. They need to think more about it as they articulate what they have learned. The availability of so many linked resources will, it is hoped, discourage the time-honored approach of producing a school report by rephrasing, or even plagiarizing, the encyclopedia entry on that topic.

Getting Lost in Hyperspace

However, what about the potential to wander aimlessly through a hypermediated environment? When students are not very conversant with the subject matter, it might be easy for them to skip valuable information as they pursue inefficient or illogical learning paths through the material. In a nonlinear environment like this, student-initiated sequencing of material can become haphazard and they may become confused. Besides, the easily distracted learner might prefer to explore some other material that appeals more to them than the assigned topic, even though it has little educational relevance to what the class is studying. Educators also need to be aware of the potential problems that students may encounter when they attempt to navigate within these instructional settings. What kinds of students may have difficulty navigating by means of hyperlinks and why?

One group that may find it too challenging to find certain kinds of material is young children. Elementary school students may not be ready to take this kind of initiative and may learn more effectively from structured, linear materials. It takes a certain level of cognitive maturity to know what material is relevant and what is tangential to a given topic. Young children may not be able to effectively make these distinctions. Even if they can do so to some extent, it may still be difficult to find relevant material in an information-rich environment like the Web, which can even overwhelm adults at times given the sheer volume of material available. It also may be difficult for young students to discriminate which links are likely to be most worth pursuing. Finally, it may be challenging for young children to read material in a nonlinear fashion, in that they may skip critical information they need in order to understand what comes later. The reading level of many educational materials is too advanced for elementary school children anyway, and asking them to follow it in a hypertext environment may be expecting too much.

Another group of students who may not fare well in a hypermediated environment are slower learners, for some of the same reasons just discussed. Likewise, many older students may not be cognitively mature enough to effectively cope in hyperspace. These students may not have the ability to clearly conceptualize the material they are interested in. It can be difficult for them to coherently pursue a topic if the links lead them astray and they become distracted by tangential material. With so much information available, it may be hard for students to decide what to include or exclude from a report, as they succumb to information overload.

One group that may experience considerable difficulty are those with attention deficit disorder. The hypermediated environment can be a very confusing place, with so many links to click on and so many distracting pictures, sounds, and animations. The myriad choices and the "bells and whistles" can make it nearly impossible for such pupils to focus effectively on the task at hand. Without sufficiently lengthy attention spans, students with ADD cannot sustain the effort to wend their way through the labyrinth of cyberspace. A structured, linear lesson is often the best approach for these students.

Nonlinearity can be a real problem for those who are not sufficiently prepared to address a topic. As already mentioned, it can provide opportunities for those with good metacognitive skills, who can navigate effectively to find the material they need. On the other hand, for those with poor learning skills and immature schema in a given topic area, processing material out of its logical sequence can be quite confusing. Attempting to comprehend advanced material before effectively grasping the basics can be very difficult and frustrating.

Pursuing hypermediated connections can very quickly take students far from the original screen where they started and far from their original topic. Like the starship *Voyager*, some may find it difficult to get back where they originally came from. Others may get into the habit of clicking and surfing aimlessly, so that they do indeed just wander through cyberspace with no sense of direction (like the *Enterprise!*). Too many links can be a bad thing if they only serve as a source of distraction and diversion.

Some have observed that the new nonlinear media may be contributing to a mentality sometimes described as "hypermind." Hypermind is characterized by a short attention span, overly divergent ways of thinking, and an inability to coherently communicate in a logical, analytic manner. Young people who spend a great deal of their free time surfing around the Web or changing channels on cable TV may be developing mental habits that will not serve them well in school or in their future choice of occupation. Because the content of these media is designed to hold young people's attention through constantly changing, flashy, superficial distraction, nothing is focused upon for any length of time or explored in any depth.

Consequently, this hypermind syndrome may include difficulties in appreciating or pursuing any topic in any real depth. It may result in an inability to work steadily on a given assignment for a sustained period of time. It is a mentality that struggles to overcome boredom through distractions, but which fails to recognize that boredom can be a by-product of such superficiality. If this hypermind syndrome has any validity, then the question for teachers is how to address it. Probably the best way to combat it would be to help pupils use the new technologies in more substantive, focused ways than they tend to use them at home. Giving students specific assignments to complete on the Web can help them develop higher levels of concentration and more persistence in their work habits. With some practice, lazy mental habits can be replaced by more productive ones.

Issues in Hypermedia Design

So how can hypermedia materials be best designed to avoid these potential pitfalls? One obvious issue is the planning of hyperlinks. These connections should be made thoughtfully. Selecting appropriate text passages and media materials for linking is the first issue. Substantive, relevant material must be chosen. Many hypertext documents are weakened by the inclusion of links to and from trivial, tangential material. Highlighting inappropriate material for linking only confuses the reader as to what is really important. Ill-advised links only serve as distractions, which may divert readers from the material the author has provided, never to return to it.

Another important issue in developing links is the quality of the material that is linked to the main topic. If it does not effectively serve to further inform the reader, then linking to it is a mistake. Again, it will only lead the learner into unproductive paths. As a technique, hypertext is effective only if the link helps elucidate. Yet there is much linking for the sake of linking on the World Wide Web. There are links to poorly designed websites. There are links to pages with material of questionable veracity. And there are, of course, annoying links to Web pages that no longer even exist. In fact, links on any Web page need to be checked periodically to see if the destinations are still active.

Speaking of the Web, there is some question as to whether it is always the most appropriate hypermediated environment for students to use for their studies. It may be better to give students who have problems negotiating non-linear environments more-limited, focused hypermediated environments like those that can be found on compact discs. Material on a CD usually focuses on a given topic and the number of links is finite, neither of which is the case for material on the World Wide Web. Students with the potential to stray off topic should fare better with the more-structured programming on a CD; they might then try the Web when they have developed better skills in cyberspace.

What approaches can help prevent confusion in nonlinear environments? Navigational aids can be quite helpful. Clear menu screens and "maps" of a website can clarify the structure and content of a CD or website. Clearly identifiable icons on each screen that link users back to the main menu or a home screen are important to include. Other links to different sections of the website provided on each screen also allow for easier navigation around the site. Standardization of the appearance of screens within a site can help learners become more quickly acquainted with the available features, and they will know where to look for navigational icons. Limiting the number of links that leave the site may help users stay focused, although it can sacrifice some of the potential richness of the hypermediated environment.

Having students design their own hypermediated environments can be a very worthwhile experience. Whether they author a HyperStudio program or develop their own Web pages, they will face these navigational issues. They will need to plan the kinds of links that allow the reader to move easily throughout the program. They can experience firsthand how a nonlinear learning environment should be structured so that users can move around it effectively. They will face the issue of what material should be linked to other sources. They will need to research which materials are worth connecting to. They will ultimately make judgments about how many links are appropriate and what kinds of links are worth including.

The process of developing a complex nonlinear environment should involve a great deal of careful thought about both its content and its design. Such experiences should be encouraged in classrooms, for they can foster both intellectual development and imagination. Might not the complex intellectual challenges involved in this kind of computer authoring enhance student learning in ways that transcend simply writing materials in a linear fashion? Designing multiple learning paths effectively is surely more challenging than simply designing a single learning path. Integrating a set of different learning paths so that different learners have appropriate choices can be a very challenging, sophisticated design task. Having students develop their own hyperlinked lessons can be a very meaningful learning experience. You might even describe it as "hyperlearning."

RECOMMENDED READING

Barab, S., B. Bowdish, and K. Lawless. 1997. Hypermedia navigation: Profiles of hypermedia users. *Educational Technology Research and Development* 45 (3): 23–41.

Campbell, R. 1998. Hyperminds for hypertimes: The demise of rational logical thought? *Educational Technology* 38 (1): 24–31.

Heller, R. 1990. The role of hypermedia in education: A look at the research issues. *Journal of Research on Computing in Education* 22 (4): 431–441.

Yang. S. 1996. Designing instructional applications using constructive hypermedia. *Educational Technology* 36 (6): 45–50.

OTHER REFERENCES

Ayersman, D. 1996. Reviewing the research based on hypermedia-based learning. *Journal of Research on Computing in Education* 28 (4): 500–525.

Becker, D., and M. Dwyer. 1994. Using hypermedia to provide learner control. *Journal of Educational Multimedia and Hypermedia* 3 (2): 155–172.

Bush, V. 1945. As we may think. *Atlantic Monthly* 176 (1): 101–108.

Corry, M. 1998. Mental models and hypermedia user interface design. *Educational Technology Review* 9: 20–24.

Dyrli, O., and D. Kinnaman. 1995. Moving ahead educationally with multimedia. *Technology and Learning* 15 (7): 46–51.

Hill, J., and M. Hannafin. 1997. Cognitive strategies and learning from the World Wide Web. *Educational Technology Research and Development* 45 (4): 37–64.

Nielson, J. 1995. *Multimedia and hypertext: The Internet and beyond.* New York: AP Professional.

Oliver, R., and J. Herington. 1995. Developing effective hypermedia instructional materials. *Australian Journal of Educational Technology* 11: 8–22.

Perelman, L. 1992. *School's out: Hyperlearning, the new technology, and the end of education.* New York: William Morrow.

Schroeder, E. 1995. Patterns of exploration and learning with hypermedia. *Journal of Educational Computing Research* 13: 313–335.

Tripp, S. D., and W. Roby. 1990. Orientation and disorientation in hypertext lexicon. *Journal of Computer Based Instruction* 17 (4): 120–124.

Tolhurst, D. 1995. Hypertext, hypermedia, multimedia defined. *Educational Technology* 35 (2): 21–26.

Wei, Chin-lung. 1991. Hypertext and printed materials: Some similarities and differences. *Educational Technology* 31 (5): 51–53.

Weller, H., J. Repman, W. Lan, and G. Roose. 1995. Improving the effectiveness of learning hypermedia-based instruction: The importance of learner characteristics. *Computers in Human Behavior* 11 (3-4): 451–465.

SCENARIO

You are a primary school teacher who is currently teaching second grade at a progressive new school. Your school, George Lucas Elementary, has formed teams to explore innovative approaches to teaching that might be implemented next year. You chair the technology team, which has decided to explore whether "hypermediated" learning environments might prove instructionally advantageous for students in grades 1 to 3. The school has a small computer lab in which each machine has a CD-ROM player and access to the Internet. There are several CDs that provide hyperlinks, including the electronic World Book Encyclopedia and Atlas. The school is considering upgrading both its software collection and its connectivity to the Internet, so that more students can access the huge hypermediated learning environment of the World Wide Web. How much of the budget is spent on technology next year may depend on what your technology team reports about the potential of hypermedia.

You have spent some time exploring hypermediated environments. In fact, rather than picking up the heavy volumes of your now dated *Encyclopaedia Britannica* at home, you prefer to use a digital multimedia encyclopedia on CD. You find it more efficient in finding information. You also occasionally surf the Web and at times, by linking, find yourself on Web pages of interest, some of which you have used in your teaching.

But you are still not convinced that hyperlinked materials are altogether appropriate for your elementary school students. When your second graders get online at the classroom computer, they seem lost when they try to look things up on the Web. It's confusing enough for them, given the fact that much of the material is too difficult for them to comprehend. Adding links that take them to other materials only further complicates their efforts to learn anything. Usually your observations of their linking have indicated that it more often takes students off on a tangent, rather than helping them find out what they were looking for. The other phenomenon you have observed on several occasions is pupils who begin to click on hypertext almost for the sake of clicking. They like to see the computer flash from screen to screen. They seem to quickly become bored with a given screen and the hyperlinks allow them to switch to something else. Is this any way to learn? You have some serious doubts.

This technology team of teachers has asked you, as the unofficial "chair" of the group, to draw up a set of guidelines for analyzing the strengths and weaknesses of hypermediated learning materials. These guidelines should list some of the potential pitfalls associated with using hyperlinked materials. They should also describe what features should be provided by a well-designed piece of hypermediated instruction to help ensure that the learner can benefit from it. Your report should also suggest how teachers might best work with students who are using such systems. Finally, your team has asked you to weigh the potential strengths and weaknesses of hypermedia and then to make recommendations about Web access for young students and about the possible purchase of more CDs for the early primary grades.

ISSUES INQUIRY

1. What have your own experiences with hypermediated learning environments been like? Do you like the instant access to related information? Does it live up to its potential? Have most links been worth activating or would you have been better off staying with what you were looking at?

2. What type of student learns most effectively in a hypermediated environment? How can you most effectively help students who struggle with this type of learning environment to benefit from it?

3. What are the instructional strengths of a hypermediated environment? Is a hypermediated learning environment best suited for certain types of learning experiences? Can unstructured paths through material be beneficial or can too much time be wasted?

4. Do you prefer a more controlled, consistently designed, self-contained hypermediated environment, like an electronic encyclopedia on CD-ROM, to the open-ended, uncontrolled hypermediated environment of the World Wide Web? Or does this depend mainly on the type of learner and the task?

5. How can a hypermediated environment be designed to maximize learning? What recommendations would you make regarding numbers of links, type of information linked to, linking within a body of material versus linking outside it, navigational aids, and so on?

CHAPTER 14

Digital Developments

TELEVISION'S TECHNOLOGICAL TRANSFORMATION

INTRODUCTION

Television has matured considerably as a technology over the course of the past half century. In the 1950s, the medium was monochrome, restricted largely to "line-of-sight" reception within a limited geographical area, not recordable, capable only of one-way transmission, and very expensive to produce. By the new millennium, television had developed a high-definition signal with accurate color rendition. It could be delivered across vast distances by a variety of different technologies in ways that preserved the fidelity of its signal. Videotape or compact disc could be recorded for convenient use. Two-way transmission systems could provide "interactive" capability. Finally, respectable production values in programming could be attained on modest budgets, using equipment that improved in quality and capability each year while its costs dropped.

The improvements in the medium of television have been truly remarkable. As we begin a new millennium, we are about to experience perhaps the most significant technological advance of all, the widespread digitization of television in a digital high-definition format. Digital television promises to be clearer, capable of more dynamic special effects, reproducible without signal degradation, and easier to edit. Were we to obtain and view some educational television programming from the 1950s, most of us would be amused at how "primitive" it would appear, compared with much of the programming available today. Those programs from fifty years ago would seem barely representative of what can be accomplished with the television medium today.

Improvements in Television Quality

A brief review of the technical transformation of television in the second half of the twentieth century will help readers appreciate how much more dynamic the medium is than ever before. What began as a black-and-white signal today provides accurate color signals representing every nuance of the rainbow. In the 1960s, color signal processing was perfected to a degree that made color the standard in television. This was achieved with the use of three separate electronic signals for each of the three primary colors of light: red, green, and blue (yellow is a primary color for pigment, but green is its counterpart for light). Combining these three primary colors produces all the colors of the rainbow. Microscopic light-sensitive dots for red, green, and blue (RGB) wavelengths of light were placed in triads on the front of the picture tube. The electron beams from the three electron guns activate these phosphorescent dots to create images, which combine colors in the ways that an impressionist painting might. For example, a purple item on television would have red and blue phosphor dots activated by the respective red and blue electron guns, and the eye would combine the two colors to produce the color purple.

The grainy TV picture of the past has evolved into the remarkable clarity of high-definition television (HDTV), which approaches that of motion picture film. The original television still frame contained 525 scanning lines. The afore-mentioned electron gun(s) would scan across the front of the picture tube 525 times, activating the phosphorescent coating, to create each frame. HDTV contains over twice that number, more than one thousand scanning lines, so its resolution is much better. The new HDTV format also will be wider than the old analog one. Traditional TV has been shown on a 4 × 3 ratio screen, while HDTV will use a 16 × 9 aspect ratio, similar to that of a wide-screen motion picture.

One problem with switching over to the high-definition, digital format is that it will be very expensive. One reason for this is that every piece of equipment involved, from shooting to viewing, will need to be replaced because the technology is so different. HDTV is digital television (DTV) and the traditional form of TV was processed as an analog signal. Analog signals use continuous waves of energy. Digital information processing consists of discrete bits of information that indicate whether energy is present or not. (For a more thorough discussion of the differences between analog and digital processing, see the introductory chapter entitled "From Video to Virtual Reality: Technology and Its Instructional Potential.") Most media formats today are switching from analog to digital; perhaps most notable is the music industry, with the audio CD replacing the analog record and digital tape formats poised to replace their analog predecessors. The television industry also is about to make this shift because a digital signal can hold more data, does not degrade when duplicated, and can be modified more flexibly.

The tinny sounds of monophonic television sound have been transformed into the hi-fidelity stereo sounds we hear today on our TV speakers, or better yet connect through our stereo systems. Balanced audio systems, such as the "pro logic" technology developed in the early 1990s, are designed to provide powerful, directional "surround sound" experiences for television viewers with the use of multiple speakers. The audio component of HDTV will be digital, so it will sound clearer than the analog audio signals we are accustomed to hearing now. Tomorrow's television image and sound quality should have the ability to capture and hold the attention of students like never before.

The physical size of the television set has long been an important issue for teachers, because they usually want to present programs to an entire class. Students in the back of a classroom will have difficulty seeing the screen clearly, if it is too small. Television screens back in the 1950s were restricted in size, given the limitations of cathode ray "picture tube" technology. The original televisions had small picture tubes in large cabinets. The width of sets gradually grew over the years, so that now very clear pictures are available on picture tubes almost a yard across.

Projection systems were then developed that enlarged the image considerably on a screen, but their images tended not to be as bright as those of picture tubes, especially when viewed from the side. The most recent development in television screen technology is the use of large liquid crystal displays. These wide, flat, so-called "plasma" screens can be conveniently hung on walls, and their image quality is superior to that of most projection systems. The magnification of the television screen has been a plus for educators, since it facilitates viewing by entire classes of students.

Sending Signals

The transmission of television signals also has changed dramatically over the years. Television in the 1950s was broadcast from a transmission tower with line-of-sight coverage, whose signal strength weakened across distance and was subject to interference. Ultrahigh frequency (UHF) transmissions, above 13 on the tuner, were even weaker than the very high frequency (VHF) signals for channels 2 to 13. Television rarely reached very far beyond the confines of major metropolitan areas. Today, however, television is transmitted via a variety of technologies that can send it to every corner of the world and still preserve its signal strength.

The satellites launched in the 1960s provided a quantum leap in television transmission. A single satellite's transmission area or "footprint" can cover one-third of the earth, and, by relaying signals, today's global satellite configuration can provide nearly instantaneous worldwide viewing of a given event. Over the years, satellites have become capable of transmitting more television channels at a higher signal strength. Consequently, receiver dishes for concentrating the satellite signal, which were once two meters across, are now less than a meter wide. These dishes can process satellite signals for very clear reception of large numbers of channels, sometimes numbering in the hundreds.

Coaxial copper cable wiring can also carry more than one hundred television channels with fine reception into the home. Now fiber optic technology is expanding this capability. Optical fiber can transmit even more channels with even higher signal quality than can coaxial cable. With these advances in transmission technology, more channels with more varied programming are available today in nearly every corner of the globe. The bandwidth and broadcasting time are available to provide millions of students with educational programming in a wide variety of subject areas.

The shift to digital television will affect its transmission. "Bandwidth" is the term for measuring how much data can be transmitted by a given system (again, refer to the "From Video to Virtual Reality" chapter for more detail). On the one hand, the high-definition signal takes up more transmission bandwidth than the older analog format. But, on the other hand, a digital signal can be compressed so that *more* programming can be transmitted in a system of a given bandwidth capacity. Compression will help provide even more programming for educators than ever before.

Television footage can be compressed by a device known as a codec, an abbreviation for *co*mpressor-*dec*ompressor. Compression can also allow more television footage to be sent via a less expensive telecommunications connection, perhaps an Integrated Systems Digital Network (ISDN) or Telecommunications-1 (T1) line, that might not be able carry the larger uncompressed regular television signal. Normally it takes a much more expensive Telecommunications-3 (T3) line to transmit television. Since the cheaper connections carry less bandwidth, to use them requires compression. Compressed video is of lower quality and may exhibit ghosting, jerky motion, and delays that desynchronize lips with speech. But compression techniques, in particular those developed by the Motion Picture Expert Group (MPEG), are improving constantly, so that it is now often difficult to tell that the signal has been compressed.

Compression techniques will allow television to be used more extensively than ever before. As the ensuing discussion will address, compression has been the key to some major recent developments in the television industry, such as the DVD compact disc, low-cost videoconferencing, and the digital editing of video footage on computers.

Television Becomes Video

The original forms of television could not be very easily preserved. Our only records of the early days of television are kinescopes, film taken of the television screen (or the performance). Of course, these recordings on celluloid were no longer "television" (an electronic signal). Now television can easily and automatically be recorded on tape for playback at the convenience of the viewer. The development of videotape was, of course, of enormous importance to the movie and television industry. The video rental business boomed. Video stores can be found nearly everywhere. Videotape can now be found in even the most remote parts of the planet, due to the popularity of movies on tape.

Videotape was also a very important advance for school television. Seldom could classes watch live programs, because they did not happen to be aired at the time when the class was meeting. No longer are scheduling problems such a major impediment to utilization of television in the classroom, because programs can be taped and shown at a convenient time. In addition, thousands of educational programs are commercially available to schools on tape, and teachers can use the resources of videotape collections available in their schools and districts.

Videocassette recorders (VCRs) also provide a variety of playback features that teachers can use to effectively present television footage to a class. They can cue the footage exactly where they wish to start presenting it. They can start and stop the program to have discussions about it. They can fast-forward past material they do not want to show. They can rewind and replay material for review purposes. Critical footage can be shown in slow motion for purposes of clarification. The VCR can help put the instructor more in control of the classroom television viewing experience.

As a medium, videotape continues to improve in quality while getting smaller and lighter. One example is the availability of Super-VHS tape, which provides higher-quality recordings than the standard VHS half-inch tape (and is roughly equivalent to the quality of the bulkier, wider three-quarter-inch tape format). Both its resolution is higher and its color fidelity is better than the VHS that most of us now watch at home. The same can be said for Hi-8 and Betacam tape formats, which have upgraded the older 8mm and Betamax formats. The next stage in the evolution of tape will be digital. Digital videotapes are gradually replacing the analog tapes we use now, because their quality is higher and they can be copied with almost no loss in quality. As the quality of videotape improves, so will the quality of the prerecorded television broadcasts we watch and the tapes we record on our VCRs.

Television has also been available on optical disc for more than a decade. In the 1980s, the twelve-inch videodisc offered a slightly higher quality signal than videotape. Its laser pickup system allowed for clearer viewing of still pictures, which tend to wiggle on a tape being held still by the playback head of a VCR. Because each second of television is composed of thirty still frames, a minute holds 1,800 stills, and one hour contains 108,000 video stills. The one-hour videodisc has been an excellent archival medium, for it can display the equivalent of 1,080 slide carousels, each filled with 100 slides! Videodisc technology also permitted rapid random access of material, avoiding the time it took a tape to fast-forward or rewind. Interactive computer-based training software could take advantage of videodisc materials, while access of taped material would be prohibitively slow. However, a major disadvantage of this format was that videodisc players could not record video footage, as VCRs did. So the twelve-inch videodisc format was never especially popular in either homes or schools. Its use was primarily in corporate and military training settings, in many cases in interactive form.

Now television is available on CDs. Low-quality video clips have been part of materials on CD-ROMs for many years. These clips have partial-screen, low-resolution, jerky images because there is not enough room on a CD-ROM to play full-screen, full-motion television signals. Television signals take up an enormous amount of memory space on any storage medium. Now, another CD format has been developed, the Digital Video Disk (DVD), which can play back two hours of good-quality full-screen television. Players for showing movies on DVD are on the market, and computers now have built-in DVD, rather than CD-ROM players. Improved data compression techniques with DVD allows for more efficient storage of television footage. Consequently, a DVD can hold over ten times as much data as a CD-ROM. This is why it can provide so much more video, of higher quality.

Television on CD can be more interactive than on videotape, because of the aforementioned rapid random access. Television segments can be integrated with computer data, including text materials, pictures, and sounds. The DVD will help "marry" television with the computer, a union that can provide very dynamic forms of instruction, combining the strengths of both media formats. DVD titles will provide more visually interesting classroom materials than ever was possible with a CD-ROM, and students should enjoy working with this new format.

Shooting in a Gallery (or Museum, Craft Fair, Garage Sale, Etc.)

In its first few decades, television was mainly produced in studios with expensive equipment by teams of trained professionals. Today television of reasonably high quality can be produced by one person in nearly any location with relatively inexpensive portable equipment. Teachers can use television to bring events into the classroom. Students can develop, shoot, and edit their own television productions to be shown to the class or perhaps to the rest of the school. Schools can produce television programs for the community and air them on local access cable channels. Why is television production so much easier nowadays? The main reason is that equipment has become lighter, more automatic, and yet cheaper.

Cameras are a good example. The quality of cameras has improved over the years as television technology has evolved. The original television cameras had large, heavy tubes, making them both bulky and fragile. But in the 1990s, the camera tube was replaced by a light-sensitive solid-state device. These "chip" or charge-coupled device (CCD) cameras were smaller, lighter, and more durable than their tube-based predecessors. Since these new cameras were also more sensitive to light, they could be used indoors more easily without extra lamps. Smaller cameras led to the development of the convenient "camcorder," with both recorder and camera in one lightweight unit, which replaced the "portapack," a two-piece unit with separate camera and videotape recorder.

The camcorder has helped make video recording a widely enjoyed family practice, and it also has expanded the amount of television used in schools. Small-tape formats have evolved along with the smaller units. Now 8-mm tape competes with half-inch VHS-C (compact cassette) for the home consumer market. Semiprofessional videographers often use higher-grade forms of these formats, Hi-8mm or Super-VHS. These tapes use a purer metal stock and have some superior signal processing, which separates color and brightness parts of the television image. The new multipin S connectors can be used to send this component (rather than composite) signal to a television set. Now the new mini-DV format allows videographers to shoot digital television footage in a camcorder, and these digital recordings are of even higher quality than the aforementioned analog formats. These high-quality small cassette formats have encouraged production efforts in both homes and schools, since a better-looking result is possible, without sacrificing the convenience of the light camcorder.

Another factor that has contributed to the growing number of amateur videographers is the degree to which most of the important camera controls have been automated. Years ago, camera operators needed to be both knowledgeable and quick to obtain professional-looking footage with their manual controls. But with today's equipment, the inexperienced videographer can often shoot fairly respectable-looking footage with little training or practice because so many of the basic camera controls have been automated. An auto iris controls exposure. An auto focus provides clear focus on objects in the center of the shot. An auto "white balance" sets the proper-looking color for the type of lighting. Recent advances can even correct operator mistakes. For example, image stabilization features automatically shift the frame in the opposite direction of the camera's movement, thereby reducing the shakiness of shots.

Another plus for those willing to read the manual is that the higher-quality camcorders allow camcorder operators to shift out of automatic mode into manual settings. This allows the videographer to control the look of the shot. Certain situations are problematic in automatic settings. For example, too much background light can close an auto iris so much that the subject will look too dark. Too much movement in a scene may prompt annoying refocusing by an autofocus system. Doing a manual white balance often provides more accurate color rendition than the automatic system. Some basic awareness of how to control light, focus, and color can help amateur videographers shoot more-professional-looking footage with today's camcorders. Home videographers can shoot video that they will not be embarrassed to show their friends. In schools, students and teachers can shoot respectable-looking television segments that they may be proud to show in the classroom.

Editing Goes Digital

Creating a television "production," however, involves more than just shooting footage. It involves editing that footage into a program. The editing process is just as important as the shooting process. Unfortunately, the absence of any editing capability in schools has discouraged more dynamic use of television by teachers and students. A few decades ago, no school could afford an editing system. But low-cost editing systems have become widely available. Small inexpensive editors can be connected to a pair of camcorders or VCRs, and footage can be assembled into a program. The video recorders must have the ability to take a remote signal from the editor, but higher end units generally have this capability. The editor allows for control over both recorders, so that raw footage in one recorder can be cued up and then copied onto the master tape in the other recorder. A good editor controller will allow for precise cueing of exactly what footage is to be copied and precision in where it is placed in the final production. It will also force both tapes to preroll back, so that they are moving at proper speed when the footage is dubbed (otherwise it will shake). Videographers can assemble programs from their raw footage that includes only their best footage, communicates that material in sensible sequences, moves at an appropriate pace, and adds voice, music, lettering, graphics, and so on.

However, an even more important video-editing development is the digitization of the television medium. Nowadays television programming is being edited on computers. Analog footage can be captured and digitized by computers with audio/visual capability. Television footage shot with digital equipment can now be directly inputted into a computer with a "Firewire" connection, a standard feature of new computers. The digitized television footage can then be processed in the computer with editing software, such as Adobe Premier, Avid Cinema, or iMovie. As with word processing of text, digitization provides considerably more flexibility in the arranging of shots than was ever before possible with analog systems. It also makes the addition of special effects easier.

Teachers and students can now take video footage and arrange it into programs on microcomputers. Relatively low cost systems, like Avid's new products, are beginning to appear in schools, with user-friendly interfaces for television editing. Television has become a means of communicating and sharing educational experiences in classrooms throughout the world. Working on their own productions can help students develop some important skills: researching, writing, scripting, visual literacy, sensitivity to the impact of music, organizing, working with others, equipment proficiency, and an opportunity to be creative. Television, with a little help from the computer industry, is becoming an increasingly important medium in our schools.

How can television be most effectively used to facilitate learning? Television's contributions to learning are potentially numerous and varied. The medium can play several different significant roles. These roles include presentation, storage, transmission, and production of learning materials. Let's examine its potential in each of these areas.

Television As a Presentation Device

Television can serve as a presentation aid for live demonstrations. The telephoto lens can magnify details of objects and show them on a large monitor to students in the back of the room who otherwise would not be able to see them. Video copystands, like those sold by Elmo, are now widely available with mounted cameras possessing macrolenses that can magnify any item placed on the platform below and send that image to a monitor. These devices can also be used to present text (and pictures) to the whole class, if the monitor is large enough. Projection systems can be used very effectively with video copystands, replacing the need for overhead projectors. Of course, such systems can also be used to present computer materials, including PowerPoint presentations.

Possibly the most common way of using television in the classroom is to show educational programming, either live or on tape. Sometimes live programming has an irreplaceable immediacy that is difficult to replicate on tape, as did the live reports on CNN from Iraq during the Persian Gulf War. But for most educational programming, there are advantages to using tape (or disk) materials associated with convenience of timing and control over the presentation of the material (see earlier discussion). Laser disc formats have the aforementioned advantages over tape of clearer still frames and much quicker random access of specific footage.

The amount of educational television footage available to schools is extensive and growing each week. With the expansion of the airtime on transmission systems, especially those delivered by cable and satellite, new information-based networks were born in the 1980s. Some of the more noteworthy include the Discovery Channel, the Learning Channel, Arts and Entertainment, and the History Channel.

There is also a set of networks devoted exclusively to news, led by the Cable News Network but now also including MSNBC and the Fox News Network. In addition, other cable networks for special audiences may present specials that are appropriate for certain school units: MTV for music class, ESPN for physical education, C-Span for government, and so on. Of course, we must mention the oldest, most experienced educational network, the Public Broadcasting Service. A great deal of entertainment programming also can be used for educational purposes, especially movies that are based on actual events or those that depict other cultures or previous historical periods. A wealth of television programming can be effectively used in the classroom.

However, over the years, a great deal of television programming has been used ineffectively in schools, giving it a bad reputation in some cases. Sometimes it did not even relate to the curriculum. Or it was shown without any effort on the part of the teacher to discuss its subject matter with the class. In the most flagrant instances of this, television has been used essentially as a classroom "baby-sitter." It is important for teachers to prepare for the use of television footage in the class. Programs shown in class should be previewed by teachers, so that they can prepare to use them in their teaching. It may help to take some notes, especially since it is not always easy to refer back to part of a video, like one might with a book. It is a good idea to prepare a class handout that outlines the key material, highlights key points, or lists thought-provoking questions.

On the day of the viewing, before presenting a segment, teachers should make some introductory remarks, indicating the relevance of this material to what is being studied. Teacher handouts and other relevant printed materials might be passed out before the program to help orient the group. Or, depending on their content, they might be more appropriately disseminated after the program is over. During a video presentation, it may make sense to stop the tape for explanations or discussions of what has just been seen. Starting and stopping a tape may be more instructionally effective than letting it play in its entirety. This makes sense, since student attention spans are only so long. Also teachers can clarify points along the way and encourage an interest in the tape's content to keep students engaged. After the program ends, the teacher should conduct a follow-up discussion that reviews key points and explores critical issues. Asking the group some thoughtful questions is important, so that they can fully process the material and develop their thinking skills. Using media effectively is an important part of any effective teacher's repertoire of skills.

Video As an Archival Medium

Television is an excellent storage medium for educational materials. Its ability to store still pictures has already been noted. Thirty still frames per second are required to produce the standard television image, so even a few minutes of television contain many stills. A one-hour videodisc can store the equivalent of a truckload of slide trays. But video can also store a great deal of moving footage, up to six hours on a VHS tape at the slower (SLP) recording speed. As such it can archive events even of lengthy duration. Hours of material can be stored on one inexpensive, compact little half-inch cassette. When the DVD compact disc can be more easily recorded upon, it will serve as an even better video storage device, for optical disc is actually a more durable medium for archiving than is tape.

Television is an excellent medium for recording events that some students may not be present at. It is also excellent for showing these educational experiences to absentees or classes in subsequent school years. Special guest presentations at the school can be taped for this purpose, as can special events, like plays, sporting competitions, and debates. Videotaping experiences outside the building also can be worthwhile. These might include class field trips or events taped by a student (or teacher) that the entire class might appreciate. Video also can be helpful for educational research efforts. Interviews can be videotaped and reviewed at a later point. For really serious studies, researchers may produce written transcripts based on the taped material.

Another role that videotape can serve very effectively is that of recording performances for purposes of individual feedback or evaluation. Videotaping of teaching performances has been used widely to help teachers hone their classroom skills. Video can also be used effectively to provide feedback to students, especially in areas of performance like sports, speech, music, dance, interview skills, and so on. Having a video recording of a performance on video can be helpful to teachers who need to evaluate it. It can be viewed again if necessary or examined more closely (perhaps in slow motion).

Video may be used to document behaviors or processes. Sometimes it makes sense for teachers to record a student's behavior in class to try to document problem areas for administrators, parents, specialists, or even the student himself or herself. Or conferences may be taped as documentation of efforts to address student difficulties or as a way of trying to address the issues in subsequent viewing.

Most processes can be presented clearly and concisely on videotape. Some processes that occur over time may be interesting to periodically videotape as a way of documenting their various stages; for example, the growth of plants, the construction of buildings, the positioning of heavenly bodies, or the shift in length of shadows. Editing can help produce dynamic time-lapse television segments.

Telecommunicating Educational Experiences

The transmission capability of television can of course be used to deliver broadcasts. Unfortunately, for a variety of reasons, school television has never attained high levels of utilization. But utilization levels are on the rise, partially as a result of technological advances. The technical capability for receiving educational programming is, of course, greater than ever, with satellite and cable systems augmenting transmission from television towers. But another factor in the expanded use of television in schools is the impact of a few special large-scale school television projects.

One of these projects is the formation of the Cable in the Classroom consortium. The cable television industry has provided some exciting new opportunities for schools to take advantage of television. Many schools have been wired for cable transmission, sometimes for free as part of local contracts worked out with cable companies. In many cases, one of the stipulations associated with a township giving their cable rights to a given provider is that it wire all the schools in the district.

The Cable in the Classroom consortium includes all of the major information-based cable networks. It was formed to facilitate the use of cable television in the schools. For example, it informs teachers what programming will be broadcast on various educational cable networks. The monthly magazine, distributed to schools throughout the country, provides a detailed schedule of that month's programming, highlights some potentially noteworthy programs, and provides feature articles on topics that relate to the use of television in the classroom.

Another important school television project is the Channel One effort, described in some detail in Chapter 5, "TV or Not TV? That Is the Question: Commercialization of the Classroom." This project has equipped more than twelve thousand secondary schools throughout the country with the television equipment they need to show programming throughout the school. This equipment includes TV sets in nearly every classroom, cable wiring throughout the building, a "head end" for presenting programming schoolwide from a VCR, and a satellite reception dish on the roof. The project also provides programming, most notably the daily newscast designed for teens entitled "Channel One" news. Some educational programs from PBS are also part of the deal.

Channel One schools have generally used television more extensively than their counterparts who did not subscribe to this project. The equipment has allowed teachers and students in these schools to use television in the classroom much more conveniently than in the past. Not only is there a TV set permanently installed, but the local cable company's wiring can be connected to it, as can a VCR for playing of tapes. Some Channel One schools have used television in ways that go far beyond the showing of the daily newscast. They have shown what can be accomplished in a school building when a sufficient amount of television equipment is made available to teachers.

But television's transmission capabilities have transcended the traditional type of broadcast. Nowadays, many transmission systems, including cable, microwave, or satellite, can provide two-way capability. These two-way systems can provide video teleconferences, wherein participants at different locations can see and hear one another. The television experience can be more interactive with a two-way transmission. Many teachers have attended videoconferences that last several hours and provide professional development. In many cases, the connection back to the broadcasting facility is not via television but telephone, because it is less expensive.

Some large-scale satellite-based distance education projects, like the Satellite Educational Resources Consortium (SERC) and TI-IN, serve schools across entire sections of the country (see Chapter 15, "Distance Education: So Far, So Good?"). They provide television-based classes, mainly of advanced high school courses, with telephone connections back to the teacher at each site. Their classes consist of scores of students, in scores of schools, separated in many cases by hundreds of miles. Many students in rural schools can receive coursework previously unavailable to them.

But full *two-way* videoconferencing is also being used more and more often for distance education. Sometimes called "interactive television," multiple classrooms can be connected via TV, so that the teacher and students can all see and hear one another. The experience can create a kind of "superclassroom" that involves three or four different locations and many students. Because full-motion, full-screen television is expensive, many of these systems now use compressed video instead. VTEL and PictureTel are two companies that specialize in providing compressed videoconferencing systems. Multiple-site institutions, like many universities and corporations, can provide classes at several locations at once or even throughout their entire system. Some school districts are using interactive television systems to share teacher expertise and equalize curricular opportunities across all schools within the boundaries of the district.

Highly compressed television signals can be sent via the Internet, despite its low bandwidth (signal-carrying capability). With a camera like the eyeball-shaped Quickcam and a mike connected to a computer, along with some special software, students can interact with their peers in other schools across the country or on the other side of the world (see Chapter 10, "It Takes a Global Village: Multicultural Studies Through Telecommunications"). They can also use this so-called desktop video to interact online with an expert on a given topic. In addition, teachers can use such systems to share ideas with one another (see Chapter 16, "Conceptual Connections: Establishing Online Learning Communities"). The most commonly used software for computer-based Internet-driven television is called CU-SeeMe (get it?). As networks improve and the Internet is able to handle more data than ever before, it will be capable of transmitting higher-quality television signals. With the global reach of the Internet, television has another means of reaching students around the world.

No Big Production

Perhaps the most exciting potential role for television in schools is to provide opportunities for classroom productions. Television production, as mentioned earlier, has become more feasible for schools with the development of light, inexpensive camcorders and digital editing software on computers. Nevertheless, producing a television program can be a challenging, complex task. It involves much more than just the technical skills to operate the television equipment. It requires a considerable amount of organization. It demands some creativity and some writing skill. It may involve research. It requires social skills, since invariably a number of people will be involved. Good productions demand a visual sense of what to shoot and how to shoot it. The show may include some music, so those aesthetic sensibilities may also come into play. Timing is important in shooting, acting, and editing. Patience will undoubtedly be necessary, and, of course, some determination. A class video production can help students develop a number of different worthwhile skills.

Teachers should be prepared to deal with student frustration as they face all these challenges. But few activities are more exciting or more rewarding than the development of a successful television production. Television can be a very creative outlet, allowing students to express themselves in very interesting ways. Some possibilities include video self-portraits, video poems, music videos, improvisation, parodies of movies or television programs, mock commercials, historical or literary dramatizations, and newscasts from the past. Other possible projects might be more documentary in nature, capturing footage of actual events, conducting interviews, or shooting scenery.

Television productions can work well as culminating experiences at the end of a unit of study. Such a production might be shown to other classes. A television production can be a powerful vehicle for learning. In fact, the excitement of working on a television production can generate a great deal of enthusiasm for exploring a given topic and thereby may enhance levels of learning. A creative teacher can use television to make the classroom a more exciting, dynamic place to be.

RECOMMENDED READING

Barron, A. 1995. An overview of digital video. *Journal of Computing in Higher Education* 7 (1): 69–84.

Committee on Applications and Technology. 1998. *Advanced digital video and the national information infrastructure.* Washington, DC: Report of the Information Infrastructure Task Force, ERIC, ED 385274.

Educational Services, Thirteen/WNET. 1995. *Eyes open! Hands on! Using video as a catalyst for learning.* New York: WNET-TV, ERIC, ED 376084.

Fleisher, F. 1995. Between postage stamps and digitalization: The changing roles of educational broadcasting. *Educational Media International* 32 (1): 18–20.

OTHER REFERENCES

Barron, A., and G. Orwig. 1997. *New technologies for education: A beginner's guide.* Englewood, CO: Libraries Unlimited.

Colella, C. 1994. TV: Foe or friend? *Momentum* 25 (3): 57–58.

Corporation for Public Broadcasting. 1997. *Study of school uses of television and video.* Washington, DC, ERIC, ED 413879.

Fink, E. 1998. *The transition to digital video: What lessons have we learned so far?* ERIC, ED 418691.

Galbreath, J. 1996. Interactive television: The state of the industry. *Educational Technology* 36 (2): 24–35.

Meyer, M. 1996. *Aspects of school television in Europe. A documentation.* New Providence, NJ: K. G. Saur Publishing.

Schiller, S. 1991. Educational applications of instructional television and cable programming. *Media and Methods* 27 (4): 20–21, 52.

Seels, B. 1996. Integrated research on learning from television. *Proceedings of the Association for Educational Communications and Technology*, ERIC, ED 397837.

SCENARIO

As part of the social studies curriculum, you are required to teach a unit to your sixth-grade class on the conflict-ridden "sixties era" (actually the decade from around 1963 to 1973). You have been disappointed in the students' lack of interest in the topic so far. Since it was well before their lifetimes and the social climate differed considerably from that of today, it seems difficult to get them to relate to this period (or maybe "dig it" or even "grok it," as one might have said back then!).

But you have an idea for getting this class more involved. Your school recently purchased four new video camcorders. Kids always seem interested in television, and many of them have doubtless already shot some footage with their family's home camera. The class could even do some primitive editing by connecting a camcorder to a VCR and copying selected footage. (You might even bring in your own VCR for this purpose.) Furthermore, four new computers in the school lab came with Avid Cinema, a digital video-editing application. Your principal has encouraged the faculty to try this software. Why not ask the class to develop creative projects about the sixties that involve the use of television? After all, Vietnam was after the first "television war" and the Watergate scandal was dramatized each night on television's evening news shows.

Students could use some television footage from historical programs in the school's tape library. In fact, you noticed that the library has a copy of the definitive ten-part, award-winning PBS series entitled "The Vietnam War" and another documentary called "Making Sense of the Sixties." Copyright shouldn't matter when nobody will make any money from these student productions. Anyway, sixties protest leader Abbie Hoffman once wrote a book entitled *Steal This Book*.

You realize that you cannot simply instruct your students, "Do a creative television project related to some sixties-era theme." Many would be uncertain as to how to begin. So you sit down to prepare a list of suggested video-based activities that your students might consider for their projects. The students can then choose which type of project to pursue. If some come up with project ideas on their own, that's fine. After some deliberation, you have a few ideas, but not enough. So you decide to contact two of your colleagues with whom you sometimes collaborate. You used to team teach with one and the other has a special interest in the sixties. He was in college back then and he remembers those days (slightly hazily, however). During the lunch break at school the next day, the three of you brainstorm a set of interesting sixties-related topics for this assignment.

Now you are ready to spring this assignment on the class. You tell them that they are going to break into teams to produce some videos about the sixties. They can be documentaries or creative fictional pieces. You say that these projects can include material that is already available on tape, but they must also include some footage shot by the team. Existing programming might be real footage from the era, as in the Woodstock movie, or Hollywood dramatizations like *Born on the Fourth of July*. You remind students that these projects need to be feasible both in scope and in terms of the capability of the equipment available. You then conduct a brainstorming session in which students identify some topics of special interest to them (which include civil rights, the Vietnam War, the protest movement, hippies, drugs, rock music, communes, assassinations, race riots, Watergate, etc.). You have a start to what could be an exciting unit.

Describe how the rest of this unit might be planned and supervised. Without some thought beforehand and some guidelines, the classroom sessions could become quite chaotic. What role do you plan to play in assisting with these projects? How will you help students when they are discouraged or unable to get the project together? How can the class best take advantage of the television equipment available? How will you help them develop the skills they need to complete their television productions? How will you encourage the development of worthwhile content? What kinds of culminating activities might accompany the final viewing of the productions? Finally, how will you evaluate the students' work and what they have learned from this experience?

ISSUES INQUIRY

1. Describe some of the advantages of television as an educational medium. What kinds of material can best be taught using television? How can it most effectively be used in the classroom to enliven and improve instruction?

2. Discuss several ways in which the "digital revolution" has improved the medium of television. Then discuss how these advances have provided enhanced opportunities to use the medium for educational purposes.

3. Describe how you would prepare to show an instructional television program to your class. What kinds of activities might you plan to make this viewing a worthwhile educational experience?

4. Discuss some of the challenges associated with producing a television program in class with your students. What kind of equipment is needed? How can a television project best be planned? What kinds of skills need to be developed? How can a team of students be encouraged to work together effectively?

5. Television has improved a great deal in its first fifty years. Think about how television may change in the *next* fifty years. What do you predict? Will these changes affect the schools in any significant way? How so?

CHAPTER 15

Distance Education

SO FAR, SO GOOD?

INTRODUCTION

Distance education has recently become an extremely important area of instructional technology. Distance education (DE) is an educational experience wherein the teacher and the student are separated by distance or in time (or both). New advances in telecommunications and computer networking have provided exciting new opportunities for course delivery both "on camera" and online. But both individuals and educational institutions need to decide whether these options are appropriate for them. One important issue is whether the instruction provided is of acceptable quality, and whether it meets accreditation standards. Another problem has been attrition, for many distance learners quit before completing their coursework. The experience can be a lonely, isolated one in which it may be difficult to maintain one's motivation. Yet another critical question is whether projects are cost-effective, given the expense associated with the technologies involved.

A Brief History of Distance Education

What today is described as "distance education" has a history that dates back more than a century. It was originally called correspondence study, because it took place through the mail. In the early 1800s, when reliable national mail services were firmly established in the United States and Europe, courses by mail began to emerge. By the end of the century, a number of well-established correspondence schools had been established. The Chautauqua Institute in upstate New York was providing adult correspondence education across the country. The International Correspondence Schools of Pennsylvania offered training in a variety of job skills, using a combination of mail delivery and some face-to-face instruction from railroad cars. The first university "extension division" was established at the University of Chicago in the 1890s, which offered courses by mail. Women were encouraged to educate themselves through "home study." One large project, entitled The Society to Encourage Studies at Home, enrolled more than seven thousand women across the nation in the late 1800s.

The University of Wisconsin became a leader in DE efforts of the early part of the twentieth century. Its extension division provided written study materials for students and experimented with educational radio broadcasts in the 1920s. A number of different universities in the United States experimented with radio broadcasts for their distant students in the 1920s and 1930s. But after World War II, the use of radio for educational broadcasts declined in the United States, partly because it was supplanted by the arrival of television. However, because it is inexpensive, ubiquitous, and can communicate effectively with illiterate audiences, radio has been widely used in many developing countries to expand educational opportunities.

Television was hailed as a revolutionary development in the field of education when it became widely available in the 1950s. The Ford Foundation spent millions of dollars on its "master teacher" project, which broadcast lessons taught by talented teachers to classroom television sets in multiple schools. The regular teachers remained in their classrooms, to follow up these televised lectures and work directly with the students. This approach was used, most notably, in a project conducted in Hagerstown, Maryland, where school television seemingly helped raise the educational level of that rural school district. However, few teachers wished to play "second fiddle" to a master teacher on television, and general teacher opposition to this idea made it nearly impossible to implement.

In the 1970s, the British Open University (OU) was established, and it soon became a model for DE efforts in higher education around the world. Thorough curriculum planning is stressed. The OU develops its materials with a team approach that includes instructional designers, content specialists, and media specialists. While much of the success of the OU has been attributed to its excellent print materials, it also uses a "multiple media" approach to course delivery, which includes radio broadcasts, audiotapes, television programs, videotapes, and so on. In the eighties, the OU began distributing lessons on computer discs, and in the nineties it has developed its own Web-based online course components. It contracts with tutors across the country, who help individual students and conduct group study sessions. The British OU attained full accreditation as an institution of higher learning, so its graduates can take advantage of the professional opportunities to which any university degree should entitle them. Today, the OU remains one of the world's most respected DE efforts, and its spin-off OUs around the globe are educating hundreds of thousands who otherwise would not be able to obtain a college education.

Teleconferencing Technologies

The telephone has been used in DE projects for a long time. For years, it was an important supplementary means of communication between DE participants. Students working at a distance could discuss assignments with classmates and talk directly with their instructor to receive guidance about their work. But two developments expanded the instructional potential of the telephone. One was the widespread availability of the speaker phone, allowing groups to converse. The other development was the "bridging" of calls, so that more than two connections could interact at once. "Audioconferencing" was born. It provides opportunities for an instructor to reach many students at several sites, and for everyone to interact. Courses can be taught in this way fairly inexpensively. With satellite services, these courses can cover extensive distances. Students can go to nearby institutions where speaker phones with the appropriate connections are available and take coursework from an institution on the other side of the state, or even in another region of the country. The lack of visuals, however, is a handicap, especially for certain subjects. So-called audiographic systems that provide limited graphics, usually on a computer screen, have been tried to compensate for this deficiency. Nowadays, Web pages can be effectively used for this purpose. Another problem is that when too many students are involved, discussions can become somewhat disjointed, with confusion as to who is speaking and who has the floor next. But at least students can interact with an instructor and their fellow students in an experience that is somewhat similar to a traditional class.

"Videoconferencing" provides a similar educational opportunity, but, of course, with the addition of a full-motion visual signal. An "interactive television" experience can come very close to duplicating the conventional face-to-face classroom experience. Participants at multiple sites can see and talk with one another, with the use of multiple cameras, monitors, and mikes. These systems allow organizations to connect their various facilities around the state or across the country. They can, of course, also allow for sharing of coursework or training between several different institutions. These two-way television signals can be sent by microwave, cable, or satellite.

Although some are sending full television signals back and forth, it is less expensive to compress the video signal using a compressor-decompressor (codec) and send it across special telephone lines, like ISDN services or on a T1 telecommunications line, which costs far less to purchase or rent than does a full cable connection (T3 line). The loss in signal quality is negligible (some possible image ghosting and voice-lip movement desynchronization). Companies like V-TEL and PictureTel have become industry leaders in providing compressed videoconferencing systems for corporations and educational institutions across the country.

Many videoconferences are "one-shot deals." A presentation on a given topic is advertised and interested parties attend the videoconference at sites that can receive the video signal. Many of these broadcasts are shown nationwide. Sometimes there are two-way video signals between sites, but this is rare, because of the costs involved. The majority of sites involved will only receive the television signal, with no return capability. However, telephone connections are usually available at each site, so attendees can ask questions or comment. Interactivity is possible, but it is usually somewhat limited, in part because thousands may participate and only so much interactivity is possible between so many.

But teleconferencing is being used in a more highly interactive way, with two-way television signals available at all participating sites in a form sometimes described as "interactive television." These systems are mostly used for regularly scheduled classes to be offered at multiple sites. The instructor has a set of monitors mounted in his or her "line of sight," one for each distant site. He or she can interact with the students at a distance almost as if they were in the room with the instructor. Likewise, students at each site have a set of monitors in front of them, displaying the instructor and their classmates at each of the different sites. Everyone can participate while seeing and hearing one another. Usually the classroom has a copystand with a special video camera that magnifies whatever is set before it. The teacher can use this video copystand to display class notes (or objects of study) for onscreen presentation through the system. Computer signals also can be incorporated into the broadcasts, so computer skills can be taught or material can be presented using PowerPoint. Networked connections allow for computer-mediated communications between all participants. And with the addition of a fax machine in each room, hard copy documents, like tests and assignments, can be quickly sent between sites.

This form of DE can effectively "expand" a class across the miles to multiple locations, while preserving most aspects of traditional, face-to-face instruction. One example of where this approach is commonly used is at multiple-site institutions, like universities with branch campuses, where course offerings at a given location can be made available to students at other campuses. Corporations can provide training sessions to workers at various plants. Public school districts also can expand their course offerings. Specialized coursework, like foreign languages and advanced placement courses that are normally taught at only one school, can be made available to other schools throughout the district.

Satellite systems can provide videoconferencing services across vast geographic expanses. For example, the Satellite Educational Resources Consortium (SERC) and TI-IN each can cover about half the continental United States. For fees paid by client schools, usually in rural areas, they offer coursework to students for whom the course would otherwise not be available. Teachers in television studios, equipped with all the apparatus of a standard classroom or laboratory, teach daily lessons that are broadcast live to their clientele. It would be very expensive to provide a video uplink from every school with a student taking the class (not to mention a nightmare for the instructor, trying to track all these sites on monitors!). So students contact the instructor by telephone. Work can be submitted online, via fax, or by mail. These satellite systems provide instruction for thousands of students across vast distances, improving their educational opportunities by means of DE.

Sometimes facilitators are hired to oversee the educational experiences at the DE sites. In many cases, this approach has proven more successful than leaving students on their own. But this may depend upon the facilitator's qualifications, and it increases the costs associated with the course. The appropriateness of providing a facilitator can depend upon the size of the group, the age of the students, the difficulty of the course, and so on.

Online Instruction

Other approaches to DE have arisen along with the widespread availability of the microcomputer. Some DE institutions mail their students entire courses on computer disks, substituting the interactivity of the programs for the interactivity with an instructor. The computer's capabilities make it an excellent delivery device for well-organized, interactive lessons that can respond appropriately to student performance. Mistakes can be remediated, and students can be shifted to other parts of the unit, depending on how well they are doing with the material. So some students can work fairly independently at a distance with computerized lessons, and they may be able to effectively complete whole units without the intervention of an instructor. Many skills can be taught effectively through computer-assisted instruction, but this approach cannot always be substituted for other critical instructional experiences. Some types of learning do not lend themselves very readily to a computerized approach. Most college coursework, for example, is conceptual, and students can significantly benefit from discussions with others. It is very difficult to program a computer to respond to the kinds of open-ended material that is often dealt with in higher education.

It is the communications potential of the computer that has really facilitated DE efforts. Computer networking provides instantaneous forms of electronic communication that can substitute for face-to-face discussion. Online "chat" sessions are less expensive than the telephone and can accommodate many participants at once. Asynchronous forms of electronic communication can also be used effectively by DE participants. E-mail can allow for ongoing communications between student and teacher, as well as between students. Assignments can be distributed and submitted electronically. Listservs and newsgroups can provide opportunities for online discussion sessions. With a listserv, each e-mail message is sent to all those who have signed up to participate in the "electronic discussion." With a newsgroup, each message is posted on a server for any participant to view. A great deal of communication can take place between members of a class "at a distance." The instructor can moderate the discussion, much as he or she would in a face-to-face situation.

If the two-way videoconference is the ideal technology for synchronous DE, then the World Wide Web is its counterpart for asynchronous DE. The Web is an enormous educational resource. For those who can access it, there is information in abundance. It can substitute, to some degree, for the availability of a library. The problem is separating the "wheat from the chaff." Because it is largely unregulated and unedited, a lot of material on the Web is not worth pursuing. There is also so much information that it may be difficult to find exactly what you are looking for. Web search engines and indices help in this regard. Instructors who provide guidance about where to look on the Web can be even more helpful.

Instructors who post their own Web pages for their students can provide a framework for courses that many can take "at a distance." Class handouts and much of the reference material can be posted on the Web. With the use of a commercial Web course development tool, like Top Class, WebCT, or Blackboard, instructors without a great deal of expertise with technology can provide DE via the Web. These systems also generally incorporate their own user-friendly interfaces for e-mail, live chat sessions, asynchronous online discussions, and so on. Many courses already exist on the Web. In fact, entire degrees can be earned online, with universities like Walden, Nova Southeastern, and the University of Phoenix.

The approaches taken by these Web-based courses often differ from a traditional course in ways that are even more radical than the synchronous DE experience. There may be no regularly scheduled class sessions. Instead, the course is conducted primarily by means of small-group encounters online, asynchronous electronic discussions, and electronic exchanges between individuals.

Learning may occur primarily through independent exploration of the Web and asynchronous interactions with others in the class. The teacher's role becomes one of facilitation, rather than being primarily concerned with the dispensing of information. He or she will seldom serve as the "sage on the stage," rarely even addressing the entire group at once. Rather, this role shifts beyond the "guide on the side" to something more akin to the "ace from cyberspace" or the "guru whom you barely knew."

Testing also tends to differ on these systems. It is somewhat difficult to create online tests that record student responses. But the greater challenge is determining whether the enrollee or an acquaintance really took the test. How can an instructor know? So "authentic assessment" is practiced in these types of courses, which involves submitting materials, often in the form of a portfolio. Or students submit test essays as they might have with a traditional "take-home" exam.

Hands-on learning can be very difficult to supervise in these online courses, making the teaching of equipment skills or specialized applications in instructional technology somewhat problematic. Thus, these online efforts have their limitations. But they offer a new form of DE that appeals to many students, and the number of offerings should expand as more people connect with the constantly growing World Wide Web.

Finally, distance education courses are often augmented by fax, a technology that brings us full circle, back to the approach used by the very first efforts at DE: the distribution of printed materials. Fax machines are extremely useful additions to DE projects, for sending both teacher handouts and student assignments. Fax eliminates the delay normally associated with the mail services, which made correspondence course instruction so awkward.

Nowadays, with the increased availability of networked connections and modem-based dial-up services, the function of fax is sometimes replaced by electronic exchanges with no "hard copy" involved. Homework can simply be e-mailed or posted on a student website for instructors and fellow students to view. But printed material is often more convenient to deal with than is its electronic version, so fax will probably remain a significant technology for some time.

Distance Education Issues

So, as a teacher, what kinds of concerns might you have about DE? Your first question might be, What do you mean by DE? As our historical review has indicated, there are many forms of DE, which differ in the type of technology, numbers of sites, total enrollment, degrees of contact with an instructor, amount of interactivity, patterns of scheduling sessions, and approach to evaluation. Although they both might accurately be described as DE efforts, there is a significant difference between the learning experience of a Latin American farmer trying to complete his high school education by listening to broadcasts on his transistor radio and that of a Norwegian technician learning new skills by taking a Web-based course developed at a postgraduate polytechnic institute in

Oslo. Thus, when you hear about DE, it is important to clarify what type of DE project is being discussed.

The second question you might ask about DE is, "Does it work?" While it is hard to generalize about DE, because it can take so many different forms, research indicates that learners in many DE projects do as well as similar students in traditional classrooms. In addition, studies show that several different types of DE have proven to be successful, as long as they are effectively designed and implemented. Although the newer forms of Web-based DE have not been very extensively investigated yet, thus far it does not appear that any one form of DE is necessarily better than another. The key issues are whether the approach selected is appropriate for the circumstances, in terms of institutional support, student access, type of subject matter, availability of staff, cost, and so on.

What might most concern you about DE, however, is how you would deal with it, if you were asked to teach "at a distance." Would this teaching experience be a potentially unpleasant one? Or would it be an exciting new challenge, with interesting gadgetry and novel approaches to instruction? Of course, the answer would depend on the situation and how you adapted to it. But there are definitely challenges associated with DE. It may be more difficult to get to know your students. It may be harder to hold their attention. It may be challenging to involve students at remote sites in discussions. It may not be easy to help them with their work when they are having problems. It may be difficult to sense when your teaching is going well, and when it is not.

Perhaps you will never be asked to participate in a DE project. But it is a rapidly growing educational enterprise. With the increasing demands for "lifelong learning" from all sectors of the population, DE programs can provide instruction to clientele for whom attendance at a traditional educational institution is impossible or inconvenient. Work skills in our economy are constantly evolving and with these changes comes the need for ongoing retraining. Often DE programs can provide this training right in the job setting. Distance education can also provide opportunities for sectors of the population, such as the disabled and the homebound, who otherwise would have no access to educational services. Even if you never actually become a "distance teacher," you will likely hear about DE from others in the field and will probably encounter people who are taking advantage of it. You might want to do so yourself some day.

RECOMMENDED READING

Gray, S. 1998. Web-based instructional tools. *Syllabus* 12 (2): 18–22.

McGreal, R. 1997. The Internet: A learning environment. *New Directions for Teaching and Learning* 71: 67–74.

Mikovsky, E. 1997. Techniques for distance learning instruction. *Media and Methods* 34 (1): 24.

Tiene, D. 1997. Student perspectives on distance learning with interactive television. *TechTrends* 42 (1): 29–35.

OTHER REFERENCES

Barker, B., and M. Dickinson. 1996. Distance learning technology in K-12 schools: Past, present and future practice. *TechTrends* 41 (6): 19–22.

Barnes, F., and B. Lowry. 1998. Sustaining two-way interaction and communication in distance learning. *T.H.E. Journal* 25 (8): 65–67.

Bates, A. 1995. *Technology, open learning and distance education.* London: Routledge Press.

Berge, Z., and M. Collins. 1995. *Computer mediated communication and the online classroom.* Cresskill, NJ: Hampton Press.

Chen, L. 1997. Distance delivery systems in terms of pedagogical considerations. A re-evaluation. *Educational Technology* 37 (4): 34–37.

Dede, C. 1996. Distance learning—distributed learning: Making the transformation. *Learning and Leading with Technology* 23 (7): 25–30.

Ehrhard, B., and B. Schroeder. 1997. Videoconferencing: What it is and how it is being used. *TechTrends* 42 (3): 32–34.

Garrison, D. 1990. An analysis and evaluation of audioteleconferencing to facilitate education at a distance. *American Journal of Distance Education* 4 (3): 13–24.

Khan, B., ed. 1997. *Web-based instruction.* Englewood Cliffs, NJ: Englewood Technologies Publications.

Laney, J. 1996. Going the distance: Effective instruction using distance learning technology. *Educational Technology* 36 (2): 51–54.

McHenry, L., and J. Bozik. 1997. From a distance: Student voices from the interactive classroom. *TechTrends* 41 (6): 20–24.

McIssak, M., and K. Ralston. 1996. Teaching at a distance using computer conferencing. *TechTrends* 41 (1): 48–53.

McManus, T. 1996. Delivering instruction off the World Wide Web. Online: ccwf.cc.utexas.edu/~mcmanus/wbi.html.

Moore, M., and G. Kearsley. 1996. *Distance education: A systems view.* Belmont, CA: Wadsworth Publishing.

Oliver, R., J. Herrington, and A. Omari. 1996. Creating effective instructional materials for the World Wide Web. Online: www.scu.edu.au/sponsored/ausweb/ausweb96/educn/oliver.

Roblyer, M. 1997. Videoconferencing. *Learning and Leading with Technology* 24 (5): 58–61.

Schrum, L. 1996. Teaching at a distance: Strategies for successful planning and development. *Learning and Leading with Technology* 23 (6): 30–33.

Spitzer, D. 1998. Rediscovering the social context of distance learning. *Educational Technology* 38 (2): 52–56.

Tiene, D. 1997. Teaching via two-way television: The instructor's perspective. *International Journal of Instructional Media* 24 (2): 123–132.

Willis, B. 1998. Effective distance education planning: Lessons learned. *Educational Technology* 38 (1): 57–59.

Wolcott, L. 1996. Distant, but not distanced: A learner-centered approach to distance education. *TechTrends* 41 (5): 23–27.

SCENARIO

Your principal has proposed that Frontier High School encourage its brighter students to explore advanced placement coursework. Up until now, your small rural school has been unable to provide this kind of advanced-level coursework because of staff shortages and a lack of expertise in some areas, like mathematics, science, and foreign language. He feels that the brightest seniors in the school are capable of college-level work and should be challenged during their last year. Furthermore, the parents of many of these honors students have requested that their children should have an opportunity to obtain some college credit through advanced placement coursework.

One option for these bright students would be to enroll in satellite-based classes for advanced placement. The school would need to subscribe to one of these services, paying fees to receive the transmissions. Several satellite services reach Frontier High School. One of them, called Advanced Placement Teaching, charges a basic rate for installation of the equipment: a satellite receiver dish, cabling, television(s), and telephone(s). Then there are add-on fees for each course subscribed to, which increase with the addition of each student who takes the class. The cost per student is approximately $950 for a 35 week course. APT, as its name aptly implies, specializes in distance coursework for advanced placement credit in high schools. There are a variety of offerings, some of which would be attractive to the gifted students at Frontier. A teacher in a studio teaches the course each day for fifty minutes, just as any high school course would be taught. A copystand camera is used to show the teacher's notes or an experiment being conducted. A computer is connected, which can provide graphic material or display of relevant Web pages. Telephone connections provide some interactivity. Students at Frontier High would have access to a toll-free number to ask the teacher a question. The phone lines also are used to fax assignments back and forth. Some teachers at Frontier saw a promotional tape about this service and feel that subscribing to APT would be a good idea.

However, the mathematics teacher, who teaches a number of computer courses, has pointed out that coursework is also available on the World Wide Web in the desired subject areas. Some of the courses are with accredited institutions. In fact, Daniel Boone University, which is only about one hundred miles from Frontier High School, has several courses posted online to fulfill freshman liberal arts requirements. The fees for this service are equivalent to those charged for regular coursework at DBU, about two hundred dollars per credit hour. Most courses, which last a fifteen-week semester, are for three credits. Much of the work is conducted asynchronously, so that students would not be bound to any schedule. Assignments are provided and submitted via electronic mail. Listservs and chat sessions are included as part of the experience. The course instructor is available at all times online, but the students will never meet her face-to-face. There are some high school teachers from a nearby town, hired by DBU as tutors, who meet with members of the class three times during the semester, for discussion sessions. The mathematics teacher has not investigated the nature of these websites, and he is not sure whether high school students will succeed with coursework that demands so much independent effort. But he assures your principal that the necessary connections are available, through the school's computer network, for students to participate in coursework of this kind.

This Web-based option appeals to Frontier's principal, who is wary of paying for the APT service, especially if very few students will take advantage of it. Yet he is also somewhat uncomfortable with the Web courses, because the approaches associated with them seem so nontraditional. The absence of actual class sessions bothers him. He places you in charge of a team of three teachers who will investigate the DE possibilities for Frontier High School. You are asked to develop a set of issues for the entire faculty to consider at a future meeting, when they plan to discuss whether this is a viable option for the school to pursue.

You must read some literature about Web-based education and explore some actual websites. You need to investigate satellite-based delivery of high school coursework. You also might explore some material about DE in general, so that you have some sense of what approaches are generally used to help students learn without face-to-face contact with an instructor or with their fellow students.

There are a number of issues related to this DE proposal for this team to consider. Does the Frontier High School faculty want a televised version of a regular classroom, using fairly expensive equipment to deliver it? Or is it comfortable with an option that demands less equipment expenditure on the school's part but would involve students in a radically different type of educational experience? Your team needs to address these issues in its examination of DE possibilities for Frontier High School. After the committee has deliberated, it will be your assignment, as chair, to write a report that describes how the high school might approach DE as a way of providing advanced coursework for its strongest students.

ISSUES INQUIRY

1. Which of the two DE systems, synchronous television-based or asynchronous computer-based, do you feel will be preferable for the gifted students at Frontier High School? What critical factors most significantly influenced your decision? Discuss the advantages and disadvantages of both the satellite-based APT project and the Web-based Daniel Boone University coursework.

2. How critical is the *social* dimension of any educational experience? What are its most important aspects: the role modeling, the intellectual exchanges, the socializing, the opportunities to build relationships, or the cooperative learning? Is this component of a class less significant for certain types of subject matter? Does it matter less to certain kinds of students? How do DE systems try to provide a social component, even if it is

not one that is face-to-face?

3. Do asynchronous learning experiences become too diluted and too disjointed? Do people lose interest when they are only exposed to a topic in small doses over a period of days? Do discussions lose coherence when contributions are made sporadically and several topics have been raised simultaneously?

4. Would you recommend the same type of DE system for Frontier High School if the principal had suggested that it be used to deliver remedial reading classes for students with learning difficulties? Is DE a good solution for this situation? How might DE efforts be best designed for these types of students and this type of subject matter?

5. Can you envision problems giving examinations "at a distance"? With television-based systems, could there not be "cheat sheets" on the floor (off camera)? With Web-based systems, how would you know who was really taking the exam (without being able to see them)?

6. From the instructor's perspective, what challenges would you face in teaching "at a distance"? Would you worry about holding and maintaining attention? Would you be concerned about being able to help students with their work? Would you want to try to teach in a DE classroom? Why or why not? Under what conditions might you consider this?

Conceptual Connections

ESTABLISHING ONLINE LEARNING COMMUNITIES

INTRODUCTION

The Internet and other computer networks offer a variety of ways to communicate online. Have you used online bulletin board systems? Usenet newsgroups? Chats? MUDs and MOOs? The Palace? Computer networks and their interconnections through the Internet have led to the development of a variety of new communications channels. Collectively, these are now often referred to as "computer-mediated communications (CMC)." Here we describe many of these new opportunities to communicate online and then discuss some of their potential applications in education.

Electronic Mail

Nowadays nearly everyone seems to have an e-mail address, and a growing number have their own Web pages. In fact, it is the increasing popularity of electronic mail and the World Wide Web that are largely responsible for the tremendous growth of computer networks. Without them, the networks would probably still be primarily the domain of techies. Originally, computer networks were developed to allow computers to send data to each other. Since humans already had mail and telephone service, there was no obvious need for using the computer networks to do something similar. The early users of the networks saw things differently, however. They quickly discovered the advantages of exchanging written information this way, and electronic mail was born. This was in the 1960s, and things really haven't been the same since. Today tens of millions use electronic mail.

Chances are you've already used e-mail, so you know quite well how it works. You connect to your e-mail account via a network connection or by means of a modem that connects through the telephone line. Your "e-mailbox" is actually memory space in a powerful computer somewhere. Within your account, you type a message on your computer and click the "Send" button. Your text is relayed across telecommunications networks to the recipient's e-mail account, again simply computer memory space on some machine. The recipient will see it when he or she logs in and checks his or her mail. The recipient reads the message and replies when he or she can. It's a lot like conventional mail, now sometimes called "snail mail" by computer-savvy types, but with the electronic speed of the telephone. In fact, e-mail might be considered a written version of a voiced telephone message. Or it could be thought of as a "paperless fax."

One convenient way to access e-mail is through a so-called POP mailer. Using the Post Office Protocol (POP), the software is designed to access a mail account and then to quickly download all the messages to the client computer's hard drive. This approach avoids tying up the server for long periods, helping to alleviate the potential delays associated with accessing e-mail on systems that tend to be overloaded, given the popularity of e-mail. The interfaces for these POP mailers are also more user-friendly than those generally found with online e-mail programs, like Pine or Elm, which lack point-and-click mouse capability and whose text processing may be somewhat primitive. POP mailers, like Eudora, allow for more efficient handing of e-mail.

Electronic mail was the first use of computers and networks for communications, and it is still the most common. Since e-mail became especially reliable in the last few years, it has offered many advantages: speed, immediacy, ease of use, and so forth. One of its advantages is the fact that it is "asynchronous." That is, the exchange does not take place with both parties participating *at the same time*. As with the postal service, you can send and receive your messages without worrying about what the other person is doing. Communications like a telephone conversation (at least without answering machines or voice mail) are "synchronous," and all parties have to be online simultaneously in order to communicate. Computerized exchanges can also be synchronous, as with various chat services.

Synchronous communication has some distinct advantages, most notably the immediate ongoing feedback that the participants provide for one another, which can facilitate clear, productive, efficient exchanges. On an asynchronous system, a comparable exchange might take much longer to complete. Participants might misunderstand one another when the sender is not available to provide immediate clarification. In fact, excessive delays between exchanges can interfere with the effort to communicate. In some cases, delayed replies are no longer even relevant, since in the meantime, circumstances have changed or a decision has already been made.

Synchronous exchanges also may engender a higher level of engagement, because the participants are interacting directly. The dialogue may benefit from a positive chemistry that develops during the exchange. It may be difficult to replicate the social dimensions of interpersonal interaction in an asynchronous mode, especially when there are long delays between exchanges. Participants in a lengthy asynchronous encounter may lose the enthusiasm they originally brought to the experience.

But asynchronous forms of communication also have their advantageous aspects. They allow participants to respond when it is convenient for them. Consequently, participants can take the time they need to fully articulate their comments, without fear of interruption or pressure to keep the discussion going. Many people write more articulately than they can extemporaneously speak, especially given the opportunity to revise their writing before the message is sent. Asynchronous exchanges may allow for more thoughtful expression, if the sender is willing to take the time and make the necessary effort. E-mail is certainly a convenient, inexpensive way to leave a message, which can be effective as long as the receiver checks his or her mail regularly (or at least before the message is irrelevant!).

In addition to providing opportunities for asynchronous exchanges, another advantage of e-mail is the ease with which you can send messages to a large number of people at once, rather than to just one at a time. There are a couple of ways to do this. The simplest way to do this is to store a set of e-mail addresses as a "distribution list" on your computer. You can then call up this list, and a given message will automatically be sent to every address on the list. For example, your list could include all of your classmates in one of your classes, so you could send around a question about the upcoming final exam. Or a manager might create a distribution list of everyone on his softball team, so that he could inform the players about upcoming practice sessions (or provide his "perspectives" on recent team performance). A group of friends or siblings could set up such lists to send groupwide messages. This is fast, easy, and convenient, but it does require that you take responsibility for keeping the list current. If you have several such lists, and if they change frequently, you might find that maintaining them becomes more trouble than it is worth.

Mailing Lists

The second way to reach many people simultaneously is to use a mailing list server, often called a "listserv" (the "e" was lost because of the eight-character limit on file names that characterized many early operating systems, including the ubiquitous MS-DOS). Many programs, such as "Listproc" and "Majordomo," allow for multiple e-mailings, but the prototype was IBM's Listserv, and that brand name has been applied to all programs of this type (in the same way that we often refer to tissues as Kleenex). The term "server" refers to a computer that is being used to provide information over a network, so anyone who wants to be part of a computerized mailing list sends a message to the mailing list server program asking to subscribe. Every message that is sent to the list goes to all of its subscribers.

A listserv is a convenient way to reach multiple parties. In education its one-to-many protocol is commonly used for online discussions. An instructor can set up a listserv for her class, so that discussions can be continued online, outside of class. Listservs are often used in distance education courses, to provide opportunities for discussions that otherwise would be difficult or expensive, given the distances between participants.

Some listservs are set up for national or international exchanges. It can be interesting to hear the opinions of others from across the continent and around the world. Often these listservs are designed for a specific topic or field of study. For example, the "edtech" listserv at Michigan State University allows for exchanges between professionals interested in the use of technology for instructional purposes. The potential disadvantage of large listservs is that they often receive scores of messages each day, and a participant must be prepared to have his or her e-mail account filled each day. Another problem is that many of the contributions on such a listserv may not be interesting to the participant, who needs to sift through the list of contributions to find those that might be worth examining.

Setting up a listserv usually requires some technical assistance from a network administrator (and probably approval from one's supervisor). But once it is running, the technical requirements for the individual who established the listserv are generally minimal. However, other demands may be placed on the person in charge of a listserv. Many electronic discussions can benefit from the intervention of a "moderator." The moderator can improve the quality of discussion by posing appropriate questions, refocusing discussion when it has gotten off topic, involving nonparticipants who are "lurking," calming tempers when they flare, and so on. Sometimes moderators actually screen messages before they are distributed to members of the list, to eliminate the inappropriate ones. The success of an online discussion often depends on the discussion leadership skills of a moderator, in the same way that the quality of a classroom discussion can depend on the abilities of the teacher who is leading it.

Newsgroups

Usenet newsgroups can serve the same purposes as a listserv. The concept behind newsgroups is simple: you send a message to the group in much the same way that you send an e-mail message. This message is kept on a server with all the other messages sent to the newsgroup, usually for a period of several weeks. It is available to newsgroup participants all over the world who access that group's message via the "usenet" protocol and who can read it and possibly respond to it. Technically, the newsgroup differs from the listserv in that the message is not actually placed in participants' e-mail accounts. It is viewed rather than actually received. But the communication process is very similar.

The newsgroup is a very public means of communicating and allows you to get your opinion, your question, or your information out to a potentially huge audience. Most newsgroups have no restrictions on what you can post, though, so there is often a lot of irrelevant, silly, and even offensive material to be found there. This can spell trouble for using newsgroups in K–12 education. Other newsgroups are moderated by people who screen what is posted. These tend to have more focused and relevant content. In general, newsgroups have a mixed reputation. On the one hand, many people find them invaluable (and sometimes almost addictive!) as ways of interacting with others and exchanging information. On the other hand, they are often despised because of specific newsgroups that deal with unusual sexual proclivities, hate messages, or other controversial topics.

One advantage of a listserv over a newsgroup is that participation in a listserv discussion can be limited to a list of specific individuals (the class roster, for example), whose names are forwarded to the network administrator overseeing the listserv. Restricted access can prevent interference and abuse by outsiders. Educators interested in participating in newsgroups can find one of interest to them by using Web directories that list hundreds and allow for computerized search of them by topic. One such exhaustive directory of newsgroups is "Deja News," found at www.dejanews.com.

Bulletin Boards

Computerized bulletin board systems (BBSs) predate the widespread use of the Internet and are fast being supplanted by other communications media, including similar technologies on the World Wide Web. Some of these systems are still around, however. An electronic bulletin board is exactly what the name implies. It is a computerized storage place that will hold messages for all to view, in the same way that a bulletin board displays posted paper messages. Some electronic bulletin boards are used like traditional ones, for posting of rides, items for sale, events, or even personal ads from singles looking to meet other people. Other bulletin boards are used for special-interest groups (like listservs and newsgroups). Some are special "clubs" that demand membership fees for access.

In general, you access one of these systems by using your modem to dial up a specific computer (not an Internet services provider). Once you are connected, you might find each BBS to be very different, with diverse software, people, and topics for discussion. One of the most famous such systems is The WELL (Whole Earth 'Lectronic Link) in California. One concept that came out of these systems is that of creating a "virtual community" online, which can be developed, nurtured, and sustained entirely through electronic communications. This idea has been extended into education, as we shall see in the following.

Although most of the time we use the World Wide Web as primarily a place to find information, increasingly it is also being used for multiuser communications. There are many Web-based discussion groups of various kinds, both small and large, whose interfaces range from extremely simple to quite complex. In many ways, these groups are the successors to the BBSs mentioned. They can be open to all, or available only to restricted groups (like a distance education class, for example). They can be used by anyone who has access to the World Wide Web, although you may need a password to enter many of them. Like bulletin boards, e-mail, newsgroups, and so forth, they are asynchronous. People can and do get online at any time of the day or night and from any computer running a Web browser. Thus, the discussions that take place here can extend over days, weeks, or even months and involve people from many different places and points of view.

"Chat" Services

Unlike the other communications technologies mentioned so far, online "chats" are synchronous. Like a telephone conversation, everyone communicating must be online at the same time, although they can be widely separated geographically. Unlike a telephone conversation, chat services are mostly text-based, although voice-based online audio services, like Webphone and ICQ (as in "I seek you") do exist as an Internet-based alternative to the telephone. The communications in chat environments like America Online's chatrooms and

Internet Relay Chat (IRC) are often fast and furious, with people typing their messages, reading those of other participants, and trying to respond before the conversation moves on. You choose your "room" or channel, read and type messages, and generally participate completely with words or other typed symbols. Other environments, as we shall see, include graphics, sounds, and other media as well. Chats can involve as few as two people or as many as dozens. With more people the experience changes and can get overwhelming. It can be very difficult, with many messages being presented onscreen simultaneously, to determine who is responding to whom. Also, given the delays often associated with typing, messages can appear out of sync with each other. By the time a message appears, the topic may have already shifted. For this reason, lengthy messages are generally avoided (unless the sender is a gifted typist!).

Another primarily synchronous online communications medium, the "Virtual World," encompasses a variety of possibilities, from text-based systems like MUDs and MOOs to two- and three-dimensional graphical gaming and conversational environments. Most of these technologies started out as places to play interactive games. Increasingly, companies, educators, and others are beginning to see their advantages in other settings. The communication process is like that of the chats just mentioned. You type messages and they appear to others in the same "rooms." The difference is that the rooms might actually look like rooms, vehicles, auditoriums, courtyards, landscapes, seascapes, or any kind of environment you might imagine. The pictures that represent the rooms could be two-dimensional, as in a program called "The Palace" (www.thepalace.com), or three-dimensional as with ActiveWorlds, Microsoft V-Chat, and Virtual Places. Most of these chat systems use their own software, which can be downloaded for a fee (or for free) from the home page.

You and the other people using a particular room are not just a name on the screen. You are represented graphically as well, as a figure called an "avatar." Once again, you have a lot of latitude in determining what you will look like today: a picture of yourself? a famous movie star? a deep sea creature? It's up to you. Many such environments also allow people to carry and manipulate objects as well. These props might include party hats, beer steins, weaponry, magic wands, or bizarre masks. The Palace provides a picture library of amusing props, but users can also design their own online accoutrements.

The graphical nature of these virtual worlds may add an extra dimension to conversations that take place online. It is up to teachers and students to figure out how to make good use of them. Otherwise the discussions can degenerate very quickly, as participants get distracted by props and backgrounds or steer the conversations into purely social paths. Environments like the original Palace site are not for minors, for they are generally frequented by exotic, risqué-looking avatars prone to typing remarks of an outrageous, provocative nature. But other palaces, like Hawaii's Zen Palace (palace://obunhawaii.com), have been established for special-interest groups, and they can be more educationally oriented than the original site. There is even a palace designed expressly for young people, called KidsNation (palace://kidsnation.com). And it is not difficult for educators with some computer background to create their own palace environment, designed to encourage more intellectual pursuits.

Applications of Computer-Mediated Communications in Education

The potential applications of computer-mediated communications (CMC) are many and diverse. Increasingly, sound educational practice demands that learners communicate effectively, ask meaningful questions, formulate their own ideas, and discuss what they are doing. These are key elements of the constructivist approach, which is discussed elsewhere in this book. Likewise these skills are critical in problem-based learning. These skills can be developed and enhanced during class discussions and in small-group dialogues. As we have seen, technology can expand opportunities for discussion outside the classroom. Some classes may be largely homogeneous, with most of the students (and probably the teacher) coming from similar backgrounds and holding similar opinions. CMC discussion can bring together much more diverse learners to talk about issues and ideas. Everyone can benefit by being challenged by other points of view.

At the same time, not all students do equally well in class discussions. Sometimes it seems that the students who dominate, drive, and direct class discussions do so more because of their assertive personalities than because of the quality of their ideas. Some research shows that CMC can help overcome this, allowing more reticent students to have a greater say and letting everyone benefit from their input. Similarly, CMC may eliminate irrelevant characteristics of the discussants, allowing everyone to forget about race, gender, disabilities, and status and concentrate on what people are saying.

Asynchronous CMC also can provide opportunities for ongoing discussions, which continue beyond the confines of the classroom and expand the otherwise limited time allowed for class discussion. How often have you gone home after class and thought of other points that might have been worth mentioning? It sometimes takes time for ideas to incubate. If the discussion were on a listserv, a newsgroup, or a Web-based discussion group, you could jump online and let everyone know your insights. This kind of discussion also gives everyone the opportunity to think more carefully and reflectively about what they want to say. Ideally, given the time to write an opinion, a comment, or a response, people should be able to craft their messages more carefully. In addition, the contributions to listservs are then available in e-mail accounts as a record of what was said. Discussion participants can refer back to previous comments quite easily or review them to refresh their memories as to what points had been made.

Furthermore, students do not have to converse just among themselves. CMC offers the chance for students to get information and direction from recognized experts in whatever fields they are interested in. It is impossible for teachers to know everything (no, really, it's true!), and frequently a student might stump a teacher with a question. Going to the library might not help, since it may not have the latest information. An online search of the World Wide Web might turn up wildly conflicting information and opinions. One possible remedy is to locate someone knowledgeable who is willing to provide worthwhile, accurate information. There are educational websites, like AskER-IC (ericir.syr.edu) or AskAnExpert (www.askanexpert.org), that will help put one in touch, synchronously or asynchronously, with experts in various fields.

Another major use of CMC is as a means of professional collaboration. People from all over the world are using online technologies to work with colleagues, some of whom they have never met in person. This raises interesting possibilities for educators. Frequently, teachers tend to be isolated in their classrooms, having little opportunity to interact with colleagues with similar interests, needs, and students. CMC can help overcome that isolation. Teachers can subscribe to listservs or check newsgroups in their areas of specialization. They can join online chat sessions with their colleagues at websites like Global Schoolnet (www.gsn.org), Teachnet (www.teachnet.com), and Webteacher (www.webteacher.org). Perhaps you will teach in a school where there are few other teachers in your subject or grade level. Or you may not find that your immediate colleagues are interested in sharing ideas or working collaboratively. CMC could provide you with a way of finding and exchanging ideas with colleagues who are more interested in collaborating. You might also be able to set up projects with teachers in other countries, which can be more exciting for students than working with the kids in the classroom next door, whom they have known for years. Groups of like-minded people communicating online, exchanging ideas, and sharing personal information are sometimes referred to as "virtual communities." For some, virtual communities result in more meaningful communications than physical communities do.

Of course, there is enormous potential for students to learn from online exchanges. Teachers can help their students get online with others in their age group all over the world at websites like Kidlink (www.kidlink.org), E-Pals (www.epals.com), or the Intercultural E-mail Classroom Connections (www.stolaf.edu/network/iecc). An e-pal is, of course, the electronic equivalent of a pen pal. In communicating with someone from another culture, students can develop their writing skills and learn about how other children live in different societies. Some can develop their proficiency in a foreign language by communicating online with a native speaker. Online projects for kids to collaborate on are also available at many websites. Many of these are science oriented, but Web-based projects can be found in every subject area.

Another type of online project that has been very successful is the "virtual expedition," wherein students can communicate with travelers and scientists who are exploring a far-off region of the world. Maps, photos, journal entries, field notes, and background information are provided at the website where the expedition is based. The team of explorers sends back materials from the expedition via a satellite uplink. This connection allows them to interact with students in classes that have signed up to participate in the project. Some websites where these virtual expeditions are based include Globalearn (www.globalearn.org), Adventure Online (adventureonline.com), and the Jason Project (www.jasonproject.org).

Limitations of Computer-Mediated Communications

Computer-mediated communications are not perfect, of course, and they are not suited to every situation. No electronic communication has quite the same immediacy and intimacy as in-person communication (often called face-to-face or f2f communication). In some cases this allows us to take a more objective look at an issue; in others, it can get in the way of communicating important feelings and beliefs. Since asynchronous CMC can often be spread out over days or weeks, it often has a very disjointed quality. It is easy to forget what previous contributions have been and to lose the thread of the discussion. In part, this may also be due to the fact that a large group of people, interacting regularly online, can generate many messages. You may find, as many of us have , that it is impossible to keep up with the amount of e-mail you get from an active mailing list, and when it comes to dialogue, "more" is not necessarily "better." You may find that a high percentage of remarks on a listserv are not clearly thought through or not relevant to your particular interests. For students, these pitfalls may be even more troublesome than they are for teachers.

Over time, new communications media will inevitably find their way into our nation's classrooms. The opportunities they afford may significantly affect how teachers approach their responsibilities. The teaching role may shift, from being the primary source of information and direction in the classroom, to helping students make the best of the resources they have available. This might include helping students find experts and other students to communicate with. It might mean getting online with a firm virtual hand to moderate discussions and keep students on track. It might mean learning alongside the students, displaying one's own curiosity and excitement about discovering new things, rather than attempting to remaining an aloof "know-it-all." It might simply mean getting out of the way while students pursue their own educationally valuable discussions.

RECOMMENDED READING

Furst-Bowe, J. 1996. MOOs for teaching and learning. *TechTrends* 41: 3–5.

Palloff, R., and K. Pratt. 1999. *Building learning communities in cyberspace: Effective strategies for the online classroom.* San Francisco, CA: Jossey-Bass.

Shedletsky, L. 1993. Minding computer-mediated communication: CMC as experiential learning. *Educational Technology* 33: 5–10.

Sherry, L. 1996. Supporting a networked community of learners. *Tech Trends* 41 (5): 28–32.

OTHER REFERENCES

Bohlen, W. 1998. Virtual learning. Online: 209.7.240.5/virtuallearning/index.html.

Dehler, C., and L. Porras-Hernandez. 1998. Using computer mediated communication (CMC) to promote experiential learning in graduate studies. *Educational Technology* 38 (3): 52–55.

Graziadei, W., S. Gallagher, R. Brown, and J. Sadiadek. 1997. Building asynchronous and synchronous teaching-learning environments: Exploring a course/classroom management system solution. Online: exon.itec.suny.edu/west/aslpaper.html.

Harasim, L., S. Hiltz, L. Teles, and M. Turoff. 1997. *Learning networks: A field guide to teaching and learning online.* Cambridge, MA: MIT Press.

Hathaway, R. 1995. Teaching and learning in the 21st century: The case for virtual schools. Online: www.cyberhigh.org/append2.html.

McCormack, C., and D. Jones. 1998. *Building a Web-based Education System.* New York: Wiley Computer.

McGreal, R. 1997. The Internet: A learning environment. In *New directions for teaching and learning,* edited by R. McGreal. San Francisco: Jossey-Bass.

Rheingold, H. 1993. *The virtual community: Homesteading on the electronic frontier.* Reading, MA: Addison-Wesley.

Tips for successful CMC. Online:
http://www.psy.uq.edu.au/CogPsych/ic320/cmc.html.

Velayo, R. S. 1994. Supplementary classroom instruction via computer conferencing. *Educational Technology* 34 (3): 20–26.

SCENARIO

Networks! Everyone at your school is talking about them, because over the summer the entire district was wired. Now, every classroom has at least one computer connected to the school network, which in turn allows your school to communicate with other schools in the district as well as with the Internet as a whole. You have some definite ideas about what you want to do with these new capabilities.

Sure, everyone is excited about using the World Wide Web in their classes, and you intend to do that, too. But at home you have long been a subscriber to an online computer service called USAMegaNet. Even before the Internet became popular, this service gave you e-mail capabilities, online information and games, bulletin boards where you could ask your most pressing questions and answer those of others, and even the ability to "chat" with other subscribers. After it was connected to the Internet, you quickly got all those same services and much more. Now you can communicate with people all over the world, not just those who subscribe to USAMegaNet. Until now, you have done all of that sort of work at home, since your school didn't provide the computers and networks that would make it easy or even possible. You want to see whether you can take all your online experience and put it to good use in your classroom.

As you think about the possibilities, you realize that, although all the online information provided by USAMegaNet and the World Wide Web is terrific, it is only part of what you want educationally. You realize that the opportunity to communicate with other people has been especially meaningful to you educationally. You have used e-mail and bulletin boards, as well as chat rooms. All of them were useful but for different things and in different ways. With each of these situations you had some problems: people who "flamed" you or were otherwise rude, superficial discussions with people who had nothing to say, time wasted that sometimes could have been better spent in other pursuits. But looking back at your experience, you think that maybe the new ways of communicating were the best part of your online time. Now you are wondering how to bring those communications into the classroom.

You would like to explore two interesting ideas: increasing your communication with other teachers in the district and providing ways for students to communicate with others outside the classroom. Several other teachers teach the same subjects you do at the same level, but they are scattered among several schools in the district. Perhaps you can use the computer networks to bring you all together and to exchange ideas. You recently read an article that mentioned the phrase "virtual community," and you like the idea. You would love to feel that there was more of a community among the teachers.

To extend that, you want to help your students become part of a "virtual community of learners." You think that if the various classes in the district that are studying similar things could get together online somehow, you might see the development of such a community. This could be a really good experience for students: to work with other people, to hear other points of view, maybe to solve problems and complete assignments online as well.

You are one of the lucky ones who has two networked computers in your classroom, so that helps a little, but you are still going to face the problem of making sure that all your students get a chance to try these things out. The big thing now is to get the other teachers in your district excited about your ideas. Write a proposal to the four other teachers who are teaching similar subjects. Describe what you want to do, both in terms of professional collaboration and opportunities for student communication. Try to be persuasive. You want to get these teachers enthusiastic enough to work with you on some online projects. You should also address any concerns that they might have about using computer-mediated communications, either professionally or with their classes.

ISSUES INQUIRY

1. What types of activities lend themselves most readily to online collaboration? What kinds of discussions will help you build a "virtual community"?

2. What factors might discourage other teachers from participating in an online experience like this, either personally or with their classes?

3. What are your biggest worries about getting your students communicating online? What can you do to make sure that things go well? What guidelines and suggestions will you have for your students?

4. What are the key things that computer-mediated communications allow you to do educationally that you cannot do in other ways? Why are they important?

5. What are the key characteristics of the different online communications media—e-mail, BBBs, chat, and so forth—that are discussed here? How do those characteristics help or hinder you in meeting your educational goals?

6. How can you assess the success or failure of your "virtual community"? For example, if you wrote a survey for your students to complete, what would you ask?

7. How large can a virtual community be and still be viable? How long might you expect it to function effectively? Should virtual communities have boundaries or time limits?

Future Possibilities

VIRTUALLY NO LIMITATIONS

Teacher Training in Technology

THE TRIALS AND TRIBULATIONS OF THE TECHNOPHOBES

INTRODUCTION

Teachers are always learning new ideas and skills. They take courses, earn degrees, participate in in-service days, and study topics on their own. Some of this learning is directly related to their teaching. Some is for their own enrichment. With the world and our knowledge of it changing so much and so quickly, it is good that teachers are like this, for it is difficult to be a good teacher without also being a good learner.

Schools, districts, and the laws covering teacher licensure also recognize the need for teachers to be lifelong learners. Salary scales often include significant raises for obtaining graduate school credit, continuing education credit, and graduate degrees. Maintaining one's license and certification often depends on showing evidence of being engaged in continuing education and other experiences. Most schools and districts sponsor in-service educational experiences for their teachers, even in times of budget problems. The teaching profession certainly seems to be committed to lifelong learning.

As schools introduce new technologies, teachers must learn how to use and apply them. Since hardware and software are changing more rapidly than ever before, there will be no point at which teachers can say that they know everything necessary. New software and upgrades of older programs are released continuously, and frequently the new capabilities and features are of real importance to students and teachers. As schools become wired and acquire a range of equipment, teachers will have to be able to make good use of e-mail, Web browsers, databases, digital cameras, video cameras, digital video editors, and much more. Teachers must keep upgrading their skills, and expanding their awareness of new technologies.

Two important areas related to technology demand teachers' attention: gaining new and improved skills in using a variety of technologies and making better use of those technologies by integrating them into their teaching. The first area is important because without good technology skills teachers will find it difficult to pass them on to their students or to integrate technology into their teaching. The second goes way beyond how to use a computer or video camera, however, and is likely to prove the more difficult of the two. The promise of technology in education is not just to teach the same way we do now but with a bit more efficiently. It is to introduce more effective and perhaps quite different ways of teaching into our work. This will be a lengthy process that requires much learning, experimentation, and effort.

Keeping Up with the Latest and Greatest

There is more to know about instructional technology than any one person can possibly cover. Add to that the fact that many technologies—computers, digital video, the World Wide Web—are changing rapidly, and it becomes clear that no one will ever fully keep up. In turn, that means we all have to make choices about the technologies that will be most important to our teaching. And we have to make choices about how deeply we will study them.

Among the skills that teachers must learn is how to use new hardware and software. Computers have new capabilities and new requirements. New input and output devices, such as scanners, cameras, and printers, will require setup, basic troubleshooting, and competent use. New versions of software appear frequently, especially in active markets like multimedia development or the World Wide Web. Useful programs that no one ever dreamed of before may be introduced tomorrow. A new version of Windows or a favorite word processor may require only a little adjustment. An entirely new program might demand serious study and practice. Do you know how to use a geographic database or a concept mapping program yet? How about the latest version of your favorite Web browser? Have you taken advantage of *all* the features of your e-mail program, including the ones to help you organize the numerous messages you receive every week? You may find that some of your students already have these skills. Will you be able to keep up?

Which of the major computer platforms do you have to know? Macintoshes long held the lead in educational settings, but that has changed with the general market domination of Windows-based computers. Some schools may even use one of several versions of Unix instead. Obviously, you will need to look carefully at your school and the directions it is headed to decide which platforms you must focus on.

Beyond learning basic hardware and software platforms, there are still a variety of choices required. You may be in a position where you will use digital cameras or scanners, so there is more hardware for you to learn. Software choices depend on many things, including what programs your school or district has standardized on, the subjects that you teach, and your own teaching strategies and preferences. For example, there are just two popular browsers for the World Wide Web at the time of this writing (these things change rapidly, though!): Netscape Navigator (part of a group of programs called Netscape Communicator) and Microsoft Internet Explorer. It probably makes little difference which one you choose in most situations, except that it can be time-consuming to keep learning different ones or to switch back and forth. Your best bet may be to stick with whatever is provided in your work setting.

To make good choices about what to learn and use, you need to keep current on what software and other technologies are available, both in general and within your school or district. Certainly most teachers will want to know how to use basic "productivity" software such as word processing, e-mail, spreadsheets, databases, grade-keeping programs, and so on. Teachers cannot be allowed to duck this responsibility, since computers, video, and other technologies are going to be an integral part of their classrooms. Students and their parents will expect that these tools will be used, and used effectively, in the teaching/learning process.

Beyond the Basics with Technology

Going beyond the basics requires moving into new and possibly unfamiliar areas. For example, you might want to switch from **showing** videos to your classes to having them **produce** videos. This change might require you to learn how to operate a variety of video equipment as well as to use complex but powerful video editing software, such as Premier. Just deciding to begin to show computerized presentations in your classes will probably mean learning to use PowerPoint or similar software. Having your class create Web pages requires learning a Web development tool such as FrontPage or Dreamweaver.

It can be overwhelming to contemplate how much there is to learn about technology. To master even a small part of the available hardware and software is beyond most of us. The best strategy for teachers (and teachers-in-training) is probably to learn enough to make good use of the technology they have available now and then add to their knowledge and skills over time as their needs expand. Some people learn the rudiments of basic programs like word processors but never go beyond them. In addition, many never learn how to make the *best* use of the programs they have. They fail to use all the features available to them and do things the hard way when the software provides other possibilities.

When word processors were first introduced, some typists pressed "Enter" at the end of each line, not realizing that the computer could now handle the tedious chore of wrapping the text to the next line and keeping the margins even in spite of changes, additions, and deletions. Some early users of spreadsheet programs did not know that they could enter an equation into a spreadsheet cell (e.g., to sum a column of numbers). They performed the calculations by hand using paper and pencil and entered the results into the cell, instead. They saw the spreadsheet as a way of formatting the numbers rather than as a way to free themselves from the need to perform tedious and error-prone arithmetic. Nowadays, it is still common for people to learn to put text slides in a PowerPoint presentation but not to know how to add pictures, sounds, or animations. To make the best use of the technologies available to them, as well as to be able to teach students how to do so, teachers must be willing to go beyond these basics and learn the advanced features, the shortcuts, and the special capabilities of the technologies.

Knowing a piece of software or other technology well still does not necessarily make you an expert. For example, you could know how to use a desktop presentation or publishing tool without necessarily being a competent graphic artist capable of making the product visually appealing and informative. Many of the first users of desktop publishing programs did not know how to use different typefaces effectively and fell prey to the "ransom note effect" in which documents had such a variety of different fonts, sizes, and styles that they looked like the cut-and-paste ransom notes of old. Trying to cram too much information onto a page or screen is another common mistake.

Learning just the mechanics of a technology does not mean that you have mastered the medium. The next step is to learn the principles of using it well. Effective design is critical, be it visual design, graphic design, or instructional design. When producing a newsletter or Web page, what design principles should you follow for layout? How do you use fonts and text styles appropriately? Have you ever considered what makes a photograph appealing? How does shot angle and distance affect the video you shoot? When you start to address these kinds of issues, you will begin to master the technology and the techniques for producing effective materials.

Integrating Technology into Classroom Instruction

As noted earlier in this chapter, it is not enough just to know how to use the technology itself. You also need to learn how to make effective use of it in your teaching. Certainly, knowing word processing or making a database to help with your grading chores can make you more efficient or productive as a teacher. Word processing programs can make handouts and reports more professional. Databases and spreadsheets can simplify record keeping. Presentation programs like PowerPoint can display information to a class clearly and concisely. However, for technology to really have an effect on student learning, you will need to go beyond that. How will your students use the technology? Will you be prepared to teach and assist them? What assignments and tasks will they use the technology for?

Many of us expect that using technology wisely and effectively in education can lead, over time, to a real revolution in how teachers teach and students learn. It will not happen quickly or easily, but it could happen. It will not happen if we simply use technology to continue our old ways of teaching. We all need to learn new ways to teach that take advantage of what the various technologies do best. Learning how to use new instructional strategies is likely to be a more challenging task than learning the technology itself.

When students learn basic word processing skills, their papers are likely to *look* better, neater, and more polished. But that does not necessarily mean that they are *writing* better. A lot of good teaching is still needed if they are going to learn good writing skills. Does the introduction of word processing change how we teach writing? Maybe so, since it makes both reading student work and revising it much easier. Also, students may be able to spend less time on the mechanics of writing (spelling, grammar, etc.) than on developing coherent ideas.

But what technologies might improve the clarity of the ideas and the quality of the writing? More thorough research through computerized searches of the World Wide Web is one possibility. The opportunity to communicate quickly and reliably through e-mail and other computer-mediated communications is another, since there is no substitute for large amounts of practice to improve one's writing. These technologies can help facilitate more effective writing.

Within most word processing programs nowadays we find advanced features that can help students if they are used well. Spell checkers are valuable, but only if students understand and work within their limitations. The same can be said of grammar checkers. Online thesauruses can be useful as well, as long as students are willing to look up words they are unsure of and not use them blindly. None of these tools should be used unthinkingly, but as students learn to question them and use them judiciously, they can improve the quality of their writing. Beyond those relatively simple tools, we can see the potential for having students write more, for having their pieces "published" to a wider audience via homegrown newsletters and Web pages, for having students critique one another's work, and for having students collaborate on written assignments more readily. All these approaches could be valuable additions to our collection of strategies for teaching writing.

Technology can provide new ways of communicating ideas as well, especially with multimedia. Whether students use simple presentation programs or complex multimedia development software, they have opportunities today to communicate with audio, video, and graphics, as well as through plain text. Students who do not express themselves well verbally will probably appreciate opportunities to try other modes of expression. They may reveal hidden talents at working with the visual arts or with music. Providing opportunities for students to make effective use of these other means of expression is the teacher's responsibility. How will you meet that responsibility?

Similarly, although we will probably still want students to learn calculation skills in math, technology might be useful in helping them go beyond the basics. Graphing calculators and computer programs can show instantly how a small change in an equation can result in a very different curve on a graph. The results of manipulating mathematical symbols can be clarified by technology. Similarly, students of statistics can analyze much larger and more complex data sets from real-world applications with the help of calculators and computers. Once we move students beyond rudimentary calculations, we can use technology to expand their actual understanding of the underlying concepts behind the equations and numbers. Perhaps the task of entering valid and appropriate equations into spreadsheets is a more useful exercise than repetitive arithmetic drills. Working within learning environments like that provided by the Geometric Supposer may clarify mathematical concepts more effectively than paper-and-pencil proofs. However, we have to develop effective activities with these tools, lest we be accused of simply helping students avoid how to do the arithmetic.

Technology and Active Learning

Educational software is moving well beyond its former focus on simple drill-and-practice programs and now offers schools complex case studies and dynamic simulations. Instead of lengthy worksheets, which can be tedious for both students and teachers, students might learn mathematics by solving the challenging problems found in the Jasper Woodbury multimedia series produced at Vanderbilt University. Biology students might learn ecology by rescuing virtual species from extinction. What kinds of skills does this sophisticated software teach? How can it be used most effectively in the classroom? Should students work individually or collaboratively on the programs? How can the goals of the software be integrated with the goals set by your state and district? These questions and many more like them will become crucial as education moves beyond the simple and obvious uses of technology toward a potential revolution in teaching and learning.

Even a well-crafted PowerPoint presentation may have a negligible effect on learning. Listening to a lecture while seeing slides or other visuals is, after all, a time-honored learning mode. There is little reason to believe that putting the information on the computer instead of on overhead transparencies or writing it on the blackboard will necessarily improve learning. But PowerPoint can be used in other ways. Most researchers and theorists are increasingly advocating instructional strategies that lead to more active learning by the students. If lectures supported by PowerPoint are deemed too passive for learners, then the solution is not necessarily to discard PowerPoint. It may be to teach students to develop their own presentations using the program.

Similarly, there is little reason to request that students look up information on the World Wide Web if the same information is available more quickly and easily in the reference books already in the classroom. But students might now wish to check their texts or reference books against potentially more up-to-date information on the Web. Conversely, they could check information they find on the Web against standard reference works like encyclopedias. In addition, it can be useful to have students solve problems collaboratively that require information available *only* on the Web. The availability of this new technology should allow, encourage, and even demand that teachers and students try new activities in the classroom.

To do this, many teachers may need to learn new ways of teaching using technology. Teachers may need to step back, become less the center of attention in the classroom, and realize that they are not the final source of information. Instead, they might become the *facilitators* of learning, as well as sometimes colearners along with their students. Their focus may shift to guiding students in the right direction, providing corrective feedback, and serving as cheerleaders and mentors, not necessarily as the "authorities." The skills to do this effectively with technology will not come easily to all teachers.

Many teachers may have to develop new attitudes toward technology. There is some resistance to the recent influx of computers, networks, and other technologies into schools. Teachers may see this development as threatening in many ways. They may be concerned about not knowing enough about how to work with the technology or may even be afraid of breaking expensive equipment. Some will surely be troubled that their students know more about the technology than they do. As students begin to work more independently on the new machines, it may bother some teachers that they are no longer the focal point of their classrooms. It may be difficult for them to relinquish, to some degree, the role of ultimate authority to the multiple sources of information that technology can provide. All of these are common sources of resistance to working with technology. They can all be overcome.

Hands-on, Not Hands-off

At first, learning how to use unfamiliar hardware and software can be daunting. It may be confusing, and it often seems to take forever to get started. You may not be sure what the technology does, there may be a profusion of features and controls, and it may not be clear how it all fits together. Many of us find it easier to learn these things if we have assistance, someone who will show us what to do, how to do it, and when to do it. At the same time, just being told or shown about technologies clearly is not enough to teach us how to use them. Also, it is not usually a good strategy to try to learn everything about a program or piece of equipment at once. Adults, especially, seem to learn best when they are doing something personally meaningful to them. Often your best bet is to learn enough to get started on a program, begin working on a real project for a class or a personal need, and then develop more advanced skills as you need them.

Teachers cannot be expected to pick up all the necessary skills entirely on their own. Certainly, some teachers with special interests in new technologies will spend their own time, money, and effort in figuring out how they work. But school administrators cannot expect the same of everyone in their building. Most teachers need more-structured, formal ongoing learning opportunities if technology is to be used more widely in the schools.

So how do we get from here to there? There are many pieces to that puzzle, of course, but one of them has to be teacher training. In all likelihood you are currently enrolled in a teacher education program. You are taking courses to learn both *what* you will be teaching and *how* to teach it most effectively. As noted earlier, however, you will not be finished learning when you graduate and find your first teaching job. You will be expected to keep learning how to excel in your teaching. This ongoing training will probably include in-service programs sponsored by your school or district, workshops of various sorts, and university-level courses.

Some of these experiences can be worthwhile, but unfortunately, much of the direct teacher training about technology seems to be ineffective, especially the in-service training. This may be because of what is taught, how it is taught, or the fact that teachers often feel forced to take classes that they aren't interested in. In-service workshops that simply tell teachers what to do are almost completely ineffective. Not only do teachers learn little in the classes, but also they cannot or will not apply what they learn back in the classroom.

On the other hand, workshops that stress learning-by-doing seem to have a much greater impact. Most experts in the technology field learned those skills by doing them. Think of your own learning history. We bet that some of the areas that you have learned best are the ones where you actively explored the ideas and skills, trying different tricks and learning a lot of them on your own.

A good training technique is to take people through using the technology step-by-step. This can be done using a variety of different media. A printed workbook can be effective, as can an audiotape. You might use a videotape that clearly demonstrates each procedure. There are even good computer tutorials that teach how to use application programs. For any school, a library of tutorials might be a useful resource for teachers who wish to update their skills with technology.

However, tutorials have their limitations. As the skills and concepts to be taught become more complex, it is harder to find effective tutorials. Often the complex skills are also more ambiguous and more in need of human intervention to explain them and evaluate the user's understanding. Finally, many people rebel against the lockstep nature of many tutorials. The tasks they do at each step seem too limiting and artificial. Teachers often want to explore on their own and try out the technology on a real-world problem that they bring to the situation.

Thus, often the best way to learn how to make good use of technology is to experience it. Choose a project to work on, and get guidance from more experienced teachers. Look for workshops where everyone has hands-on access to the technology being taught. Although you might need some of the material explained to you, you also should be given plenty of time to explore on your own. The trainers should serve as resources to keep you on track, to answer questions, and to model the best ways of performing the tasks. Frequently such an approach leads to both better learning and a better attitude toward technology and its possibilities.

Knowing It, Hands Down

When you put it all together, it is clear that even after you become a teacher, you must still be a learner. Mastering the mechanics of specific equipment and software is important but still only the first step. Before you can write the Great American Novel or even the perfect lesson plan, you will need to master at least parts of a word processor. Before your students can produce that professional-quality video that they imagine in their heads, you must have enough command of the cameras, sound equipment, and editing software to help them realize their vision. Clearly these basics do not go far enough, however. Creating a great Web page cannot be accomplished solely by knowing some Web development software.

Effective media materials are produced by people using the technology to apply skills, vision, and principles to the problem at hand. Thus, you need to learn the principles as well as the skills to make your vision succeed and to help your students do the same. Even when you have these skills, you have one more step to take and that is to integrate the use of technology into your teaching. You may have to change how you teach. This may mean learning to step back a bit from a position of authority and becoming more of a facilitator of learning through various mediated sources. It may mean providing more active and meaningful projects for your students to work on in class, so they can take advantage of different technologies. It may mean rethinking your entire approach to planning your school day. But take heart, it could all be quite exciting.

RECOMMENDED READING

Boyd, E. 1997. Training-on-demand: A model for technology staff development. *Educational Technology* 37 (4): 46–49.

Holzberg, C. 1997. Teach your teachers well: Successful strategies for staff development. *Technology and Learning* 17 (1): 81–96.

Maddin, E. 1997. The real learning begins back in the classroom: On-the-job training and support for teachers using technology. *Educational Technology* 37 (5): 56–59.

OTHER REFERENCES

Bradshaw, L. 1997. Technology-supported change: A staff development opportunity. *NASSP Bulletin* 81: 86–92.

Brown, G., and J. Henscheid. 1997. The toe dip or the big plunge: Providing teachers effective strategies for using technology. *Techtrends* 42 (4): 17–21.

Gillespie, K. 1998. The impact of technology on faculty development, life, and work. San Francisco: Jossey-Bass.

Milone, M. 1998. Staff development success stories. *Technology and Learning* 18 (7): 20–28.

Northover, M. 1999. Developing a successful information technology competency strategy for faculty and staff. Online: horizon.unc.edu/TS/development/1999-01.asp.

Rups, P. 1999. Training instructors in new technologies. *T.H.E. Journal* 26 (8): 67–69.

Vojtek, R., and B. Vojtek. 1996. Technology in staff development. "Net"working: Staff development online. *Journal of Staff Development* 17 (4): 60–62.

Wolinsky, A. 1999. What works in staff development. *Multimedia Schools* 6 (2): 37–40.

SCENARIO

Your school has been adding technology as fast as it can, given the funds the state is providing and the budget that is available at the local level. Right now, at Ford Prefect Middle School (about five hundred students), you have two computer labs with relatively new Windows computers. In addition, each of the thirty-two classrooms has at least one computer, although some of them are pretty old. Some classrooms have as many as four computers, and more are being added whenever possible. Due to a recent state initiative, all the classrooms are now wired into a network, which, in turn, is connected to the Internet. Some of the oldest computers cannot access the Web, but the rest can, and they all have e-mail capabilities. Printers and scanners also are available in the labs, which can be used by anyone who knows how.

Personally, you would like to have all the computers and connections you can get your hands on, so you consider yourself lucky to have four good machines in your classroom. But not all of your colleagues are making good use of this equipment, so many of the computers just gather dust. And if the truth be known, you aren't fully aware of the many functions included in some software applications, let alone how to use them effectively with your students.

When you talk to them, the other teachers have a variety of reasons for not using the technology. Some see this as solely the responsibility of the computer teacher who runs the lab. Others seem to be nervous around the machines. They don't know how to use them and don't seem to want to try, at least not in front of anyone else! Others admit that they use computers themselves for such tasks as word processing, e-mail, and grades, but have no idea how to use them in teaching the curriculum.

Your principal, Arthur Dent, seems to consider you a "rising star" among the faculty, and he has recently asked you to develop a plan for your own professional development, with an emphasis on learning how to plan to use technology in your classroom. When he approached you about this, he indicated that he may have some money to send you to workshops or maybe even a conference. For some reason, he insists on using the term "milliways" for "millions of ways" when referring to the potential of technology, as in "there are *milliways* to take advantage of the new conductivity of the Web." You feel he's slightly eccentric, but that's all right. Besides, he's your boss. You have to listen to him.

Dent also has said that he hopes you will be a school leader in encouraging others to use technology in their classrooms. He clearly believes that technology should be a major focus of the school, so he is planning an in-service training on it. You fear that he is counting on you to get others to sign up (don't panic).

Not all the teachers agree with Dent's game plan. There is considerable resistance to being "forced" to use technology in the classrooms. When you ask around, a few of your colleagues advise you against getting caught up in another of the principal's "pet schemes." They don't think it will go anywhere and this latest technology fad will just die down soon, as did other such fads before them. Miss Trillian, who has the classroom next to yours, says, "Honey, just ignore it. He'll forget all about it, and you can just concentrate on being with the kids."

You're not convinced. You think that technology can make a real contribution to your teaching, but you know that you have a lot to learn. Even though you doubt that you're up to the leadership role that the principal seems to have in mind for you, you do want to take advantage of his offer for more training and learning opportunities. And who knows? Maybe you'll be able to win over a few of your colleagues (with the probable exception of Miss Trillian).

The question now is, What do you need to learn? Principal Dent has asked for a professional development plan for developing skills with technology. He gave you no particular format for it, saying simply to write up a description of what you know and what you believe you need to learn. You should include some indication of how you might most effectively learn these skills. Dent also encouraged you to describe how you plan to use technology in your classroom. List some possible activities wherein technology might play a useful role. Develop some creative suggestions, if possible. After all, your boss seems to be counting on you to show some of your sluggish colleagues how a classroom can be energized by technology.

ISSUES INQUIRY

1. There are many skills that teachers might need to know that could increase their ability and willingness to use computers. What are some of the basic technology-based skills that every teacher should have?

2. What skills go beyond the basics (see previous item), but might be next on a list of what every teacher might know? Finally, list a few competencies that the most technology-savvy faculty members in your school might possess.

3. Analyze your own learning style, and describe how you feel you learn best. Then apply your observations to show how you might most effectively learn how to use instructional technologies.

4. List some of the most effective ways teachers can use technology in the classroom. What applications would be involved, and how would each be utilized to facilitate learning?

5. Discuss how you might encourage your students or other faculty members to take advantage of available instructional technologies. Would your approach vary, depending on the individual? How so?

CHAPTER 18

Is Artificial Intelligence Better Than Authentic Stupidity?

INTRODUCTION

The definition of "artificial intelligence (AI)" has been discussed and debated for many decades. In fact, it is difficult for psychologists and philosophers to define what "intelligence" is, and even more challenging for them to operationalize how it can be documented or measured. Attempting to address the "artificial" dimension only serves to further complicate the issue. Consequently, definitions of AI may vary, and there is programming described by some as AI that others would not consider sophisticated enough to be defined as such.

However, nearly everyone in this field acknowledges a seminal definition provided over half a century ago by the man who many consider the "father" of AI. That man was the British mathematician Alan Turing, who worked with a powerful computational device called the Colossus to crack the Nazis' secret communications code during World War II and thereby helped the Allies win the war. His "Turing Test" for AI was that the person conducting the test would exchange messages on a computer with what could be either another person or a computer. If this person were unable to distinguish whether the messages came from the other person or not, the computer would have achieved artificial intelligence. In this way, the Turing Test examines the ability of a computer to mimic a human being.

A number of programs have been developed over the years that could interact successfully with a human user in ways that approximate human conversation. But none of these have been widely acknowledged as having convincingly passed the Turing Test. These programs are designed to recognize certain verbal patterns in the sentences that the user inputs, like common words or phrases. Some programs have a large database of prepared statements written into the code, which might be appropriate rejoinders to the word or phrase that the user entered. The better programs drew on databases of information and placed the word or phrase into grammatically correct sentences.

Other programs, like the counseling program called "Eliza," are designed to take material from the user's entries and place it in their replies, thereby seeming to "understand" what has been communicated. However, while clever, these approaches were seldom foolproof. One such program designed to get the client talking about his father was programmed to use this strategy. It would ask, at some point, "What does your father do for a living?" It would then take whatever job title the client indicated in a reply like, "He is a (job title)," and feed it back by asking, "How to you feel about (job title)s?" But the approach backfired whenever the clients responded that their fathers were dead. The reply "How do you feel about deads?" clearly did not pass the Turing Test.

Expert Systems: Smart but Specialized

One type of AI that has been widely publicized is the so-called expert system. An "expert system" is a program that deals with a very specific area of expertise. For example, expert systems exist for medical diagnosis, automobile repair, oil prospecting, chemical analysis, and investing in the stock market. An expert system works in the following general way. It will ask users a series of specific questions. The expert system program code is designed to react to the answers, with a series of If . . . Then programming commands. For example, "if" A has been entered, "then" the computer will perform a particular part of its program. But if B is entered, then it will perform a different part in the program. Response C might send it to still another line of code and so on. If the response does not match anything in the program, it skips on to the next item. In this way, the program can recognize certain meaningful answers to its questions and react according to how it has been programmed.

The set of possible responses needs to be clarified carefully in the questions, so that the users will type in a response that is recognizable to the program. For example, the system might be foiled when users enter a synonym like "heat rash" that is not in the program code, for a term like "sunburn." Providing multiple choices can solve this problem. The expert system's programming should also, of course, reflect the diagnostic expertise of the human specialists who helped design it. The data retrieved by the "then" statements should help identify a condition or perhaps make a recommendation. If the program is effectively designed, each user response helps it make an eventual determination, by narrowing down the potential possibilities.

Let's use a fairly famous expert system as an example, the program Mycin. It was designed to help doctors identify blood infections and might begin a session by asking a doctor about the patient's symptoms, the results of blood tests, and so on. After Mycin is given all the relevant information about the patient, it would make a diagnosis. Some diagnoses can be quickly made, based on a few questions, but for certain ailments many questions are required. The protocol depends mainly on the nature of the data. Toward the end of the interview, after asking about any allergic reactions to particular medications, Mycin will prescribe a drug to address the infection, if one is indicated. In certain cases where Mycin is unable to make a clear diagnosis, the patient is referred to a living, breathing blood specialist. But Mycin has been evaluated as being as accurate as most specialists and more accurate than general practitioners.

How are such expert systems developed? Basically, the expertise of many human experts is collected by a so-called knowledge engineer, who interviews and observes them. This "knowledge engineer" then articulates the set of rules by which human experts make their decisions. A programmer takes these rules and develops code for a production. The program is tested and its recommendations checked by human experts. When it reaches a high level of reliability approaching that of human experts, the program can be used on real clients.

This computerized expertise can be very helpful, especially when human experts are not available (or their consulting fees are too high!). This form of AI, like any form of automation, may eliminate some work for humans. And, on the positive side, it can free up human experts to focus on tasks more complex than making straightforward diagnoses.

Expert systems have played a limited role in the training field. They can be used to double-check the appropriateness of diagnoses or recommendations made by trainees. Their expertise can also be used to help train employees in specific tasks, wherein performance can be prescribed based on specific circumstances. But they have rarely been used in schools or universities, because the knowledge required of pupils obtaining a basic education is neither so specific nor so comprehensive as the information programmed into a typical expert system.

In fact, this is the primary limitation of these programs. They can function quite effectively within a very narrow knowledge domain but are utterly useless outside of that particular area of expertise. So although they are a form of AI, expert systems are very topic-specific. The more general the knowledge demanded of an AI system, the more difficult it is to program. This is why general purpose robots are still the stuff of science fiction.

Pattern Recognition: Making Machines More Perceptive

Some devices used in factories have been called "robots," because they can perform mechanical operations without human control. They are driven by AI programs and are especially common on assembly lines, their metal "arms" repetitively and tirelessly attaching parts to manufactured items. These so-called robots serve extremely useful functions, generally performing their specialized tasks with an efficiency superior to that of a human being. They can be very precise, do not make mistakes (barring a malfunction), can keep at the job twenty-four hours a day, demand neither wages nor benefit packages, and never go out on strike. But these mechanisms are not robots in the sense that the average person thinks of the term. Like expert systems, these devices are capable of very little beyond the specific task for which they were designed (although a broken robot would probably be a good door stopper or possibly an effective paperweight).

Robots and androids like the ones in the *Terminator* and *Alien* movies are still well beyond our technological capability at this point. Several critical challenges must be met, which have proven quite problematic. One is the issue of perception. The Turing Test is based on an ability to process language, and some "transformative" AI programs that can feed back parts of the user's statements have come close to passing it. But these programs could never answer the question, "What am I now holding in my hand?" Perception is a biological capability that is difficult for a machine to replicate.

Television cameras and microphones can serve as the eyes and ears of a robotic device. In fact, television technology is advancing in ways that will help it better serve this function. New high-definition TV (HDTV) has about twice the resolution of the television we are used to seeing and can thereby "see" better. It is also processed digitally rather than in analog form, so that its signals can be picked up, manipulated, and duplicated far more effectively by computers (see the introductory chapter entitled "From Video to Virtual Reality: Technology and Its Instructional Potential"). Also, a digital television signal is compatible with the computer's digital processing, eliminating the need for conversion from analog to digital with a codec. The progress made by television technology should contribute to advances in robotic systems in the coming decades (see Chapter 14, "Digital Developments: Television's Technological Transformation").

But some serious fundamental problems remain in getting the computer to recognize objects. Studies of pattern recognition indicate that the human capability of establishing what is figure and what is background is quite difficult. A television camera can show a series of shapes and colors, but how can a computer program make sense of this? This figure-ground problem is exacerbated by the fact that objects change size and shape as they move. Viewed at other than a ninety-degree angle, a circle looks like an oval and a square appears to be a rectangle. You cannot simply program the shape of an object into the computer and expect it to easily recognize that item, because the shapes of objects rarely stay constant in the real world. Of course, as objects move farther or closer they grow smaller or larger in our visual field. The way distance changes size introduces yet another complication into the challenging task of getting computers to recognize objects.

Along with shape and size, color is another potential cue for object recognition. But colors are rarely monochromatic-looking in real life, given the play of light and shadow on them. Their appearance can also change dramatically as the lighting changes, growing lighter with brighter light sources and darker as they dim. Even different types of light cause colors to look somewhat different. Household lightbulbs emphasize reds and institutional fluorescent lights make objects look greenish. Television cameras are so sensitive to these changes that they have "white balance" controls to compensate for indoor versus outdoor shooting. It is therefore difficult to effectively program a computer to recognize an object's colors, given how they are constantly changing.

Movement of objects, while problematic in some ways, may also help computers to recognize them, for movement can serve as a cue to help establish figure-ground. What's moving can be identified as an object separate from its background, and it can even be tracked by a camera with remote controls that pan, tilt, and zoom to keep the object in its frame. In some ways, this is akin to the way predators sometimes identify their prey (remember the Tyrannosaurus Rex in *Jurassic Park*?).

As chip technology advances and raw computer processing becomes ever more powerful, AI efforts will benefit, because critical data about shape, size, color, and movements of objects can be programmed into a machine. If the programming is sophisticated enough to account for some of the complications just described, a computer will be able to recognize and track specific objects, based on this kind of data. If the machine has a powerful enough processor, it will be able to react with sufficient speed to changes in angle, distance, lighting, or velocity, so as to keep the object within its sights and not confuse it with its surroundings or with other similar objects.

Speech Recognition: My Machine Just Doesn't Understand Me

Another important type of perception that is very challenging for computers is speech recognition. Some programs do exist that provide limited speech recognition capability, usually a set of basic commands. But, at this point, a computer's ability to hear and recognize specific sounds is fairly primitive. Again the issue is one of pattern recognition. As with the figure-ground issue in visual pattern recognition, aural identification of a word depends on the machine's ability to separate that word from other background sounds. Noisy conditions can confound today's speech recognition systems. Another problem may be distinguishing between words that sound alike. A request for "rum" can easily set a computer in motion, if it is mistaken for "run." Even more problematic are homonyms. What would an AI system make of this limerick?

> Two tooters who tutored the flute,
> Tried to tutor two tooters to toot,
>   Said the two to the tutors,
>   "Is it harder to toot
> Or to tutor two tooters to toot?"

Even though these systems have improved a great deal in the past few years, speech recognition is only a subset of language recognition, and computers are still a long way from being able to respond sensibly to everything that is typed on their keyboards. Most of today's systems depend on the use of certain "key words" that the machine has been programmed to recognize. Identifying any word in the English language is a more challenging proposition, given the huge number of words that exist. However, powerful computers can very rapidly peruse lengthy lists of words, as they do with spell-check programs. The more difficult problem is programming machines to know how to *react* to each word after they identify it. They must be programmed to provide meaningful responses to that word.

This is problematic because many words have multiple meanings and they can only be accurately understood within a given context, which brings us to the issue of phrase recognition. As difficult as it is to get a computer to recognize a word, it is even more difficult to get it to respond sensibly to a series of words, because combining words can change their meanings, and following rules of grammar and syntax can be difficult for a machine. Thus, very sophisticated programming would be necessary. In fact, this area may be where computers and their programmers face their ultimate limits. One must wonder whether AI programs will ever be as sophisticated as human beings in understanding "natural language" (language presented in the way it is commonly used).

These issues all have dealt with computer input issues, but output issues are also important. How effectively will a computer be able to communicate with humans? This is the "litmus test" of an AI program's comprehension. In a sense, computers will never have cognition exactly like humans, but if they can respond in similar enough ways to a given request, then that should be enough for the machine to pass the Turing Test and be classified as "intelligent."

Text processing programs may be the most important computer applications ever developed, probably even surpassing the machine's computational contributions to our society's productivity. Today's computer software includes some very dynamic writing aids. Word processing and spell-check capabilities have become fairly sophisticated. Grammar checkers are less reliable, but they have improved over the years. The computer has helped many of us improve the quality of our writing.

Computers also are advancing in terms of their ability to talk aloud to us. Digitized sound is simply computer storage of audio data. It used to be difficult to work with digital sound files because they took so much more memory space and processing power than text. But improved compression techniques now allow more data to be stored in smaller memory spaces. As the memory capability and processing power of machines have improved, computers have become more proficient with digitized speech. They also are now capable of more sophisticated synthesized speech. To synthesize speech, a computer uses a data set of noises that approximate the phonemes used in speech, combining these sounds to create words. Unfortunately, this process has not been perfected, so synthesized speech still sounds artificial. One advantage, however, of synthesized speech over digitized speech is that it can more automatically convert text to speech and thereby read it aloud. Probably the talking computers of the future will be able to use digital speech the way synthesized speech can be used today, integrating the realistic sound of a human being's prerecorded digitized voice with the voice generation capability of synthesizer systems.

As computer interfaces become more sophisticated, AI will improve and its applications will become more widely available. The area we are most concerned with is, of course, education. While training programs in the corporate and military sectors have attempted to use AI-type software to augment their efforts, so far there have been few dramatic developments. Applications in school and university settings are even fewer in number and less sophisticated in their capabilities. But there may ultimately be many opportunities for "smart" programs to assist students with their learning in our nation's schools. Already computer aids like word processing, spell checking, search engines, and multimedia authoring tools have begun to affect how children learn. More-sophisticated programs that take advantage of advances in AI development should also have a significant impact some day.

Intelligent Computer-Assisted Instruction: How Smart?

So what role might be played by AI in education? The term "intelligent computer-assisted instruction (ICAI)" was coined years ago to refer to instructional software that attempted to incorporate elements of AI. In the upcoming scenario for this chapter, many basic elements of ICAI are described, which would take certain features of today's software a step or two further. Here are some of the possibilities.

In the past, some computer-assisted instruction (CAI) has included diagnostic tests that determine student skill levels. The software then places users at a point in the instructional sequence appropriate for their level of expertise. ICAI programs might have a much more extensive, sophisticated questionnaire that pupils would need to complete before proceeding. This "learning style" survey would be designed to provide the computer with important information about the individual student. Some of the sections might include reading skill level, mathematical aptitude, attitudes about learning, preferred sensory mode, cognitive style, degree of independence, favorite subject areas, topics of interest, and so on. This inventory of items would help the computer software select appropriate approaches and content materials for teaching this particular student.

ICAI would have greater flexibility than today's CAI in adjusting to student needs. A more extensive set of options also would be available to the program, for presenting material in dynamic ways, in providing appropriate forms of feedback, for effectively reinforcing responses, for testing levels of skill or knowledge, for remediating problematic parts of the lesson, and so on. It would be better able to individualize instruction. For some time, the so-called branching built into some programs has allowed them to adjust somewhat to pupil performance. If students are doing poorly, the program will review, and if they are performing well, it might skip on to more advanced material. ICAI would monitor pupil progress far more closely than today's software. It also would be capable of addressing specific skill deficiencies more effectively by providing more ongoing remediation as well as be more able to keep gifted students involved in work at their own level of sophistication.

The most fundamental principle associated with ICAI is that the software will be smart enough to learn about the student. Some of its information about pupils will come from the aforementioned initial inventory. But it will also learn as it works with students on a daily or weekly basis. Users will be asked to indicate their preferences for the next assignment or for the kind of examples they need. How they perform on exercises and tests will be recorded. All of this data about each student will be stored in a database for that individual. Each student's database will grow as he or she works with the program, allowing ICAI programs to become more knowledgeable and sophisticated about how to work with each student in the class.

As each student opens up the program, he or she identifies himself or herself. The program then attempts to personalize the presentation of material to that particular student. Of course, it will try to start at an appropriate level of difficulty. But, in addition, it will use examples that should be of interest to the individual child (as he or she has indicated previously). The nature of the examples it presents also will depend on learner characteristics. Concrete learners may see a video, whereas those who can operate effectively with more abstract material may be given text passages. The ICAI program will also try to customize its lesson to fit preferred learning modes. For example, it could present the material in either visual or auditory form (or both), depending on expressed pupil preferences. Its ability to motivate students should be enhanced by what it has learned about them. For example, to keep attention levels high, it might show an amusing clip from a student's favorite TV comedy or play a few bars of a favorite song. Thus, ICAI would be able to relate more effectively to the individual user than is possible with today's software.

Artificial intelligence might also play a role in constructivist lessons. For example, it might assist students in choosing a topic to research by suggesting potential themes based on the aforementioned databases of information it has collected about the students in the class. Or it might conduct a "virtual brainstorming session" prompting pupils to come up with topics on their own, through a series of questions or suggestions. Once a topic has been selected, AI programming might help the student search for some interesting, relevant materials on the Web or on compact disc. Or it might serve as a kind of digital "agent" that automatically keeps track of materials it finds on an ongoing basis, by searching electronic resources and then saving material for the student to examine. These twenty-four-hour daily searches could be based on the report topics that students have selected, and each student in the class could have an electronic file of materials gathered by the computer.

In many ways, AI might actually be more helpful to the teacher than to the student. For example, it can serve as an effective teacher's aid, helping students in ways a teacher would like to if she had the time to devote to each child. If the teacher is busy with another student, a child can ask his or her computer for guidance. AI applications could also keep the teacher closely informed about each pupil's progress. They might help the teacher personalize and individualize instruction by serving as a source of information about each pupil's learning style. AI programs developed expressly for the teacher could provide curricular suggestions, resources, and ideas for interesting lesson plans.

To what degree AI programs might actually replace teachers is an interesting question. It is certainly hard to imagine a computer program addressing the emotional and social needs of elementary-aged children the way a sensitive teacher can. School is far more than just studying, and the human dimensions will always be best addressed by human beings. It also is difficult to envision a computer effectively leading a class discussion or reprimanding students whose behavior has been disruptive. But these roles can be left to teachers. One challenge for future educators will be to determine the most appropriate ways in which AI can best be used in the classroom.

Another interesting issue is how the teaching role might be affected by the availability of AI programming in the classrooms of the distant future. It is likely that ICAI will play a significant role in the pupils' skill development, and AI will also help deliver much of the curriculum content. As a consequence, teachers will probably be less involved in preparing worksheets, administering tests, and keeping student records. Teachers should be freed from some of these responsibilities to focus on other important aspects of teaching that may be somewhat neglected in today's classrooms. For example, they should have greater opportunities to work directly with individual students on a one-to-one basis. Or they could work with small groups on special projects. They might also have the time to develop projects with other classes, so that students can share what they have done or benefit from experiences with other age groups. With assistance from AI programs, the teaching role could be potentially more exciting than ever before.

Deep Blue and Beyond

Artificial intelligence is really still in its infancy. Yet it has already captured some headlines. Most notable was the chess victory recorded by IBM's computer program Deep Blue over the otherwise uncontested human champion, Gary Kasparov. This feat impressed many of us who have played some chess, for the game demands a high level of concentration, imagination, and mental manipulation of possible game sequences. Chess champions have long been considered geniuses, because they need to hold so many things in their heads to calculate the next best move. In addition, chess champions must have the ingenuity to develop a strategy that will surprise their opponents. Yet here was a genius like Kasparov being beaten by a machine. Not since John Henry lost to the pile driver has there been such a triumph for machine over human.

How could Deep Blue have won? One reason is that it does not get nervous or fatigued. A chess championship can be a very tiring, grueling, nerve-racking event that includes many matches over a period of several days or even weeks. So the computer had those advantages over Kasparov. The other clear advantage it had was its ability to quickly process all the possible sequences of moves that might result from a given move. Of course, it first needed to be programmed to understand the objectives of the game, its rules, and the movements of all the different pieces. Then Deep Blue, with its gigahertz processor conducting its billions of operations per second, could determine the thousands of conceivable final game outcomes more quickly than any human being. But what was most amazing was that the program could be so sophisticated about deciding which move was the best and that it was able to develop a winning strategy against so formidable and experienced an opponent. Deep Blue's victory raises the question: Can a computer be creative? Or is creativity only an issue for mere humans, who cannot know all the possible ramifications of a given move as can Deep Blue?

Despite the success of Deep Blue, some computer scientists have questioned whether concentional computer programming will ever be able to give the machine all of the aforementioned capabilities it needs for true AI: perception, voice recognition, natural language processing, effective speech production, and so on. Some computer scientists have decided that another approach might offer more potential. That was to model AI on the way the human brain actually works. If you want to simulate the mind, then imitate its "wetware" or brain organization. Most neurologists think that the brain functions by means of complex combinations of multiple brain cells firing together. It is known that brain cells, called neurons, can be activated or inhibited by the firing of other neurons. It may be the pattern with which neurons are activated in these so-called neural networks that is the physical manifestation of thought.

A computer can be programmed in much the same way. The equivalent of the neuron would be the switch, which can go on or off. Sets of switches can be activated in a pattern, which models how the brain cells fire (or don't)[11]. With parallel processing of the electrical current, multiple switches in multiple circuits can go on or off simultaneously. If the computer can then be "taught" that a given configuration of circuits and switches represents something, then this may be the beginnings of a semiconductor-based "neural" network. The real trick, however, would be to get the machine programmed so that it can teach itself. Experiments with parallel processing have shown some success. The computer has first been "trained" and then it has exhibited some aspects of AI. But as yet, attempts to get a computer's electrical networks to act like neural networks are still in their formative stages. Only the future will tell us whether this approach is ultimately worth pursuing.

As digital technology advances into the distant future, computers will unquestionably get smarter and smarter. They will more accurately perceive their surroundings, better understand human communications, and will respond more similarly to the ways humans typically react. Artificially intelligent robots will no doubt assist humankind some day in a variety of capacities. But it is debatable whether they will be ever be as clever as the cute ones in Isaac Asimov's classic 1950s novel *I Robot*, and we hope they will never become as powerful as those depicted in the *Terminator* films, in which Deep Blue's descendants have enslaved the human race.

RECOMMENDED READING

Frick, T. 1997. Artificial tutoring systems: What computers can and can't know. *Journal of Educational Computing Research* 16 (2): 107–124.

Moore, J. 1996. Making computer tutors more like humans. *Journal of Artificial Intelligence in Education* 7 (2): 181–214.

Negroponto, N. 1995. The new engines of learning. *Executive Educator* 17 (1): 25–27.

OTHER REFERENCES

Arruarte, A. 1996. The CLAI model: A cognitive theory of instruction to guide ITS development. *Journal of Artificial Intelligence in Education* 7 (3-4): 277–313.

Bringsjord, S. 1998. Chess is too easy. *Technology Review* 101 (2): 23–28

Copeland, J. 1993. *Artificial Intelligence: A philosophical introduction.* Oxford, UK: Blackwell.

Ford, N. 1987. *How machines think: A general introduction to artificial intelligence.* Chichester, UK: Wiley.

Meek, J. 1995. Intelligent agents, Internet information and interface. *Australian Journal of Educational Technology* 11 (2): 75–90.

Montazemi, A., and F. Wang. 1995. On the effectiveness of a neural network for adaptive external pacing. *Journal of Artificial Intelligence in Education* 6 (4): 379–404.

Ray, R. 1995. Adaptive computerized instruction. *Journal of Instruction Delivery Systems* 9 (3): 28–31.

Ritter, S., and K. Koedinger. 1996. An architecture for plug-in tutor agents. *Journal of Artificial Intelligence in Education* 7 (3-4): 315–347.

Rose, E. 1998. Talking Turing: How the imitation game plays out in the classroom. *Educational Technology* 38 (3): 56–61.

Schofield, J. 1995. The GPTutor: Artificial intelligence in the classroom. In *Computers and classroom culture,* edited by J. Schofield. Cambridge, UK: Cambridge University Press.

Snyder, R. 1996, June. Neural networks for the beginner. Association of Small Computer Users in Education (ASCUE) Summer Conference Proceedings, North Myrtle Beach, SC, ERIC, ED 405832.

Witbrock, M., and A. Hauptmann. 1998. Speech recognition for a digital video library. *Journal of the American Society for Information Science* 49 (7): 619–632.

SCENARIO

One day in the teacher's lounge, the conversation turned to computers. Mr. Moore, who always enjoys a lively discussion, provocatively asserted that computers might some day "revolutionize education." But Mrs. Payne countered that she felt computers "would never replace teachers, that's for sure!" Others joined in with various opinions on this issue, most agreeing with Mrs. Payne, but some admitting that the computer was a remarkable device that might take on more sophisticated human qualities in the far distant future.

Finally, Mr. Moore described a computer capability that he found out about in a university course he took last fall. He said that his instructor, Professor Pierce, had shown a television program in which a computer was able to assist a student in mathematics by asking him a series of questions. This computer was capable of using digitized speech, so it actually "talked" to the student while it presented the lesson material on the screen. It was also "voice activated," so the student could give certain commands aloud (although the student's answers were generally keyboarded).

The computer's initial set of questions was designed to determine how much this particular student, named Johnny, knew about trigonometry. Then, after the lesson had begun, the computer periodically asked questions about the material, to see if Johnny could answer correctly. If he was unable to do so, the computer would provide review, including some examples related to the topic. If Johnny was able to answer correctly, the computer might ask him a harder question or two. If he was able to answer a series of difficult questions correctly, the computer told him that it would move on to some more difficult material or perhaps even on to a more advanced unit. In addition, the computer would periodically praise Johnny, especially when he had answered a challenging question. It asked whether he felt the material was too easy or too hard. Furthermore, the machine periodically asked him if he was getting tired and needed a break. It even offered to give Johnny a "brain teaser," to break up the lesson with an activity that might be fun. Occasionally the computer used current, hip vocabulary, which sometimes sounded a bit ridiculous, but which at least was lively. When he indicated that he was ready to stop, the computer congratulated Johnny on whatever progress he had made and said he looked forward to working with him again. Then it said, "Adios, amigo," with a slightly Spanish accent before shutting down.

As Johnny continued to work on this instructional sequence, the computer would "learn" how he learned. It would store information on various aspects of the instructional experience with him. As Johnny worked with this software, it came to understand his strengths and weaknesses. It noted how many items for practice he needed before moving on to the next sequence. It tracked what kinds of examples worked best for him. It asked him about his interests and then incorporated those topics into the scenarios that contained mathematics problems. Over time, it gradually developed a "learning profile" on Johnny, which it stored in a database, designed to hold relevant information about individual learning styles. As it worked with him, it checked with this database, before deciding on the next course of action. The longer Johnny worked with this software, the more sophisticated it became about the best ways to teach him.

Another way in which the computer used this "learning profile" was to find materials of interest to Johnny in databases or from the World Wide Web. It functioned as a sophisticated computer search tool, which responded to his requests for certain types of information by only suggesting materials that were appropriate for Johnny, given his aptitude, degree of expertise in this area, level of interest, and so on. It served as his electronic "agent," by routinely searching for electronic resources that it knows Johnny is interested in. The computer could help Johnny research material and would provide him with an ongoing source of information on topics that he wanted to explore.

Computers can also be programmed to serve as so-called expert systems. A computerized expert system contains an extensive database of information about a given topic. It also is programmed to explore that database to diagnose problems, provide information, and even to suggest solutions. Johnny worked with the school's biology expert system to explore the workings of the human immune system.

Mr. Moore described these computer capabilities as examples of artificial intelligence (or AI, for short). He concluded his remarks with the point that, if this type of behavior is already a possibility, how can we know how effectively computers will be able to mimic human beings by the middle of the next century. Perhaps some day computers will be able to act far more like teachers than we might suspect today. Furthermore, they might well be smarter than the average teacher. After all, hasn't the Deep Blue computer already defeated Gary Kasparov, the world's best chess player?

While most of the group, especially Mrs. Payne and Miss Scott, continued to disagree with Moore, you had to admit to yourself that you were impressed with what he claimed this computer could do. Perhaps a computer with AI could some day oversee very significant aspects of a student's daily school experience. Could an expert system be even more pedagogically astute than the average teacher, about some topics? Could an electronic agent be as helpful as a teacher in providing students with suggestions for resources to explore? Describe your thoughts about this issue. Explore both sides of the argument, focusing on how "human" a computer might someday become, but also examining the ways in which a computer might never replicate what a person can do in the teaching role. Even though computers will probably never completely replace human teachers, how extensive and important a role might you envision them playing in the schools of the twenty-first century?

ISSUES INQUIRY

1. In the next few decades, do you envision computer-assisted instruction (CAI) playing an increasingly significant role in the schools? What will the advantages be for teachers if CAI can become more "intelligent"? How might intelligent CAI (ICAI) best facilitate instructional efforts?

2. What problems may be associated with an increasingly important role for computers in the schools? Will there be negative consequences, some of which cannot be foreseen at this point?

3. How dynamic do you imagine AI may someday become? To what extent will machines be able to imitate teachers? In what ways will computers be less effective than human teachers? In what ways might a computer be superior to a human instructor?

4. In the distant future, several centuries from now, will there be androids who serve as teachers, even for young children? Might this be the case in remote, inhospitable regions where there are teacher shortages (the Gobi Desert, the Antarctic ice cap, the plains of Mars, etc.)?

5. Are you concerned about the degree to which we are increasingly dependent on machines? Or is this simply a way of improving our lives? Should machines deliberately be limited in certain critical disciplines, like education, where their influence may not be entirely positive?

CHAPTER 19

That's Virtually Impossible!
(or Is It?)

VIRTUAL REALITY IN THE CLASSROOM

INTRODUCTION

Virtual reality (VR) is a term used to describe a computer application that uses computer graphics images, often with accompanying sound, to animate a simulation of some phenomenon or setting with which the user can interact. VR programs can be run on standard computer configuration, with the user on a mouse or joystick, watching the animation on a monitor. More-sophisticated systems attempt to "immerse" the user in the experience by employing goggles, gloves, and even bodysuits as input devices. VR, as it name implies, is a way of providing experiences that feel realistic.

In interacting with the computer graphics, the user can experience and experiment with the programmer's model of "reality." Such models have been developed for many different fields: for example, the human body for medicine, car engines for engineering, and buildings for architecture. Instructional applications of VR are mostly for training in specific skills: realistic flight simulators for pilots, simulated medical procedures for interns, specialized tests for nuclear engineers, and so on. In many cases, practicing on real people or with real equipment might be dangerous, impractical, or expensive, so using a simulated computerized version makes a great deal of sense.

How VR Became a Reality

How was such an amazing technology developed? As with other complex technical achievements, VR evolved as a result of several different developments in the computer industry that ultimately provided this sophisticated capability. First, advances in the computer graphics field led to the development of very realistic animation. Another development was the improvement in the user-friendliness of computer input systems, allowing for more natural ways of interacting with programs than keyboarding. Also, as computer systems became more powerful, with greater storage capacity, it became possible to run very large programs efficiently. Meanwhile software developers were able to produce increasingly realistic simulations of a variety of different phenomena. All these developments in the computer industry contributed to the birth of VR.

The field of computer graphics began decades ago with modest low-resolution screens composed of rectangular picture elements, or pixels for short. Early graphics were boxy, with unnatural-looking spikes on curved edges and "staircase" effects on diagonal lines. Monochrome images evolved into colored pictures, but the number of colors was limited at first, because graphics required more processing power and memory space than text. But as computer capabilities improved, the number of pixels available per screen increased and higher-resolution graphics with greater numbers of colors became possible. With faster processing capability and larger memory storage, the movement in computer animations became much faster and more lifelike. By the 1990s, computer animation was capable of presenting realistic-looking dinosaurs in the blockbuster movie *Jurassic Park. Toy Story*, the first film created entirely on a computer, was also a hit with the public. The graphics for creating realistic simulations in a VR environment had been developed. By the end of the millennium, many personal computers had sufficient processing power to run the animation in simple VR programs.

A critical element of any VR system is its interactive capability. Realistic VR requires a computerized input interface that is as naturalistic as possible. The earliest computer input systems relied on the preparation of punched cards. Keyboarding had become a standard interface by the time the microcomputer was developed. The arrival of the Macintosh in 1984, with its object-oriented operating system and its mouse-based input, allowed users to work more easily and efficiently with applications. Joysticks, stylus pads, and touchscreens were other user-friendly input devices. In the early 1990s, some video games worked with gloves that allowed the user to activate a specific screen icon by simply pointing. Such gloves were eventually used with VR programs to allow the user to actually manipulate virtual items onscreen, like they would move real objects. Head-mounted displays, such as helmets or goggles with implanted monitors in the eye sockets, were developed to immerse the user in the VR program. Swivel chairs have been used to allow users to look or move in any direction. Bodysuits with sensors have even been developed to simulate touch. Some of the kinesthetic applications of VR get pretty wild.

A simulation is an effort to replicate a real-world experience. The programming of simulations dates back to the days when all computers were giant mainframes. Programs that modeled complex processes were developed to be used on computers at many "think tanks," whose responsibilities included trying to understand phenomena like the global economy, international politics, ecological trends, and weather. Users could input data from the real world and the programs were designed to predict how the system itself might react, providing output data about how the phenomenon might be affected. Formulas were developed that reflected the relationships between factors in the real world. Random events might even be included, with varying levels of probability. All these calculations could be modified as the simulation was tested and used. In fact, the computer simulation became a way of developing models for complex phenomena and testing their accuracy.

At first, simulations were entirely text-based. But as the graphics and audio capabilities of computers became increasingly sophisticated, simulations that provided fairly realistic animation and sounds became possible. For example, computerized flight simulators could show all the instruments on the front panel, as well as the changing landscape below as viewed through the windshield of the cockpit. The simulation was designed to present a realistic flying experience for pilot trainees, wherein their manipulation of graphic representations of the standard flight controls would affect the plane's performance, as demonstrated on the animated instruments (and scenery viewed "outside"). The combination of these somewhat realistic computer-animated simulations and increasingly naturalistic input capability led to the applications we now call VR.

Real World Applications of VR

The term "virtual" came to be used in the mid-1980s to refer to any computer representation of a real phenomenon. However, many of the early VR programs were not so realistic looking. The graphics were fairly crude and the sounds limited. But it was the degree of interactivity that excited everyone, more than the look or sound of the simulation. The goggle-and-glove systems made users feel so involved in the virtual experience that they might actually get dizzy if the program had them flying or falling. The ability to manipulate virtual objects in such realistic ways also seemed to have a great deal of potential. Like every other computerized application, the potential of VR grew rapidly in the nineties. With the quantum leaps in computer processing power and memory storage capacity, VR programs became increasingly complex, sophisticated, and realistic. The potential of applications grew along with the improvements in VR, so that now it is used in many different fields for a number of different purposes.

What has VR been principally used for? One very important application has been in the design of commercial products. VR representations of items can be accurately rendered in considerable detail. Computer renderings may be less difficult and costly to develop than actual models or prototypes. VR combines the sophisticated graphics and multiple perspectives provided by computer-aided design (CAD) programming with its interactive capability. This interactivity allows designers to test their products with potential customers, who can use the virtual product and react to the way it has been designed. In fact, VR is most appropriately used in cases where the actual user-friendliness or ergonomic viability of the item needs to be tested. Finally, it is much easier to modify the design of a virtual product in the computer than it would be to rework or rebuild an actual model. With this flexibility, a greater variety of possible designs can be experimented with in a shorter period of time than was the case before VR was available.

Another important application of VR is in modeling systems, which the user can then actively experiment with. Virtual anatomical models allow medical students to practice procedures before performing them on real patients. Detailed virtual models of complex electrical or hydraulic systems can be developed as training aids or to help engineers practice troubleshooting a malfunction. Again, an advantage of a virtual model is that it can be modified to reflect recent changes in the system's design or to depict new features. Some VR models try to portray what has never really been seen or experienced. For example, physicists and chemists can manipulate virtual molecular models to better display how atoms bond, electrons leave their orbits, radioactive decay progresses, and so on.

One of the most ambitious applications of VR is in the depiction of entire environments. For these programs, the use of an immersive interface is more important than in some of the previous types of VR use, because these virtual worlds have often been developed to test their practicality, their aesthetic appeal, and so on. Users can navigate around the virtual space and manipulate virtual items within this environment. Architects often use VR for this purpose. The interior design of a new building can be explored and tested in a virtual model. The clients would be able to examine and experience their new space before it was actually constructed. They might have worthwhile suggestions as to how to modify the design so that it fits their needs or appeals more suitably to their sensibilities. Large-scale virtual environments also have been developed to test the design of public spaces. For example, a proposed renovation of the Seattle waterfront was programmed as a virtual environment and tested by the primary parties involved before any actual construction began.

Finally, VR is used for training purposes in many different fields. Nuclear power plants must train their workers to certain standards established by law. On-site VR programming helps train staff, so that they know how to most effectively and safely run the plant. The U.S. military uses VR to train those who will be operating sophisticated equipment. For example, VR programs were developed to help train the NASA space shuttle crew to repair the Hubbell space telescope. Medical interns do "mock" operations on virtual patients. A significant advantage of VR for training is that it can provide an experience very similar to the real task. It can also present trainees with a variety of possible problematic scenarios, thereby preparing them for the most likely challenges they will face. VR systems also allow users to practice their skills repeatedly, in fact as long as it is deemed necessary, before they try the real thing. Realistic feedback about trainees' performances is provided. If mistakes are made, trainees can experience the disastrous consequences in a firsthand way, but in a way that does not actually harm anyone or destroy anything.

Multiuser VR on the Web

Virtual reality has made its way onto the World Wide Web. Virtual reality modeling language (VRML) allows for placement of VR applications on the Web. There are applications that provide user-friendly ways of authoring with VRML, like Virtual Home Builder, Fountain, and EZ3D. Placing VR programs on the Web has several advantages. One is, of course, global accessibility to them. A second advantage is to allow multiple users to explore and interact with one another within the environment at the same time. With some VR applications, this is highly appropriate, since they are attempting to simulate environments in which many people will circulate, investigate, share, come into conflict, and so on. Examples might include VR designs for public squares, parks, or workspaces. The best way to test these programs may be to have many people enter them, as they would in real life.

The primary disadvantage to placing VR on the Web is naturally the amount of bandwidth required for it to operate efficiently. Sophisticated VR programs can be huge, and when multiple users are attempting to work with them the system can become overtaxed very quickly. Not only is a powerful server required to run the program, but the individual users who log on must have sufficient bandwidth in their connections and sufficient processing power in their microcomputers. Only individuals with relatively new computers and robust Web connections, through cable services, for example, should probably attempt to use certain VR programs online.

While VR can be a tremendously dynamic approach, there are some potential drawbacks to using it. It can be very expensive. The equipment involved can be costly, especially since state-of-the-art computing power is often necessary to run the programs and special peripheral devices may be used to provide a sense of immersion. The software development also can be very costly, in that its design may be complex, the size of the programs can be huge, and the programming required can be nontrivial.

Another potential problem with VR is that it may not provide as accurate a virtual experience as was hoped (or promised!). The more complex the situation to be simulated, the more challenging it can be to fully replicate it. Because of complexity or cost, compromises may need to be made in its design. Many VR programs use graphics that are not photographically realistic. Even if the appearance of program elements is adequately rendered, realistic interactions with its features may be difficult to develop. In some cases, the approximations for what things look like or act like can be good enough. But this depends on the level of accuracy or precision required. Unfortunately, in other cases, differences between VR representations or reactions and the real experience can ultimately lead to mistakes by designers, trainees, and theoreticians.

Experience Is the best Teacher: VR in the Schools

Today there is very little of what most people would consider VR in our nation's schools. The most obvious reason for this is VR's considerable cost. Another reason is that few classroom tasks require the level of training generally associated with the use of VR; for example space shuttle assignments, nuclear power plant maintenance, and so on. Also, VR may be an inappropriate approach for many school activities. For example, purely conceptual work does not require the use of graphics or physical manipulation. The VR that one might find in a school would probably be a low-level version, using standard input devices, displaying simple animation, and with limited amounts of interactivity.

Nevertheless, each of the previously mentioned applications of VR has its educational aspects and might find its way into the school curriculum. Product design is practiced in art and technology classes, where computer graphics and CAD applications are learned. VR software can help students both develop and test their concepts. VR modeling might be used in a science class to demonstrate how a system functioned. Such a VR program might allow pupils to experiment with aspects of this system, to see how its overall performance was affected by changes in one of its subsystems, for example. Virtual environments might be used in a social studies class to depict scenes in other countries or from other historical periods. In literature classes, VR programs could simulate characters and settings in famous works of fiction. In a science unit on astronomy, VR programming could place pupils on the landscapes of other planets or their moons, as has already been done with a Martian surface simulation. Or in biology, pupils might dissect a virtual frog.

One problem with schooling is that students are often given material to study that they have difficulty visualizing and appreciating. It may be dry and abstract. It may not be anything to which they can relate. VR has the capability of immersing pupils in a certain type of environment and allowing them to get an immediate sense of this world, one that would be impossible to attain by just reading or talking about it. Experiencing something can be much more exciting and instructive than simply discussing what it might be like. VR could help motivate students and engage them more meaningfully in a variety of different types of study.

The famous educator John Dewey once described experience as the best teacher. Many others in the field of education over the years have agreed with him. The most effective way of learning is through active involvement. VR applications can involve students in a variety of different types of experiences. They allow for active interaction and experimentation with objects and exploration of environments. VR can potentially deliver some very dynamic educational experiences, which may result in meaningful instructional outcomes.

Imagine a VR program that can place students in Napoleon's tent at the Battle of Waterloo. Other parts of the VR environment could include the campground of the French troops, the field where the actual battle was fought, the campground of the allied troops fighting the French, some of the generals opposing Napoleon, like the Duke of Wellington, and so on. How might students explore different aspects of this important historical event? The pupils might interact with Napoleon in some way. His character might be programmed to answer some typical questions. The pupils could examine the uniforms, the weapons, artillery, the terrain, maps of the area, battle plans, and other elements of the impending battle. VR programming would also be capable of placing users in the battle itself, allowing them to move around and fire their muskets. Pupils could experience the Battle of Waterloo (although they might not survive it!). They might also be able to pretend they were commanders and experiment with different battle plans. A sophisticated VR program might show different outcomes of the battle that might result from different military strategies. These simulated experiences could teach students a great deal about the battle and its importance in world history.

Constructivist educators should appreciate the potential of this type of "virtual" experience. It allows students to actively guide their own learning and to discover what this historical event was like. It also might allow them to draw some of their own conclusions about the state of warfare or Napoleon's historical role. Rather than just being told about this famous man and his final battle, students would be able to appreciate the event in a more interesting, meaningful way.

From Pacman to Holodeck

Unfortunately, the Waterloo program just described is unlikely to be available for schools for a very long time, if ever. The long-term future may witness the development of sophisticated historical reenactments using VR, but today's schools will have to settle for scaled-down versions of VR, such as educational simulations and video-game-style software.

An educational simulation like "The Oregon Trail" is about as close to an interactive historical reenactment as a teacher will find these days. It places pupils in the mid-1800s in Independence, Missouri, and asks them to plan an expedition along the Oregon Trail up to the northwest region of the United States. They have a certain amount of money to begin with and need to buy a wagon, animals to pull it, their food, and whatever other supplies may be necessary for the journey. Along the way they must ford rivers, cross mountains, and perhaps deal with Indians or wild animals. A map shows their progress along the route. They meet other pioneers along the way, too, who speak with them in video clips. They can get advice, purchase items, or just converse with these characters. The object of this simulation game is to make it all the way, without perishing in the face of the many dangers involved. The simulation gives students a sense of what this country's pioneers might have encountered on their way west and how difficult the journey must have been. It is not as exciting as a VR immersion experience, but it includes many of the basic features of VR: user-initiated activities, encounters with realistic characters, and appropriate consequences for actions taken.

Video games can be about as mindless an activity as one can find. Many teachers feel these games detract from their students' educational experiences by distracting them from completing their homework. But the latest video games are very slick, in terms of both their animation and their interactivity. The most recent generation of games display a realistic-looking environment from the player's point of view, rather than from the objective, omniscient perspective we used to get of SuperMario's adventures. This approach mimics VR, as does the immediacy with which player input can affect the elements of the game. If educational simulations use some of the same techniques as VR, video games provide some of the same technical capabilities as VR. Unfortunately, at this point, few games have any meaningful instructional value (apart from encouraging users to be perceptive and develop winning strategies). But they could be developed, if there were a market for them. At least the equipment platforms for presenting a low-quality form of VR are widely available and reasonably priced, courtesy of Nintendo, Sega, and Sony.

Another way to introduce VR in schools is to have students create their own simple programs. Software, like Virtus VR, is available for this purpose, and high school students with some computer background can work with it. Such experiences could develop a variety of skills. They would involve computer authoring skills, of course, and pupils might also learn how to more effectively work with computer graphics. In developing the content for such a program, they would need to use their research skills. They would need to exercise

certain design skills in the program's implementation. Developing a VR program could be a very challenging experience in a variety of ways.

Who knows how significant a technology VR will some day become in our
society? It is a potentially compelling medium and would be even more so with
the introduction of holographic images (like Star Trek's famous Holodeck).
Many individuals in the future may spend hours in VR environments in the
same way that they currently spend their leisure time watching television,
playing video games, browsing the Internet, or participating in electronic chats.
To what degree such a dynamic medium will ultimately be used for educational purposes in both schools and homes is anyone's guess. But we have the technical capability to provide many interesting and educationally worthwhile
experiences, through this digital format known as VR.

RECOMMENDED READING

Andolsek, D. 1995. Virtual reality in education and training. *International Journal of
Instructional Media* 22 (2): 145–155.

Milheim, W. 1995. Virtual reality and its potential application in education and training. *Machine-Mediated Learning* 5 (1): 43–55.

Moore, P. 1995. Learning and teaching in virtual worlds: Implications of virtual reality
for education. *Australian Journal of Educational Technology* 11 (2): 91–102.

OTHER REFERENCES

Bellan, J., and G. Scheurman. 1998. Actual and virtual reality: Making the most of field
trips. *Social Education* 62 (1): 35–40.

Brown, E. 1998. VRML industry: Microcosms in the making. *NewMedia* 8 (3): 21–22.

Chiou, G. 1995. Learning rationales and virtual reality technology in education. *Journal
of Educational Technology Systems* 23 (4): 327–336.

Cornell, R., and D. Bailey. 1996, February. Virtual reality: A dream come true or a nightmare. *Proceedings of the Association for Educational Communications and Technology.*
Indianapolis, IN, ERIC, ED 397786.

Dede, C. 1995. The evolution of constructivist learning environments: Immersion in
distributed, virtual worlds. *Educational Technology* 35 (5): 46–52.

Dennen, V., and R. Branch. 1995. Considerations for designing instructional virtual
environments. Presentation at the International Visual Literacy Association, Chicago, IL, ERIC, ED 391489.

Dowling, C. 1997. Simulations: New "worlds" for learning? *Journal of Educational Multimedia and Hypermedia* 6 (3-4): 321–337.

Dunning, J. 1998. Virtual reality—Learning by immersion. *Technos* 7 (2): 11–13.

Durlach, N., and A. Mavor, ed. 1995. *Virtual reality: Scientific and technological challenges.*
Washington, DC: National Academy Press.

Freeman, O. 1997. Virtual reality in education: The emerging innovative technology for
delivery of public and home based instructional materials. *Journal of Instruction
Delivery Systems* 11 (4): 19–26.

Hoffman, H., and D. Vu. 1997. Virtual reality: Teaching tool of the twenty-first century? *Academic Medicine* 72 (12): 1076–1081.

Johns, J. 1998. Improving perceptual skills with interactive 3-D VRML scenes. *Journal of Interactive Instruction Development* 10 (4): 3–11.

Lewis, S. 1995. Student-created virtual tours. *Learning and Leading with Technology* 23 (2): 35–39.

Psotka, J. 1995. Immersive training systems: Virtual reality and education and training. *Instructional Science* 23 (5-6): 405–431.

Rheingold, H. 1991. *Virtual reality.* New York: Simon & Schuster.

Schank, R. 1997. *Virtual learning: A revolutionary approach to building a highly skilled workforce.* New York: McGraw-Hill.

Winn, W. 1995. Semiotics and the design of objects, actions and interactions in virtual environments. Paper presented at the annual meeting of the American Educational Research Association, San Francisco, CA, ERIC, ED 385236.

SCENARIO

You are attempting to teach a seventh-grade history class about the Middle Ages. "Attempting" just about describes it perfectly, since there is more commotion than you would like, especially in the back of the room. You finally wander toward the back to see what is going on. As your sentence about "the medieval concept of unrequited love . . ." trails off, you notice, to your considerable annoyance, that Luke is playing with the latest portable Nintendo unit. He is attempting to conceal it within his desk, but you have already spotted it. As you confiscate this unit, you notice that he was in the middle of playing a fantasy game. There on the little screen is a knight, fully clad in armor, attempting to kill a dragonlike creature with his lance.

After class, you speak with Luke about his inappropriate behavior. He apologizes but also begins telling you how excited he is about this game entitled "Medieval Mission." You try to convince him that he might learn more about the Middle Ages by listening in class, and then he could more fully appreciate the world of "Medieval Mission." But he hardly seems convinced, and you realize, as the next class files in, that perhaps you could learn a lesson from him.

Might you not somehow integrate "Medieval Mission" into the unit on the Middle Ages? The kind of interactive experience that a video game provides can really involve a teenager. In fact, many of these games allow users to immerse themselves in an artificial environment. Now that you think about it, the last time you went to a large downtown mall, you saw a sign in a video arcade about virtual reality games, which involved wearing goggles and using a wired glove. Your nephew was with you, and he said that he had tried one once and it was "way cool."

Maybe this technology has some potential for instruction. Couldn't VR be used to provide experiences in other historical eras that might be more educational than a duel to the death with a giant dragon? Couldn't there be quests that forced students to explore the medieval castle, wander through peasant fields, and perhaps be part of a real joust? These experiences might be assigned as homework, since many students had game units and, in the future, might have VR-like equipment upon which this software might be run.

The agenda for the weekly teachers' meeting has been for members of the staff to discuss "an idea for the classroom." Your turn is coming up in two weeks, and you were starting to get nervous about what idea you would present. This VR idea seems like it has possibilities. Develop a presentation about VR for the upcoming teachers' meeting. Discuss not only the present-day potential of using interactive computer simulations in the classroom, but the long-range potential of sophisticated VR software for the field of education. Or at least attempt to do so!

ISSUES INQUIRY

1. Have you ever tried out a VR program? Simulation? Video game, at least? Describe your experiences. How sophisticated a program was it and was any special equipment involved? How engaging was the experience? How realistic do you think it was? How might it be improved?

2. Imagine a simulation that you would like to have for one of your classes. Describe how it would work. How feasible do you think it would be to develop such a simulation with today's technology?

3. How do you feel about the potential of simulation as an instructional approach? Is experience the best teacher? Do you think that computer simulations and VR will soon play a more important role in schools, as the technology develops? Why or why not?

4. Project far into the future. Will Star Trek's Holodeck become a reality? Will schools of the year 2525 provide a great deal of VR for teaching purposes? Will VR become so engaging that a significant percentage of the population will ultimately become preoccupied with escapist behavior? If so, will the boundaries between VR and reality eventually begin to blur for these people?

CHAPTER 20

The Third Millennium School

FROM INDUSTRIAL TO INFORMATION SOCIETY

INTRODUCTION

Today, every country the world over has a mass public education system at the primary school level that students are required by law to attend. Most of the world's industrialized nations have compulsory mass education through the age of 15. Most of us tend to take the existence of public education for granted, but historically, mass public education is a relatively recent phenomenon.

In fact, compulsory schooling dates back only about a century and a half. In the first half of the nineteenth century within the industrializing parts of the world, schools began to be built with public funds on a mass scale. These areas included many countries in western Europe and the United States, where industry and the mass production of goods had evolved on such a scale that factories began to employ large numbers of citizens who previously had worked on farms. This phenomenon is known historically as the "Industrial Revolution," and it marked a major shift in the work efforts of large masses of people, the growth of capital, the more widespread availability of goods, the rise of living standards, technological advances, and so on. Modern society, as we know it, is the byproduct of this Industrial Revolution. Sometimes it has been described as the "industrial society," to distinguish it from the "agricultural society" that preceded it. Today, the economies in many parts of the "developing" world are still characterized by a reliance upon agriculture, for industry has not yet appeared on a significant scale. These nations are still struggling to achieve higher levels of literacy, and their education systems are still in their early stages of development.

Schools in a Changing Society

Why should mass public education have risen in conjunction with industrial development? Like any other large-scale historical phenomenon, the reasons are complex. But most historians and educators agree that our modern educational infrastructure arose, to some degree, to provide the skills and knowledge needed by an emerging economy. With the growth of business enterprises, there was a greater need for a literate workforce, which schooling could provide. This literacy contributed to advances in science and technology, which in turn contributed to the industrial growth of society. Literacy led to the growth of a set of professions associated with modern society, including medicine, law, banking, trading, management, and so on. Another of these professions was, of course, teaching.

Another contribution of mass schooling to industrial development was more subtle. Industry demands that its laborers work long hours at repetitive, boring tasks. What better way to prepare young people for an eight-hour day of tedious, repetitive activity than to expose them to the public schools, which until fairly recently were characterized by assignments that involved a great deal of rote drill? Schools served to "socialize" the population into the factory.

In fact, the modern public school is like a factory in many ways. The teacher is the boss and the students are, of course, the workers. There is a set schedule, regulated by bells. There are breaks allowed, including lunch. Work is relatively constant throughout the day. Most of the work is assigned, and students are expected to complete it as efficiently as possible. Much of the work is repetitive and involves little creative thought. Productivity is rewarded. School is in session five days a week, for six hours a day. There are some vacations (in fact, one of the few holdovers from the agricultural era is the summer vacation, which allowed for work in the fields during the growing season).

As an institution, the public school is very much a by-product of industrialization. It is structured much like an industrial workplace and serves the needs of that setting. However, the most heavily industrialized countries of the twentieth century have recently witnessed a dramatic shift in the character of their economies. The most highly developed economies no longer devote the major portion of their business activity to manufacturing, and they are no longer characterized by a predominantly working-class population. In the last half of the twentieth century, the world's leading economic nations are now running the global economy, and their workforce is primarily engaged in professional, service-oriented occupations. By the close of that century, the United States, Japan, and most of the countries of western Europe had more "white-collar" than "blue-collar" workers. Their service sectors had grown larger than their industrial sectors. They had shifted from being industrial societies to what many have called "information societies," wherein the information processing involved in financing and managing businesses is the main activity, not the actual production of goods and materials.

Yet the world's population continues to obtain consumer goods in record numbers. Where are these products coming from, if the most economically developed nations are no longer focusing on their production? The answer is that formerly less-developed countries are moving into the industrial age. Their societies are evolving from an agricultural base to an industrial one. Countries such as Mexico, Brazil, China, Indonesia, Korea, Thailand, and Malaysia have all become more industrialized in the past half century. This economic development has been assisted by the increased levels of literacy and demand for consumer goods in these countries. But it has also been fostered by the multinational corporations themselves, who have relocated plants to these areas, where the labor costs are cheap, the pollution standards are minimal, the protection of natural resources is limited, and corrupt government officials can be "compensated" in exchange for favorable legislation on zoning, taxes, and tariffs.

The New Curriculum

In these newly industrializing societies, one might expect public schooling to continue to reflect the factory model. But what should schooling be like in those nations whose economies are now more information-based? Unfortunately, there is always a high degree of inertia in public institutions, and many public schools in these countries are still run much like factories. But there is a clamor in the business sectors of these countries for schools to modernize, so as to provide the kinds of skills needed in the new information-based society. Young people seek educational experiences that will develop these professional skills. If schools are to serve the larger society, should they not evolve along with that society? What should an information society school be like? How might it differ from the type of school we have been more accustomed to, which arose to serve the needs of industry?

A school designed to prepare skilled white-collar workers in service industries should provide students with the kinds of experiences that they will face in those job descriptions and might model itself on the professional work environment (rather than the factory). So the information society school should probably be less authoritarian than its industrial society predecessor. While most factories are run by the management, and workers basically complete tasks that are assigned to them, employees in professional positions generally have more responsibility over their own work schedules and assignments. So it might be expected that an information society school would be less tightly controlled by administrators.

Like many of the most successful corporations in information-based fields of endeavor, much of the initiative in an information society school could come from the "bottom up," rather than always coming from the higher levels of the organization on down. Teachers and students probably should have more input into how the school is run. Their perspectives should be considered and their initiatives should be taken seriously by school administrators. Committees of teachers (and students) might provide ongoing recommendations about how to improve the school, in the same way that quality circles of employees in the corporate world help reexamine how the company can most effectively be run.

What might the curriculum be like in this new type of school? The traditional curriculum will doubtless undergo some revision, for it dates back to an era when information was not so plentiful, and it attempted to cover the knowledge in a given field in a relatively comprehensive way. Now, much more information is available in nearly every field than ever before, a phenomenon that some have termed the "information explosion." This situation makes it more difficult to constrain a subject area within the curriculum to a given set of concepts and facts. Subjects will not be able to be "packaged" as neatly as they have been in the past. New findings will be included and older, obsolete material dropped. Emphases will change as each field evolves. Curricula should change more rapidly than ever before to keep pace with rapidly expanding knowledge bases.

Curricula will continue to include the *basic* concepts associated with a given discipline. But a truly dynamic curricular experience will also allow students to explore some areas in more detail. Opportunities for students to do their own research will be important in the school of the future, for the ability to effectively find information will be an important skill for any graduate seeking a professional, corporate position. Being aware of the most recent developments is extremely important for companies that hope to provide effective services. If future schools are to be modeled on the new corporate situation, they must also encourage their students to keep current with the latest developments. They will also need to allow for more open-ended exploration of topics by students, so as to encourage independent learning and the development of research skills.

How might assignments in the school of the third millennium differ from those of the past century? The emphasis should not be on repetitive tasks, which are more characteristic of assembly-line work than of professional duties. Assignments should instead encourage student initiative and creativity, because these abilities will lead to success in the professional world, where a number of different challenges may arise on a daily basis that will call for imaginative solutions. Creativity can be encouraged in a variety of ways. There are of course opportunities in the arts for creative expression; for example, writing stories, composing songs, painting, taking photographs, and producing videos. But there are also opportunities for imaginative problem solving and the creation of interesting projects in the core subject areas: developing a proof in mathematics, designing a science experiment, researching an historical incident, critiquing a body of literature, and so on. These kinds of assignments will encourage students to think imaginatively and critically, thereby developing the kinds of intellectual skills that will prepare them for their professional lives.

Information-Processing Skills

Other assignments should focus on the development of information-processing skills. Students should be asked to complete research projects that involve not only finding relevant information but also communicating clearly what they have discovered in a report or applying what they have learned in the completion of a project of some kind. In this way, students can learn, through actual experience, the critical skills that the corporate world will demand of them later in life. The intellectual skills associated with successfully completing such assignments are numerous and can be complex. For example, researching technique can involve a number of different subskills. First, pupils must know where to look for information and how to most efficiently search for it. A computerized search will entail some basic computer skills. Recognizing material that is likely to be most highly relevant to the topic under investigation is yet another skill. Sorting through scores of sources to narrow down a list of the best material is another challenge, involving judgments about various issues, such as complexity of material, reliability of certain types of sources, clarity of the writing style, and how current the information is. And all of this will depend on the individual's reading proficiency. Slow readers can be seriously handicapped, and even competent readers need to develop their ability to efficiently skim material to see if it warrants closer examination in the next phase of the project.

Once sufficient material is found about the topic, other skills come into play. Students will need to process what they have found in an efficient, effective way. With really challenging material, just clearly comprehending it can be a struggle for some. And for most students, being able to conceptualize the key points and critical issues is another intellectual skill that needs to be developed. Learning to narrow the focus in on the most critical information can be challenging. Staying on topic can be another challenge, for many students inadvertently pursue material that has veered off tangentially into unrelated areas. Taking notes on the most relevant, interesting information is another skill that young researchers need to develop. Organizing those notes into a coherent outline can be a major effort, especially when many sources have been found and when source materials themselves are not organized clearly.

Clearly communicating the information obtained is yet another important information-processing skill. Many students find it difficult to restate the material in their own words. Others find it difficult to synthesize all the information that they have obtained from various sources. Still others find it difficult to express it in ways that allow the reader to clearly distinguish the key points from the supporting detail. Some find it difficult to come up with clear examples, and others may find it more challenging to articulate the important generalizations to be made. Writing formal papers that demand specific styles of formatting and referencing of material can be a challenge for some. Unfortunately, only a few students will likely be able to express themselves in ways that enliven their writing. Finding a personal style of writing that makes one's work special can take years, and many will never reach this level of writing skill.

The third millennium school may find that it stresses skill development over content acquisition. Learners' levels of sophistication in a given field of knowledge will always depend to some extent on the background information they already possess. But when students know how to learn and how to communicate effectively, they should be better able to more efficiently learn *any* content. Information can be gathered on an "as-needed" basis, rather than memorized just in case it comes into play. In many professional job situations, much of the information that employees need to deal with will be new to them. But if they have strong information-processing skills, they can learn about it quickly and be ready to make informed decisions in their work. Content may be taught less for its own sake in the future.

There will also probably be a shift in emphasis from product to process. While the quality of a final product is important, more significant may be the issue of what aspects of the process need to be worked on to improve future instructional outcomes. Students should be encouraged to examine the process they pursued in completing the assignment and to identify any trouble spots or areas for future improvement. By so doing, the critical information-processing skills they need should develop over time, so that by the time they graduate, these students are ready to take on professional responsibilities.

Instructional Technology in the Schools of the Future

If there is one aspect of future schools that we can bet will differ significantly from the situation today, it is the forms of technology that will be available to assist pupils with instruction. Based on the pace with which communications technologies have advanced in the past few decades and assuming this rate of development will continue to accelerate, the digital technologies available to future schools should be far more powerful and dynamic than what we see today. These new technologies will be capable of more-sophisticated instructional tasks. How might advanced technologies impact the school of the future?

Perhaps the most obvious role that technology might play in a third millennium school would be in facilitating the processing of information. A variety of different applications could help students in their efforts to research and to communicate their findings. Researching could be somewhat automated through the use of computerized search of large electronic databases, either online or on CD. Disk-based materials might be specialized by content and also designed appropriately for different age groups. Online connections to the Internet would provide access to huge amounts of up-to-date information, indexed by topic. These connections might also be used to contact experts in the field, to obtain their perspectives.

Communications could be "technology enhanced" in a number of different ways. Word processing, with available digital assistants to provide guidance about spelling, grammar, and word choice, will help students express themselves articulately. Networking will allow for convenient communications with those at a distance. Some students may wish to develop a media production to disseminate their research findings in a dynamic way. This approach might be especially effective if there are sounds or visuals involved that could help communicate the material more effectively and enliven its presentation. Audio-taped footage or photographs could be incorporated. Video material could be edited into a television production. Computer authoring systems might be used to create interactive lessons that include multimedia resources. Or some presentation software like PowerPoint might be used to do this, and students could present their report with a projection system to an entire class. Maybe a good way to communicate the information would be to develop a Web page, which would be available to interested parties on the Internet. In this age of dynamic communications technologies, students should be encouraged to develop their skills in using various technologies, so as to communicate that information in the most dynamic possible way.

Artificial intelligence (AI) may be applied more extensively in the field of education during the next century. For a review of this advanced computer application, see Chapter 18, "Is Artificial Intelligence Better Than Authentic Stupidity?" AI could be used to effectively deliver units of instruction and might be especially effective with skills-based instruction in areas like language arts and mathematics. Students would work on their own and at their own pace. Expert system software could be used to develop a profile on each learner, and it could then recommend forms of instruction that would be appropriate for each student, both in terms of pace and style. A computerized management system would oversee each student's movement through units of material, keeping track of their progress and storing it in a database. AI-based intelligent computer-assisted instruction (ICAI) could provide lesson materials at an appropriate level of difficulty for each individual student, adjusting to performance so that remediation would be provided when difficulties arise. Students doing very well might be skipped ahead in the instructional sequence. Testing would be conducted periodically by the program and the results would be stored and used to determine whether the student progressed to the next level or not.

Technology promises to provide students with access to exciting sources of information that will include not only text but also sounds, pictures, and videos. The incorporation of multimedia resources into instruction will enliven that instruction and help motivate students. These multimedia materials can also prove instructive in ways that text cannot. Sometimes a picture really is worth a thousand words. Video sequences can effectively communicate dramatic sequences for the teaching of literature or history. Audio can be invaluable for certain subject areas like language and music. The school of the future should have access to a great deal of multimedia resources, and they should enhance instructional efforts in significant ways.

Computer graphics can represent reality very effectively, as we all know from our trips to the movies. They also can be used to represent environments that we might not normally encounter, but from which we might be able to learn, like the inside of an atom, a swamp in the Jurassic Age, or the landscape of Mars. Combine sophisticated computer graphics with dynamic interactive programming and you have an application called virtual reality (VR) (see Chapter 19, "That's Virtually Impossible (or Is It?): Virtual Reality in the Classroom"). VR has potential in the school of the future for providing advanced simulations. Students can be placed in artificial environments and interact with them in ways that prepare them to deal with the real thing. VR environments might also be created for the schools of the future, to allow students to learn about phenomena that they might never otherwise encounter. VR programs could represent other periods in history, other cultures across the globe, or deep sea grottoes filled with exotic creatures. Students would have opportunities to learn through their virtual experiences, an approach that might prove far more effective than simply reading about these phenomena.

Technology will afford other exciting opportunities to students in the coming decades. With the increasing degree of computerized connectivity available through the Internet, students will be able to communicate with others outside their own classroom. They can become involved in projects with other groups of students at a distance. International exchanges are possible, and these can be both stimulating and informative. Students can learn about other cultures in an exciting, experiential way. Some of these exchanges will be ad hoc and temporary, but others might be perpetuated for a long time. Virtual learning communities could connect groups across distances to work on projects for months or even years (see Chapter 16, "Conceptual Connections: Establishing Online Learning Communities"). Many of these online groups would doubtless be based on mutual topics of interest or fields of specialization. Such virtual communities could be sources of both support and stimulation for the students of the twenty-first century.

From the Student's Perspective

How will students' learning experiences change in this new type of school? Students might be expected to have more choice in what they wish to study. They might spend more of the school day on work that *they* have initiated, rather than assignments provided by a teacher. They might be expected to work with new technologies more often and develop skills with a variety of different computer applications. They should have extensive learning resources available to them on magnetic and optical formats that hold huge amounts of information or through networked connections to the enormous resources of the Internet. As such, they should be able to explore a great number of topics on their own. They also ought to be able to communicate what they learn in more dynamic ways through the use of technology, and they will be able to present these materials to others beyond the walls of their classroom via computerized connectivity.

Working with others is a critical part of most white-collar professional positions. So an information society school should encourage collaborative projects. Students will probably work more often with each other in partnerships or small groups. Cooperative learning skills will be important if students are going to work effectively in teams. Interactive exchanges between students will be encouraged, so that they can learn from one another. A dialogue also can provide valuable feedback from others about one's ideas, or stimulate new perspectives that had not even been considered. Technology should expand the possible range of these collaborative efforts, as previously discussed. Virtual teams may work together online and their efforts should benefit from the combined contributions of students from different locations and diverse backgrounds.

The school of the third millennium may also be more effectively designed to address the needs of the individual student. Some parts of the curriculum, most notably those which are skills based, may be delivered via technology and designed so that all students will be able to proceed through material at their own pace. Such an instructional approach can be more motivating for students and more efficient. Slower pupils will not become confused as easily because they cannot comprehend the material, and faster learners will not be held back or gradually become bored with school. If AI techniques have reached sophisticated levels, then students could work quite independently, relying on the teacher only when they need special assistance. This instructional approach is sometimes referred to as "mastery learning," because the student must master a given set of skills before moving on to more difficult material.

Third millennium schools will probably need to respond to the increasing specialization of job descriptions in the business world. Many of the most successful corporations offer expertise in complex, changing fields, in which knowledge bases may be rapidly expanding. Certainly this is true in the fields of new technology, scientific research, and the engineering of new products. Consequently, in schools of the future, a more extensive set of higher-level course offerings may be available for advanced students. If some of the innovative educational approaches already described in this chapter are successful, the overall pace of learning in the schools might be accelerated. The intellectual level of many future high schools may become comparable to that of our present-day colleges.

New Roles for Teachers

What might the teacher's role be like in this new type of school? If some of the aforementioned changes in the curriculum take effect, teachers may play a more significant role in course development. Teachers may have more freedom to develop units that respond to student interests or that address timely issues, rather than being forced to adhere closely to a state or locally mandated curriculum. If so, teachers will need to research new topic areas and develop new sets of teaching materials.

If much of the coursework is delivered in individualized fashion using technology and students are given more opportunities to explore topics on their own, there will be less call for teachers to serve as the primary source of information in the classroom. Teachers in future schools will probably lecture less often. They will spend less time addressing the entire class at once. There will be less performance pressure on them to hold their students' attention. So, in some ways, the teaching role may be less demanding than it has been in the past.

However, some new demands will be placed on teachers. One challenge will be to manage a more complex classroom environment that involves students engaged in a variety of different activities at once. If this classroom learning style is to succeed, it will probably demand more planning on the part of the teacher. If students are going to do more independent work, the teacher may need to find materials, arrange time on computers, reserve the library, and, in general, provide the kind of support for independent activities that allows students to succeed and to proceed in an efficient manner. One of the great misconceptions in education is that teaching in a less-structured environment is necessarily less work for the teacher. Rarely can an entirely unstructured learning environment succeed. Providing choices for students generally means that the teacher must provide *more* suggestions, find *more* learning resources, and engage in *more* one-on-one sessions with students. All of this requires that the teacher plan ahead carefully and be very active in assisting students during class time.

The style with which teachers interact with their students is also likely to change. In the past, teachers have tended to tell students what to do. They have given them information. They have given tests that students must complete. The teaching role under the industrial model was akin to that of the factory boss. The teacher's role in the future will probably be less authoritarian. There will be less need for the teacher to provide information. There will be less need to direct students on a constant basis. Testing will probably be less formal. Teachers in future schools will serve in a more facilitative role. They will be providing more individual assistance to students. They will be learning alongside their students and will see how technology can assist in the learning process. Teachers will be observing how their students are progressing on a daily basis.

Another potential change for teachers might be in the degree to which they work with their own colleagues. In the past, most teachers have worked alone in their own room. But with a growing emphasis upon collaboration between students, there may also be more communication between teachers. Some of this might occur at a distance, across computer networks, but much of it might take place within the school building. Teachers in the school of the future may team together more often to share ideas. This could make teaching a less isolated profession and, in that sense, might be a healthy phenomenon.

Actually, teaching may become a more attractive profession in the school of the twenty-first century. There should be fewer hassles associated with trying to control the class and motivate students, assuming the school's learning environment has successfully taken advantage of technology and that students respond positively to their new opportunities to learn independently. More opportunities should be available to work individually with students and to get to know them personally. Teachers can learn how to address the different learning styles of their different pupils. And teachers may be able to spend more time enhancing their own professional development, which most of them should find rewarding.

New Approaches to Evaluation of Student Progress

Evaluation of high school students may change in the upcoming decades. In fact, changes in instructional approach should affect how students are evaluated. For example, it has been mentioned that, with the increasing availability of computers, more students may be learning skills with computerized packages. Some of these software packages may include entire units of study. Advanced algebra skills, for example, may be taught with computer-assisted instruction modules. The testing in such units is likely to be designed to measure whether students have achieved a reasonable level of competence with the material. If they have, they can proceed on to work with more complex material in the next module. Evaluation is more likely to be based on how far along a student has progressed through the materials than on how they have done compared with others on a general exam. There may be fewer tests given to the entire group. With this type of "mastery" learning, the focus can be more on how the individual student has progressed in relation to his or her past performance, rather than on how he or she has fared compared with other students.

Independent learning is also more difficult to assess by means of a class-wide test. If students are focusing their efforts on a particular topic, it makes more sense to test their knowledge of that topic than to test their general knowledge. Evaluation can be based on the work submitted and on whether students can demonstrate what they have learned in class presentations, discussions, or interactions with the teacher. It has been proposed that in the future, teachers might spend more time working with individual students, as facilitators. If this is the case, they should be in a position to gauge how much pupils have learned in the course of completing their independent projects.

Some have described this ongoing evaluation of the student's actual work as "authentic assessment," arguing that this is a more genuine, accurate way to judge achievement than performance on an objective test, which might not be effectively designed to demonstrate what the pupil has really learned.

In fact, students in the information society school may be asked to create portfolios of their work for a given semester or school year. These portfolios can then be examined and evaluated on an agreed-upon set of criteria. Some of the issues might be how comprehensively they have covered the topic, whether the material is interesting, how clearly it has been explained, and whether media materials have been developed with it. Assuming technology will play a more significant role in the schools of the future, some of this portfolio material will include computer programs, Web pages, video productions, and so on. The development of a portfolio makes sense for students looking to be admitted to a preferred college or, later on, in their job searches, for what better way for students to represent themselves than to show others what they have accomplished, bundled into a professional-looking portfolio.

Changes in School Structure

It is difficult to speculate how the administrative structure of a school of the future might change. In today's schools, the administrative staff spends most of its time managing the various activities associated with running the institution. Only a small percentage of their time is spent dealing with actual educational matters. It is possible that with computerized processing of records, less administrative time will be needed to manage the institution, so that principals might become more involved in improving the curriculum, helping teachers, and addressing the needs of individual students. This kind of leadership is very important for schools, and it would mirror what happens at successful corporations. The executives running a company should do more than simply keep the business going. They should provide a sense of the organization's mission, keep abreast of changes in the market, help introduce new technology, and develop a positive image for the institution. Like their corporate counterparts, school principals should be educational leaders, not just bureaucrats.

Many successful corporations have developed a "culture" that fosters ongoing communication throughout the institution. Ideas flow freely from bottom to top and back again. In this way, decisions by executives are informed by suggestions from the rank-and-file staff. Likewise, management-level decisions can be effectively implemented because their rationale has been communicated to staff well in advance of the issuing of any new policies. Such an institutional culture allows for healthy airing of concerns, provides ongoing "reality checks," and allows for the discussion of new ideas. The information society school would do well to copy this business model. More openness on the part of principals to teacher concerns and suggestions would improve many schools. Empowering teachers, parents, and students to become involved in important school decisions can benefit the school in many ways. A school has its own "culture," and school administrators need to develop a positive atmosphere, rather than seeking compliance with a set of arbitrary rules. If a strong sense of community is effectively established within the building, there may be less need for the enforcement of rules because there may be fewer problematic circumstances.

Finally, one of the limitations of the present school model is its insularity. Rarely do students get involved in community activities, work with businesses nearby, or even communicate with many adults, besides their parents and teachers. The information society school will have the means to extend its mission beyond its own four walls. Its computers will be networked to outside institutions and individuals. It can check out resources on the Internet. It will have video equipment that can be used to record experiences outside the building. Its mission should be expanded to include meaningful involvement with the local community. Meaningful projects can be developed that allow students to accomplish worthwhile tasks in the real world. Student learning experiences can occur in real contexts, which will help prepare pupils to take on professional responsibilities in the future. The school of the future should use its resources to enrich the community and, in so doing, enrich itself.

RECOMMENDED READING

Hancock, V. 1998. Creating the information age school. *Educational Leadership* 55 (3): 60–63.

Reigeluth, C. M., and R. Garfinkle. 1992. Envisioning a new system of education. *Educational Technology* 32 (11): 17–23.

Ringsted, M. 1998. Open learning in primary and secondary schools—Towards the school of tomorrow in the information society. *Educational Media International* 35 (4): 278–281

November, A. 1998. The school of the future. *Principal* 78 (1): 18, 20, 22.

OTHER REFERENCES

Bell, D. 1973. *The coming of post-industrial society: A venture in social forecasting.* New York: Basic Books.

Center for Educational Leadership and Technology. 1995. *America's 21st century school: Linking education reform and technology.* Marlborough, MA: CELT, ERIC, ED 393396.

Cetron, M. 1997. Reform and tomorrow's schools. *Technos* 6 (1): 19–22.

Council of Europe. 1989. *The information society: A challenge for education policies?* Strasbourg, France, ERIC, ED 327211.

Dede, C., ed. 1998. *Learning with technology. 1998 ASCD yearbook.* Alexandria, VA: Association for Supervision and Curriculum Development, ERIC, ED 416857.

Gibbons, A. 1998. Reform reconsidered. *Technos* 7 (2): 32–36.

Jones, B., and R. Maloy. 1997. *Schools for an information age: Reconstructing foundations for learning and teaching.* Westport, CT: Praeger.

Kerr, S. 1996. *Technology and the future of schooling. Ninety-fifth Yearbook of the National Society for the Study of Education*, Part II. Chicago, IL: University of Chicago Press, ERIC, ED 412917.

Lauber, G. 1997. Preparing students for a changing future: How one New York school district restructured its educational focus with technology. *T.H.E. Journal* 24 (8): 63–65.

McGraw, J., and C. Frank. 1995. *Schools in the age of technology: Ideas for instructional innovation*. New York: McGraw-Hill, ERIC, ED 382171.

Reigeluth, C. M. 1992. The imperative for systemic change. *Educational Technology* 32 (11): 9–13.

Toffler, A. 1980. *The third wave*. New York: Bantam Books.

SCENARIO

You are offered a rather lucrative consulting opportunity with an organization called "Third Millennium Education." This recently formed enterprise intends to develop a new kind of school that will offer an educational program supposedly designed to provide students with skills for the coming centuries. "Ed-3M," as it is nicknamed, was founded by a group of chief executive officers, most of whom head firms that specialize in digital technologies. This board of directors drafted a mission statement that states:

> "Today's school should prepare students for jobs in the twenty-first century economy, which will witness an accelerated utilization of new technologies, not only for product development, but in the processing of information and in the management of corporate activities."

Ed-3M intends for this prototype school to serve as a model for a network of such schools to be established throughout the country. These schools will require private tuition, but these fees should be kept reasonably low through grant activity and a significant level of corporate sponsorship. These schools hope to attract pupils from a wide socioeconomic range and thereby serve as legitimate national models, not simply another opportunity for society's elite. The key distinction between this new school and traditional schools is its problem-based, information-processing emphasis. The corporate executives involved in the project have caustically referred to traditional schools as "factory-based schooling."

Ed-3M's chairman of the board stated at the last meeting: "A complete overhaul of our nation's public schools is long overdue. The present model of mass education has remained frozen in time for well over a century. It is a nineteenth-century model, based on the needs of the industrialized society that existed at that time. Children were provided with literacy skills for the workplace, but they were also socialized into an environment of long hours involving repetitive tasks. When they left school, they were well prepared for a factory job. Today's modern economy is no longer based on manufacturing. White-collar positions in America now outnumber blue-collar jobs. The advanced world economies have seen their primary focus shift from industrial, production-based activities to managerial, information-based professional positions. This is the paradigm shift from 'industrial society' to 'information society' that the pundits have described for well over a decade. But educators have not responded to these societal changes. We now need an educational model that prepares our young people for the kinds of positions they are now likely to take up. They need information-processing skills and an ability to problem solve. This is the impetus for the 'Third Millennium Education' project."

A critical component of this plan is to use technology extensively in the new schools. Some of this equipment and software may be donated by companies that have invested in Ed-3M. If the first school is successful as a model, it is hoped that both hardware and software manufacturers will be willing to donate their products to the project as a way to test their effectiveness. This equipment is not to be found only in a laboratory, although the school would likely have several hi-tech labs. But, in addition, each classroom will be outfitted with the up-to-date technology necessary for students to engage in extensive researching, thoughtful processing, and dynamic presentation of material.

Your assignment is to begin developing a blueprint for this "information society school." You need to advance this project beyond the rhetoric and operationalize how an information society school might actually function. How might such a school be organized? How might class sessions differ from those of a traditional school? How might the teacher's role change? Most importantly, what role might technology play in this school of the future?

ISSUES INQUIRY

1. Do schools really need to change? If so, need every aspect of the institution be altered: organization, staffing, curriculum, instruction, evaluation, use of technology? If not, which kinds of changes might be most important?

2. Are schools already changing to any significant degree? Have you had any experience at unique schools, as a student, visitor, or teacher? Why is institutional change so slow? How might its pace be accelerated?

3. How important will the role of technology be? What kinds of technologies will be most important in an information society school? How can they be most effectively be utilized

4. How will the teacher's role need to change? Will teachers need to abdicate the "sage on the stage" role or will that function still be important? Will teaching become easier or more difficult?

5. Will these new approaches work well with all students? If not, which types of students do you think will respond best to these changes?

Glossary

acceptable use policy (AUP)   A written description of the procedures and policies regarding appropriate use of computers and *networks* in an organization. Most institutions probably need an AUP nowadays to help discourage misuse.

advance organizer   An instructional strategy that clarifies a point by relating new information to prior knowledge. For example, an analogy between U.S. Post Office mail and *e-mail* may help people learn *e-mail* functions better.

agent   A computer program that can be set up to perform tasks for a user independently. These tasks might include searching the Web, performing backups, or scheduling meetings.

analog   A message or signal that is continuous. For example, a "classic" clock represents time as the continuous movement of its hands around the dial. This is in contrast to a *digital* clock, which presents data as separate units (in this case numbers).

artificial intelligence (AI)   The attempt to duplicate or even surpass human intelligence with computer programs. There are many ways of producing such programs, but the field has so far had real success in only limited areas (like chess).

assistive technology   Technological devices that help individuals overcome specific disabilities. These include computer systems that can read to a person with visual impairments, special input devices for those with physical disabilities, software that provides guidance for the learning disabled, and so on.

associative learning   Learning that is characterized by the linking of ideas, concepts, and facts. These links can facilitate memory and understanding.

asynchronous   Communications that take place independent of time and space, so that the parties to the communications do not have to all be communicating at the same time. Examples include leaving a note, regular mail, *e-mail, listservs, electronic bulletin boards,* and *newsgroups.* Conversely, face-to-face conversations and mediated interactions that occur live are *synchronous.*

attention deficit disorder (ADD)   A condition marked by difficulty in concentrating, which often includes hyperactive, restless behavior.

audioconferencing   Live *telecommunications* exchanges in which audio signals are sent back and forth between two or more sites. With speaker telephones, groups can interact with one another.

audiographics   A *telecommunications* system that allows for simultaneous communication of both audio signals (such as voice) and visual data (such as *graphics* or text).

authoring system   A computer program designed for the development of *multimedia* programs. This software allows a user to integrate text, graphics, animation, audio, and video. It can also provide interactive sequences. Some examples are Director, Authorware, Toolbook, and HyperStudio.

bandwidth   The amount of information that can be transmitted simultaneously over a given communications link, generally measured in *baud* (*bits* per second). Bigger is better when it comes to bandwidth. *Optical fiber* has higher bandwidth capability than copper *coaxial cable*, for example.

baud   The number of *bits* per second that can be telecommunicated. The higher the baud rate of a device, the faster it can transmit information and the greater the amount of information it will be able to send in a given amount of time.

behaviorism   The psychological theory that maintains that the key to understanding animals and people is to predict and control their behavior, using stimuli and *reinforcements*.

bit   Abbreviation for binary digit—the basic unit in digital information processing. A single bit of information has one of two possible states: on or off (often represented by the digits one and zero). When combined into *bytes* and larger units, bits become a powerful way of representing information.

bozo filter   An *e-mail filter* set to reject messages from known clowns.

branching   An instructional strategy used in *programmed instruction* and *computer-assisted instruction* in which learner performance determines the difficulty of the next instructional sequence.

browser   A *client* computer program used for navigating the *World Wide Web*. The two current favorites are Netscape Navigator and Microsoft Internet Explorer.

byte   Eight *bits* grouped together by a computer. Measurement of computer memory capacity and communications speed are based on bytes. (Four bits grouped together are called a "nibble" in case you were wondering, but nibbles aren't used for much of anything anymore, apart from snacking.)

cable modem   *Networking* hardware that enables a computer to communicate at high speeds with the *Internet* via standard cable television connections. It is something of a misnomer, since it does not operate like a standard telephone line *modem*.

camcorder   A lightweight television recording unit that combines the camera with the videotape recorder. All consumer models and most professional units use this configuration now.

capital expense   An accounting term referring to expenses incurred for the purchase of property, major equipment, and other items associated with an organization's physical plant, which depreciate over a period of years. *Operating expenses,* by comparison, are associated with a set of ongoing activities and do not depreciate.

CD-ROM   Compact Disc–Read Only Memory. A computer laser-based storage device based on the same CD technology we use for music. At the time it was introduced, it was considered an extremely high capacity storage medium. However, CD-ROMs have now been surpassed in this regard by other technologies such as *DVD* and very large *hard disk drives*.

central processing unit (CPU)   The core processor of a computer that does the main work—calculating, storing data, transferring signals, and generally making things happen inside the machine. In a microcomputer, it is called the *microprocessor*.

Channel One   A commercial secondary school television venture that equips schools, free of charge, with televisions in each classroom, a schoolwide cable system, *satellite* dish, and so on. It also provides daily a free twelve-minute newscast designed for teenagers. All of this is funded by fees charged for two minutes of advertising in the newscast.

chat   *Synchronous* computer communications in which individuals exchange messages by typing them into their computers and sending them almost instantly to one or more other people online. Chats often take place in "chat rooms," which are *virtual* places on a computer *network*.

client   A computer program whose primary purpose is to communicate with another program on another computer. Clients generally send requests to *servers* and receive information in return.

coaxial cable   The thick copper cable used in cable television systems to carry the signals into homes. Its *bandwidth* is lower than that of *optical fiber*, however, so it is gradually being replaced by fiber. But today the vast majority of connections into homes and companies are still via coaxial cable.

codec   Abbreviation for *compressor/decompressor*. A hardware device or software program that compresses and decompresses video signals. This is done to make those signals smaller, thereby reducing the amount of space they take on a *hard drive* or the amount of communications *bandwidth* that they require. Neither *digital video* editing nor *videoconferencing* would currently be possible without codecs.

collaborative learning   An educational strategy in which learners work together on tasks that help them learn. Effective collaboration generally is characterized by common goals, mutual sharing of information and tasks, and the spirited exchange of ideas (hopefully!).

compact disc (CD)   A five-inch *optical disc* that contains *digital* data read by a laser beam. The CD has become the standard medium for optical storage of music, computer data, and now even video (*DVD*).

computer-aided design (CAD)   The use of computers in design-related fields such as architecture, engineering, and manufacturing. Specialized programs assist this process by providing flexible means of modification, 3-D imaging, rotated perspectives, and so on.

computer-assisted instruction (CAI)   Instruction delivered by a computer. CAI can include *drill-and-practice* programs, tutorials, *simulations*, and many others. Similar terms include computer-aided learning and computer-based training.

computer graphics   Images that are produced and/or manipulated using computers running specialized painting/drawing software, such as Paintshop Pro or Photoshop.

computer laboratory   A room within a school, library, or other institution that is devoted to computer use. Usually a computer lab will have a large number of computers and often contains other shared equipment, such as printers and *scanners*. There may also be a teacher's station with the ability to project the instructor's computer screen for class viewing.

computer literacy   The set of competencies necessary for successfully utilizing a personal computer. The definition of what constitutes computer literacy changes as the technology evolves.

computer-mediated communications (CMC)   Any of a variety of means of communicating through a computer via computer *networks*. Possibilities include *e-mail, listservs, chats, audioconferencing, and videoconferencing*.

computer memory   The microchips within a computer that store information in circuits are generally termed "primary memory" or *random access memory*. This data storage is "volatile," since it is lost when the computer is shut off or restarted, necessitating the use of "secondary" memory storage devices, like magnetic or optical disks.

constructivism   An educational philosophy that stresses the learners' active involvement in making sense of information, understanding concepts, and expanding their awareness. The term also can refer to teaching strategies that support students in these efforts to learn independently.

copyright   The ownership of media materials by those who created them (or paid for their creation). Copyright can be secured for any type of creative work, including written materials, music, graphic arts, computer code, videos, and so on. Copyright establishes the owners' rights to compensation for use of their materials.

cost-benefit analysis   Analysis that compares the costs of programs with their expected benefits to discover whether they are ultimately "worth it."

CU-SeeMe   A widely used computer program that allows low-quality *videoconferencing* over low *bandwidth* computer *networks*. This low-budget form of *telecommunications* also requires an inexpensive video camera, a computer, and a network connection.

database   A structured collection of information stored in a computer. Databases can range from simple (i.e., address books) to complex (i.e., kinds of pharmaceuticals). In a computerized database, specific information can be rapidly retrieved through the use of subject descriptors and computer search functions.

descriptive research   Research that is aimed at describing some phenomenon rather than testing hypotheses (as is the case with *experimental research*). Some examples are histories, case studies, and ethnographic investigations.

desktop publishing   The process of producing professional-quality publications on a personal computer using specialized software such as PageMaker, Quark Express, or Microsoft Publisher.

digital   The use of separate *bits* of information, rather than a continuous representation (*analog*). For example, a digital clock has separate numbers, rather than moving hands. Digital *information processing* is superior to analog in a variety of ways, including ease of manipulation, accuracy of duplication, and reliability of transmission.

digital camera   A camera that stores images in *digital* form in *computer memory* rather than on film. This might occur in a chip or on a magnetic disk.

Digital Service Line (DSL)   A high-speed *telecommunications* service that provides data at many *megabytes* per second. It is still in its formative stages but may ultimately compete with the *cable modem* in providing dynamic connections to the *Internet*.

digital television (DTV)   Video equipment that transmits and displays programs in a new *digital* format rather than the *analog* format commonly used until recently. The Federal Communications Commission has mandated that all broadcast television be digital by 2006.

Digital Video (or Versatile) Disk (DVD)   The evident successor to *CD-ROMs*, it can hold over ten times as much information and can be used to store high-quality video as well as sound, data, and computer programs.

digitization   The process of converting from some *analog* medium to a *digital* one. For example, a *scanner* might convert an analog photograph to a digital file, or a video capture card could convert an analog videotape to digital form.

Direct Broadcast Satellite (DBS)   A commercial television *satellite* service that provides *programming* to those who rent or purchase a satellite dish to receive it. It furnishes even more channels than cable systems, but customers cannot receive their local channels on it.

discovery learning   An instructional approach in which learners are encouraged to discover basic facts, concepts, and principles on their own, rather than having them explained to them.

discriminative stimulus   A term from *operant conditioning (behaviorism)* used to refer to the particular conditions in the environment that elicit a response from a person (or animal).

distance education (DE)   Any teaching and learning that takes place when the teacher and learner are separated. The original distance education used the mail system, but newer *telecommunications* forms, like *audioconferencing, videoconferencing,* and the *Internet,* have provided faster, more dynamic ways to make this connection between teacher and students.

document camera   A camera with a close-up (macro) lens, mounted on a stand, that can be used to present images of documents or objects for viewing or transmission (essentially a really cool overhead projector). Sometimes called an "Elmo," after the company that dominates the market for these cameras.

drill-and-practice   An instructional strategy that involves having learners repeatedly practice simple facts and/or skills using textbook exercises, worksheets, computer programs, and so on.

electronic bulletin board system (BBS)   A *computer-mediated communications* system in which users leave messages to be read by others. These may be accessed by anyone *online* or restricted to specific groups (like a college class, for example). Although these systems used to run as separate programs on computer *servers,* they are almost all implemented through the *World Wide Web* now.

electronic mail (e-mail)   Text messages sent between computers across computer *networks.* Increasingly, e-mail systems are allowing users to send pictures, sounds, and videos, as well as text.

experimental research   Research that is aimed at testing some phenomenon, usually through comparing results attained by one group with those of another very similar group that was not exposed to the process being examined. Hypotheses about outcomes should be established beforehand. All conditions and variables but the one being tested should be as similar as possible across the groups being tested. Nonexperimental research is usually called *descriptive research.*

expert system   A type of *artificial intelligence* that uses an extensive computer *database* and a set of programmed procedures to carry out a specific task. It uses a set of rules for interpreting data that human experts have provided to guide its operation. Some well-designed expert systems have addressed problems more effectively than their human counterparts.

fair use   A policy established by the courts interpreting *copyright* law that allows parts of a copyrighted work to be used free of charge by educators, under certain very specific conditions having largely to do with the amount of the work used and the degree to which this use would financially penalize the copyright owner.

filter   A computer program, or part of one, that selectively screens out some information before it reaches the user. In an *e-mail* program, a filter might be used to store messages on certain subjects in special directories. On a *network*, a filter may screen out some objectionable Web material, such as pornography, so that the user is not subjected to it.

First Amendment   The first provision of the Bill of Rights, which amended the United States Constitution. It guaranteed freedom of speech to citizens and freedom of the press to journalists.

flame   A highly emotional and hostile *e-mail* or other *CMC* message.

floppy disk   A disk with a magnetic coating used to save computer data. Older versions were about five inches, but were replaced by three-inch versions that were faster and stored more information (up to 1.4 *megabytes*). While "floppies" have been the standard means of saving portable files for years and still are adequate for text, they cannot hold many audio files and are totally inadequate for *digital video*. New formats for these large kinds of files have been developed: the *Zip disk* and the *Jaz disk*.

gigabyte (gig)   One billion *bytes* of information. It is equivalent to one thousand *megabytes* and one million *kilobytes*.

global village   A term originally coined by Marshall McLuhan to refer to the way global telecommunications media allows faster, more immediate, more extensive communications worldwide. Those on the other side of the world might thereby come to seem as familiar as neighbors in your village.

graphics   This term can mean visual images of almost any kind, but it is most often used to refer to those produced artificially, like drawings, rather than to realistic images that are captured photographically or electronically.

hard copy   Printouts on paper of computer information (as opposed to its less tangible electronic version).

hard drive   A set of magnetic disks that store computer information. This storage is more permanent than *computer memory* because it persists after the computer is turned off. But it is somewhat less permanent than information on an *optical disc* (*CD-ROM* or *DVD*), in that it can be erased or altered by the computer user. All computers come with a hard drive encased and *external* hard drives can be added to a system to increase the amount of total memory storage capability.

high-definition television (HDTV)   The *digital television* system that will be adopted by commercial broadcasters within the next five years. HDTV's picture resolution is over twice that of today's *analog* system, and it has a motion-picture-style framing (16 x 9 ratio) that is more rectangular than the present system (4 x 3 ratio).

Holodeck The holographic re-creation and training environment first introduced in *Star Trek: The Next Generation*. Amazingly, the *holograms* are not only highly intelligent (presumably through advances in *artificial intelligence*), but they are also as solid as real objects. This is science fiction that advanced technology may someday approximate.

hologram An imaging medium that produces three-dimensional images that one can view from any angle. Their quality is still relatively poor but improving.

hyperlink Computer text or graphic that, when clicked on by a user, calls up a new piece of information for display on the computer screen. Nearly all computer software now provides such links, and it is, of course, one of the important characteristics of the *World Wide Web*, allowing users to browse efficiently *online*.

hypermedia A generic term referring to *multimedia* that is organized through the use of *hyperlinks* in a nonlinear manner, which distinguishes it from traditional linear media like books or videotapes. The *World Wide Web* is the largest-known hypermedia system.

hyperspace A currently fashionable term used to refer to an information "environment" that uses *hypertext* and *hypermedia* (like the Web) .

hypertext Electronic text materials connected via *hyperlinks*. Hypertext allows readers to move efficiently through reading material in a nonlinear manner or to quickly link to another document.

hypertext markup language (HTML) This is the basic language of *World Wide Web pages*. Some fairly simple codes are used to define the type of text, format the page, provide sound or *graphics*, link to another document, and so on. In the early days of the Web, people would actually add these codes to the pages they were posting. But nowadays few see these codes, since today's Web development programs automatically provide them.

inclusion Placing students with disabilities in regular classrooms, rather than in special education classrooms.

individualization Instruction that is appropriately designed for the individual student who is working with it. One potential advantage of the computer medium is its ability to interact in unique ways with different learners and *branch* to material best suited for the person at the keyboard.

Individualized Education Program (IEP) A plan that identifies all services and supports necessary for meeting the educational needs of an individual child with a disability. Mandated by the federal government since 1975, a new plan for each special education student must be developed each year by the classroom teacher, a special education teacher, a school administrator, and the parents.

information processing The way in which information flows throughout a system. Cognitive psychology has used the information-processing capabilities of a computer as a model for how people perceive, think, and remember.

information society A stage of economic development that characterizes societies which have already passed through agricultural and industrial phases, and whose dominant enterprise is now the processing of information and the provision of services, rather than the cultivation of crops or production of goods.

infrastructure The facilities and equipment that allow large-scale systems to properly function. Roads, bridges, tunnels, rail lines, stations, and airports would all comprise a transportation infrastructure. For computers to be useful in schools, there must be an infrastructure that includes reliable electrical power as well as *network* cabling and computer equipment.

instructional design   A structured process of analyzing, designing, developing, implementing, and evaluating instructional materials. This approach has been widely used in business and by the military to train people in specific, job-related tasks.

Integrated Services Digital Network (ISDN)   A fast *digital telecommunications* line that operates at about 128 *kilobytes* per second, about twice the speed of a normal telephone connection. Now ISDN is being superseded by faster, more dynamic *telecommunications* technologies, like the *cable modem* and *Digital Service Line* (DSL).

intelligent computer-assisted instruction (ICAI)   *Computer-assisted instruction* that is combined with *artificial intelligence* techniques to make it more personalized, more responsive, and more effective.

interactive multimedia   *Multimedia* that responds to user input by presenting different information based on choices, responses to questions, and so forth. These interactions allow for *individualization* of the learning experience and potentially greater instructional effectiveness.

interactive television   *Videoconferencing* connections that allow people to interact with one another via television. This term is often used to describe video-based *distance education* systems with multiple sites, wherein the instructor and students rely on a two-way television *network* to see and hear one another.

Internet   The vast global *network* that is fast connecting most of the computers on the planet and which houses the World Wide Web, newsgroups, listeners, e-mail services, and so on.

Jaz disk   A portable magnetic computer disk, used with an associated Jaz drive, which can hold one or two *gigabytes* of data. This type of disk is most often used for really large computer files, which generally contain many *multimedia* resources (audio, *graphics*, video, etc.).

keypal   The electronic equivalent of a penpal, in which someone exchanges *e-mail* messages (rather than letters) with another person living far away whom they probably have never met in person.

kilobyte (K)   One thousand *bytes* of information. It is one-thousandth of a *megabyte* and one-millionth of a *gigabyte*.

knowledge engineer   A person involved in *artificial intelligence* (and especially *expert systems*) who uses a variety of techniques to encode knowledge and intelligence into a computer program.

laptop computer   A small, lightweight portable computer, run off a battery or plugged into an outlet and used almost any place. Sometimes called a *"notebook"* computer.

laserdisc   This term generally is used to refer to the twelve-inch-wide videodiscs that contained *analog*, not *digital*, information. It is less often used to refer to five-inch-wide *compact discs*.

learning styles   The tendency of people to differ in how they learn best and how they respond to different learning situations. Many different types of learning styles have been described in the research literature, which include issues such as sensory orientation, cognitive style, sociability, intuitiveness, and so on.

least restrictive environment (LRE)   A legal provision mandating that students with disabilities be placed in classrooms that least restrict their educational opportunities. This mandate has led to the widespread practice of *inclusion* in regular classrooms, special education classes having been deemed potentially "restrictive."

licensure   Official certification by a state that one has certain skills. It generally is granted through an institution of higher learning. For example, an instructional technology licensure might qualify an educator to be hired for certain types of technology specialist positions in school districts.

lifelong learning   Learning throughout one's entire life. Often this process is in response to the demands of a career, which today often involves shifts in position with new responsibilities, different skills, and higher levels of expertise.

listserv   An *e-mail* service often used for *online* group discussions, in which each e-mail message sent to the listserv address is distributed to everyone who has subscribed to it. (It has no "e" at the end, because it was originally restricted to the eight-character limit imposed by the MS-DOS operating system).

local area network (LAN)   A computer *network* that connects computers and other devices within a relatively small area, often a single institution or small group of organizations. A network that covers a wider geographical area is generally called a *wide area network (WAN)*.

mailing list   A list of people who will all receive any *e-mail* messages sent to that address. This works like a *listserv*, but usually it is established by the sender, rather than necessarily subscribed to by the recipients.

mainframe   A large, very powerful computer that can handle an entire institution's computer tasks or even those of multiple organizations. Its capabilities include large-scale data processing, storage of considerable amounts of information, housing of large *websites*, and other tasks beyond the capability of smaller machines.

mainstreaming   The practice of including children with disabilities in regular educational classes and experiences. This can also be referred to as *inclusion* and relates to a legal mandate termed *least restricted environment*.

mastery learning   An instructional strategy that aims at ensuring learners master one skill or concept before moving on to the next one. Mastery learning tends to be highly individualized and self-paced.

megabyte (meg)   One million *bytes* of information. It is one thousand *kilobytes*, but only one-thousandth of a *gigabyte*.

microprocessor   The specialized computer chip that serves as the *central processing unit* of a microcomputer. Microprocessors are also placed in many electronic consumer devices to add functionality. Their speed and processing power has increased enormously over the past two decades.

microwave transmissions   The use of transmission and receiver dishes to send signals for voice, data, radio, television, etc. Dishes not only provide reception capability but also serve to relay signals across vast distances.

modem   Abbreviation for *modulator/dem*odulator. A computer *peripheral* that allows computers to communicate with each other over telephone lines, by modulating transmitted *digital* computer signals into *analog* signals that the telephone system can handle and, conversely, demodulating the analog signals received by a computer back into the digital form that the computer can interpret.

MUD   Multi-user Dimension (formerly Dungeon). This is an *online virtual* environment that one can explore while interacting with other participants by *chatting* with them. The entire environment as well as all messages are text-based descriptions rather than actual pictures, sounds, or video.

multimedia   The combination of a variety of different media types in a single program. The media might include text, *graphics*, photographs, sounds, voice, animation, or video.

network   The hardware and software comprising a *telecommunications* system that connects computers together and allows them to communicate with one another.

newsgroup   An *Internet*-based way of exchanging information around the world, somewhat analogous to a massive *electronic bulletin board (BBS)*. Newsgroups are usually topic-based, like *listservs*. But while listservs involve *e-mail* messages sent into individual accounts, newsgroup messages remain on a server and are viewed, rather than received.

nonlinear editing   Video techniques that use new *digital* technology to make video editing more flexible. *Analog* video footage is digitized (or digital footage is captured) and edited on a computer system using specialized software like Premier or Avid.

"notebook" computer   Another term for a *laptop computer*, which is small and portable and run by a battery when away from any electrical outlets.

online   A very general term referring to any activity taking place on a computer *network*.

operant conditioning   A *behaviorist* technique used to modify human behavior by focusing on discriminative stimuli, responses, and *reinforcement*. When certain desirable responses are reinforced with some kind of reward in the presence of a certain stimulus, they can be strengthened so as to nearly automatically be elicited by that stimulus.

operating expense   An accounting term that refers to the day-to-day expenses needed to keep an organization running. These costs are generally separated for accounting purposes from *capital expenses*, which are associated with an organization's tangible assets and depreciate over time.

opportunity cost   Refers to the fact that we often give up the chance to do other things or purchase other items once we decide to spend our time and/or money on something specific. If we go to a movie, then we cannot simultaneously attend a baseball game. If our school buys computers, it may not have the money to hire another teacher.

optical disc   A general term that includes any disc (twelve-inch *laser disc* or *compact disc*) that relies on lasers to read the microscopic marks inscribed on the discs that store *digital* data. Some specialized discs now combine optical and magnetic storage techniques (magneto-optical technology).

optical fiber   A *telecommunications* line made of fiberglass that uses laser signals to encode messages. Its *bandwidth* is greater than that of *coaxial cable*, so it can carry more television channels and its signals are clearer. Consequently, cable television companies are gradually replacing their coaxial cable with optical fiber.

pattern recognition   The process of selecting specific pieces of information from a mass of data. Object recognition depends on this process. Computers still find this process difficult and often remain unable to accurately separate a given figure from its background. Improving pattern recognition is a key challenge facing efforts in *artificial intelligence*.

peripheral   Any computer-related hardware that exists apart from the main computer (on the periphery). Classifying a piece of hardware as a *peripheral* is becoming less straightforward nowadays, however, since some devices that used to be separate, like modems, disk drives, and even monitors, are now included in the computer case itself.

portal   A *World Wide Web site* that serves as an entry point for services on the rest of the Web. Yahoo! is a popular general Web portal, and there are increasing numbers of education-specific portals as well. (Not to be confused with a porthole!)

portfolio   A collection of an individual student's work that can be assessed to determine the amount of learning that has taken place or to gauge that individual's levels of skill and talent.

presentation software   Computer programs that can be used to develop visual support for a professional-looking presentation. The most commonly used is Microsoft's PowerPoint.

problem-based learning (PBL)   An instructional strategy that involves giving learners real-world problems to solve. Usually groups of students work together to gather information, understand the issues, and develop solutions.

programmed instruction   An instructional strategy that involves breaking down the material to be taught into small steps and then developing paper-based or computer-based materials that take learners through the steps. An important feature is the ongoing use of questions to elicit frequent responses from learners to check their comprehension. In addition, a great deal of feedback is provided for students about their progress.

programming   The set of instructions that tell a computer what to do. Programs can be written in many computer languages, some of which are specially designed for specific types of applications. Some commonly used languages are Fortran, Cobol, Basic, C, and Pascal. A newer class of languages, which are "object oriented" began to be used widely in the nineties. These facilitated design of objects that could be manipulated in mouse-driven user interfaces.

proxy server   A *server* that functions as an intermediary "traffic-control" device for a *network*. For example, a proxy server might hold *Web pages* that are popular on its network for faster delivery. Or it might serve as a *filter*, to keep offensive information off of a school's network.

qualitative research   Research that looks at aspects of the world that are not easily converted into numbers, such as the quality of student *portfolios* produced in *constructivist* learning environments. Much *descriptive research* is of a qualitative nature.

quantitative research   Research in which numerical data are collected. Much *experimental research* is of a quantitative nature, since statistical significance must be documented quantitatively.

random access memory (RAM)   Information stored so that it can be retrieved in any order, without delay. The chip-based memory of a computer functions this way and is consequently often referred to as RAM.

random assignment   A key to good *experimental research* in which subjects are placed by chance into groups for purposes of comparison, thus hopefully avoiding any differences between these groups that might affect outcomes. The objective is to have nearly identical groups, so that any differences in outcomes can be attributed to the "treatment" that is being tested.

read only memory (ROM)   An information storage medium that the user cannot save (write) material on, but can only get (read) material off. Since early compact discs could only be read from, they were called CD-ROMs.

reinforcement   A term in *behaviorism* that refers to the fact that behavior that is rewarded, or positively reinforced, tends to be repeated, and behavior that is discouraged, or negatively reinforced, should diminish. The proverbial "carrot" would be a positive reinforcement and the "stick" a negative reinforcement.

red green blue (RGB)   The three primary wavelengths of light: (yellow is a primary color in the mixing of *pigments*, not light). Three separate signals for these colors (RGB) are then displayed on a monitor as a set of microscopic red, green, and blue dots. The human eye cannot separate these dots, so all of the colors of the spectrum can be presented with RGB. Areas with both red and blue dots glowing will be perceived as purple, for example.

satellite   A device launched into space above the earth that can be used for *telecommunications*. Satellites are placed in geosynchronous orbit so they orbit over the same spot above the planet and can thereby be easily located for purposes of transmission and reception. A satellite's footprint is the geographical expanse that its signals cover (which can be as large as one-third of the earth's surface).

scanner   A computer *peripheral* that can be used to convert text and images on paper to *digital* form in a computer. An intense light is passed over the paper and light-sensitive sensors record the patterns. Computer chips digitize this information, so it can then be manipulated and viewed on a computer.

schema   A hypothesized cognitive construct that represents one's knowledge about a topic. A strong schema for "political campaign," for example, might include concepts for candidate, party, election, primary, caucus, platform, and so forth, all of which would help us understand this phenomenon.

search engine   A computer program, usually accessible through a *website*, that indexes vast numbers of *Web pages* and provides opportunities for users to find specific information on the Web.

server   Computer hardware, and its accompanying software, that stores files and sends information upon request across a *network* to *clients* on the system.

simulation   The attempt to re-create some aspect of reality, usually on a computer, for purposes of providing vicarious experiences. Simulations can be very useful in education and training, especially when the actual experience could be dangerous, difficult, or expensive. For example, pilots in training usually practice new maneuvers on a flight simulator before going up in a plane. Simulations can also re-create interesting experiences for students, as with the "Oregon Trail" program that allows them to pretend they are nineteenth century American pioneers.

situated learning   A key concept of much *constructivist* thinking, in which learning is thought to occur best when it is grounded in real situations. As such, problems are presented in their actual context, rather than as isolated, abstract exercises.

spam   *E-mail* that is sent simultaneously to large numbers of people, without being requested. It is widely frowned upon, and often results in *flames*. Aptly named for the unappetizing mixture of meats that soldiers often find in their rations.

speech recognition   Computer hardware and software that can recognize human speech. Many corporate phone services now use this software to direct calls, requesting callers to *say* what they seek rather than selecting a number on the keypad. In the future, accurate speech recognition software might be used to capture dictated messages directly into a word processor, skipping the keyboarding process altogether.

spell checking A feature now built into most word processors that compares each word in a body of text to a large *database* of correctly spelled words (dictionary) and then highlights those that do not match. It also provides a list of words similar to any word it cannot find in its list, as "suggested spellings."

spreadsheet A computer program that allows one to enter numbers and equations into a large grid and perform calculations. It accepts variables, for which the user can enter specific data. Then the spreadsheet's equations will automatically determine certain quantitative outcomes. For example, in a business operation, higher wages might be entered and the spreadsheet would calculate how this expense would affect a company's profit margin.

statistical analysis The process of taking quantitative data from a research study and describing it numerically. The objective is to discover significant relationships within the data or between the data and the conditions under which it was gathered. One of the most common approaches to analyzing an experimental study is to conduct an analysis of variance (ANOVA).

statistical significance A common concept in *quantitative research* that refers to the probability of the results occurring by chance. Results are generally considered statistically significant if statistical analysis determines that there is a less than 5 percent probability that they could have happened by chance.

synchronous Communications that occur in "real time." A face-to-face encounter is synchronous, as are telephone conversations, live exchanges *online* in *chat* rooms, or the interactions during an audioconference (or videoconference). Conversely, *asynchronous* communication involves delays between the exchanges (as with *e-mail* messages).

telecommunications The entire process and *infrastructure* for communicating at a distance via voice, computer, video, and so on. Telephone calls, radio broadcasts, television transmissions, and computer *networking* are all forms of telecommunications.

telecommunications-1 line (T1) A high-speed *telecommunications* service that operates at 1.5 *megabytes* per second (that's an enormous number of telephone calls). These lines are often used to carry compressed television signals for *videoconferencing*.

telecommunications-3 line (T3) A very high speed *telecommunications* service capable of transmitting a full, uncompressed television signal or a huge number of phone calls, data, audio, and so on. Its *bandwidth* is about thirty times that of a *T1 line*. (Don't worry, you can't afford it!)

teleconferencing Interacting live with other people over *telecommunications networks*. The two most common forms of teleconferencing involve the use of audio equipment (*audioconferencing*) or video equipment (*videoconferencing*).

transponder The device on a *satellite* that receives and transmits signals. The communications capability of a satellite depends largely on the number and type of transponders it has.

uniform resource locator (URL) The common way of specifying an address on the *Internet*. *World Wide Web sites* often begin with www. The type of institution is indicated by the final suffix. Commercial sites are .com, military are .mil, educational are .edu, and so on. For example, the URL for Kent State University is www.kent.edu.

usenet   The *Internet*-based collection of *newsgroups* that people can use to exchange messages. A large directory of these newsgroups is available at the www.dejanews.com *web site*.

videocassette recorder (VCR)   The common videotape technology found in many homes (often with its clock repeatedly blinking 12:00!), which is used to record and play back videotapes. Professional units are used in *analog* editing systems. Some consumer models also have special connections allowing them to be used with a *camcorder* as an inexpensive television editing system.

videoconferencing   Live *telecommunications* exchanges in which video signals are sent back and forth between two or more sites. Computer screen data can also be converted to television signals and transmitted as part of this type of *teleconference*.

videographer   A person who shoots and edits video footage. The analogy is to a photographer who shoots photographs and a cinematographer who shoots movies.

virtual   Almost any process that takes place by means of a computer rather than in reality. A virtual field trip, for example, could be created by authoring a computer program containing digitized television footage taken at a site, which the user could then navigate and explore, presumably in lieu of actually going there.

virtual reality (VR)   The *simulation* of a real environment using a computer wherein an individual can navigate through and manipulate objects to such an extent that he/she gets the subjective feeling of being in a real place. VR often includes the use of special *peripherals*, like gloves and goggles, which allow for more realistic interaction and contribute to a sense of "immersion" in the environment.

Web editor   Specialized software used to create *Web pages*. Web editors have graphic interfaces with icons for each function, allowing even amateurs to create appealing Web pages by automatically providing the *hypertext markup language (HTML)* used in the *programming* of Web pages. Some popular Web editors are PageMill, Front-Page, and Dreamweaver.

Web page   A body of information encoded using *HTML* and residing on the *World Wide Web*. A Web page can be as small as a single computer screen or very large, so that one must scroll to see it all.

web site   A collection of *Web pages* produced by a single person or organization and residing on a single Web *server*. Websites have addresses (or *URLs*) by which they can be accessed. They also generally provide a "home page," an initial Web page that provides links to and from other pages within the site.

wide area network (WAN)   A computer *network* that connects computers and other devices across a relatively wide geographical area. A network that covers a smaller geographical area is generally called a *local area network (LAN)*.

World Wide Web (WWW)   The full collection of interconnected Web *servers* that hold the billions of pages of information currently available using *HTML* and related technologies. The Web is a subset of the *Internet* as a whole, which also includes *e-mail* services, *listservs*, *newsgroups*, and so on.

word processing   The process of producing written documents on a computer rather than with pen and paper or typewriter. The *digital* electronic files it produces can be modified far more easily than the *hard copy* approaches that preceded it. Language aids like *spell check*, electronic thesaurus, and grammar check are generally included with commercial word processors. The most popular available products are Microsoft Word and WordPerfect.

Zip disk   A portable magnetic computer disk, used with an associated Zip drive, to store information. *Zip disks* are only slightly larger than a *floppy diskette*, but hold about seven times as much data (about 100 *megabytes*). *Jaz disks*, however, can hold 10 times as much information as Zip disks.

Index

Acceptable use policies (AUP),
  142–142, 305
Active learning
  educational technology for,
    258–259
  requirement for, 65
ActiveWorlds, 244
Adobe Premier, 217
Advance organizer, 305
Adventure Online, 81, 156, 247
Agent, 305
Alta Vista, 54, 55
America Online, 243–244
Analog, 212, 305
Ancient Egypt, 80–81, 83
Anderson, Richard, 31
Aphasia, 169
Artifacts, 48
Artificial intelligence (AI)
  Deep Blue and, 273–274
  expert systems and, 265–267
  explanation of, 23, 265, 305
  future outlook for, 274, 294
  intelligent computer-assisted
    instruction and, 23, 32, 270–273,
    312
  pattern recognition and, 267–270
Arts and Entertainment, 92, 218

Asimov, Isaac, 274
AskAnExpert, 77, 246
AskERIC, 246
Assistive technology
  explanation of, 305
  for physically impaired students,
    170–171
  selection of appropriate, 175–176
Associative learning
  explanation of, 305
  linking and, 202–203
Asymmetric digital service line
  (ADSL), 22, 306
Asynchronous, 240, 305
Attention deficit disorder (ADD), 169,
  306
Audioconferencing, 228, 306
Audiographics, 228–229, 306
Ausubel, David, 30, 203
Authoring
  explanation of, 78, 306
  impact of, 20

Bandwidth, 21, 213, 306
Baud, 306
Behaviorism
  background of, 25–26

Behaviorism—*Cont.*
  explanation of, 28, 306
  impact of, 26–28
Berniers-Lee, Timothy, 201
Bit, 306
Blindness, 168. *See also* Visual
    impairments
Bloom's taxonomy, 59–60
Bozo filters, 144, 306
Braille, 171
Branching, 306
British Open University (OU), 228
Browser, 306
Bruner, Jerome, 203
Buggy, 32
Bush, Vannever, 200, 202
Butz, Arthur R., 140–141
Byte, 306

Cable in the Classroom consortium,
    220–221
Cable model, 306
Cable News Network (CNN), 92, 218
Cable television, 218–219
Camcorders
  explanation of, 306
  obsolescence and, 125
  operation of, 216–217
Cameras, 216
Capital expense, 307
Captioning, 173
Case studies, 46
Cataract, 168
CD-ROMs
  digitized views on, 156
  encyclopedias on, 77–78, 81, 113, 118
  explanation of, 113, 307
  video clips on, 215
Central processing unit (CPU), 307
Cerebral palsy, 167
Channel One
  advantages of, 91–93
  commercialism and, 90–95
  effects of, 93–95

explanation of, 90, 221, 307
  opposition to, 90–91
  schools using, 93
Charge-coupled device (CCD), 216
Chats, 77, 243–245, 307
Christie, Jack, 112
Clark, Richard, 41–43
Classroom productions, 222–223
Classrooms
  advantages of computers in,
    102–103
  curriculum integration of
    computers in, 103–104
  integrating technology into,
    257–258
  virtual reality in, 283–286
Client, 307
Clinton, Hilary, 160
Coaxial cable, 307
Codec, 17, 213, 307
Cognitive impairments
  explanation of, 167
  types of, 168–169
Cognitive skills, 58–60
Cognitive theories
  application of, 30–32
  background of, 28
  explanation of, 28–30
  linking and, 202–203
Collaborative learning, 67, 307
Colossus, 265
Commercialism, 90–95
Communications disorders, 169
Compact discs (CD)
  design of, 206, 207
  explanation of, 307
  multicultural awareness through,
    155–156
  television on, 215
  use of networking *versus*, 117–118
Compression techniques
  function of, 214
  video, 159–160, 214
Computer-aided design (CAD), 281,
    307

Computer-assisted instruction (CAI)
  artificial intelligence and, 23, 271,
    272
  background of, 27, 28
  explanation of, 307
Computer graphics
  applications for, 296
  explanation of, 279–280, 308
Computer laboratories
  advantages of, 100–101
  explanation of, 308
  teaching in, 101–102
Computer literacy
  classroom computer use to
    enhance, 104
  computer use and, 107
  explanation of, 308
Computer location
  classrooms as, 102–103
  computer laboratories as, 100–102
  curriculum integration and,
    103–104
  miscellaneous factors influencing,
    106–107
  overview of, 100
  in various types of schools, 104–106
Computer-mediated communications
  (CMC)
  applications for, 245–247
  drawbacks of, 247
  explanation of, 308
Computer memory, 308
Computers
  cognitive theories and, 28
  development of, 18
  instructional roles of, 18–19
  obsolescence and, 125
  physical impairments and, 170–171
Computer software
  assistive, 170–171
  comparisons of, 43
  copyright issues and, 187, 188
  filtering, 145
  for students with learning
    disabilities, 173–174

Computer specialists, 102
Conditioned operant, 26
Constitution, U.S., 137–138
Constructivism
  background of, 33
  communications technologies and,
    76–78
  educational technologies and,
    34–35
  explanation of, 32–34, 64, 104,
    308
  hypermedia and, 203–204
  impact of, 76
  lesson planning and, 69–72
  media studies applying, 82–83
  projects using, 67–69, 78–79
  sample unit applying, 80–82
  situated learning and, 66–67
  teaching strategies and, 64–66
  virtual reality and, 284
Cooperative learning, 67
Copyright Act of 1976, 181, 190, 191
Copyrights. See also Fair use
  distance education and, 189–190
  enforcement of, 186–187
  explanation of, 308
  financial issues related to, 185
  function of, 181–182
  hyperlinks and, 188–189
  permission requests and, 185–186
  technology and, 187–188, 191–192
Cost-benefit analysis, 127–130, 308
Cover Concepts, 95
Cultural awareness. See Multicultural
  awareness
Curriculum
  in future schools, 291–293
  integration of computers in,
    103–104
  multicultural awareness and,
    152–153
CU-SeeMe software, 81, 159, 308
CyberPetrol, 144
Cybersitter, 144
Cystic fibrosis, 167

Databases
  explanation of, 308
  function of, 20, 115
Deafness, 168
Deep Blue, 273–274
Deja News, 242
Descriptive research, 46–49, 308
Desktop publishing, 20–31, 308
Detached retinas, 168
Dewey, John, 35, 103, 284
Digital, 308
Digital camera, 309
Digital information processing, 212
Digitalization
  explanation of, 309
  of television, 17–18
Digital television (DTV), 211, 212, 268, 309
Digital video disk (DVD)
  availability of, 78
  benefits of, 156, 215
  explanation of, 113, 309
Digital videotapes, 214–215
Digitized speech
  explanation of, 172, 270
  students with learning disabilities and, 173
Direct broadcast satellite (DBS), 309
Disabilities. See Students with disabilities
Discovery Channel, 92, 218
Discovery learning
  explanation of, 35, 309
  hypermedia and, 203
Discriminative stimulus, 309
Distance education (DE)
  background of, 227–228
  concerns regarding, 232–233
  copyright issues and, 189–190
  explanation of, 227, 309
  online instruction and, 230–232
  teleconferencing technologies and, 228–230
Document camera, 309
Down's syndrome, 169
Dreamweaver, 79, 256

Drill-and-practice software
  explanation of, 309
  students with learning disabilities and, 173

Ear infections, 168
Educational technologies
  creative projects using, 78–83
  information access through, 76–78
Educational technology
  for active learning, 258–259
  advances in, 15
  copyright issues and, 187–188, 191–192
  cost-benefit analysis for, 127–130
  cost categories of, 123–125
  estimating costs for, 125–127
  future outlook for, 294–296
  research on, 40–42 (See also Research)
Educational Technology Research and Development, 42
Education of All Handicapped Children Act, 165, 166
Electronic bulletin boards, 22, 243, 309
Electronic discussion groups, 22, 158–159
Electronic encyclopedias
  on CD-ROMs, 77–78, 81, 113, 118
  hyperlinks and, 200
Electronic textbooks. See also Textbooks
  advantages of, 115–117
  proposal to switch to, 112–114
Elementary schools, 105–106
Eliza, 265
Elm, 240
E-mail (electronic mail)
  advantages of, 240–241
  background of, 239–240
  explanation of, 309
  hearing impaired individuals and, 172
  impact of, 22

international contacts through, 157–159
misuse of, 143–144
Encephalitis, 168
Encyclopedias. *See* Electronic encyclopedias
E-Pals, 158, 160, 246
Epilepsy, 167
Epstein, Sheldon L., 141
ERIC database, 115
Ethnographies, 46
Excite, 54
Experimental research, 46, 49, 309
Experiment system, 310
Expert system, 23, 265–267

Facsimile (fax), 22, 230
Fair use. *See also* Copyrights
explanation of, 182–183, 310
interpretations of, 183–185
teacher knowledge regarding, 186–187
Fetal alcohol syndrome, 169
Field trips, online, 81
Films, 153–155
Filters, 144–146, 310
Firework card, 217
First Amendment, 137, 138, 310
Flame, 310
Floppy disk, 310
Ford Foundation, 227–228
Foreign exchange programs, 152
Foreign language study, 152–153
Fox News Network, 218–219
Free and appropriate education (FAPE), 165, 166
Freedom of press, 137, 138
Freedom of speech, 137, 138
FrontPage, 79, 256

Gagné, Robert, 31–32
German measles, 168
Gigabyte (gig), 310
Glaucoma, 168

Globalearn, 81, 156
Global SchoolNet, 81, 156–157, 160, 246
Global village, 310
Goal-based scenarios, 70–72
Goal-directed scenarios, 68
Graphical user interfaces (GUI), 25
Graphics, 310
Griffith, D. W., 154
Groliers, 200
Guidelines for Off-Air Recording of Broadcast Programming, 187–188

Hard copy, 310
Hard drive, 310
Hearing impairments. *See also* Students with disabilities
devices for students with, 172–173
explanation of, 168
learning disabilities and, 169
Hearing tests, 168
High-definition television (HDTV)
audio component of, 212
capabilities of, 267
explanation of, 16–17, 211–212, 310
impact of, 25
Histories, 46
History Channel, 218
Hoax of the Twentieth Century, The (Butz), 140–141
Holocaust, 140–141
Holodeck, 311
Hologram, 311
HyperCard, 200
Hyperlinks
background of, 200
copyright issues and, 188–189
costs associated with programming, 116
explanation of, 202–203, 311
planning of, 206
Hypermedia
background of, 200–201
challenges of, 204–206
constructivism and, 203–204

Hypermedia—*Cont.*
   design issues related to, 206–207
   explanation of, 200, 311
   function of, 201–202
Hypermind, 205–206
Hyperspace, 311
HyperStudio, 66, 78, 207
Hypertext, 116, 200, 311
Hypertext markup language (HTML),
   311

ICQ, 243
Inclusion
   explanation of, 165, 311 (*See also*
     Students with disabilities)
   legislation promoting, 166
Individualization, 311
Individualized Education Program
   (IEP)
   development of, 174–175
   explanation of, 311
   function of, 165
   selection of devices and
     applications for,
     175–176
Individuals with Disabilities Act
   (IDEA)
   function of, 166
   IEP requirements and, 175, 176
Information Infrastructure Task Force
   (IITF), 188, 189
Information processing
   development of skills in, 293–294
   digital, 212
   explanation of, 29, 311
Information society, 311
Infrastructure, 311–312
Injury, 167
Instructional design
   explanation of, 312
   research and, 41, 42
Instructional technologists, 41
Integrated Services Digital Network
   (ISDN)

   explanation of, 22, 312
   use of, 213
Intellectual property. *See* Copyright;
   Fair use
Intelligence Quotient Test (IQ),
   168–169
Intelligent computer-assisted
   instruction (ICAI)
   applications for, 271–273
   cognitive theories and, 32
   explanation of, 23, 270, 312
Interactive multimedia, 312. *See also*
   Multimedia
Interactive television, 312. *See also*
   Television
Intercultural E-mail Classroom
   Connections (IECC), 158, 246
International Correspondence
   Schools of Pennsylvania, 227
Internet. *See also* World Wide Web
   (WWW)
   acceptable use policies for, 142–143
   censorship issues and, 141–142
   as communications medium, 77
   constructivism and, 34
   copyright issues and, 187, 190
   explanation of, 312
   filtering, 144–146
   freedom of speech and freedom of
     press issues and, 138–140
   resources available on, 54
Internet Relay Chat (IRC), 159, 244
Interviews, 47–48
I Robot (Asimov), 274

Jason Project, 156
Jasper Woodbury series, 34–35, 67,
   69
Jaz disk, 312
Journal keeping, 48

Kasparov, Gary, 273

Keypals
  constructivism and, 34
  explanation of, 22, 77, 312
  multicultural awareness through,
    157–158
Kidcafe, 158, 159
Kidlink, 158–160, 246
KidsNation, 244
KidsTown, 159
Kilobyte (K), 312
Kinescopes, 214
Knowledge engineer, 266, 312

Laptop computers, 112–119
Laserdisc, 218, 312
Lawrence, T. E., 154
Lawrence of Arabia, 154
Learning Channel, 92, 218
Learning disabilities. *See also* Students
    with disabilities
  software for students with,
    173–174
  types of, 169
Learning style, 312
Learning theory
  behaviorism and, 25–28
  cognitive psychology and, 28–32
  constructivism and, 32–35
Least restrictive environment (LRE),
    166, 313
Legal blindness, 168
Licensure, 313
Lifelong learning, 313
Likert scale, 47
Lisp, 32
Listproc, 241
Listservs, 77, 241–242, 313
Local area network (LAN), 313
Long-term memory, 29
Lycos, 54

McLuhan, Marshall, 41, 150
Macular degeneration, 168

Mager, Robert, 26
Mailing lists, 241–242, 313
Mainframe, 313
Mainstreaming. *See also* Students with
    disabilities
  background of, 166
  explanation of, 165, 313
Majordomo, 241
Mastery learning, 299, 313
Mathematics instruction, 105–106, 258
Megabyte (meg), 313
Memory
  computer, 308
  long-term, 29
Meningitis, 168
Mental retardation, 168–169
Michigan State University, 241
Microprocessor, 313
Microsoft V-Chat, 244
Microwave transmissions, 313
Mini-DV, 216
Modem, 313
MOOs, 244
Motion Picture Expert Group
    (MPEG), 214
Motor impairments. *See also* Students
    with disabilities
  assistive devices for students with,
    170
  explanation of, 166–167
MSNBC, 218
MTV, 219
MUD, 244, 314
Multicultural awareness
  compact discs to increase, 155–156
  curriculum and, 152–153
  films and videos to increase,
    153–155
  importance of, 150–152
  international exchanges to
    promote, 157–159
  Web use to increase, 156–157
Multimedia
  in classrooms, 103
  electronic texts and, 115–116

Multimedia—*Cont.*
    explanation of, 314
Muscular dystrophy, 167
Mycin, 266

Nelson, Ted, 200
Net Nanny, 144
Networking
    in computer laboratories, 101
    distance learning and, 231–232
    explanation of, 21, 314
    use of compact discs *versus*,
        117–118
Newsgroups, 77, 242, 314
Nonlinear editing, 314
Northwestern University, 68, 69,
        140–143
Notebook computers, 314

Online, 314
Operant conditioning, 26, 314
Operating expense, 314
Opportunity cost, 314
Optical discs
    explanation of, 77, 314
    technological developments and,
        113
    television on, 215
Optical fiber, 213, 314
Oregon Trail, The, 285
Osteogenesis imperfecta, 167

Palace, The, 159, 244
Pattern recognition
    artificial intelligence and, 267–268
    explanation of, 314–315
Pavlov, Ivan, 25
Peripheral, 315
Phenylketonuria, 169
Physical disabilities. *See also* Students
        with disabilities
    assistive devices for students with,
        170–171

    students with, 166–167
Piaget, Jean, 31, 35
PictureTel, 222, 229
Pine, 240
POP mailer, 239–240
Popular culture, 82–83
Pornography, 139
Portal, 315
Portfolios, 300, 315
Post Office Protocol (POP), 239
PowerPoint, 78, 256, 258–259
Presentation software, 315
Problem-based learning (PBL)
    explanation of, 68, 315
    function of, 33–34, 72
Programmed instruction, 27, 315
Programming
    explanation of, 315
    skills associated with, 18–19
Proxy server, 315
Public domain, 116

Qualitative research, 46, 49, 315
Quantitative research, 46, 49, 315
Quickcam, 222

Random access memory (RAM), 315
Random assignment, 315–316
Read only memory (ROM), 316
Recreational Software Advisory
        Council (RSAC), 145
Red green blue (RGB), 316
Reinforcement, 316
Research
    challenges regarding, 42–44
    descriptive, 46–49, 308
    determining type of, 49–50
    experimental, 46, 49, 309
    guidelines for experimental design
        and, 44–46
    overview of, 40
    qualitative, 46, 49, 315
    quantitative, 46, 49, 315

on role of technology in instruction, 40–42
Researchers, 48–49
Retinitis pigmentosa, 168
Rubella, 168

SafeSurf, 145
Satellite Educational Resources Consortium (SERC), 221, 230
Satellites
explanation of, 213, 316
videoconferencing and, 230
Scaffolding, 66–68
Scanners, 316
Schank, Roger, 35, 68, 70
Schema, 31, 316
Schools
change in structure of, 300–301
in changing society, 290–291
freedom of speech and freedom of press issues in, 139–141
future applications for students in, 297–298
new curriculum in, 291–293
placement of computers in various types of, 104–106
School to Encourage Studies at Home, The, 227
Search engines, 54–56, 316
Secondary schools, 105–106
Sensory impairments. *See also* Students with disabilities
explanation of, 167
special devices for students with, 171–174
types of, 167–168
Server, 316
Simulations. *See also* Virtual Reality (VR)
background of, 279–280
explanation of, 280, 316
students with learning disabilities and, 173
Situated learning, 66–68, 316
Skinner, B. F., 26

Spamming, 143–144, 316
Speech recognition, 269–270, 317
Spell checkers, 19, 317
Spina bifida, 167
Spreadsheets
applications for, 256
explanation of, 317
influence of, 19–20
Statistical significance, 317
Students
approaches for evaluation of, 299–300
future applications for, 297–298
Students with disabilities
assistive devices for, 170–171
background of education for, 165–166
cognitively impaired, 168–169
common disorders of, 166–167
individualized education programs for, 174–175
selection of devices for, 175–176
sensory impaired, 167–168, 171–173
software for, 173–174
Super-VHS tape, 214, 216
Surveys, 47
Synchronous, 231, 240, 317
Synthesized speech, 172, 173

Tay-Sachs disease, 169
Teachers
attitudes towards computers by, 107
new roles for, 298–299
as supervisors of Internet access, 145
Teacher training
beyond the basics, 255–256
by experiencing technology, 259–261
to integrate technology into classroom instruction, 257–258
overview of, 254–255
to use technology for active learning, 258–259

Teaching machines, 27
Teachnet, 246
Technology. *See* Educational
    technology
Telecommunications
  explanation of, 317
  impact of, 21–22
  multicultural studies through,
    150–160
Telecommunications-1 line (T1)
  explanation of, 22, 317
  use of, 213
Telecommunications-3 line (T3)
  explanation of, 22, 317
  use of, 213–214
Teleconferencing
  distance education and, 228–230
  educational applications of,
    221–222
  explanation of, 317
Teletypewriter (TTY), 172
Television. *See also* Channel One
  access to, 16
  background of, 211
  captions for deaf on, 173
  classroom productions and,
    222–223
  commercialism and, 90–95
  digitization of, 17–18, 217–218
  early educational programs on,
    227–228
  educational opportunities using,
    220–222
  multicultural awareness through,
    154–155
  as presentation device, 218–219
  program production for, 79,
    215–217
  programs on Ancient Egypt on, 82
  signal transmission and, 213–214
  as storage medium, 219–220
  technical transformation of,
    211–213
  technological background of, 15–17
  videos and, 214–215
Terminator, The (films), 274

Texas, 112, 116
Textbooks. *See also* Electronic
    textbooks
  computers to replace, 112–113
  as instructional medium, 114–115
  obsolencence issues and, 116–117
Thorndike, Edward, 26, 202
TI-IN, 221, 230
Toolbook, 200
Transponder, 317
Travel
  multicultural awareness through,
    153
  virtual, 156–157
Turing, Alan, 265
Turing Test, 265, 267

Ultrahigh frequency (UHF)
    transmissions, 213
Uniform resource locator (URL),
    317–318
University of Chicago, 227
University of Wisconsin, 227
Usenet, 318
Usher's syndrome, 169

Very high frequency (VHF)
    transmissions, 213, 214
Video
  compression techniques for,
    159–160, 214
  multicultural awareness through,
    153–155
  as storage medium, 219–220
  television and, 214–215
Videocassette recorder (VCR), 214, 318
Video clips
  on CD-ROMs, 215
  explanation of, 172
Videoconferencing
  distance education and, 229
  educational applications of,
    221–222
  explanation of, 318

Video copystands, 218, 229–230
Videodiscs, 215
Video editing, 217–218
Video games, 285
Videographers, 216, 318
Video productions, 222–223
Virtual, 318
Virtual expedition, 246–247
Virtual Places, 244
Virtual reality (VR)
    applications for, 103, 281–282
    background of, 279–280
    in classrooms, 283–284
    examples of, 285–286
    explanation of, 23, 279, 318
    students with learning disabilities
        and, 173
    on Web, 282–283
Virtual reality modeling language
    (VRML), 282
Virtus VR, 285
Visual impairments. *See also* Students
    with disabilities
    devices for students with, 171–172
    explanation of, 168
    learning disabilities and, 169
Voice-activated systems, 171
Voice recognition systems, 172–173
VTEL, 222
V-TEL, 229
Vygotsky, Lev, 35, 65

Watson, John B., 25–26
Web-based courses, 231–232
Web editor, 318
Web pages, 79, 318
Webphone, 243
Web site, 318
Webteacher, 246
WELL, 243
Wheelchairs, 170

Whittle, Chris, 90–92, 94
Whole language approach, 19
Wide area network (WAN), 318
Word prediction software, 170–171
Word processing
    advanced features of, 257
    explanation of, 318–319
    impact of, 19
World Wide Web (WWW). *See also*
        Internet
    acceptable use policies for, 142–143
    browsers for, 255
    bulletin boards on, 243
    censorship issues and, 141–142
    constructivism and, 34
    copyright issues and, 187, 190
    creative projects using, 78, 79, 81
    explanation of, 23, 318
    filtering, 144–146
    freedom of speech and freedom of
        press issues and, 138–140
    hypermedia and, 204
    multicultural awareness through,
        156–157
    multiuser virtual reality on,
        282–283
    resources available on, 54, 56–58,
        103, 118–119
    search engines and, 54–56

Xanadu, 200

Yahoo!, 54, 55

ZapMe! Corporation, 95
Zen Palace, 244
Zip disk, 319
Zone of proximal development,
    65–66